Nelson History

Britain in the 20th Century World

John Traynor
Eric Wilmot

*For Carole, Linda,
Hannah and Patrick*

I 1276174

Thomas Nelson and Sons Ltd
Nelson House Mayfield Road
Walton-on-Thames Surrey
KT12 5PL UK

51 York Place
Edinburgh
EH1 3JD UK

Nelson Blackie
Wester Cleddens Road
Bishopbriggs
Glasgow
G64 2NZ UK

Thomas Nelson (Hong Kong) Ltd
Toppan Building 10/F
22A Westlands Road
Quarry Bay Hong Kong

Thomas Nelson Australia
102 Dodds Street
South Melbourne
Victoria 3205 Australia

Nelson Canada
1120 Birchmount Road
Scarborough Ontario
M1K 5G4 Canada

© John Traynor and Eric Wilmot 1994

First published by Thomas Nelson and Sons Ltd 1994

ISBN 0-17-435089-9
NPN 9 8 7 6 5 4 3 2 1

All rights reserved. No paragraph of this publication be reproduced, copied or transmitted save with written permission or in accordance with the provisions of the Copyright, Design and Patents Act 1988, or under the terms of any licence permitting limited copying issued by the Copyright Licensing Agency, 90 Tottenham Court Road, London, W1P 9HE.

Any person who does any unauthorised act in relation to this publication may be liable to criminal prosecution and civil claims for damages.

Printed in Spain.

Acknowledgements
The publishers are grateful to the following
for permission to reproduce copyright material:

Photographs
Associated Press: p.102 (2), 124, 135, 148, 149, 161, 170, 177; B T Archives: p.203; Colour Processing Lab.: p.35; Commission Des Communautés Européannes: p.159; Daily Sketch Newspaper: p.15; David King Collection: p.94, 132, 143; Greater London Photograph Library: p.185; Hulton Deutsch: p.6 (top), 8, 9 (right), 10 (top), 10 (bottom), 13 (top), 14, (top), 15, (top), 21 (middle right), 25, 27, 28, 34 (2), 37, 38, 39 (top), 39 (bottom), 41, 48, 51 (top), 53, 56, 57, 60 (2), 61, 62, 63, 65, 68, 69, 71, 72 (bottom), 73, 74 (top), 74 (bottom), 75 (top), 75 (bottom), 77, 79 (bottom), 84 (top), 88, 89, 91, 98 (2), 99 (top), 100, 102, 104, 105 (2), 100, 108, 109, 110, 111, 113, 114, 116 (top), 129 (2), 131, 133, 140, 141, 153, 157, 160, 163, 165, 166, 167, 168, 169, 174, 176, 180, 181, 183, 187 (3), 188 (2), 189, 192, 193, 194, 197, 203, 205 (2), 208, 209, 211, 213, 214, 215 (2), 220; J Allan Cash: p.152, 198, 204, 206; John Frost Newspapers: p.30 (top), 154, 191; Lon Cartoon: p.7; Mary Evans Picture Library: p.11, 13, 20, 21 (top), 21 (bottom right) 23, 78, 79(top), 93, 214; Museum of London: p.6 (bottom), 9 (left), 11 (5 pics), 14 (bottom); National Museum of Ireland: p.42; National Portrait Gallery: p.21 (bottom left); Novosti Press: p.97; Panos: p.145; Paul Popper: p.18, 48 (2), 70, 124, 137, 138, 142, 152; Retrograph Archive Collection: p.72 (top), 207, 210; Rex Features: p.37 (top), 44, 50 (bottom), 219, 221 (2); Robert Harding: p.120, 147; Science Photo Library: p.95, 203; Sygma: p.155; Syndication International: p.50 (top), 197, 199 (2), 210, 216; Topham Picture Source: p.61, 117, 122, 123; United Nations Photo: p.128 (2).

Text excerpts
Andromeda Oxford Ltd for material from *Wealth and Poverty* by Sydney Pollard, © Andromeda Oxford Ltd, 1990; A.P. Watts Ltd on behalf of John Stevenson and Chris Cook for material from *The Slump* published by Quartet; Batsford for material from *Women* by Katherine Moore; Croom Helm for material from *Women in Europe since 1750* by Patricia Branca; John Wiley & Sons Inc for material from *America's Longest War* by George C. Herring; Kenneth D. Morgan for material from *The People's Peace: British History 1945–1989* published by Oxford University Press; Longman for material from *England, 1868–1914* by Donald Read, *The Eclipse of a Great Power* (Foundations of Modern Britain Series) by Keith Robbins and *Britain and Europe 1848–1980* by Martin Roberts; Methuen & Co. for material from *Between the Wars* by C.L. Mowat; Michael Joseph Ltd for material from *The Korean War* by Max Hastings, © Romdata, 1987; Newspaper Publishing Plc for extracts from *The Independent* and *The Independent on Sunday*; Orbis Publishing Ltd for material from *The Vietnam Experience*, vol.1, © Orbis Publishing Ltd; Oxford University Press for material from *Black and British* by David Bygott; Pimlico for material from *Vietnam* by Stanley Karnow; Stanley Thornes for material from *Changing Horizons: Britain 1914–1980* by W.O. Simpson; The Irish News Ltd for material from *Irish News*.

Although every effort has been made to trace original sources and copyright holders, this has not been possible in all cases. The publishers will be pleased to rectify any such omission in future editions.

Contents

1 **The Development of British Democracy** 4
   The right to vote 1900–1969

2 **Political Parties 1900–1929** 20
   The rise of the Labour Party and the decline of the Liberal Party

3 **A United Kingdom?** 34
   Britain and Ireland, and devolution

4 **Boom and Bust** 60
   Economic change in the 1920s and 1930s

5 **The State in Society** 74
   The development of the Welfare State

6 **Superpower Relations since 1945** 94
   The Cold War, the Cuban Missile Crisis and Vietnam

7 **The United Nations** 128
   The UN, the Middle East, the Congo and Zimbabwe

8 **European Unity: 1945–1975** 150
   Britain and the European Community

9 **The End of European Empires** 164
   The British and French experience – India and Algeria

10 **Destination Britain** 178
   Migration and the immigrant experience

11 **Shrinking the World** 202
   Mass communications and popular culture

1 The Development of British Democracy

SOURCE 1
The campaign for votes for women was vital both for establishing 'universal suffrage' – votes for all – and for helping women to become more equal in society at large.

The right to vote 1900–1969

The right to cast a vote in national elections is an essential feature of any democracy. In modern Britain no government can remain in power for more than five years without calling a general election. By voting in such elections, citizens are able to play their part in choosing how their country will be governed. Since 1969 all British citizens over 18, who are included on a list called the electoral register, have been entitled to vote in local and national elections.

Who could vote in 1900?

People in Britain have not always been entitled to vote upon reaching adult age. In 1900, the right to vote depended upon a number of other qualifications. Consider the five profiles at the bottom of this page.

In a modern election, all of these people would be entitled to vote. Which of them could have cast a vote in the election of 1900? You might be surprised to learn that only Alfred Smith and Charles Sleigh had the necessary qualifications to vote in 1900. If you look carefully at the profiles, you can work out what these qualifications were.

Name: Alfred Smith
Age: 40
Occupation: Brewery worker
Place of residence: Union St, Burton-on-Trent (lodger)
How long at this address: 12 months

Name: Emily Green
Age: 28
Occupation: Teacher
Place of residence: Ferme Park Road, London (owner)
How long at this address: 15 months

Name: Thomas Lowe
Age: 21
Occupation: Soldier
Place of residence: None. On active service in South Africa.

Name: Charles Sleigh
Age: 72
Occupation: Retired farmer
Place of residence: Hope Cottage, Lincolnshire (owner)
How long at this address: 25 years

Name: Albert Bruce
Age: 24
Occupation: Dock worker
Place of residence: Hessle Road, Hull (lodger)
How long at this address: 11 months

From the list which follows, choose the combination of qualifications which entitled a person to vote in 1900:

- Over 21
- Male
- Female
- Working
- Resident in Britain for at least 12 months at the same address
- Wealthy
- House owner, or a lodger living in rooms worth at least £10 per year

---

DATAPOINT

The right to vote

Percentage of all adults (people over the age of 21) allowed to vote in British parliamentary elections.

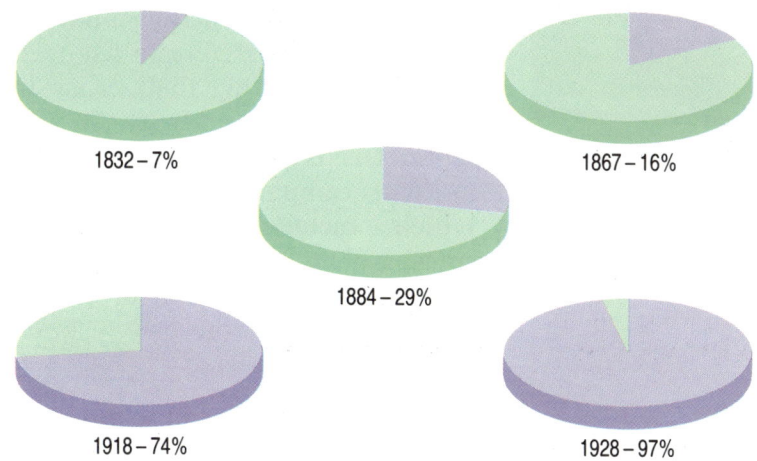

1832 – 7%
1867 – 16%
1884 – 29%
1918 – 74%
1928 – 97%

Developments in the 20th century

1918 *Representation of the People Act*
- Gave the vote to all men over the age of 21
- Gave the vote to women over the age of 30 who were householders or the wives of householders

1928 *Representation of the People Act (Equal Franchise Act)*
- Extended the right to vote to women over the age of 21
  Women could now vote on the same terms as men

1969 *Representation of the People Act*
- Reduced the age at which adults could vote from 21 to 18 years

People excluded from voting: people under 18, members of the House of Lords, involuntary mental patients, prisoners, people convicted of corrupt practices in the last five years, non-citizens – e.g. foreign workers.

A full franchise

Before 1918, no women and only 58 per cent of adult males in Britain had the *franchise* (the right to vote). During the course of the 20th century this position changed and Britain became more democratic (see **Datapoint: The right to vote**, left). The key which unlocked the door to a more democratic Britain was the Representation of the People Act of 1918. This Act entitled women to vote for the first time and, by abolishing the property qualification, also allowed all adult males to vote. The reasons why Parliament decided to extend voting rights in 1918 are considered in the rest of this chapter.

The need to vote

Although many men were unable to vote in 1900, few of them made an issue of this. Most men enjoyed favourable legal rights and were paid the same wage as each other for the same work. The trade unions looked after their interests in the workplace, and Parliament made laws to tackle important social issues such as poor housing. The need to extend the vote to all men was not seen as urgent. For women, however, obtaining the right to vote was vital. Since they were denied the vote, issues that particularly effected women were largely overlooked by a male Parliament. By the turn of the century, in spite of some improvements, the legal position of women and their conditions of work were clearly inferior to those of most men. Unlike men, women could not obtain a divorce on the grounds of adultery. In all areas of employment, women were paid less than men for the same work. Some of Britain's poorest and most exploited workers came from amongst the country's five million wage-earning women. The vote was seen by women as a means of forcing Parliament to take seriously the issues which effected the lives of half the population.

The activists

Women who campaigned for the female franchise were commonly known by one of two names: *suffragists* or *suffragettes*. The suffragists were moderate and law-abiding and used peaceful persuasion to try to win the vote. They were organised by Millicent Garrett Fawcett who, in 1897, had brought together various local groups to form the National Union of Women's Suffrage Societies (NUWSS) (**Source 2**). In 1903 a group of suffragists, impatient with the methods of the NUWSS, broke away to form a new women's organisation. It was called the Women's Social and Political Union (WSPU) and was led by Emmeline Pankhurst (**Source 3**). The WSPU believed that it was too easy for men in Parliament to ignore the polite appeals of the moderates. They decided therefore to use tactics which would bring their cause into the full glare of publicity. With the motto 'Deeds not Words' they began a militant campaign of direct action which included arson, window smashing and mass demonstrations. Before long, the name of the suffragettes had become known throughout the land.

A woman's place

It took many years for Parliament to accept that women should have the same voting rights as men. Millicent Garrett Fawcett was a young woman of 20 when, in 1867, Parliament first debated and rejected a proposal to give women the vote. A lifetime later, at the age of 81, she was finally able to celebrate the passing of a new law giving women the right to vote on the same terms as men. The main reason why women waited so long for the vote was because they had first to overcome deep-rooted male prejudice. Women were seen as being inferior to men and destined for different roles in society (**Source 4**).

SOURCE 2

Millicent Garrett Fawcett, leader of the National Union of Women's Suffrage Societies. By 1914 her organisation had 100,000 members. Mrs Fawcett was not the only outstanding woman in her family. Her sister, Elizabeth Garrett Anderson, was the first woman in Britain to qualify as a doctor.

SOURCE 3

Emmeline Pankhurst addressing a crowd in Trafalgar Square, London. She spoke at hundreds of public meetings, bringing her demand for the vote to a wide audience. It took courage and commitment to express these controversial views in public.

SOURCE 4

This extract from *The Times* newspaper appeared in May 1867 at the time when a Parliamentary Reform Bill was being debated in the House of Commons. The Bill proposed to extend voting rights to working class men. John Stuart Mill attempted to amend the Bill to give women the vote also.

Ever since the world was created, the great mass of women have been of weaker mental power than men with an instinctive tendency to submit themselves to the control of the stronger sex. Their destiny is marriage, their chief function is maternity, their sphere is domestic and social life.

SOURCE 5

This extract comes from an article titled 'An Appeal Against Female Suffrage' which appeared in a periodical in June 1889. It was signed by a group of women famous either in their own right, or as the wives of prominent men.

To men belong the struggle of debate and legislation in Parliament. It is often urged that certain injustices of the law towards women would be easily and quickly remedied were the political power of the vote conceded to them. We reply that during the past half-century all the principal injustices of the law towards women have been amended by means of the existing constitutional machinery; and with regard to those that remain, we see no signs of any unwillingness on the part of Parliament to deal with them.

Such views of the position of women in society went on being repeated throughout the suffrage campaign, and not just by men. Many women believed that female suffrage campaigners were misguided and should leave the business of politics to men (**Source 5**).

Above all, it was the misgivings of men in Parliament which delayed the extension of the vote to women for so long. MPs were fearful of how women would vote once they obtained the franchise. Conservatives were concerned that women would vote in large numbers for the Liberals, or for the newly formed Labour Party. The Liberals were equally worried in case the female franchise gave the Conservatives an unbreakable majority. Politicians from all parties feared a 'petticoat government' which would be dominated by 'emotional' women incapable of making rational political decisions (**Source 6**).

SOURCE 6

With women outnumbering men in the aftermath of the First World War, the results of granting the female franchise were taken to extremes in the imaginations of some Members of Parliament, aware that their jobs might be under threat.

THE PARLIAMENT OF THE FUTURE?

'Deeds not words': a profile of the suffragette campaign

The stubbornly held belief that a woman's place was in the home was not easy to challenge. It required a special kind of courage and determination to take on the prejudices of Britain's Parliament of men. By the early 20th century a group of women equal to the task had emerged: the suffragettes. The women of the WSPU used very different tactics from their moderate sisters in the NUWSS. The suffragettes were militants, prepared to break the law and to go to prison for their cause. They were often described as lady terrorists, earning both admiration and contempt from the British public. They have been accused of setting back the struggle for votes for women, the public outrage caused by their violent and destructive methods giving Parliament the perfect excuse to deny women the vote. By contrast, they have been praised for making 'votes for women' a high-profile issue which could not easily be ignored or dismissed. This profile may help you to decide which assessment you prefer.

Key events in the suffragette campaign

1903
The Women's Social and Political Union was founded in Manchester by Emmeline Pankhurst and her daughters Christabel and Sylvia.

1905
In October Christabel Pankhurst and Annie Kenney were thrown out of a Liberal meeting in Manchester's Free Trade Hall for interrupting the speakers with the question 'Will the Liberal Government give the vote to women?' Outside they were arrested for spitting at the police and both went to prison. This incident began the WSPU's deliberate policy of militant activity.

1906
The election of a Liberal government gave encouragement to the WSPU. It was hoped that they might be more sympathetic to the female franchise than the Conservatives had been. WSPU members took their demands direct to the law-makers with a demonstration at the House of Commons. Many of the protestors were arrested and sent to prison. The *Daily Mail* newspaper christened the women who used these shocking new tactics the 'suffragettes'. By the end of 1906 the WSPU had moved to London and set up their national headquarters.

1908
In April H.H. Asquith became the new Liberal Prime Minister. He was opposed to votes for women and challenged the suffragettes to prove that there was a widespread demand for the female franchise. In June the WSPU staged 'Women's Sunday' in Hyde Park. More than 500,000 people attended the demonstration! In the same month 122 suffragettes were arrested after disturbances in Parliament Square. Twenty-nine women were sent to prison, including the first two 'window-smashers', Mary Leigh and Edith New.

Militant tactics
- MPs were heckled at meetings
- Slogans were daubed onto walls
- Golf courses were damaged with acid
- Women chained themselves to railings
- Reservoirs were polluted with dye
- Women refused to complete the 1911 census
- Windows were smashed
- Chemicals were poured into postboxes
- Protest meetings and marches were held
- Women went on hunger-strike in prison
- Empty buildings were fire-bombed

SOURCE 7
St Catherine's Church, Hatcham, London, in 1913. The building is engulfed by flames following an arson attack by militant suffragettes. Such action did little to win the support of those in power; 'it was hardly a tactful way to convert us by burning down our churches or putting bombs in our homes and cathedrals', said the Bishop of London in 1918.

SOURCE 8

For the authorities, force-feeding was a way of preventing hunger-striking suffragettes in Holloway prison from becoming martyrs (see **1909** below). This Source explores the women's experience of this brutal practice.

This illustration appeared on the front cover of the WSPU newspaper, *The Suffragette*, on 31 July 1914.

An artist's impression of forcible feeding in Holloway Prison.

This is an account by Lady Constance Lytton of her experience of being forcibly fed. She was fed in this way on seven occasions. This account comes from a speech she made at the Queen's Hall on 31 January 1910, eight days after being released from prison.

The doctor and four wardresses came into my cell. Two wardresses held my hands, one my head. Much as I had heard about this thing, it was infinitely more horrible and more painful than I had expected. The doctor put the steel gag in somewhere on my gums and forced open my mouth till it was yawning wide. As he proceeded to force into my mouth and down the throat a large rubber tube, I felt as though I were being killed – absolute suffocation is the feeling. You feel as though it would never stop. You cannot breathe and yet you choke. It irritates the throat, it irritates the mucus membrane as it goes down, every second seems an hour, and you think they will never finish pushing it down. After a while the sensation is relieved, then the food is poured down, and then you choke, and your whole body resists and writhes under the treatment; you are held down and the process goes on, and finally, when the vomiting becomes excessive the tube is removed. I forgot what I was in there for, I forgot women, I forgot everything except my own sufferings, and I was completely overcome by them.

1909

In June, suffragettes who had been refused a meeting with Asquith went on the rampage, smashing windows – 108 women were arrested and 14 were sent to Holloway prison. In prison the women started a campaign to obtain the status of political prisoners. When this was refused the women went on hunger-strike. The authorities responded by forcibly feeding the women (**Source 8**).

1910

A Conciliation Committee was established to draw up a bill to give women the vote. The WSPU called a truce to enable discussions to go on in an atmosphere of calm and goodwill. During the summer the Conciliation Bill successfully passed its first two readings in the House of Commons. But then, Asquith suspended parliament until November. The future of the Bill looked uncertain, and angry suffragettes staged a demonstration outside the House of Commons. The protest became a riot with assaults on the women committed by the police and men from amongst the crowd of onlookers (see **Investigation: Black Friday** on pages 18–19).

1911

On 17 June the suffragettes staged the Women's Coronation Procession to mark King George V's accession to the throne. Sixty thousand women took part in the procession which stretched for seven miles! In November the Government announced its intention to introduce a new Reform Bill which would give the vote to more men and would consider women in an amendment to the Bill. The WSPU reacted with fury. There had been no real agitation for an extension of the male franchise – why should women be considered only as an after-thought to a bill giving more men the vote? The WSPU called off their truce for good. On 21 November, 200 women were arrested after an angry window-smashing attack on government offices and West End shops. Militant activity was

10 The Development of British Democracy

intensified and continued until the outbreak of the First World War in the summer of 1914.

1912
At the beginning of the year the government postponed discussions on the proposed new Reform Bill. In March the Conciliation Bill was defeated in the House of Commons.

1913
Under pressure to do something about the forcible feeding of hunger-striking suffragettes, the government introduced the Prisoner's Temporary Discharge for Ill Health Act. The measure was quickly nicknamed the 'Cat and Mouse Act'. Women who refused food were now to be released on a special licence to prevent them from gaining any propaganda value from hunger-striking in prison. After a specified time the woman would be re-arrested and taken back to prison to serve another part of her sentence. In this way the authorities were seen to resemble a cat cruelly 'playing' with a mouse: allowing the woman to go free and then recapturing her.

On 4 June Emily Wilding Davison became the first and only suffragette martyr. During the running of the Derby at the Epsom racecourse, she dashed out onto the track and made a grab for the reins of the King's horse, Anmer (**Source 9**). The sickening collision was seen by many of the spectators and was recorded on moving film, so it reached an even larger audience. Emily received terrible head injuries and died four days later in hospital. Her funeral procession through London attracted thousands of supporters and even greater numbers of onlookers (**Source 10**). In her fight to obtain votes for women she had been to prison eight times and had been forcibly fed on 49 occasions. She died as she had lived, totally committed to the cause of votes for women.

In spite of the dedication of women like Emily Wilding Davison, and the headline-grabbing activities of the militants, the Government continued to refuse to give women the vote.

SOURCE 9
4 June 1913, Derby Day. Emily Wilding Davison and the racehorse Anmer crash to the ground at the Epsom race-course. There were potentially hundreds of eye-witnesses to this event. How many of the crowd shown in this photograph appear to have seen the collision? What do most of the crowd have their attention fixed on? Can these spectators be considered as reliable witnesses?

Anmer struck her with his chest, and she was knocked over screaming. Blood rushed from her nose and mouth. The King's horse turned a complete somersault, and the jockey, Herbert Jones, was knocked off and seriously injured. An immense crowd at once invaded the course.

Daily Mirror, 5 June 1913.

SOURCE 10
Part of Emily Wilding Davison's spectacular funeral procession through London. Huge crowds lined the route from Victoria Station to King's Cross. Why do you think so many people came out onto the streets? Does the huge turn-out tell us anything about the suffragette movement?

SOURCE 11
The propaganda war
Supporters of the female franchise constantly published propaganda materials to convince people of the justice of their cause. At the same time, those groups who opposed votes for women produced their own cartoons and posters to counter the women's claim. This source reproduces six propaganda items. Study the pictures and the captions carefully. There are some questions on page 11 for you to investigate.

Knowledge and understanding

Use pages 4 to 11 to investigate the following questions:

1 List the qualifications needed to vote in a British general election in 1900.

2 Show how these qualifications had changed by (a) 1918, (b) 1928 and (c) 1969.

3 Why were women more active than men in putting pressure on Parliament to extend the franchise?

4 Explain why Parliament was so reluctant to allow votes for women.

5 What do Sources 4 and 5 tell you about attitudes towards women in Victorian times?

6 Write a brief profile of the NUWSS and the WSPU. For each organisation include: (a) the year it was set up, (b) the name of the leader, (c) the type of methods they used, (d) the popular name given to their supporters.

7 Write a description of the key events in the suffragette campaign, 1903–14.

8 Carefully examine Source 8.
a What do these sources tell you about:
  i the attitude of the government to the hunger-strikers?
  ii how strongly the suffragettes felt about their cause?
b In what ways would Lady Lytton's account of forcible feeding be useful to a historian?
c Examine each part of Source 8 in turn. In each case point out the advantages in using this type of source to investigate forcible feeding.

d Look at the front page illustration from *The Suffragette*.
  i What image of forcible feeding has this artist tried to present?
  ii Select four features from this picture which the artist has used to create this image.
  iii Bearing in mind the newspaper in which this picture was printed, how reliable do you think this image of forcible feeding is?
  iv What can a historian learn from this source about the attitudes and tactics of the suffragettes?

9 Study Source 11.
a Picture 1 is a postcard by a group in favour of votes for women. Picture 2 is a postcard by a group opposed to votes for women. In both cases the original caption has been removed. Show your understanding by selecting the appropriate caption for each picture from the list below:
• Give my mummy the vote!
• I trust Parliament to protect us working women.
• They have a cheek, I've never been asked.
• I behave like a suffragette.
• Mummy's a suffragette.
Justify your choice of caption and explain the message behind the postcards.
b Decide which of the remaining pictures were published:
  i in favour of votes for women,
  ii against votes for women.
In each case, describe the ideas and attitudes of the artists who produced them.

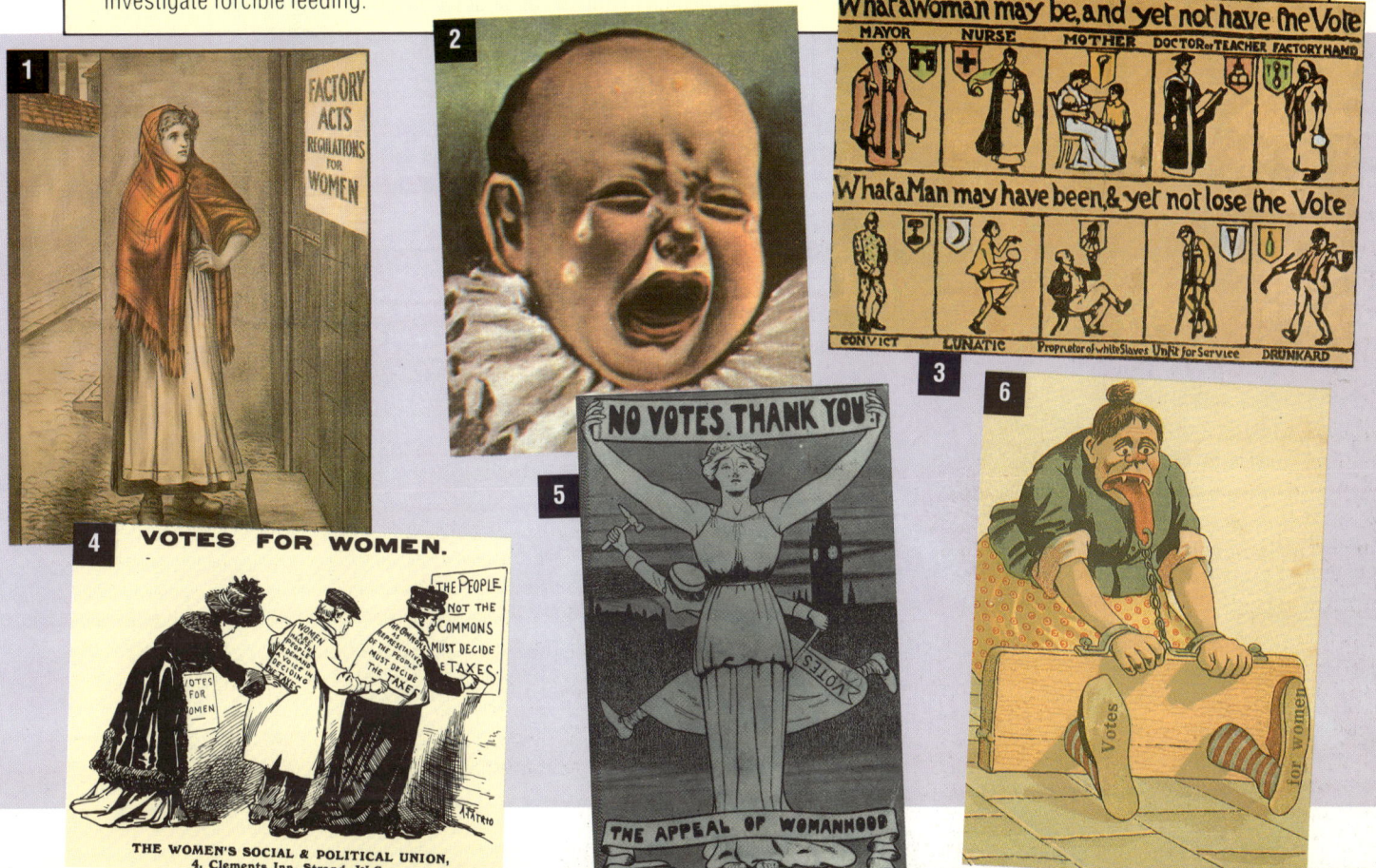

Investigation

Evaluating the suffragette campaign

SOURCE A

The militant suffragettes made themselves repulsive to the majority of women's advocates. Anti-suffrage leagues were formed, with significant female participation. Mrs Humphrey Ward was an outspoken leader of women who believed that the crusade for the vote did women more harm than good. Yet the WSPU did serve to bring the 'woman question' to a position of top political priority, particularly between 1905 and 1912. After this the extremism of the radicals clearly outweighed their positive impact, as a public beleaguered by labour agitation, Irish unrest, and fear of war, sought calm. After World War 1, the women's cause was taken up again in a quieter fashion, and in 1918 the vote was won.

Patricia Branca, *Women in Europe since 1750*, 1978.

SOURCE C

Mrs Pankhurst claimed in her memoirs ... that militancy had been proved right because it gained notice for the agitation. The limited militancy of the early years could be justified in this way; but later excesses only provoked sufficient anger to lose support without generating enough fear to force concession. The narrowness of the Pankhursts' demand – their concentration upon winning the vote – also drew much attention away from the needs of women for equality in other respects, at work and in the home. [The war] saved them from continuing along an increasingly dangerous course. The contribution made by women to the war effort greatly reinforced their claims to full citizenship but ... it was the absence of agitation which made it easy in wartime finally to concede votes for women.

Donald Reid, *England 1868–1914*, 1979.

Questions

1. According to these interpretations how did the suffragette movement:
   a. help,
   b. obstruct,
   the campaign to obtain votes for women?

2. Suggest reasons why historians might interpret the role of the suffragettes in different ways.

3. Why is it difficult for historians to give an accurate and unbiased assessment of the suffragette campaign?

SOURCE B

These women certainly showed that they were capable of losing themselves in a cause, but they did both harm and good to it. Undoubtedly they alienated many sympathisers and often turned what had been a dignified campaign for justice into a sex war. Like most fanatics, in spite of their courage, they were in danger of defeating their own ends. But that same courage also won them some support and one result of their notoriety was that the vast majority of those women who had worked quietly for the suffrage, and in other practical ways for women, in hospitals, schools and workhouses, were now forced to argue in support of their beliefs which had been brought into disrepute by the suffragettes. From 1906 to 1914 the country was obsessed by the suffrage question. In 1910 alone sixty new branches of the Society came into being. It is impossible to say how long Parliament would have held out had not the 1914 war changed the whole situation.

Katherine Moore, *Women*, 1970.

Turning point: the First World War 1914–18

The activities of the suffragettes won them both admiration and contempt, but by 1914 their high-profile campaign had failed to win them the vote. Those people who believed that the country would become unstable if women entered politics pointed to the 'irresponsible' behaviour of the suffragettes as proof that women were emotional and irrational and could not be trusted with the vote. If women were ever to win this precious right, they had first to break down the prejudices which condemned them to live in Britain as second class citizens.

The opportunity to begin this process came with the outbreak of the First World War in the summer of 1914. The War was a turning point in the campaign to win the vote for women. Britain was overwhelmed by a wave of patriotism as the whole country rallied to prepare for the fight with Germany. Without hesitation Emmeline Pankhurst and Mrs Fawcett called off the campaign for the vote and instructed their supporters to help with the war effort. The suffragettes soon discovered new ways to impress the British public.

The right to serve

At the beginning of the War thousands of women came forward to volunteer their services. Many were disappointed to find that there was little work available for them to do. Only gradually were women taken on in new occupations. They became van drivers, ticket collectors, lift attendants, tram conductors and munitions workers. The frustration felt by those women for whom no position could be found was made clear in July 1915. Thirty thousand women assembled in the centre of London in a rally organised by the WSPU. This time, however,

SOURCE 12
February 1917. A female bus conductor at work during the First World War. Twelve months earlier there had been just 100 women employed as conductors in London. By the time this photograph was taken there were 2,500. Half of these were former domestic servants.

SOURCE 13
Women provided essential support to front line troops during the First World War. They worked as nurses, drivers, cooks and clerks. This picture shows a unit of female carpenters constructing barracks.

14 The Development of British Democracy

SOURCE 14
On August 20th 1915, the *Engineer* magazine reported with astonishment that 'women can satisfactorily handle much heavier pieces of metal than had previously been dreamt of.' The women making axles in this photograph were not at all surprised by their ability to perform the same work as men. Their only complaint was that it had taken so long for such opportunities to be given to them.

they did not demand the right to vote, but the 'right to serve'. In the summer of 1916 the Government introduced compulsory military conscription. This measure turned thousands of working men into soldiers and left serious gaps in Britain's wartime economy. For the first time on a large scale, the government now began to exploit the willingness of women to serve their country. Within months, thousands of women were recruited to fill the jobs left vacant by men departing for the battlefields. As a result, there was a dramatic increase in the numbers of women employed in almost every occupational group (see **Datapoint: Working women 1914 and 1918** below).

DATAPOINT

Working women 1914 and 1918

Occupation	1914	1918
Transport	18,200	117,200
Agriculture	190,000	228,000
Industry	2,178,600	2,970,600
Commerce	505,500	934,500
Hotels, public houses and entertainment	181,000	220,000
Self-employed and employers	430,000	470,000
Domestic service	1,658,000	1,258,000
National and local government (including teaching)	262,200	460,200
Others	542,500	652,000
TOTALS	**5,966,000**	**7,310,500**

Number of women (thousands)

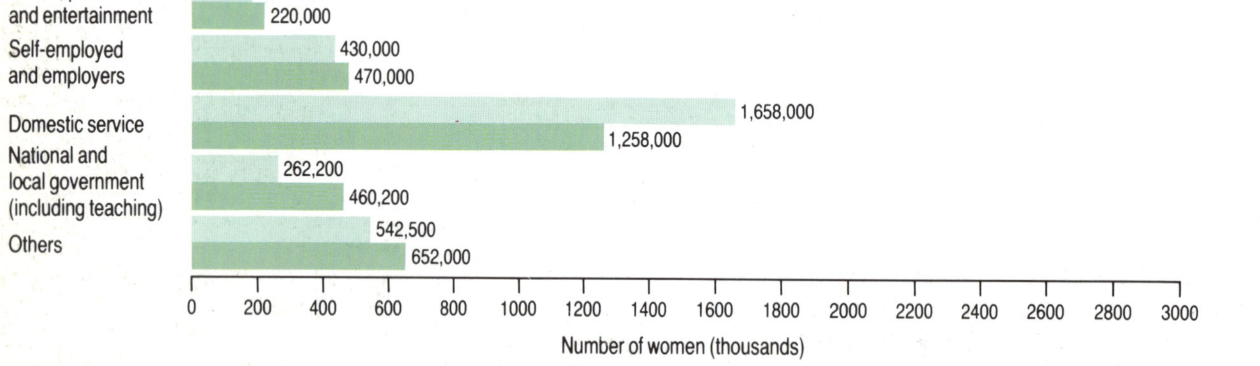

The Representation of the People Act 1918

As the War progressed, it became obvious that the old rules for deciding who could vote would have to be changed. With millions of men fighting overseas or working away from home on war contracts, it was absurd to retain a voting qualification which required the unbroken occupation of a property for 12 months. Champions of female suffrage were quick to seize this opportunity. They argued that if men deserved the vote for their loyal service to the country, then surely women, through their magnificent efforts, had also earned this right? It was a compelling argument which even Asquith found difficult to resist:

> Have not the women a special claim to be heard on the many questions which will arise directly affecting their interests ... ? I cannot think that this House will deny that, and I say quite frankly that I cannot deny that claim.
>
> H.H. Asquith, The House of Commons, 14 August 1916.

On 12 October 1916 a committee of MPs called the Speaker's Conference, began to discuss changes to the voting system. The Conference reported at the end of January 1917. It recommended that the existing property qualifications should be ended and that the vote should be given to some women. The recommendations were quickly shaped into a bill which proposed to give the right to vote to all men over 21 and to women over 30 who were householders or the wives of householders. On 6 February 1918, the bill became law.

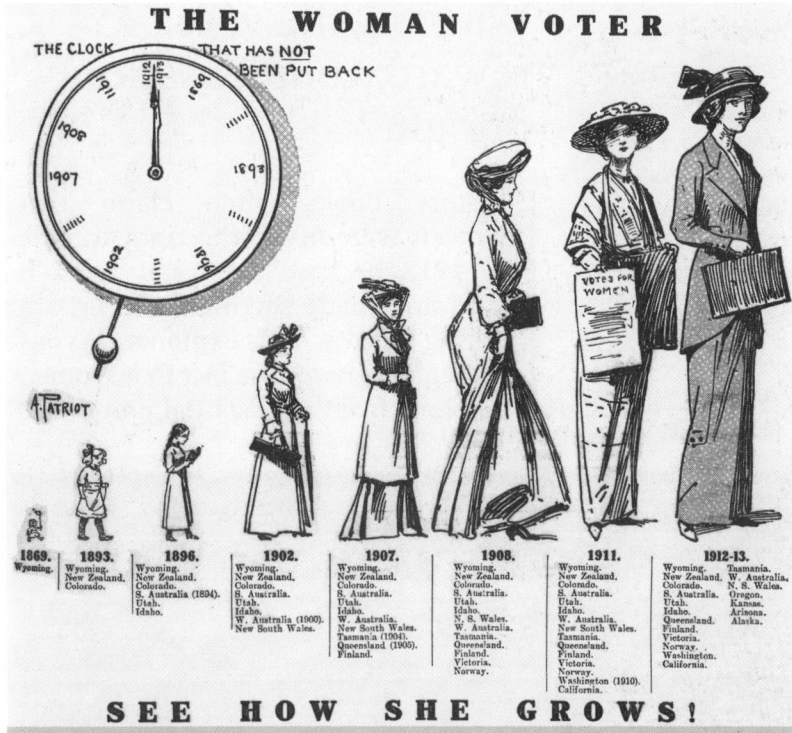

SOURCE 15

Suffragette propaganda showing the progress of the female franchise in other parts of the world. How might British women have used this information in their struggle to win the right to vote? The woman in the cartoon carried on growing during the 20th century. The franchise was granted on the following dates around the world – 1919: The Netherlands and Czechoslovakia, 1920: Canada, 1922: India, 1930: Greece, 1932: Spain, 1945: France, Hungary, Italy and Japan, 1955: Peru, 1971: Switzerland.

SOURCE 16

At the General Election of 1918 women in Britain voted for the first time. It was to be another ten years before women could vote at the same age as men.

Winning the vote: reward, compensation or right?

History books often claim that women were given the right to vote in 1918 because they had worked hard and made sacrifices for Britain during the War. This explanation conveniently ignores the fact that women had long been an essential part of the workforce. Centuries of toil and loyal service to the country had not brought them the vote by 1914; why should four years of the same thing make any difference? It is also worth remembering that thousands of women who had endured hardship and danger as nurses, munitions workers or factory hands were not rewarded with the vote in 1918 because they were under 30 years of age. Only six million out of a total of 13 million adult women were given the vote. In spite of their efforts, women were still not trusted with the vote on the same terms as men. The vote was not a simple reward for service to the nation. Look at the alternative explanations below. What reasons lay behind the decision to allow votes for women in 1918?

> **SOURCE 17**
> The passing of the Equal Franchise Act in 1928 gave women the right to vote on the same terms as men. Now all adults over the age of 21 were, like the young women in this picture, able to play a part in the democratic process.

> **SOURCE 18**
> In recognition of the broader education and earlier maturity of young people, the Government dropped the voting age from 21 to 18 years of age in 1969. Here the 19 year old actress Sally Geeson goes to the polls for the first time in the General Election of 1970.

I don't believe we are being given the vote simply because the government thinks we deserve it. We women know that our employment contracts are only valid for the duration of the War. When the fighting ends and the men return home we will be forced to give up our jobs and return to our kitchens or to employment considered more 'suitable' for a woman. There are about four million men waiting for this War to end so they can hang up their uniforms and return to civilian life. We are being given the vote to compensate us for what we are about to lose!

Now is a very good time to give women the vote. Those dreadful suffragettes have abandoned their lawless campaign so no one can say that we are giving in to violence. If we don't act now I dread to think what will happen when this War ends. If the militants resume their campaign, to what extremes will they be prepared to go? Let's give them the vote and ensure peace at home once there is peace in Europe.

We would be very foolish to continue to exclude women from politics after this War is over. We have lost 750,000 of our most able-bodied men on the battlefields; now more than ever we need the talents of women to rebuild our country. Without women it would not have been possible to continue with the War; we will need them when the fighting ends to help build the peace. We should stop thinking of women in politics as a threat. As voters and MPs they will work with men for the good of the country. In the reconstruction of Britain we need the talents of women in the economy and in politics.

The conduct of the women during this War has seriously weakened many of the old prejudices against them. Dozens of well-known politicians such as Winston Churchill, Lloyd George and even Asquith have now accepted that women are the equals of men. The newspapers have also been converted. The Times, The Daily Mail *and* The Observer *have all acknowledged that Britain's future depends on both men and women. The female anti-suffragists have also been silenced. Women will be given the vote because the War has forced influential people to acknowledge that women are both able and resourceful. Many of the old prejudiced attitudes have been shown to be completely ridiculous.*

Knowledge and understanding

Use pages 13 to 17 to investigate the following questions.

1 Why did the NUWSS and the WSPU call off their campaigns when the First World War began?

2 How did the introduction of conscription in 1916 change the position of women in society?

3 Use the Datapoint on page 14 to calculate the change in the employment of women from 1914 to 1918 in each of the named occupational groups. Express your answers in percentages.

4 Name the three types of occupation which experienced the largest increases. Which type of employment declined during the war years?

5 Why did 'votes for women' become an issue once more during the First World War?

6 In what ways was the Representation of the People Act of 1918 unfair to women?

7 Consider the following statement: 'Women were given the right to vote in 1918 as a reward for their loyal service to Britain during the War.'
a What truth is there in this statement?
b Give a detailed account of the other reasons a historian would use to explain why women were given the vote in 1918.

8 Which of the reasons identified in question 7 were: (a) political, (b) economic or (c) social?

Investigation

'Black Friday', 18 November 1910

On 18 November 1910 a deputation of women, angry at Asquith's interference in the Conciliation Bill, attempted to gain admission to the House of Commons to see the Prime Minister. The violent scenes which followed as women tried to break through the police lines, caused the day to be remembered as 'Black Friday'.

SOURCE A

120 Arrested

Suffragist Attack on House of Commons

DISGRACEFUL SCENES

True to their word, the Suffragists marched on the House of Commons yesterday, and the scenes witnessed exceeded in violence the utmost excesses of which even these militant women had previously been guilty. It was an unending picture of shameful recklessness. Never before have otherwise sensible women gone so far in forgetting their womanhood.

Here a ... campaigner sprawled in the mud to the obvious disgust of decent men and the obvious delight of some others. There an obese champion of the vote flung her bedraggled self against smiling policemen until lack of breath beat her. There again a few of the still more desperate pushed at the police in rugby style until they were swung back by a powerful neck or waist grip.

The police behaved with their usual tact, but during the afternoon mounted police had to be sent to help to maintain order. The police kept their tempers admirably, notwithstanding the fact that several were rather badly hurt or assaulted by angry women.

Daily Sketch, Saturday 19 November 1910.

SOURCE B
A suffragette is arrested and led away by the police.

SOURCE C

Sir, – I notice in your account of the reception given to the deputation from the WSPU to the Prime Minister on Friday last it is stated that the police behaved with great good temper, tact and restraint.

This may have been the case on previous occasions on which deputations have been sent; on the present one it is absolutely untrue. The women were treated with the greatest brutality. They were pushed about in all directions and thrown down by the police. Their arms were twisted until they were almost broken. Their thumbs were forcibly bent back, and they were tortured in other nameless ways that made one feel sick at the sight.

I was there myself and saw many of these things done. The photographs that were published in your issue of November 19 prove it. And I have since seen the fearful bruises, showing the marks of the fingers, caused by the violence with which these women were treated. These things were done by the police. There were in addition organised bands of well-dressed roughs who charged backwards and forwards through the deputation like a football team without any attempt being made to stop them by the police; but they contented themselves with throwing the women down and trampling upon them.

Yours faithfully

C. Mansell-Moullin

Vice-President, Royal College of Surgeons and Consulting Surgeon to the London Hospital.

Letter in the *Daily Mirror*, 22 November 1910.

The Development of British Democracy

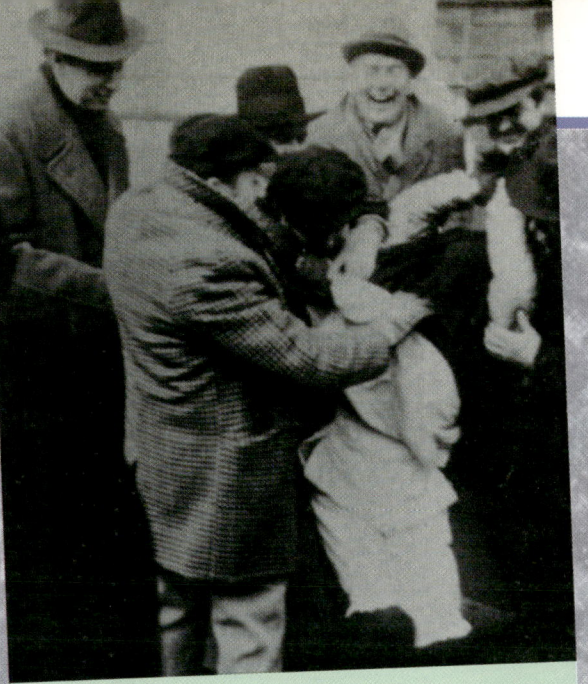

SOURCE D
Photograph of a woman being assaulted by a group of men. The men are trying to raise her skirts above her head.

SOURCE E
Orders were evidently given that the police were to be present in the streets, and that the women were to be thrown from one uniformed or ununiformed policeman to another, that they would be so rudely treated that sheer terror would cause them to turn back. The Government very likely hoped that the violence of the police towards the women would be emulated by the crowds, but instead the crowds proved remarkably friendly. At intervals of two or three minutes small groups of women appeared in the square. They carried little banners inscribed with various mottoes. These banners the police seized and tore in pieces, then they laid hands on the women and literally threw them from one man to another. Some of the men used their fists, striking the women in their faces, their breasts, their shoulders. One woman I saw thrown down with violence three or four times in rapid succession, until at last she lay only half conscious against the curb. For a long time, nearly five hours, the police continued to hustle and beat the women, the crowds becoming more and more turbulent in their defence.

Emmeline Pankhurst, *My Own Story*, 1924.

Questions

Work as a group, assuming the responsibilities of a Committee of Inquiry set up to investigate the events of 'Black Friday'. Study the evidence which has been presented to your committee (Sources A–E).

1 Use the evidence to establish as many facts about 'Black Friday' as you can find. For example; the date of the event, where it took place, who was involved, how long the incident lasted.

2 Consider the following points of evidence. Decide which are reliable facts, and which are the opinions of the author.
- The women were treated with the greatest brutality.
- They carried little banners inscribed with various mottoes.
- The government very likely hoped that the violence of the police towards the women would be emulated (copied) by the crowds.
- The police kept their tempers admirably.
- The Suffragists marched on the House of Commons yesterday.
- Their arms were twisted until they were almost broken.
- It was an unending picture of shameful recklessness.
- Orders were evidently given that the police were to be present in the streets.

3 Consider Source D. How useful would this photograph be to you in trying to resolve the following claims:
- The suffragettes were treated with brutality by the police.
- The crowds of spectators supported the suffragettes.
- The crowds were hostile to the women and some men in the crowd assaulted the suffragettes.

Your committee now calls for other evidence in an attempt to settle the three claims above. How useful would the following sources be in this part of the investigation?
Source A – Report from the *Daily Sketch*
Source B – Newspaper photograph
Source C – Letter by C. Mansell-Moullin
Source E – Mrs Pankhurst's memoirs

4 **Issue: Did the police behave with excessive force?**
Look at Sources A, B and C. Your committee should decide which source they trust the most to help them decide whether or not the police used excessive force. Rank the three sources into an order of reliability. When deciding your ranking, you must take into account the following points:
- Mansell-Moullin is a surgeon.
- Mansell-Moullin was an eye-witness.
- The *Daily Sketch* is unsympathetic to the suffragette cause.
- The *Daily Sketch* is bought by a readership largely opposed to the suffragettes.
- A photograph captures only a single moment in time.
- The man holding the left arm of the woman in the photograph was a plain clothes detective.

Did the police behave with excessive force? What is the conclusion of your committee on the basis of this evidence? Justify your conclusion.

2 Political Parties 1900–1929

Disaster!

On 15 April 1912, the pride of the White Star fleet, the *Titanic*, struck an iceberg in the North Atlantic and sank to the bottom of the ocean. This terrible tragedy claimed over 1500 lives. One week later the left wing newspaper the *Daily Herald* published an analysis of the disaster:
- Proportion of 1st class saved: 61 per cent
- Proportion of 2nd class saved: 36 per cent
- Proportion of 3rd class saved: 23 per cent
- Proportion of crew saved: 22 per cent

Three millionaires and the Managing Director of the White Star Line were saved in the first lifeboat, but only 20 of the 180 Irish (mostly 3rd class) passengers survived.

To the outspoken *Daily Herald*, the *Titanic* disaster perfectly reflected Britain's class-ridden society: even in the life-or-death situation of a sinking ship, the struggle to survive seemed more likely to be won by those with wealth and privilege.

While people with money and influence were able to enjoy life, those without fought a constant battle against poverty and want. Many argued that the only way to change this situation was to elect working class MPs and find a political voice outside the old parties.

This impulse was behind the birth and rapid growth of the Labour Party and the dwindling of the Liberals as a political force. Between 1900 and 1929 Labour replaced the Liberals as one of the two main parties, while Conservative support held firm. How did these changes come about?

The roots of the Labour Party

In February 1900 delegates from various trade unions and socialist organisations met at London's Memorial Hall. The conference had been organised by the TUC to consider ways of 'securing a better representation of the interests of Labour in the House of Commons', and led to the creation of the Labour Representation Committee (LRC).

The LRC agreed to sponsor candidates who, once elected, would form a group of MPs to work 'with any Party engaged in promoting legislation in the direct interests of Labour.' The Memorial Hall meeting marked the founding of the Labour Party, and brought together groups which shared the common cause of promoting working class concerns.

The Labour Representation Committee

The LRC consisted of 12 members:

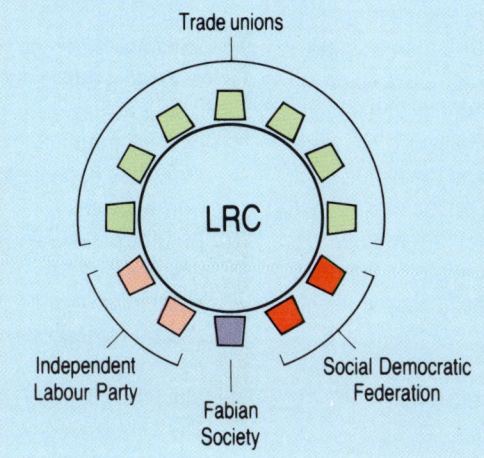

Secretary: James Ramsay MacDonald (ILP).

Funding for the LRC came from trade unions (94 per cent) and socialist organisations (6 per cent)

In 1901 the two SDF members withdrew from the LRC. Their seats on the Committee disappeared with them.

The Fabians

My name is Beatrice Webb and I am a member of the Fabian Society.
Our movement was founded in 1884 and includes many famous writers and thinkers such as George Bernard Shaw, H. G. Wells and my husband, Sydney Webb. We believe that Parliament should adopt socialist policies in the interests of working people and we reject revolutionary tactics. We aim to persuade people through speeches and pamphlets and we have members on local councils, in the trade unions and on education committees. We have tried to persuade the major political parties to adopt socialist policies and even now, in 1900, there are many among us who still think this is the best policy; so we Fabians are cautious in our support for a Labour Party.

The Social Democratic Federation (SDF)

My name is Henry Hyndman and I set up the SDF in 1881 after studying the works of the founder of Communism, Karl Marx. Marx convinced me that British society will change when the workers seize power from the wealthy ruling class. We want major changes in the way this country is governed. We want to see votes for all adults, free education for all children, the abolition of the House of Lords, a wage for MPs, an eight hour working day and the public ownership of land, factories, railways, banks and mines. We have taken part in demonstrations in support of the workers and have sometimes been involved in violent clashes with the police. At the Memorial Hall we asked the LRC to declare that its main aim was the creation of a socialist state, and to recognise that a class war would have to be fought to achieve it. The conference rejected this proposal.

The Independent Labour Party (ILP)

My name is Keir Hardie. In 1891 I became Britain's first independent working class MP, and two years later in Bradford I helped set up the ILP. The policies of the ILP are strongly socialist. We believe in public ownership of important industries, the railways, banks and farms and we want to see a state welfare programme to assist the needy. Our methods are peaceful and are based on educating the people about socialist ideas. Six hundred of our supporters have been elected onto local councils but

we have yet to make an impression in general elections. In 1895 we put up 28 candidates, but none were elected. My aim in recent years has been to get the trade unions to work with the ILP and other socialist groups to back the idea of creating a separate Labour Party in Parliament. The Memorial Hall meeting has gone some way towards achieving that goal.

Trade unions

My name is Richard Bell and I am Secretary of the Amalgamated Society of Railway Servants. It was my union which proposed the Memorial Hall conference. We did this because we have been unable to get the employers to recognise our union. We want to get MPs into Parliament who can put our case. Other unions have, like ours, begun to call for representation in Parliament. The 'new unions' of unskilled workers are largely in favour of a Labour Party, and even some of the

more established unions are beginning to take the idea seriously. In the last ten years employers have been trying to curb the power of the unions. Recent legal cases have cast doubt on the security of union funds and the right to picket. Trade unionists have begun to realise that without Labour MPs they have no means of defending their interests in Parliament. However, most of the big unions representing skilled workers have stayed away from the Memorial Hall.

The rise of Labour, 1900–1924

The LRC fought its first general election in October 1900. It did badly. Only two MPs, Keir Hardie and Richard Bell, were elected. The future did not look promising, even to a committed Labour spokesman like Philip Snowden (**Source 1**). From 1901, however, a combination of good fortune and careful planning transformed 'Labour' into a major force in British politics. How was this achieved?

1 The Taff Vale case

In 1900 members of the Railway Servants' Union went on strike against the Taff Vale Railway Company in South Wales. The company took the union to court and in 1901 the House of Lords ruled that the union had to pay damages amounting to £23,000. The judgement dealt a serious blow to the union movement. Their ability to go on strike was placed in grave doubt since no union could afford to pay such punishing legal costs. More and more unions now began to give their support to the LRC as they realised the need to have direct representation in Parliament. By 1902 the only large unions which had not joined the LRC were those representing the mine workers.

2 The political fund

In 1903 the LRC took the important decision to set up a political fund. Each union or socialist organisation which

SOURCE 1

The new movement [the LRC] did not begin auspiciously. At the end of the first year only 40 Trade Unions out of about 1,100 then existing had affiliated [joined] with a membership of 353,000. The three Socialist bodies had joined up [the SDF, the ILP and the Fabians]. The great organisations of the miners and the textile workers stood aloof, looking on the new movement with suspicion. The first Annual Conference was held in Manchester in February 1901, and I well remember the feeling of despondency which prevailed. It looked as if this new effort was going to share the fate of previous attempts to secure the direct representation of Labour.

Philip Snowden, *An Autobiography*, 1934.

DATAPOINT

Support for the main political parties, 1900–1924

1900 Conservative government

	MPs	share of vote
Conservative	402	50%
Liberal	183	45%
Labour	2	3%
Irish Nationalists	82	3%

1906 Liberal government

	MPs	share of vote
Conservative	156	43%
Liberal	399	49%
Labour	29	5%
Irish Nationalists	83	1%

1923 Labour government

	MPs	share of vote
Conservative	258	38%
Liberal	158	30%
Labour	191	31%

1924 Conservative government

	MPs	share of vote
Conservative	412	47%
Liberal	40	18%
Labour	151	33%

British elections use a first-past-the-post system: the candidate with the most votes wins the seat. The following election result is thus technically possible:

Number of voters	30,000
Candidate A	10,001
Candidate B	10,000
Candidate C	9,999

Candidate A wins the seat in spite of the fact that almost two thirds of the electorate did not vote for that candidate. This 'winner takes all' system accounts for the fact that the number of MPs is not directly related to the share of the votes gained by a party.

The need for a Labour Party: long term reasons

- Manual workers were given the vote in the reforms of 1867 and 1884, so working people and labour issues became more important in politics. Some people became dissatisfied with the way the existing parties tackled (or ignored) these issues.
- The Education Act of 1870 created an educated working class who were more critical of political leaders and were better able to voice their complaints.
- From the 1880s there was mounting impatience with the problems of poverty. Poverty affected working class people more directly than any other social group. The failure of the existing political parties to address these problems led to demands for a new party to represent the working class.
- Some working class MPs (known as Lib-Lab MPs) were sponsored in Parliament by the Liberal Party after 1867. However, since the Liberals were chiefly business and professional people, Lib-Lab MPs were unable to persuade them to make changes in the interest of the working class.

Political Parties 1900–1929

FORCED FELLOWSHIP
SUSPICIOUS-LOOKING PARTY. "ANY OBJECTION TO MY COMPANY GUV'NOR? I'M AGOIN' YOUR WAY" — (*aside*) "AND FURTHER."

SOURCE 2
Some observers saw the Labour Party as a dangerous threat to the established parties. There was a real fear of socialism. Contrast the figure holding the 'socialist club' with the gentlemanly character representing the acceptable face of political reform.

Labour MPs in Parliament

Year	MPs
1900	2
1906	29
1910 (January)	40
1910 (October)	42
1918	57
1922	142
1923	191
1924	151
1929	287

belonged to the LRC had to contribute one penny per year for each of its members. The money was used to finance election campaigns and MPs' salaries. In this way the LRC was able to ensure the loyalty and discipline of its MPs. By 1906 the political fund had topped £10,000.

3 The Gladstone – MacDonald pact

In 1903 Ramsay MacDonald met for secret talks with the Liberal Whip, Herbert Gladstone. Both men were worried about constituencies where Conservatives could get elected if Liberal and Labour candidates stood against each other. So they devised an election strategy which would allow the LRC to put up most of its candidates without the need to face Liberal opposition. The Gladstone – MacDonald pact was of real significance for Labour in the general elections of 1906 and 1910. In 1906, only 18 of the 50 Labour candidates were opposed by Liberals and as a result the LRC won 29 seats. This was a remarkable achievement for such a new party and it caused a political sensation. One leading Conservative even suggested that the new Liberal Prime Minister was a 'mere cork' holding back the 'Socialist tide'.

In 1906 the LRC changed its name to the Labour Party – acknowledging its emerging role in British politics.

4 The Osborne judgement

The Labour Party suffered a set-back in 1909 when a legal ruling, known as the Osborne judgement, prevented union funds from being used for political purposes. The main source of funding for the Labour Party suddenly dried up. Many Labour MPs were only saved from resignation by the decision in 1911 to start paying all MPs a salary of £400 per year.

In 1913, the Trade Union Act restored the right of unions to take contributions from their members for political purposes, provided this political fund was kept separate. Union members who chose not to make political contributions could 'contract out' of this arrangement by putting their wishes in writing. Thus, the Trade Union Act of 1913 gave the Labour Party financial security.

5 The First World War

The First World War has been described by the historian John W. Derry as 'the biggest single factor in bringing about Labour's emergence as a major political force'. This was the result of two developments: the reorganisation of the Labour Party, and the divisions within the Liberal Party.

Before the War the appeal of the Labour Party did not extend much beyond the working class. In addition, it was difficult for Labour to advance its own policies since the Liberals dominated in Parliament. From 1906 to 1914 the Labour Party was effectively little more than a pressure group within the Liberal Party. In 1917 this began to change. Arthur Henderson, the Labour Party secretary, set about restructuring the Party.

Political Parties 1900–1929

With the help of Sidney Webb and Ramsay MacDonald he prepared a new constitution for the Labour Party. He aimed to bring the politicians and trade unionists within the Party closer together, and to open up the Party to all social classes. People not eligible to join a trade union could now join the Labour Party. The constitution of 1918 declared Labour's interest in all people, men and women, and workers 'by hand or by brain'.

In June 1918 the Labour Party adopted a policy statement called *Labour and the New Social Order*. This socialist plan was the work of Sidney Webb and was of great significance because it formed the basis of Labour Party policy for the next 30 years (see **Datapoint: The new Labour policy** below).

The work of Henderson, Webb and MacDonald prepared the Party to become serious contenders for government, rather than remaining as the third party in British politics. They provided clear, shared objectives and made the Party more appealing to different social groups, notably the middle class and women.

The Liberals emerged from the First World War as a divided party. Some supported Asquith while the others rallied around Lloyd George. In the years after 1918 the reorganised Labour Party exploited these divisions and made its bid for political power. In the election of 1922 Labour won 142 seats and beat the Liberals into third place for the first time. In 1924, the first Labour government took office.

DATAPOINT

The new Labour policy

Labour's policy statement *Labour and the New Social Order* was based on four broad principles:

The Surplus for the Common Good
Expansion of opportunities in education for all people

A National Minimum
Full employment
Minimum wages
Minimum standards for working conditions
Maximum 48 hour working week
Equal pay for equal work for women

A Revolution in National Finance
Heavy taxation on large incomes to pay for social services

The Democratic Control of Industry
Public ownership and control of major industries (nationalisation)

Knowledge and understanding

Use the information on pages 20 to 24 to investigate the following questions.

1 Study the Datapoint on page 22.
a Name the political party whose performance in the period 1900-1924;
  i was most consistent;
  ii showed the greatest decline;
  iii showed the most impressive growth.
b How do these election results help to support the view that the Liberal Party was the victim of Britain's voting system?
c The Labour government formed after the 1923 election was a minority government. Use the election results to explain what this means.
d Why have some political parties been critical of the first-past-the-post voting system?

2 How and why was the Labour Representation Committee formed in 1900?

3 The following factors can be said to have helped transform the Labour Party into a major political force:
- the Taff Vale case
- the political fund
- the Gladstone – MacDonald pact
- the Trade Union Act of 1913
- the First World War

a In each case explain how the Labour Party was strengthened.
b Rank these factors into an order of importance. Explain your decisions.

Division and decline: the Liberal Party 1914–1924

In the election of 1922 the Liberals trailed a poor third behind Labour and the Conservatives, and they were never again to get out of third place. The party had become a shadow of its former self. The great election victory of 1906 was now a fading memory. By the 1920s, the Party had lost its unity and direction, and its appeal to voters. The decline of the Liberal Party was the result of two broad developments:

1 Party divisions

During the First World War the Liberals suffered a leadership crisis. Asquith, the Liberal Prime Minister, was severely criticised for his handling of the war effort by the other great Liberal politician of the day, David Lloyd George. In December 1916 Asquith resigned as Prime Minister, although he remained leader of the Liberal Party. Asquith was replaced by Lloyd George, also a Liberal, who led a new coalition government. Asquith's supporters refused to serve in the new cabinet ...

> The country was therefore faced with the extraordinary spectacle of a Liberal Prime Minister whose government was made up mainly of Conservatives, supported in the House of Commons by one section of Liberals; while the leader of the party, supported by the majority of the Liberals, sat on the opposition benches.

Paul Adelman, *The Decline of the Liberal Party 1910–1931*, 1981.

The two sides became increasingly divided and the personal feud between Asquith and Lloyd George became increasingly bitter. In 1917 Asquith turned down an offer to serve in the coalition government – 'Under no conditions', he wrote, 'would I serve in a government of which Lloyd George was the head.'

The 'coupon' election

In November 1918 the guns fell silent on the battlefields of Europe and peace returned to the world. Within the Liberal Party, however, the hostilities continued. In December a general election was held and Lloyd George waged war on Asquith's supporters. He made a deal with the Conservatives to fight the election together. Lloyd George and the Conservative leader Bonar Law drew up a letter of endorsement or 'coupon', which was issued to all candidates who were known to be supporters of a continued coalition. Voters were invited to support these 'coupon' candidates and a massive coalition victory was achieved. Coalition supporters won 478 seats and destroyed the opposition. Asquith's Independent Liberals won only 28 seats

SOURCE 3

Herbert Henry Asquith, Liberal Prime Minister from 1908–16, presided over many of the Liberal reforms, including the Pensions Act. However, his lack of decision as a wartime leader resulted in his replacement as Prime Minister by his political rival, Lloyd George.

and Asquith himself was defeated. Although a personal victory for Lloyd George, the coupon election left the Liberal Party more divided than ever. The real victory belonged to the Liberals' political enemies (**Source 4**).

> ### SOURCE 4
> The Liberals were now a weak and divided force: faced on the right by a triumphant and remorseless Conservative party, and on the left, by the independent rising power of Labour.
>
> Paul Adelman, *The Decline of the Liberal Party 1910–1931*, 1981.

The deepening rift

The divisions in the Liberal Party became worse in the two years following the coupon election. Asquith's Independent Liberals established their own party organisation separate from the Coalition Liberals. Before long Liberals were opposing each other at by-elections, locked into a downward spiral of political in-fighting. In 1922 the Conservatives decided to end their political alliance with the Liberals. Lloyd George resigned but the damage was done, and despite re-uniting to fight the 1923 election, the Liberal Party came third at this and all subsequent elections.

2 The challenge of Labour

The foundations of Liberal political power began to be undermined with the rise of what historians call 'working class consciousness'. People who lived in towns and worked in industry began to discover a range of issues and concerns such as poor housing, poverty and dangerous working conditions which applied only to them. The working classes therefore began to come together to fight for improvements. This was most clearly seen in the rise in trade union membership – from two million in 1910 to four million in 1914. This increase was of direct benefit to the Labour Party. The Liberal Party did not have this sort of link with a mass-movement, and increasingly came to be viewed as a middle class party with little to offer working class voters.

New voters

Until 1918 the development of working class consciousness was not enough to damage the position of the Liberals at elections. This was in part because the vote was denied to women and an important sector of the male working class population. This changed in 1918 with the Representation of the People Act. The numbers entitled to vote trebled and, for the first time, the industrial working classes outnumbered all other sections of the electorate. Having no loyalty to the Liberal Party, many of these new voters were captured by Labour.

A 'land fit for heroes'?

Voters who turned to Labour after 1918 wanted a government which would bring real change to Britain. During the First World War people had been prepared to make sacrifices because they were promised 'a land fit for heroes' after the victory. The ending of government controls in 1918 led to rapid price increases. Wage levels stagnated and some employers, such as the railway companies, threatened to cut wages. Unemployment began to rise sharply in 1920 and by the following year had passed two million. Large sections of the working class concluded that they had been betrayed by the government.

Against this background, working class consciousness became increasingly defined. Trade union membership rose from 6.5 million in 1918 to 8.3 million in 1920. Industrial disputes became more common, with major strikes in the mines, railways and engineering works. As British society became more aware of its class divisions the Liberal Party lost out. It had no definite class basis or class appeal. By contrast, Labour, with its strong trade union links and socialist programme, was seen as the party of the working class.

The first Labour Government, 1924

In the general election of December 1923, no party managed to gain a majority. The Conservatives were the largest party, but Labour and the re-united Liberals were able to outvote them in the Commons (see **Datapoint: Support for the main political parties** on page 22). Therefore, in January 1924 the King asked Ramsay MacDonald to form the first Labour government (**Source 5**).

The government lasted for only nine months. Its main weakness was that it was a 'minority' government, dependent upon Liberal support for its continuing existence. Since many Liberals were afraid of socialism, MacDonald had little opportunity to introduce Labour's programme into Parliament. However, there were some successes. One important measure was Wheatley's Housing Act, put through by John Wheatley, Labour's Minister of Health. This increased the government building subsidy to local authorities and enabled the construction of more council houses. In education, a maximum of 40 children per class was achieved and the number of free places in secondary schools was increased. The transfer of children at the age of 11 from primary to secondary schools was introduced giving all children at least 3 years of secondary education.

In spite of these achievements, the Labour government soon found itself in grave difficulties. Industrial disputes in the docks and on the buses put the government to the test. When the cabinet authorised the use of the army to drive public transport during the bus strike, the TUC was furious. The more radical voices in the union movement criticised the government for failing to tackle working class problems such as poverty and unemployment. Over a million people were without work during 1924. The government set up some work creation schemes but this made little impact on the problem as a whole. Labour promised much but without a majority in Parliament it was unable to deliver.

The government finally fell on a foreign policy issue. MacDonald had been quick to give diplomatic recognition to the Communist regime which had seized power in the Russian Revolution of 1917. Soon after he made a generous trade loan to the Soviets. The Conservatives, Liberals and the press immediately created a 'red scare' (**Source 6**). This came to a head in July 1924 when J. R. Campbell, the editor of a small Communist newspaper, published an article urging soldiers not to 'turn your guns on your fellow workers' in industrial disputes. The Attorney General decided to prosecute but later dropped the case. The Liberals demanded a Committee of Investigation to look into the case. In the vote which followed the Liberals and the Conservatives defeated Labour, and Ramsay MacDonald decided to call a general election.

In the election campaign, the Conservatives continued their 'red scare' tactics. They claimed that Labour were plotting to introduce Communism by the back door. Five days before polling day, the notorious Zinoviev letter was published by the *Daily Mail*. Although probably a forgery, it alarmed the public by calling upon the British Communist

SOURCE 5

The Labour leadership summoned to Buckingham Palace to form the first Labour government: *left to right*, Ramsay MacDonald, J. H. Thomas, Arthur Henderson and J. R. Clynes are seen here surrounded by jubilant supporters.

Much Ado About Next To Nothing.

Case study: the General Strike of 1926

The most serious industrial dispute in recent British history began on 4 May 1926. The General Strike lasted for nine days and involved more than three million workers. The strike was the result of a long-running dispute between mine workers and pit owners over pay and conditions of work (**Source 7**). The background to the strike can be examined in the timetable of events opposite.

Party to organise an armed uprising. The Conservatives gained most from the scare. They won a huge majority with 412 seats (see page 22) and Stanley Baldwin became Prime Minister of a new Conservative government. Less harm came to Labour than might have been expected. Although they lost 40 seats, over a million more people had voted for them than in 1923. The real losers were the Liberals. They returned to the Commons with just 40 seats, 118 fewer than in the 1923 election.

SOURCE 6

The Communist threat was wildly exaggerated by the Tories in order to undermine the Labour Party. In this cartoon their efforts to discredit the left are ridiculed. The actual scale of the Communist threat is shown by the tiny figure representing the British Communist Party.

SOURCE 7

Stanley Baldwin, Prime Minister 1924–29 and 1935–36.

Knowledge and understanding

Use the information on pages 25 to 28 to investigate the following questions

1 What happened to the Liberal Party during the First World War?

2 Why was the 1918 general election known as the 'coupon' election?

3 How did the disagreements within the Liberal Party assist the other parties at elections?

4 How did the Representation of the People Act damage the Liberal Party after 1918?

5 Why did the Liberals fail to benefit from the development of 'working class consciousness' in Britain?

6 How far was the decline of the Liberal Party the result of the disagreements between Asquith and Lloyd George?

7 Why did the first Labour government last for only nine months?

Government preparations for the Strike

In preparation for the General Strike the government:
- Built up coal stocks to last for five months.
- Increased the number of special constables from 98,000 to 226,000.
- Drew up detailed instructions for the army, navy and police to guard docks, telephone exchanges and power stations.
- Made subsidy agreements with the owners of haulage firms to put 200,000 vehicles at the government's disposal.
- Divided the country into ten areas, each under a Civil Commissioner (usually a member of the government) who would take over the powers of local government in a state of emergency.
- Set up 88 Voluntary Service Committees. The Civil Commissioners were to work with the VSCs to co-ordinate local services.
- Supported the Organisation for the Maintenance of Supplies. About 100,000 volunteers joined the OMS ready to keep essential services going when the strike began.

Countdown to the Strike

March 1921
Mines returned to private ownership after being run by the government during the First World War. Mine owners immediately declared their intention to cut pay.

April 1921
The miners decided to strike in protest at the proposed pay cut. Their partners in the unions' Triple Alliance, the railwaymen and transport workers, agreed to support the miners but on 'Black Friday' (15 April) they backed out of their agreement. The miners went on strike but were forced back to work as union funds ran out. The mine owners then proceeded with the threatened pay cuts.

April 1925
Winston Churchill, the Chancellor of the Exchequer, returned Britain to the Gold Standard, linking the value of the pound to the value of gold. This raised British export prices, including the price of coal. Mine owners found it impossible to sell coal on foreign markets without cutting prices.

May 1925
The price of coal fell below £1 a ton (in 1920 the price had been £5.75 a ton) and the mine owners faced the prospect of falling profits.

June – July 1925
Mine owners announced their intention to cut wages, increase working hours and break the national minimum wage. The miners drew up plans for a strike.

Baldwin intervened, giving a subsidy of £23 million to prevent the proposed wage cuts. The subsidy was to operate until 1 May 1926 while a Royal Commission (the Samuel Commission) examined the coal industry. The unions claimed a victory for the power of labour and called July 31st 'Red Friday'.

August 1925 – May 1926
The government had no intention of paying another subsidy and accepted that a strike could break out in 1926. They made extensive preparations to cope with the effects of a strike.

March 1926
The Samuel Commission recommended that the miners take a pay cut. Arthur Cook, the Secretary of the Mine Workers' Federation, took up the battle-cry: 'Not a penny off the pay, not a minute on the day.'

1 May 1926
The government subsidy expired. As the miners were still set against the employers' terms, there was a *lock out* – the mine owners prevented the miners from getting to work.

The General Council of the TUC met to discuss co-ordinated strike action in support of the miners. A ballot of trade union members showed huge support for a national strike.

Result of the TUC ballot on strike action
For 3,653,527
Against 49,911

2 May 1926
Workers at the *Daily Mail* offices refused to print an anti-union article. Baldwin saw this as a serious challenge to the freedom of the press and called off negotiations with the unions.

4 May 1926
First day of the Strike. Ninety per cent of trade union members who had been called out on strike, obeyed their leaders and stopped work.

The General Strike 4–12 May 1926

On strike	Not on strike
Miners	Health workers
Railway workers	Water, sewage and sanitation workers
General transport workers	Food suppliers
Printers	Emergency services
Builders	
Shipbuilders	
Power workers (gas and electricity)	
Iron and steel workers	
Engineers	
Chemical workers	

BBC radio
- The BBC broadcast five strike bulletins a day
- The government checked all broadcasts
- Stanley Baldwin broadcast to the nation on several occasions
- TUC spokesmen and Labour leader Ramsay MacDonald, who was also the Leader of the Opposition in Parliament, were banned from the BBC.

Incidents of disorder	1289
Number of strikers	3,000,000
Prosecutions of strikers	3146

SOURCE 8

In the 1920s the coal industry was in serious difficulties. The extent of its problems are summarised in the following account.

In 1925 the British coal industry was in an acute, deep-rooted depression. It was still the country's largest industry with a labour force of one million men, but from a prosperous period in the early 1920s it had declined to a condition in which 79 per cent of pits were producing at a loss. In the first six months of 1926 the industry lost £2 million. Its structure was archaic [out of date], with some 2,500 pits operated by 1,400 different owners. It was under capitalised [lacked investment], machinery was antiquated, management was largely incompetent. These native weaknesses were [made worse] when cheap Polish and German coal flooded the market after 1923, forcing world prices down … The industry sank into crisis, forcing the miners into poverty.

Michael Hughes, *Cartoons from the General Strike*, 1968.

Political Parties 1900–1929

SOURCE 9

On the morning of Tuesday 4 May, the nation awoke to a transformed Britain. The cities discovered it first - the silence. No buses or trains ran, the factories were still, nothing moved on the docks. On the railways the stoppage was almost 100 per cent. The London Omnibus Company owned 3,933 buses. None of these left the garages during the first day, and even with OMS drivers only 526 were later to take to the road.

Only fifteen of London's underground trains ran, and the trams were at a standstill. At the London docks no ships were unloaded or cargoes moved until by OMS volunteers under protection of armed soldiers.

Michael Hughes, *Cartoons from the General Strike*, 1968.

SOURCE 11

The government used armoured vehicles including tanks to protect vital food supplies at the docks and in transit. Here an armoured car provides an escort for food trucks passing through central London. The convoy was on its way to a huge food depot and milk distribution centre in Hyde Park. The centre was organised and protected by armed troops.

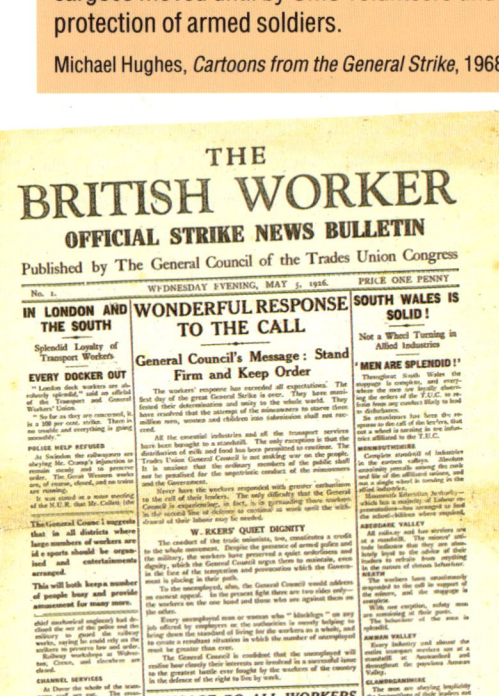

SOURCE 10

'Unfounded rumours and false news are put into circulation. Take no notice. Your officials have authentic news.'

The TUC produced its own newspaper, *The British Worker*, throughout the Strike. The paper cost one penny and had a circulation of about 700,000

'Many false rumours are current. Believe nothing until you see it in the *British Gazette*.'

The government produced its own newspaper, the *British Gazette*, throughout the Strike. It was supervised by Winston Churchill, cost one penny, and had a circulation of about two million.

Pedestrian. "I'm afraid you're fully loaded aren't you?"
Owner-Driver. "Not at all, Madam. There's still one knee vacant at the back, if you don't mind letting your legs dangle outside."

SOURCE 12

By 1926 there were over a million private cars on British roads. With public transport at a standstill, many well-off car owners put their vehicles to use as taxis, keeping thousands of office and shop workers on the move.

Political Parties 1900–1929

Volunteers

The OMS (Organisation for the Maintenance of Supplies) quickly allocated volunteers to take over some of the jobs of the strikers. They helped to keep a skeleton transport service going and some worked in the docks unloading cargo. OMS volunteers were more common in the south of England:

London and Middlesex	25,803
The South	17,775
The South West	3,830
E. Midlands and E. Anglia	16,148
The North	8,124

SOURCE 13

The Home Secretary W. Joynson-Hicks made a number of appeals for volunteers to act as special constables:

Give the government enough Special Constables to enable me to allot two to every vehicle that is, or thinks it is, in danger, thus releasing the regular police for perhaps sterner work. Give me men in such numbers that we may have mobile forces of young and vigorous Special Constables available in any London area where trouble is anticipated. Give us this and there will be little fear of serious trouble.

The British Gazette, 10 May 1926.

The end of the Strike

During the nine days of the General Strike, Baldwin's government refused to talk to union leaders until they ordered their members back to work. Meanwhile, the TUC's resolve crumbled. Its leaders were concerned about the strike's legality, and feared arrest and the confiscation of union funds. So on 12 May a delegation from the TUC met with Baldwin and called off the Strike. They were given no guarantees about miners' pay and conditions.

The miners stayed on strike for the next seven months before hunger forced them back to work. Many were victimised by the mine owners and all were forced to take pay cuts and work a longer day.

SOURCE 14

For the thousands on strike it was a time of holiday; for office workers and others not directly affected by the strike there was an excitement of the unusual. For those who volunteered to do the work of the strikers there was the exhilaration of adventure, the spirit of a lark. The subsequent cliché, that strikers and police spent their time playing football matches against each other, had a good measure of truth in it. Parades, meetings, speeches, long hours in committees, took up the time of many; other people pursued the daily round as if nothing more than a prolonged Bank Holiday was occurring.

C L Mowat, *Britain Between the Wars*, 1955.

SOURCE 15

Popular accounts of the strike have perhaps exaggerated the orderliness prevailing during the strike and the good relations between police and strikers. Trams were overturned, windows broken and buses immobilised by removing vital engine parts. There were police baton charges against pickets or gatherings of onlookers. The TUC received many complaints about provocative and violent behaviour by special constables. Many people were injured and the number and extent of violent clashes were accelerating in the last days of the strike.

Margaret Morris, *The British General Strike*, 1973.

Knowledge and understanding

Use the information on pages 28 to 31 to investigate the following questions.

1 How did the following contribute to the outbreak of the General Strike in 1926?
a The return of the mines to private ownership in 1921.
b The flood of cheap Polish and German coal after 1923 (see Source 8).
c The outdated structure of the industry and the lack of investment in it (see Source 8).
d Britain's return to the Gold Standard.

2 What short-term factors caused the General Strike (focus on the period May 1925 to May 1926)?

3 How did the government's advance preparations help to defeat the Strike?

4 What methods did the government use to ensure that the Strike would be beaten?

5 How far could the TUC claim that the General Strike was a success?

6 In what ways did some sections of the general public help to defeat the Strike?

7 Why did the TUC call off the Strike after just nine days?

Investigation

The General Strike: industrial dispute or revolution?

SOURCE A

This extract is taken from the *Daily Mail* editorial of 3 May 1926. The press, including the *Daily Mail*, was generally hostile to the trade unions.

The general strike is not an industrial dispute; it is a revolutionary movement, intended to inflict suffering upon the great mass of innocent persons in the community and thereby put forcible constraint upon the Government.

SOURCE B

The *British Worker* newspaper was produced by the TUC. It reported the Strike from the point of view of the unions.

The General Council [of the TUC] does not challenge the Constitution. It is not seeking to substitute unconstitutional government. Nor is it desirous of undermining our Parliamentary institutions. The sole aim of the Council is to secure for the miners a decent standard of life. The Council is engaged in an Industrial Dispute. There is no Constitutional crisis.

The British Worker, 7 May 1926.

SOURCE C

MESSAGE FROM THE PRIME MINISTER:

Constitutional Government is being attacked.

Let all good citizens whose livelihood and labour have thus been put in peril bear with fortitude and patience the hardships with which they have been so suddenly confronted.

Stand behind the Government who are doing their part confident that you will co-operate in the measures they have undertaken to preserve the liberties and privileges of the people of these islands.

The Laws of England are the People's birthright.

The laws are in your keeping.
You have made Parliament their guardian
The General Strike is a challenge to Parliament and is the road to anarchy and ruin.

STANLEY BALDWIN.

SOURCE D

A *Punch* cartoon from the issue following the collapse of the General Strike.

THE LEVER BREAKS.

SOURCE E

In August 1925 the miners' leader A J Cook, a self confessed 'follower of Lenin', made a defiant speech following the victory of 'Red Friday'.

Next May we shall be faced with the greatest struggle we have ever known, and we are preparing for it. I am going to get a fund, if I can, that will buy grub so that when the struggle comes we shall have that grub distributed in the homes of our people. I don't care a hang for any government, or army or navy. They can come along with their bayonets. Bayonets don't cut coal. Our hearts are strong, and we will beat Churchill, the Government, the employers and the OMS.

SOURCE F

This extract comes from *The Pageant of the Years* by Sir Philip Gibbs. The book was published in 1946 and contains the author's personal view on great events which happened in his lifetime.

My sympathies have always been on the side of the underdogs and the underpaid, but they were not in favour of this general strike, which was an attempt by the TUC to coerce the Government of the country and take over its power. It was an attack on our Parliamentary system and tradition.

SOURCE G

This extract comes from a book published to coincide with the centenary celebrations of the TUC.

In both the government and industry there were many who saw the growth of the left and the strengthening of trade union power as a menace to the nation, and they hungered for a conflict in which the left would be irretrievably damaged. Government preparations were massive, extremely thorough and deadly serious, and had half the energy expended been directed towards solving the mining dispute the industry's problems would have been over.

Michael Hughes, *Cartoons from the General Strike*, 1968.

Questions

1 What are the strengths and weaknesses of Source D as an interpretation of the General Strike?

2 How reliable is Source C as evidence about the nature of the General Strike?

3 Explain why Sources A and B present the General Strike in different ways.

4 If you wanted to present an interpretation of the General Strike which was unfavourable to the trade unions, which of these sources would you select? Explain your choice.

5 Would this selection of sources prove that the trade unions were planning a revolution?

6 Look at Source F. Explain how you think Sir Philip Gibbs arrived at this interpretation of the General Strike.

7 Explain why Sources F and G give different interpretations of the General Strike.

8 Why would it be difficult for a historian today to write an account of the General Strike which all other historians would agree with?

3 A United Kingdom?

SOURCES 1 AND 2

8 March 1973 The terrifying force of an IRA car bomb as it explodes in Whitehall, London. Shrapnel flies through the air in every direction and glass showers down from the offices lining the street.

The aftermath
Debris from the blast litters the streets. The wreckage of the George pub and the car parked outside show something of the force of the explosion. Almost every pane of glass has been blown out of the office block in the background. One person was killed and 250 were injured in the attack. On the same day there were six other bomb alerts in central London.

Ulster's 2,000th victim

Loyalist gunmen yesterday shot dead a shopkeeper in Belfast, the 2,000th civilian victim of Northern Ireland's bloodshed since 1969. Larry Murchan, a Catholic father of three, was shot at point-blank range by two masked men as he burned rubbish at the back of his shop at the junction of St James's Place and St James's Road near the Falls Road. Police blamed Loyalists and said they believed that the killing was in retaliation for the IRA murder of a Protestant three weeks ago. Loyalists said they shot Mr Murchan because he sold copies of the IRA's newspaper, *Republican News*. The dead man's family denied the allegation. The gunmen and a third man, who had been waiting at the wheel of a white Astra, drove off across the M1 motorway and then abandoned the car.

The Independent on Sunday, 29 September 1991.

On Sunday 29 September 1991, *The Independent on Sunday* newspaper reported the horrifying murder of a Belfast shopkeeper.

That Sunday, every other national newspaper in Britain also printed details of this shocking incident. Media coverage of violence in Northern Ireland has become a familiar feature of life in modern Britain. Hardly a day goes by without news of a terrorist attack in Ireland or on mainland Britain making the headlines. But how much of this news do you really understand? When the IRA claims responsibility for detonating a bomb at a London railway station, or a Loyalist para-military group admits to the shooting of customers in a Belfast betting shop, are you able to explain who these groups are and why they commit this violence?

Understanding the news from Northern Ireland is not easy. Try this simple experiment. Read again the news item on 'Ulster's 2,000th victim', this time leaving out the underlined sections of the report.

You will have discovered that the basis for the story is the cold-blooded murder of a Belfast shopkeeper by two masked gunmen. Now try to work out *why* this man was killed using the details which are underlined. No doubt you will have found that to fully understand the reasons for the murder you have to ask some basic questions about the underlined sections.

> The gunmen were Loyalists.
> Who are the Loyalists?
>
> The victim was a Catholic.
> Why do Loyalists murder Catholics?
>
> The Loyalists claimed the victim had IRA connections.
> What is the IRA?
>
> Police believed the murder was in retaliation for an IRA murder of a Protestant.
> Why does the IRA murder Protestants?
>
> The victim was the 2000th civilian to die in Northern Ireland's bloodshed since 1969.
> What is the significance of 1969?
> Why has there been bloodshed in Northern Ireland since that date?

The answers to these key questions are central to your understanding of the problems facing Northern Ireland today. These answers are to be found by examining the historical background to the present situation which has produced the terrible catalogue of violence outlined in **Datapoint: The 'Troubles' since 1969** (see page 36).

Who are the Loyalists?

In 1800 the Act of Union made Ireland part of the United Kingdom. The Irish parliament was abolished and responsibility for the government of Ireland was transferred to London. During the 19th century Irish nationalists tried to restore Irish independence. Moderate nationalists worked from within Westminster trying to persuade Parliament to allow 'Home Rule' for Ireland, with the revival of an Irish parliament responsible for Irish affairs. Home Rule became a major bone of contention in the early part of the 20th century, and led to divisions among the Irish people which persist to this day.

An independent Irish parliament was viewed by Irish Protestants with alarm. They feared being overwhelmed by Ireland's Catholic majority (see **Datapoint: Religion in Ireland**, page 38). In the Protestant stronghold of Ulster fears of a Catholic takeover were most apparent. The Ulster Protestants are fiercely Unionist, meaning that they want to preserve the Union created in 1800. Ulster Unionists are also known as Loyalists because of their loyalty to the British Crown. The resistance of the Ulster Protestants to independence from Britain led directly to the division of Ireland and the creation of the Northern Ireland state.

SOURCE 3

A cartoon comment by Irish nationalists on the prospects for Ireland as an independent state or as a member of the United Kingdom.

DATAPOINT

The 'Troubles' since 1969

Londonderry
15 August 1969: British troops arrive to restore order following a week of serious rioting between Catholics and Protestants which has left 5 dead and hundreds injured.

Belfast
9 February 1971: First British soldier killed since the arrival of troops in Northern Ireland in 1969.

Londonderry
30 January 1972: 'Bloody Sunday'. British paratroopers open fire on a banned civil rights march killing 13 demonstrators.

Aldershot
22 February 1972: IRA bomb attack on the barracks of the 16th Parachute Regiment: 7 people killed in the blast.

Belfast
21 May 1972: 8 people killed in exchange between Catholic gunmen on the Ballymurphy Housing Estate and armed Protestants in the adjoining Springmartin Estate.

M62 near Bradford
4 February 1974: IRA bomb explodes on a coach carrying servicemen and their families: 12 die.

Dublin
17 May 1974: 23 people killed in 3 car bomb explosions, more than 100 injured.

Guildford
5 October 1974: 5 people killed by IRA bombs in 2 pubs.

Birmingham
21 November 1974: The Mulberry Bush and The Tavern in the Town pubs are torn apart by IRA bombs: 21 people die in the attacks.

Newry, County Down
31 July 1975: 3 members of the Dublin group the Miami Showband are killed in an ambush.

London
27 November 1975: Television personality and anti-IRA campaigner Ross McWhirter shot dead at his home by Irish gunmen.

Belfast
17 February 1978: 14 killed in a bomb attack on the Le Mons restaurant.

London
30 March 1979: Car bomb kills Tory MP Airey Neave as he drives out of the car park of the House of Commons.

Mullaghmore, County Sligo
27 August 1979: Lord Mountbatten, a cousin of the Queen, is killed by an IRA bomb on board his boat; 3 others on board also die.

Warrenpoint, County Down
27 August 1979: 18 soldiers from the Parachute Regiment and the Queen's Own Highlanders killed in IRA ambush.

London
20 July 1982: 6 members of the band of the Royal Green Jackets killed by an IRA bomb under the Regents Park bandstand.
2 guardsmen and 7 horses killed in an IRA bomb attack on a procession by the Blues and Royals in Hyde Park.

London
17 December 1983: 5 shoppers killed in IRA bomb attack on Harrods department store in Knightsbridge.

Brighton
12 October 1984: IRA bomb attack on Conservative Party delegates staying at the Grand Hotel during their Party conference. 4 people killed. Prime Minister Margaret Thatcher narrowly escapes injury.

Enniskillen, County Fermanagh
8 November 1987: IRA bomb explodes during a Remembrance Day parade: 11 killed.

Murders in Northern Ireland	
1966	3
1990	71

Victims of the violence
August 1969-May 1987

	Killed	Wounded
Royal Ulster Constabulary	243	2398
Army	549	4168
Civilians	1785	14517

A United Kingdom?

SOURCE 4

A history lesson and political message in gloss paint. The Union Jack and the flag of Ulster fly together on a Belfast mural which celebrates the victory of the Protestants over the Catholics at the Battle of the Boyne on 12 July 1690. On the blue-painted wall, the shape of Ulster is picked out as a Union Jack, clearly showing Ulster's commitment to the Union with Britain. The Loyalist gunman with the raised fist vows never to accept a united Ireland.

How was Ireland partitioned?

Protestant resistance to Home Rule was organised by the Unionist MP, Sir Edward Carson (**Sources 5 and 6**). In 1912 he invited people loyal to King George V to sign a document called Ulster's Solemn League and Covenant. There was an immediate and overwhelming response. At one stage 150 people a minute were signing the Covenant in Belfast City Hall, some even signed in their own blood! In doing so they vowed to use all means to defeat the plans for a Home Rule parliament. Eventually almost 500,000 had pledged their support.

SOURCE 5

Sir Edward Carson, a Dublin Protestant and gifted lawyer. He became MP for Dublin University in 1892. From 1911 he led the Ulster Unionist Council which organised the Protestant resistance to Home Rule in Ulster. At a meeting of Unionists at Craigavon near Belfast in September 1911, he declared his intention to defeat Asquith's Home Rule proposals; 'You and I joined together', he told the crowd, 'will yet defeat the most nefarious conspiracy that has ever been hatched against a free people.'

SOURCE 6

Part of an anti-Home Rule speech by the Unionist leader, Sir Edward Carson, February 1914.

They [the Unionists] are fighting for a great principle and a great deal. They are fighting to stay under a government which they were invited to come under, under which they have flourished, and under which they are content, and to refuse to come under a government which they loathe and detest ... I am not going to argue whether they are right or wrong in resisting ... but I say this: if these men are not morally justified when they are attempted to be driven out of one government with which they are satisfied and put under another which they loathe, I do not see how resistance can ever be justified in history at all.

DATAPOINT

Religion in Ireland

Key:
- Mostly Protestant
- Mostly Catholic
- Mixed Catholic and Protestant

Catholic / Protestant

1 Antrim, 2 Armagh, 3 Cavan
4 Donegal, 5 Down, 6 Fermanagh
7 Londonderry, 8 Monaghan, 9 Tyrone

Londonderry, Belfast

SOURCE 7

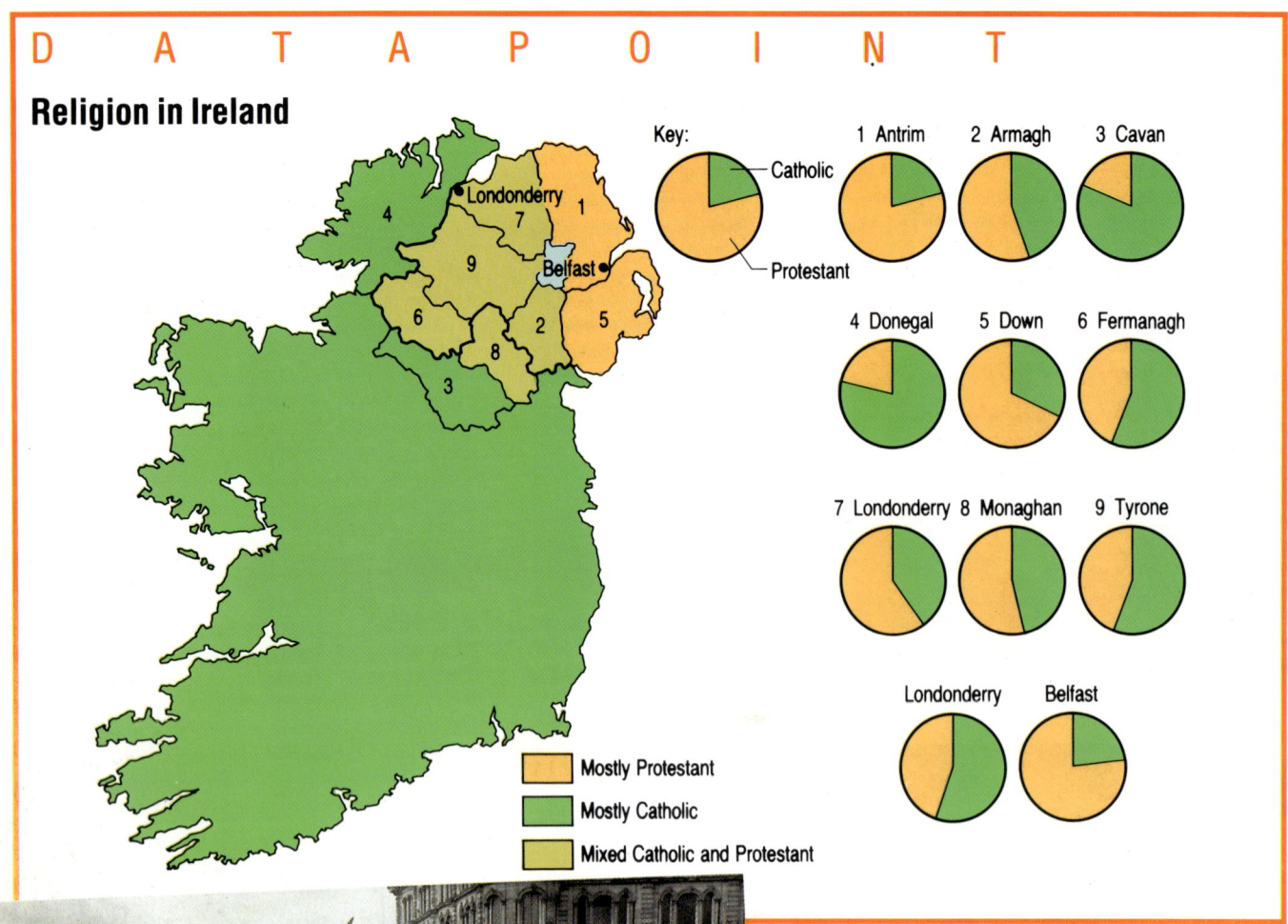

Ulster Day in Belfast, 28 September 1912. The statue of Queen Victoria looks out across a huge crowd of people assembled to declare their loyalty to her grandson George V. This was the queue to sign Ulster's Solemn League and Covenant which was kept at Belfast City Hall on a table covered with a Union Jack. By the end of the following year, many of the men pictured in the crowd had taken their objections to Home Rule a stage further by joining the 100,000-strong Ulster Volunteer Force.

In January 1913 the Ulster Volunteer Force (UVF) was formed: 100,000 men joined. Through gunrunning operations, the UVF soon began to arm itself. Almost inevitably the Catholics and Irish nationalists retaliated by setting up a para-military organisation of their own, the Irish Volunteers. With 200,000 volunteers, they too began to arm themselves. Civil War looked likely in Ireland, but the issue was avoided by the outbreak of the First World War in 1914.

In the first general election after the War the republican Sinn Fein party won three quarters of the Irish seats in the British Parliament. Sinn Fein went beyond the moderate demands of the Home Rulers and campaigned for the establishment of an independent Irish Republic. In January 1919, they declared the independence of Ireland and established a parliament in Dublin which they called Dail Eireann (**Source 8**). In 1919 the Irish Volunteers became the Irish Republican Army (IRA). The IRA was led by Michael Collins, a nationalist of uncompromising views. Shortly after the declaration of independence he announced that,

> The sooner fighting is forced and a general state of disorder created throughout the country, the better it will be for the country. Ireland is likely to get more out of a general state of disorder than from a continuance of the situation as it now stands.

Ireland rapidly fell into this 'state of disorder'. By 1920 a full-scale war between the IRA and the British authorities was being fought (**Source 9**). At first, officers of the Royal Irish Constabulary (RIC) were the main targets of the IRA and by June 1920, 55 constables had been killed. Reinforcements for the RIC began to be recruited in England, and about 7000 were eventually brought to Ireland. These were the notorious 'Black and Tans' (**Source 10**), so-called because of the colours of their uniforms. The Black and Tans were aggressive and often undisciplined, and their hard-line treatment of republican sympathisers produced fear and resentment. The Crown forces and the IRA now set upon each other without mercy, bringing terror and bloodshed to the busy streets of

SOURCE 8

Sinn Fein leaders at the first Dail Eireann, January 1919.

Michael Collins (*first row: 2nd from left*) Fought with the Easter Rebels in Dublin 1916 and was imprisoned for six months. Became Minister of Finance in the Dail and at the same time organised the activities of the IRA.

Arthur Griffith (*first row: 4th from left*) A journalist who championed the cause of an Irish parliament through the newspaper *Sinn Fein* (Ourselves Alone). Griffith helped form the political party of the same name.

Eamonn de Valera (*first row: 5th from left*) Fought in the Easter rising of 1916 but escaped execution because he was born in the USA. Became President of the first Dail.

SOURCE 9

Eamonn de Valera (*the tallest man on the platform*) reviews IRA volunteers at Six Mile Bridge, County Clare in the early 1920s. Mobile units of between 15 and 30 IRA men formed 'flying columns' which carried out ambushes on Crown forces. In return, the Black and Tans organised ferocious reprisals.

SOURCE 10

These are the words of a song popular in Ireland around 1920.

The Bold Black and Tan

The town of Balbriggan they've burned to the ground
While bullets like hailstones were whizzing around;
And women left homeless by this evil clan
They've waged war on children, the bold Black and Tan.

From Dublin to Cork and from Thurles to Mayo
Lies a trail of destruction wherever they go;
With England to help and fierce passions to fan,
She must feel bloody proud of her bold Black and Tan.

Ah, then not by the terrors of England's foul horde,
For ne'er could a nation be ruled by the sword;
For our country we'll have yet in spite of her plan
Or ten times the number of bold Black and Tan.

We defeated conscription in spite of their threats,
And we're going to defeat old Lloyd George and his pets;
For Ireland and Freedom we're here to a man,
And we'll humble the pride of the bold Black and Tan.

---

the cities and the quiet lanes of the countryside. At the same time the British Government tried to resolve Ireland's problems by passing a new measure. The Government of Ireland Act of 1920 proposed to partition Ireland into two states, each with its own Home Rule parliament, one for the six counties of northern Ireland and one for southern Ireland.

In July 1921, with the two sides bleeding each other white, a truce was arranged. Soon after, negotiations began in London between delegates of the British government, including Lloyd George and Winston Churchill, and the Dail Eireann, including Arthur Griffith and Michael Collins. The talks eventually produced an agreement known as the Anglo-Irish Treaty which was signed in London on 6 December 1921 and which followed the broad terms of the Government of Ireland Act. The Treaty had the effect of dividing Ireland into two parts; Northern Ireland and the Irish Free State (see **Datapoint: The partition of Ireland 1921**, below).

DATAPOINT

The partition of Ireland 1921

Six of the nine counties of the northern province of Ulster voted to opt out of the Irish Free State and became Northern Ireland.

The remaining 26 counties, including the Ulster counties of Donegal, Cavan and Monaghan, formed the Irish Free State.

Northern Ireland had a population of 1.5 million people; 66 per cent were Protestant and 34 per cent were Catholic. The Irish Free State had a population of 3 million; 10 per cent were Protestant and 90 per cent were Catholic.

Northern Ireland had its own parliament at Stormont in Belfast. The Irish Free State had its parliament in Dublin.

Northern Ireland's first Prime Minister was Sir James Craig. Arthur Griffith was elected as President of the Dail following the resignation of Eamonn de Valera in protest at the Treaty.

Northern Ireland remained part of the United Kingdom and was governed from Westminster on all major areas of policy.

The Irish Free State became a Dominion of the British Empire with the same status as Canada, Australia, New Zealand and South Africa. The Irish were granted self-government, taking control of their own domestic and foreign affairs and organising their own armed forces. However, they were required to join the British Commonwealth, the Royal Navy retained four naval bases in Irish ports and all MPs in the Dail were compelled to swear an oath of allegiance to King George V and his heirs.

The Anglo-Irish Treaty was passed in the Dail on 7 January 1922 by just 64 votes to 57.

SOURCE 11

1922: Civil war breaks out in Ireland. A field gun of the Irish Free State army shells anti-Treaty rebels in a Dublin street. Not being designed for use in an urban environment, such guns were enormously destructive.

Civil War

The partition of Ireland in 1921 led directly to a bitter civil war. The two sides were divided over the Anglo-Irish Treaty. Some were prepared to accept partition, others bitterly opposed the creation of a Northern Ireland state. These divisions were evident at every level in Irish society. In the Dail, de Valera was totally opposed to the Treaty, whilst Collins and Griffith, who had negotiated and signed it, were prepared to try to make it work. Even the IRA was split over the partition issue. In April 1922 anti-Treaty IRA forces occupied the Dublin Law Courts and set up their headquarters there. Soon after, Irish Free State forces began to bombard their positions and the Irish Civil War began (**Source 11**). It took eight days to subdue the anti-Treaty forces in Dublin at a cost of 60 lives.

Fighting continued across the country with the republicans employing guerrilla tactics against government troops. The Civil War continued until the end of April 1923 when the dwindling resources of the IRA made it impossible for them to continue their campaign. Six hundred people died during the conflict and over 3000 were wounded. When the bloodshed ended, Ireland was still divided. This division is at the heart of the present situation in Ireland. The IRA, who rejected partition in 1921, continue to reject it to this day. The main goal of the IRA is to end the political division of Ireland. To understand what inspires them we must focus in on a turning point in Irish history, the Easter rising of 1916.

SOURCE 12

This description of the Civil War is by the playwright Sean O'Casey. O'Casey had strong views about the war and wrote a play called *Juno and the Paycock* which examined the tragedy and futility of the struggle.

After the capture of Dublin by the Free Staters, ambushes began to blossom red from many a street corner: and the joyful killing spread over the whole country. Houses went up in flames, exploding often with a wild hurrah, and bridges sank sullenly down into the rivers they spanned. Republicans put land mines under road barriers, so that when the Free Staters tried to remove them, they ascended into heaven; and when Free Staters captured Republicans, they fixed up barricades of their own, laden with land mines, compelling the Republicans to remove the road block, so that they too were blown to pieces.

Sean O'Casey, *Autobiographies*, 1963.

A United Kingdom?

An unfinished legacy: The Easter rising 1916

When the First World war broke out Irishmen from north and south, Catholics and Protestants alike, marched together in their thousands to slaughter on the battlefields of Europe. Some 200,000 Irishmen served in the British Army between 1914 and 1918. By contrast, a very different response to the War was organised from a small tobacconist's shop in the centre of Dublin. The shop was owned by a Republican activist named Tom Clarke and it became the meeting place for a small number of dedicated Irish patriots. They regarded England's war with Germany as an opportunity to throw off British rule. The leaders of this group met shortly after the outbreak of war and decided to carry out an armed rising against the British government.

On Easter Monday 24 April 1916, Republican rebels occupied strategic buildings in Dublin. The rebel headquarters was established at the General Post Office in Sackville Street (**Source 13**). From the Post Office Patrick Pearse read to an astonished crowd of onlookers the Proclamation of Irish Independence and declared the creation of an Irish Republic (**Source 14**).

The British authorities had been caught off guard when the rising began. Many of the 2500 troops garrisoned in the city were enjoying a Bank Holiday

SOURCE 13
Inside the rebel headquarters at the General Post Office in Sackville Street. An artist's impression of the rebels under attack from British forces. The wounded James Connolly gives orders from a stretcher as the fighting rages around him. What does this picture tell us about the political sympathies of the artist who produced it?

SOURCE 14
Irishmen and Irishwomen ... We declare the right of the people of Ireland to the ownership of Ireland, and to the unfettered control of Irish destinies. We hereby proclaim the Irish Republic as a sovereign independent state and we pledge our lives ... to the cause of its freedom, of its welfare and of its exaltation among the nations.

Patrick Pearse, 24 April 1916.

outing at the Fairyhouse races when the rebels declared Irish independence. The advantage did not remain with the rebels for long. Martial law was declared to discourage looters. Troop reinforcements were sent and heavy artillery was moved into position.

Prolonged and indiscriminate shelling set the city centre ablaze. On Friday night the rebels made a final stand in King's Street but the situation was hopeless and surrender was only a matter of hours away. One by one during Saturday the rebel garrisons around the city put down their weapons and were taken into custody by the military authorities. On Sunday morning the prisoners were escorted through the city to the Richmond Barracks. At times they were jeered at and spat upon by the crowds. On the whole the people of Dublin had not supported the rising and had little sympathy with the rebels. What happened next caused a profound shift in Irish popular opinion.

Kilmainham jail stands in a western suburb of Dublin. Its bleak granite walls immediately betray its grim purpose, though today it is not a prison but a museum. It was to this place that the leaders of the rising were taken after they had surrendered. The British authorities regarded the rebels as traitors, murderers and enemies of the people. In dealing with them the Cabinet in London showed no mercy, nor any political common sense. Over a ten day period the 15 rebel leaders held in Kilmainham were executed by firing squad. The last to die was James Connolly. Unable to stand because of a bullet wound to his ankle, he was carried on a stretcher to the prison yard, placed on a simple wooden chair and executed by firing squad like the rest.

A wave of revulsion at the executions swept across Ireland and began to unite Irish people against Britain. The rebels who had so recently been dismissed as fanatics became patriotic martyrs, the victims of a brutal foreign government (**Source 16**). In a short time they became,

SOURCE 15

The aftermath of the Easter rising in Dublin. This part of the city was shelled from the River Liffey by the gunboat *Helga*. But the bulk of the damage was caused by two 18-pounder field guns firing at close range in the streets. More than 400 people were killed in the fighting and a further 3000 were wounded. Almost 200 buildings were gutted by fire and hundreds of people were made homeless. The rising caused £3 million worth of damage.

SOURCE 16

This source is an extract from a speech by the Irish Nationalist MP John Dillon. The speech was made in the House of Commons in May 1916 and was a warning to the government about the consequences of its decision to execute the leaders of the Easter rising.

I admit they were wrong; I know they were wrong; but they fought a clean fight, and they fought with superb bravery and skill ... The great bulk of the population were not favourable to the insurrection, and the insurgents themselves, who had confidently counted on a rising of the people in their support, were absolutely disappointed ... What is happening is that thousands of people in Dublin, who ten days ago were bitterly opposed to the whole of the Sinn Fein movement and to the rebellion, are now becoming infuriated against the government on account of these executions and, as I am informed by letters received this morning, that feeling is spreading in a most dangerous degree.

Hansard, 5th series, vol 82.

as they have remained, Irish heroes. By July 1917 the British government had released all the remaining prisoners held after the rising. On their return to Dublin they were welcomed by thousands of cheering and flag-waving admirers. The contrast between this reception and the jeering which they had suffered on their way to prison a year before showed how the actions of the British government had turned many ordinary Irish citizens into republican sympathisers.

The events of Easter week 1916 made permanent British rule in Ireland an impossibility. The pressure for Irish independence gathered momentum in the aftermath of the rising. It is to this week in Irish history that we must turn if we are to understand the 20th century background to the continuing problems in Ireland. The terrorist activities of the modern IRA are seen from within the organisation as a continuation of the work begun by the Easter rebels in 1916 (**Source 18**).

Even the name sometimes used to describe the IRA, the 'Provisionals' or 'Provos', is a reference to the events of 1916. The IRA took the name in 1969 proudly naming themselves after the 'Provisional' government of Ireland announced by Pearse at the Dublin GPO in 1916.

SOURCE 17

A Republican mural in the Catholic Bogside area of Belfast. To this day the events of Easter 1916 have a special significance to Irish nationalists. The united and independent Irish state proclaimed by the rebels remains the goal of the Republican movement. The mural asks defiantly, 'Who fears to speak of Easter week?'

Knowledge and understanding

Use pages 35 to 45 to investigate the following questions.

1 Look at the Datapoint: The 'Troubles' since 1969 (page 36).
a Identify the main groups who have been the targets of terrorist violence since 1969.
b Suggest reasons why such targets have been chosen.
c Why have many terrorist atrocities occurred on mainland Britain?
d According to the casualty figures for August 1969 to May 1987, who has suffered most as a result of the 'Troubles' in Northern Ireland?
e Suggest reasons why the murder rate in Northern Ireland between 1966 and 1990 has increased dramatically.

2 Look at Source 3.
a In what ways was this artist critical of British control of Ireland?
b What improvements for Ireland does the artist foresee if Ireland were to become independent?

3 What was meant by Home Rule for Ireland?

4 a Explain the terms *Loyalist* and *Unionist*.
b Why is 12 July an important date in the Protestant calendar?

5 Some of the key people and groups in Irish history in the early part of the 20th century are listed below. In each case describe their role and significance in Ireland 1900–21.

Sir Edward Carson	Sinn Fein
Eamonn de Valera	IRA
Michael Collins	Dail Eireann
Arthur Griffith	Ulster Volunteer Force
Sir James Craig	Irish Volunteers
James Connolly	Black and Tans

A United Kingdom?

SOURCE 18

In November 1969 the IRA split into two groups, the Official IRA and the Provisionals. The following month the 'Provos' made clear their objective.

We declare our allegiance to the Thirty-two-County Irish Republic proclaimed at Easter 1916 ... suppressed to this day by the existing British-imposed Six-County and Twenty-six-County partition states ... What Pearse and Connolly began ... on April 24 1916, is an unfinished legacy – but a clearly defined responsibility.

---

6 Look at the Datapoint: Religion in Ireland (page 38).
Explain why Irish Protestants were so alarmed by the prospect of Home Rule.

7 Look at Source 10.
a Choose four descriptions which tell you how the writer felt about the Black and Tans and their actions.
b What would be the value of this source to a historian who was interested in anti-British opinion in Ireland?
c How far does this source give a reliable impression of Irish public opinion around 1920?

8 Look at the Datapoint: The partition of Ireland 1921 (page 40).
a What were the main differences between the Irish Free State and Northern Ireland?
b What links continued to exist between the Free State and Britain after the partition?

9 Give reasons why the British government decided to partition Ireland in 1921 rather than grant independence to the whole of Ireland.

10 Why did a Civil War break out in Ireland in 1922?

11 Look at Sources 14 and 18. What is the historical link between the modern IRA and the Easter rising?

12 In the weeks after the Easter rising, why did so many Irish people become supporters of the nationalist cause? (Use Source 16 to help you with the answer).

The Protestant domination of Ulster 1921–1969

The present 'Troubles' in Ireland began in 1969 when the British government authorised the use of the army to bring a serious outbreak of violence between Catholics and Protestants under control. Although the Easter rising and the partition of Ireland formed the historical background to this confrontation, these were not the issues over which the two communities clashed in 1968 and 1969. At the heart of this dispute were Catholic complaints against the Protestants who were accused of abusing their majority in Ulster to obtain unfair advantages for themselves. Catholic civil rights organisations demanded fair treatment and an end to the policies of discrimination which had kept them under Protestant control since 1921.

The Northern Ireland parliament

In the first elections to the Northern Ireland parliament in 1921, the Unionists won 40 of the available 52 seats. The Unionists, who were dedicated to maintaining the union of Northern Ireland and Great Britain, remained in power until direct rule of Ulster was imposed from Britain in March 1972. In every election for 51 years the Protestant Unionists outnumbered the Catholic Nationalists by about four seats to one in the Stormont parliament. It was almost impossible for Catholic interests to be adequately protected in the face of such domination. In the decades which have followed the creation of Northern Ireland, the Unionist priority has been to maintain and strengthen ties with Britain and to preserve Protestant supremacy in Ulster. This was achieved by using unfair tactics at the expense of the Catholics.

1 The vote

When Northern Ireland was created, the British government set up a voting system based on proportional representation. This system was designed to ensure that all the different parties in a constituency would be represented in parliament in proportion to the number of votes each party won. In this way the voice of the Catholic minority would not be silenced. However, the Unionists removed this protection by abolishing proportional representation in local elections in 1922 and general elections in 1929.

2 Local elections

Not everyone was entitled to vote in local elections. The right to vote was restricted to those adults who owned a house or were tenants. This excluded people such as lodgers and people over 21 who lived in their parents' home. The situation was made worse by the fact that the better-off sections of the local community were entitled to more than one vote. These special conditions tended to favour the Protestants since more of them owned property, and had a bigger share of the wealth, than the Catholics.

3 Gerrymandering

One of the most widely practised abuses was the tactic known as 'gerrymandering'. This involved drawing electoral boundaries to ensure a Unionist majority on local councils regardless of the political views of the population (see **Datapoint: Gerrymandering in Londonderry, 1969** below).

The results of discrimination

The domination of Ulster by the Protestants produced widespread discrimination against the Catholics. Protestant-controlled local authorities were often reluctant to allocate council houses to Catholics, especially since becoming a householder qualified a person to vote. The employment of council officials and general workers was controlled along sectarian lines. In 1969 for example, 97 per cent of council workers in Belfast were Protestants. Separate schools developed to educate the youngsters of the two communities, and when funds were directed to Ulster for business development, the local authorities made sure most of the money went to help Protestant areas. Ulster Catholics became increasingly bitter about their treatment and, in the 1960s, they began to demand changes.

DATAPOINT

Gerrymandering in Londonderry, 1969

Londonderry was divided into three wards for local elections returning different numbers of councillors.

South: 8 councillors — 10,047 / 1,138 — Total 11,185

North: 8 councillors — 2,530 / 3,946 — Total 6,476

Waterside: 4 councillors — 1,852 / 3,697 — Total 5,549

In the 1969 local elections 8 Nationalist (Catholic) councillors and 12 Unionist (Protestant) councillors were elected.

This Unionist 'victory' resulted from an overall vote across all three wards of 62% for the Nationalists and 38% for the Unionists.

Nationalist: 14,429
Unionist: 8,781

Civil rights and the beginning of the 'Troubles'

In 1967 the Northern Ireland Civil Rights Association (NICRA) was founded. It demanded equal rights for all citizens of Ulster and called for fair elections. A wave of protest marches and meetings swept across Ulster in 1968 and 1969 (**Source 19**). The protests began in the summer of 1968 after a council house in Dungannon, County Tyrone, was allocated to a young Protestant girl following the eviction of a squatting Catholic family. The Dungannon March prompted a similar protest in Londonderry. This demonstration on 5 October 1968 was savagely broken up by the police. As a result a student movement called People's Democracy was set up at Queen's University in Belfast.

In January 1969 People's Democracy organised a march from Belfast to Londonderry. On 4 January the 500 marchers, having walked 70 miles, approached Burntollet Bridge on the outskirts of Londonderry. Here they were ambushed by Protestants who attacked the marchers with stones, bottles and spiked cudgels. Off-duty members of the Ulster Special Constabulary, the B Specials, were identified as being part of the Protestant mob. The regular police of the RUC (Royal Ulster Constabulary), who provided the escort for the marchers, failed to protect the Catholics. None of the attackers were arrested and there were even suggestions that the RUC was involved in the ambush (**Source 20**).

That evening there was violence in the Catholic Bogside district of Belfast. When the police went in to bring the disturbances under control they used excessive force, beating up Catholics, damaging property and shouting sectarian slogans. For the rest of the year there was violence in Ulster as Catholics clashed with Protestants. The rioting came to a head in August 1969 in Londonderry and Belfast. In two nights five people died and 300 houses were set on fire (**Sources 21 and 22**). The situation was out of control and so on August 14th British troops were deployed in Londonderry. Two days later the army took to the streets of Belfast.

At first the Catholics cheered the soldiers. They believed they had come to protect them from the Protestants and the police. But in April 1970 the army fired 104 canisters of CS gas into a Catholic riot in the Ballymurphy area of Belfast, persuading many Catholics that

SOURCE 19

Was the civil rights movement in Northern Ireland inspired by the genuine wish to improve conditions for Catholics, or was it part of a more sinister conspiracy to wreck the future of Northern Ireland? This source presents two interpretations of the issue. The first is the view of the Unionist MP, Ian Paisley, the second that of Michael Farrell, a civil rights activist in the late 1960s.

Paisley: The first salvoes in the fight of the revolution was on the civil rights front, as a softening propaganda weapon, in order to carry out further, to the bitter end, the murder and mayhem we have seen since.

Interviewer: Who was behind civil rights in your view?

Paisley: The Irish Republican Army, or at that time those that were dedicated to the views and objectives of that army.

Farrell: There were a number of Republicans (IRA members) and the proportion of them varied from time to time but they never dominated it. They were never in control, at least not until maybe later on. They were also used as stewards on civil rights marches ... but the stewards on the marches always played the role of trying to prevent trouble ... and in fact the younger PD [People's Democracy] demonstrators often had clashes with the stewards because we felt that the stewards were co-operating too much with the police.

Both extracts taken from the BBC *Timewatch* programme, *The Spark That Lit the Bonfire*.

SOURCE 20

This source was written by Michael Farrell, who organised of the march which ended in violence at Burntollet Bridge.

There was no doubt it was a trap. The RUC knew that an ambush had been prepared. Heaps of stones had been collected the night before and crowds of cudgel-wielding men had been gathering since early morning while the RUC men stood among them laughing and chatting. During the ambush some of the RUC joined in and attacked the marchers too.

M. Farrell, *Northern Ireland: The Orange State*, 1976.

48 A United Kingdom?

SOURCES 21 AND 22

Londonderry, August 1969
The police lose control of the city. Rioters on the streets by night and by day. Fire lights up the night sky as buildings and vehicles are torched by street gangs. Daytime brings no relief as crowds in the Bogside district bombard RUC officers with stones and bottles. Later that day the decision was taken at Westminster to send in troops to restore order.

Londonderry, 13 August 1969

Londonderry, 14 August 1969

the army was working with the Protestants and the police. Some Catholic communities now turned to the IRA for protection.

In November 1969 the IRA had split into two groups, the Official IRA and the Provisionals. The 'Provos' were committed to a terrorist campaign designed to end the partition of Ireland and to fight for the united Irish Republic declared by the Easter rebels in 1916. In time the Official IRA melted away, but the Provisionals continue their fight against British rule in Northern Ireland to this day.

Failed initiatives 1971–1977

In the search for answers to the crisis in Ulster, the authorities and the people themselves have tried a variety of approaches.

'Get tough'

During 1971 the IRA campaign of violence intensified. Each month the number of bombings increased; 37 in April,

SOURCE 23

Civil rights demonstrators pass British soldiers on Leeson Street in Belfast in the summer of 1970. The initial welcome received by the troops had by this time turned sour. Many Catholics believed that the army was in Ulster to prevent them from obtaining equal rights with the Protestants. A section of the crowd shows their contempt for the troops with the Nazi salute.

rising to 91 in July. In response to the worsening situation, Brian Faulkner, the Prime Minister of Ulster, introduced internment (the imprisonment of suspected terrorists without trial). By the end of the first day of internment (9 August 1971), 342 IRA suspects were behind bars. Most observers concluded that internment was a disastrous policy. The violence in Ulster which internment was supposed to reduce, became much worse (**Source 24**). In addition, the British Army was criticised in an official investigation (the Compton Report, November 1971) for ill-treating internees. The arrest of suspects was also carried out ruthlessly (**Source 25**).

The Catholics were angry at internment and became increasingly concerned for their safety. In Belfast and Londonderry they created 'no-go' areas to keep the police and the army out of their communities.

On Sunday 30 January 1972 the violence in Northern Ireland plumbed new depths. A civil rights march in Londonderry was halted by the army and a crack paratroop regiment was sent in to make arrests. The soldiers chased a crowd into the Rossville Flats in the Catholic Bogside area. Here they opened fire killing 13 unarmed civilians, a fourteenth victim later died in hospital. Catholics were shocked and outraged by the events of 'Bloody Sunday' and the IRA stepped up its terrorist campaign. At the same time extreme Protestants showed their determination to resist the Republicans by forming the Vanguard Movement (9 February 1972). William Craig, the founder of the movement, made the position of his followers quite clear in a speech the following month: 'We are determined ... to preserve our British tradition and way of life. And God help those who get in our way.'

The British Government now decided that Northern Ireland was out of control

SOURCE 24
The effects of internment

Numbers killed in IRA violence, April–November 1971.

	Soldiers	Police	Civilians
April–July	4	0	4
Aug–Nov	30	11	73

SOURCE 25

This statement by Henry Bennett, a Catholic man from Belfast, was made to the organisers of a Campaign for Social Justice. Their self-appointed task was to put together a record of army brutality at the time of internment.

At 3.45 am on Monday 9 August 1971, four soldiers broke down my front door and came upstairs with guns at the ready. There were six soldiers outside.

I was told that I was being arrested under the Special Powers Act. I was given thirty seconds to get a towel and shaving kit into a sandbag which they gave me.

I said: 'I'm not the one you are looking for as I only moved into this house a couple of days ago.' I showed them a letter to identify myself. I was taken downstairs and made to lie prone on the floor while they radioed HQ. A little while later they said: 'Come on, you'll do.' I was dressed in shirt, pants, one shoe and one sock. My other shoe and sock were in the sandbag ...

About an hour and a half later I was taken by four military policemen along with four other prisoners. I was forced to run over broken glass and rough stones to a helicopter without shoes. I spent only 15 seconds in the helicopter and then I was pushed out into the hands of military policemen.

I was forced to crawl between these policemen back to the building. They kicked me on the hands, legs, ribs and kidney area. They threw me up the steps into the building, all the time they kept saying things like: 'You are good Catholic dogs and we are your masters.' As a result of the abuse I was injured on my sides and face.

Campaign for Social Justice, *The Mailed Fist – A Record of Army Brutality*, 1971.

50 A United Kingdom?

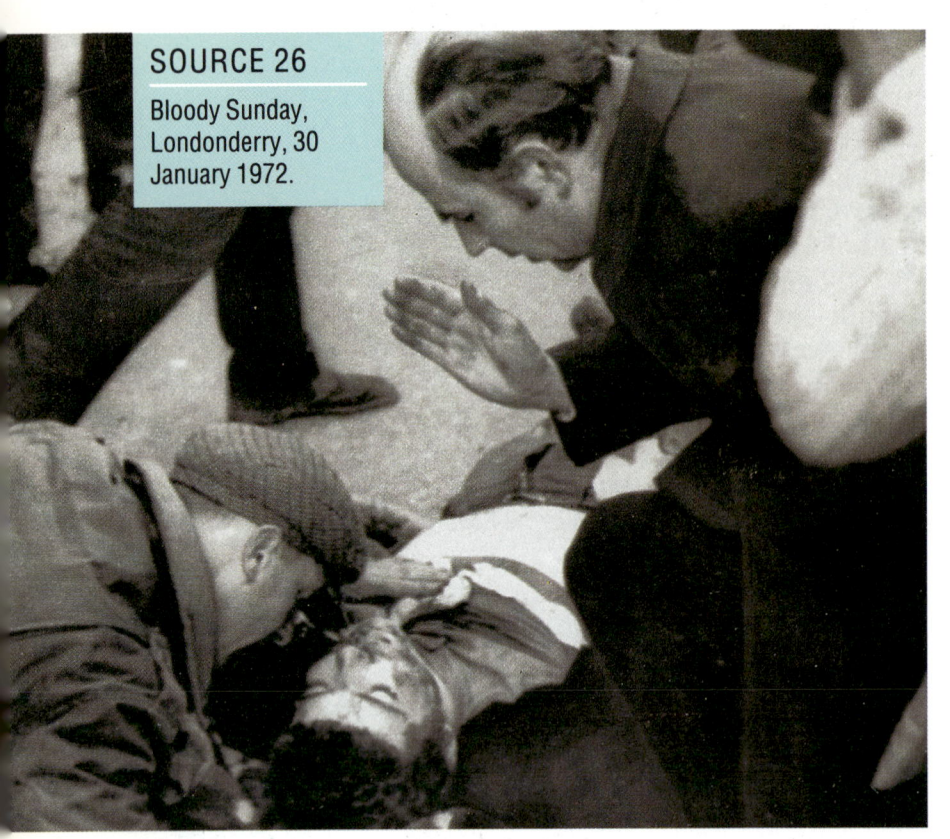

SOURCE 26
Bloody Sunday, Londonderry, 30 January 1972.

and on 24 March Edward Heath, the British Prime Minister, suspended the Ulster parliament at Stormont. He appointed William Whitelaw as Secretary of State for Northern Ireland and 'direct rule' from Westminster began. Four months later, in Operation Motorman, the Army moved into 'Free Derry' and other 'no-go' areas and cleared the barricades.

Co-operation

William Whitelaw met with Ulster politicians during 1972 in an effort to find a way forward. Two new proposals emerged from these talks. First, the Ulster parliament would be restored in the shape of a Northern Ireland Assembly. The Assembly would have to contain both Protestant and Catholic representatives. The second initiative was to create a Council of Ireland, a forum in which politicians from north

SOURCE 27
With drums beating and banners flying, Protestant Orangemen parade through the streets. The original Orange Society was formed in 1795 and took its name from the Protestant King William of Orange (William III) who had saved Ulster Protestants from the tyranny of the Catholic King James II. Members of the Orange Order were amongst the first to sign up to fight against Home Rule at the beginning of the century. Towards the century's end, they remain loyal to the British Crown and determined to resist a united Ireland.

A United Kingdom? 51

SOURCE 28

IRA 'justice' at work in Belfast. Two 15 year old Catholic girls are left tied to railings with their heads shaved, their punishment for being 'touts', Ulster slang for informers. The IRA 'police' Catholic communities to ensure loyalty and secrecy.

and south of the border could meet to discuss Ulster's affairs.

Elections to the new Northern Ireland Assembly were held in June 1973. In the following November an Executive of Chief Ministers was appointed. The Executive was based on the idea of power-sharing. Four of the eight key posts went to Unionists. Three went to members of the Catholic Social Democratic and Labour Party (SDLP) and one member of the non-sectarian Alliance Party was also given a position. In December 1973 at the Sunningdale Conference the Council of Ireland was officially established. The power-sharing experiment lasted for just five months. It was destroyed by a general strike organised by the Protestant Ulster Workers Council. For two weeks (14–28 May 1974) the strikers brought Ulster to a virtual standstill and Brian Faulkner, the leader of the new Assembly, was forced to resign. With his departure the power-sharing initiative collapsed.

The Peace People

Ulster's only mass peace campaign of recent times began in August 1976. It was led by two friends, Mairead Corrigan and Betty Williams. They called their organisation the Women's Peace Movement, but its supporters soon simply became known as the Peace People. The Peace People organised mass rallies in Belfast and other cities, and for a time the movement attracted huge support from Protestants and Catholics who

SOURCE 29

The Ulster Peace People proudly show their Nobel Peace Prizes following a ceremony in Oslo City Hall. On the left is Mairead Corrigan and on the right, Betty Williams. In the centre is Ciaran McKeown.

wanted to see an end to the bloodshed of recent years. The movement got worldwide media attention and donations began to pour in. In December 1977 the leaders of the movement were awarded the Nobel Peace Prize (**Source 29**). By this time, however, the initiative was losing its appeal. Many ordinary people turned away from it because it seemed to be becoming exclusively anti-IRA, and the leaders were distanced from their supporters as they became international celebrities. In spite of this the work of the Peace People was brave and sincere. In a speech at a Peace rally in Belfast in 1976, Mairead Corrigan urged the crowd to reflect on the tragedy of Ulster's recent past, and to work for new solutions:

> We have lived in war for seven years; and war and violence solve no problems. Not one single life has been worth what has happened in Northern Ireland. Never repeat our mistakes.

Sadly, the mistakes have been constantly repeated since that time, and Ulster remains to this day the most troubled part of the United Kingdom.

From Free State to Republic: Anglo-Irish relations 1921–1949

> The defeat of the IRA forces in 1922–23 gave those who supported the Free State the opportunity to make it work. William Cosgrave, the new President, began the difficult task of restoring law and order and rebuilding the economy.

Opposition to the partition of Ireland continued to be organised by Eamonn de Valera. In 1926 he established a new political party, Fianna Fail ('Soldiers of Destiny'). De Valera and Fianna Fail gained a victory at the General Election of 1932 and remained in government for the next sixteen years.

Under de Valera relations with Britain fluctuated and the constitution of the Free State was significantly altered. The much disputed oath of loyalty to the British Crown was removed from the constitution and the Irish government refused to make any further interest

Knowledge and understanding

Use pages 45 to 53 to investigate the following questions.

1 In what ways did the Protestants dominate Northern Ireland following partition?

2 Why did Catholics feel that they were unfairly treated in Northern Ireland?

3 Look at the Datapoint: Gerrymandering in Londonderry 1969 (page 46).
 a What is meant by the term gerrymandering?
 b Why were Catholics in Londonderry unhappy about the way in which local councillors were elected?

4 Look at Source 19. Explain why Ian Paisley and Michael Farrell have different views on the involvement of the IRA in the civil rights movement in the late 1960s.

5 Explain why British troops were sent into Londonderry and Belfast in August 1969.

6 a What was the policy of internment and when was it introduced?
 b Look at Source 24. Use this Source to show that the policy of internment was a failure.
 c Look at Source 25. Given the purpose of the Campaign for Social Justice, would Henry Bennett's statement be of any use to a historian?

7 What events led to the British Government's decision to impose 'direct rule' on Ireland in 1972?

8 What proposals emerged from the meeting between William Whitelaw and Ulster politicians in 1972?

9 Why did the Northern Ireland Assembly and the Council of Ireland collapse in 1974?

10 How did the relationship between Britain and the Irish Free State (a) change, (b) remain the same under de Valera's government, 1932-1938?

11 How did the Irish decision to remain neutral during the Second World War affect relations between Britain and Eire?

12 What was the significance of the Ireland Act of 1949 for (a) Eire, and (b) Northern Ireland?

payments to Britain on debts owed from the land purchases of the 19th century. Britain retaliated with high tariffs on Irish goods and a trade war began. The trade war lasted for six years and caused particular distress in Ireland. It was finally ended in 1938 with the signing of the Anglo-Irish Agreement. Britain reduced or abolished the tariffs on Irish goods and returned the Irish naval bases which the Royal Navy had maintained since 1921. In return, the Irish government removed the duty on imported British coal and made a final payment of £10 million to Britain for loans made to Irish farmers in the 19th century.

In the previous year (1937) de Valera had introduced a new constitution. This re-named the state Eire (Gaelic for Ireland) and claimed sovereignty over the whole of Ireland including the six counties which made up Northern Ireland. The new constitution made Eire a republic in all but name, though for the time being Ireland remained within the Commonwealth.

Irish neutrality 1939–45

When the Second World War broke out in September 1939 Eire declared itself neutral and took no part in the fighting. The declaration of neutrality helped to reinforce Ireland's new status of sovereign independence but it also had the effect of souring relations with the British Government. Earlier in 1939 the IRA had begun a bombing campaign on the British mainland and this continued into 1940. Seven people were killed and 139 injured in attacks on London, Birmingham, Manchester and Coventry (**Source 30**). The IRA also began to collaborate with Nazi Germany. A German agent Hermann Goertz, parachuted into Ireland in May 1940 to co-ordinate an IRA–Nazi offensive against Britain. His mission ended in total failure since the IRA could not provide him with a working radio transmitter. He was arrested in 1941 and held as a prisoner of war.

The decision to remain neutral confirmed de Valera's status as a popular national leader. In spite of this, de Valera was defeated in the 1948 general election. He was replaced by John Costello, leader of the Fine Gael Party who worked in coalition with Sean MacBride of the extreme republican party, Clann na Poblachta. Almost immediately, Costello took Ireland out of the Commonwealth, cutting the last remaining link with Britain. The Labour Government in Britain confirmed the loss of Ireland from the Commonwealth in the Ireland Act of April 1949. Eire was now fully established as an independent republic. By contrast, the Ireland Act strengthened the ties between Britain and Northern Ireland. It stated that on no account would Northern Ireland, or any part of it, cease to be part of the United Kingdom without the agreement of the Northern Ireland parliament.

SOURCE 30

The scene in Broadgate, Coventry following an IRA bomb attack in August 1939. Five people were killed in the blast and 60 were injured by shrapnel and flying glass. Today the fashions, car designs and street signs may be different, but the tactics of the terrorists remain the same.

Investigation

The Easter Rising, 1916

SOURCE A

... fifteen of the death sentences were carried out and it was these executions ... which more than anything else served to sway Irish opinion towards the [rebels] ... [General Maxwell] misjudged the situation and went too far. Some of those who were shot ... had fought as soldiers and had fought cleanly ... they deserved a better fate ... to shoot James Plunkett, who was dying anyway, and James Connolly, who was so seriously wounded that he had to be tied to a chair, was not only grossly inhumane, it was psychologically inept.

F. S. L. Lyons, *Ireland Since the Famine*, 1973.

SOURCE B

The execution of the leaders ... has often been taken as an indication of the ferocity of the [British] government. In fact it is difficult to see what else could have happened. The country was at war and appeared to have been literally stabbed in the back. The rebels had clearly appealed to Germany [for help] ... In the prevailing conditions Maxwell might even be represented as having shown considerable restraint ... In the event the rebels got off rather lightly ...

Edward Norman, *A History of Modern Ireland*, 1971.

SOURCE C

[At the height of the Rising] the Dublin poor were having a glorious spree, smashing shop windows and grabbing goods they could never afford to buy ... Women from the tenements strutted up O'Connell Street in leather boots and tweed skirts with a diamond ring on every finger. Shawlies danced along the streets in evening dress and satin shoes, Cinderellas for a day. Clery's department store was an ant heap as people swarmed from the slums and took as much as they could carry. One man, not waiting to miss the chance of a lifetime, filled up his donkey and cart. A woman stripped naked and starting with silk underwear, chose a new wardrobe. Gold watches were selling for sixpence. Pubs were targeted and drunken Dubliners, grasping liquor bottles, zigzagged up the street ... They built a bonfire ... and danced around it, letting off fireworks. A piano was wheeled out of a shop window for a sing-song.

Suzanne Breen, *Irish News*, 27 March 1991.

SOURCE D

... the public had to put up with a lot ... Dublin was cut off for the whole week ... food ran out, pets were killed and eaten. The police disappeared from the streets. For the public [the Easter Rising] meant squalor and hardship. Nearly a third of Dublin's population needed public relief by the end of the week. Property to the value of £2 million was destroyed.

Edward Norman, *A History of Modern Ireland*, 1971.

SOURCE E

Part of a speech made in the House of Commons by John Dillon, deputy leader of the Irish Nationalists, on 11 May 1916.

I am proud of their [the Easter rebels'] courage and if you were not so dense and stupid, as some of you English people are, you could have had these men fighting for you. It is not murderers who are being executed; it is insurgents [rebels] who have fought a clean fight, however misguided.

SOURCE F

Part of an editorial from the right-wing *Daily Telegraph* newspaper commenting on the arrest of the rebels in Dublin.

The arrested persons [the Easter rebels] have been seized at a single stroke, and we heartily congratulate the Government on the fact that, having determined at last to put an end to open treason in Ireland, they have cast their net wide. But it is not enough to deprive these conspirators of the liberty which they have so foully abused.

The Daily Telegraph, 18 May 1916.

QUESTIONS

1. What was the impact of the Easter Rising on Dublin and its citizens according to:
   a Source C; b Source D?

2. Why do you think Sources C and D differ?

3. Sources A and B reach different conclusions about the treatment of the rebel leaders. Does this mean that one of them must be right and the other wrong? Explain your answer.

4. Explain why sources E and F present the Easter rebels in different ways.

5. Explain why the leaders of the Easter rising are regarded as heroes by the IRA and as traitors by the Loyalists.

Scotland and Wales: nationalism and devolution

By the beginning of the 20th century Scotland and Wales had long been established as part of the United Kingdom. The Union suited most inhabitants of these regions. The popular demand for Home Rule in Ireland was not repeated in Scotland or Wales. Of course, the Scots and the Welsh displayed a strong national pride and both had their fair share of historical, cultural and political heroes. In Wales a sense of cultural nationalism had begun to develop from the 1880s based around the distinctive Welsh language. An annual festival of the arts, the eisteddfod, helped to stimulate the cultural identity of Wales through music, poetry and song. Political nationalism was not so evident, but by the end of the 1920s both Wales and Scotland had national political parties.

In 1925 Plaid Cymru (the Party of Wales) was established. The leaders of this party aimed at securing self-government for Wales but their immediate concern was to protect and encourage the distinctive Welsh language and culture. In 1928 The National Party of Scotland was launched (re-named the Scottish National Party (SNP) in 1934). The SNP wanted self-government and independent national status for Scotland. During the next two decades neither party attracted much popular support and their demands were largely ignored by Westminster. By 1939 Plaid Cymru had just 2000 members and had received its greatest publicity in 1936 when three of its leaders were jailed after being convicted at the Old Bailey for an arson attack on RAF property on the Lleyn peninsula.

In April 1945 the SNP won its first parliamentary seat in a by-election at Motherwell but the seat was quickly lost at the General Election three months later. The SNP now entered a period of decline. In every election from 1950 to 1959 the Party polled less than one per cent of the votes cast in Scotland. At the same time a new initiative was launched by moderate nationalists. They canvassed support for the idea of a Scottish parliament within the UK. The suggestion proved attractive to some two million Scots who signed a covenant calling for a Scottish Assembly. The Scottish Covenant was copied in Wales where a petition in favour of a 'Parliament for Wales' was begun in 1950. By 1956 250,000 signatures had been collected. Both documents failed to raise a response at Westminster.

In 1951 the newly elected Conservative government made two minor adjustments to the existing political set-up. A Minister for Welsh Affairs was appointed, giving a member of the Cabinet special responsibility for Wales for the first time. In addition, a Minister of State for Scotland was appointed to

SOURCE 31

16 November 1967. Winifred Ewing arrives in London to take her seat in the House of Commons. Mrs Ewing was the first Scottish National Party candidate to be elected to Parliament since 1945. Supporters behind the new MP hold aloft the flag of Scotland with the name of Bannockburn printed across it. It was at Bannockburn in 1314 that the Scots won a famous victory over the English armies of Edward II and secured independence for Scotland.

A United Kingdom? 57

SOURCE 32

November 1967. With membership of the SNP and Plaid Cymru rising, delegates of the two nationalist parties held a joint conference at Caxton Hall in London. There was much optimism that the Scots and Welsh people were at last waking up to their potential to exist as separate nations. Excitement among the Party faithful ran high and there was much talk of devolution for Wales and Scotland.

the Scottish Office. In 1956 Wales at last acquired a capital city. The choice of Cardiff, the largest city in Wales, was logical and represented a symbolic step towards national recognition. It was only in the late 1960s, however, that the constitutional structure of the United Kingdom began to be seriously challenged by the Welsh and the Scots. In 1964 Wales followed the example of Scotland in acquiring its own Secretary of State and Welsh Office which began to co-ordinate such areas of responsibility as agriculture, transport and education. But this development was overshadowed by a national economic crisis which was exploited at the polls by the SNP and Plaid Cymru in spectacular fashion.

In 1966 Plaid Cymru set Welsh nationalism alight when it won its first parliamentary seat in a by-election at Carmarthen. This historic victory was a personal triumph for Gwynfor Evans who captured the seat for the Party he had led since 1945. In the following year an even more sensational result was recorded in the by-election at Rhondda West. Plaid Cymru did not win the seat, but came second to the Labour candidate by just 2306 votes. Since Rhondda West was regarded by the Labour party as one of its safest Welsh seats, the result began all sorts of speculation about the future of the traditional political parties in Wales. The Labour Party was in for an even bigger shock in the Hamilton by-election in November 1967. Hamilton was the Labour government's safest seat in Scotland; they had secured 71.2 per cent of the votes cast in the General Election of 1966. Astonishingly the seat was taken from Labour by the SNP candidate Winifred Ewing (**Source 31**). The SNP offices were swamped with applications for membership which soared within a year to 125,000. People were turning to the nationalist parties in protest at the successive failures of governments to manage the economy and be sufficiently sensitive to the needs of the regions. When, in 1970, oil was discovered in the British sector of the North Sea, just 110 miles east of Aberdeen, the

58 A United Kingdom?

DATAPOINT

Scottish Assembly

To comprise about 140 members.

To have law-making powers on the following matters:
- education
- housing
- social services
- local government
- health
- roads
- the environment
- planning
- private and criminal law

Assembly would be controlled by a Scottish Executive, a team of Assembly members.
The Assembly would be headed by a Chief Executive.

Welsh Assembly

To comprise about 70–75 members.

Would not have law-making powers.

Would have the power to administer the same matters as the Scottish Assembly, with the exception of the law.

Assembly would be controlled by an Executive Committee, a team of Assembly members. The Assembly would be headed by a Chief Executive.

---

economic arguments for Scottish independence became extremely attractive.

The progress of the nationalist parties in Scotland and Wales prompted the Labour government to appoint a Commission on the Constitution in April 1969. This body, known as the Kilbrandon Commission reported in October 1973 to a Conservative government under Edward Heath. The Commission rejected the division of Great Britain into three sovereign states but did recommend that regional assemblies be established at Edinburgh and Cardiff to take responsibility for domestic affairs. Here were the first concrete proposals for devolution; the transfer of powers from Westminster to regional seats of Government. The Conservative government reacted unfavourably to the Commission's recommendations and refused to act on them. The Labour Party might have done the same had it not been for the results of the General Election in October 1974. Labour obtained a majority and formed the government, but it was the performance of the nationalist parties, particularly the SNP, which grabbed the headlines. In Wales Plaid Cymru won three seats, their best ever performance with an 11 per cent share of the vote. In Scotland the SNP startled political commentators by winning 11 seats and in the process taking a 31 per cent share of the votes cast. The SNP was now the main challenger in 42 seats, 35 of which were held by Labour. For the Labour government devolution became an urgent priority for if it lost its Scottish electoral base, it stood little chance of ever again securing a parliamentary majority.

By November 1975, the Government was ready to make its devolution proposals (see diagram). The plans were far-reaching and were of real significance for the constitution of the United Kingdom. However, opposition to devolution was evident in many quarters. There were anti-devolutionists within the Labour Party and by 1976 the Conservatives had taken the decision to officially oppose the government's proposals. In addition

A United Kingdom? 59

there was hostility from certain English regions which resented the expanding influence and importance of Wales and Scotland. It was pointed out that many English regions had larger populations and economic and social difficulties equally serious to those in Scotland and Wales. A real concern developed that the new devolved assemblies might be able to command an unfair share of government assistance at the expense of the English regions. The Devolution Bill which emerged from the Labour proposals of 1975 was defeated in Parliament in 1977. The government began again, this time with separate bills for Wales and Scotland. A referendum was organised for each region to allow Welsh and Scottish voters to judge the proposals for devolution. It was decided that 40 per cent of the electorate would have to register approval for the plans before they were accepted by Parliament. On 1 March 1979 voters in Scotland and Wales made their decisions. In both cases the devolution proposals failed.

The nationalists' attempt to separate Wales and Scotland from the United Kingdom had succeeded only in dividing opinion within those nations. For the time being, devolution ceased to figure on the political agenda and the United Kingdom remained intact.

Knowledge and understanding

Use pages 56 to 59 to investigate the following questions.

1 What were the aims of Plaid Cymru and the Scottish National Party?

2 What changes between 1951 and 1964 gave recognition to the special status of Wales within the United Kingdom?

3 Why did the by-election results at Rhondda West and Hamilton in 1967 cause concern within the Labour Party?

4 How did the discovery of oil in the British sector of the North Sea encourage Scottish nationalism?

5 What is meant by the term 'devolution'?

6 Why did devolution become an important issue for the Labour Party following the General Election of October 1974?

7 Why did Scotland and Wales fail to obtain separate assemblies to look after their own affairs?

Devolution referendum, 1 March 1979

	Yes	No
Scotland	33%	31%
Wales	12%	47%

These figures are percentages of the whole electorate, not just those who voted.

SOURCE 33

In the late 1970s and early 1980s a series of arson attacks on English-owned holiday cottages was carried out by the extreme Welsh nationalist organisation Meibion Glyndwr – 'the sons of Glyndwr'.

However, most of the owners refused to be driven out, and the terrorist actions brought strong condemnation from Plaid Cymru.

4 Boom and Bust

SOURCE 1

Charles Lindbergh receives a hero's welcome in Croydon, England, arriving after his flight across the Atlantic in 1927.

Myth and reality: the 'roaring twenties'

The race began on a muddy runway on Long Island, New York, in May 1927. The challenge was to fly from America to Paris on the first non-stop transatlantic flight. Thirty-three hours after it had disappeared into the dark American skies, the successful plane touched down on a landing field near Paris. The victorious pilot emerged, blinking, into the car headlights which were lined up on the field. He made a simple announcement: 'I am Charles Lindbergh.' The prize money of $25,000 was enough to make this twenty-five year old man from Minnesota rich for life.

Images of prosperity

Heroic escapades such as the Lindbergh flight have been very attractive to historians writing about the 1920s. They have been depicted as representing a perfect snapshot of the so called 'roaring twenties'. Within this one event are conjured up images of glamour, wealth easily gained, economic self-confidence and a spirit of adventure. This was also the period of cross-channel swimming records, sky-scrapers soaring to new heights and new films playing to packed houses in the cinema. It also seems appropriate that our image of the 1920s concerns an American, because at this time the United States was not only the world's most powerful nation in economic terms but also the country which

Boom and Bust **61**

SOURCE 2
Bond Street in the 1920s. Then, as now, this was one of London's most exclusive shopping areas.

SOURCE 3
For those who couldn't afford Bond Street, magazines like this one offered patterns for women to make their own clothes in the latest fashions.

SOURCE 4
Enough room for the whole family. A Ford Sedan in 1923.

seemed to set the social trends which others soon followed.

First in the United States, and then elsewhere, wealthier families equipped themselves with newly developed gadgets such as hoovers, washing machines, sewing machines, typewriters and wirelesses. Many of these items were purchased from mail-order catalogues, and paid for in monthly hire-purchase instalments. Outside their homes, more and more Americans parked the mass-produced automobiles which were pouring out of the factories of Ford and General Motors (**Source 4**). On the advertising billboards a famous poster showed a prosperous American family with the slogan 'There's no way like the American Way: The World's highest standard of living.' In their leisure time many middle class Americans spent money at dance halls and cinemas. Packed sports stadiums witnessed the exploits of heroes such as baseball legend Babe Ruth and boxing world champion, Jack Dempsey. Those who still had cash to spare could invest on the stock market. As more and more people bought 'shares' in companies the cost of these pieces of paper soared, and Wall Street seemed to reflect the prosperity of the country at large. The prosperous image of the 1920s has been added to by novels, such as *The Great Gatsby* by F. Scott Fitzgerald, which portrays an era of glamorous women, dashing men, glittering dances and daring fashions.

The Western European economy

Closely linked to the US economy were the fortunes of its Western European competitors. In the 1920s these countries appeared on the surface to share American economic prosperity. However, in reality they were coming to rely more and more upon American financial support and commercial ideas.

Britain

Britain was the first nation to experience the Industrial Revolution (**Source 5**). By the turn of the century, although Britain remained a major agricultural producer, its economy had become predominantly industrial. This change had been based on the rapidly developing heavy industries of coal, iron and steel. In addition, Britain had constructed an extensive railway network. Britain had the world's largest empire and had assembled the most powerful navy. However, the massive cost of waging the First World War had a drastic impact on the British economy. Although Britain still appeared to be prosperous in the 1920s, the fact was that it was now depending, to a considerable extent, on American loans and support.

SOURCE 5
The foundations of Britain's industrial economy were laid in works like this one. This photograph was taken at the height of the Industrial Revolution in 1865.

Germany

Before the First World War, Britain's economic supremacy had come under concerted attack by a new and dynamic economic force. Germany not only rivalled Britain in the heavy industries but also in developing new areas of modern industrial production. Massive chemical works, advanced companies such as Telefunken Wireless and efficient automobile producers such as Daimler and Mercedes all helped to put Germany at the forefront of the European economy. However, the traumatic experience of defeat in the First World War cost the Germans dearly. In the 1920s, German economic recovery was largely built on American money.

It appeared that in the 1920s, the United States and Western Europe were sharing a period of tremendous economic prosperity and consumer confidence. The leading industrial nations had become predominantly urban rather than rural, had developed massive markets for their industrial goods, and met high production levels by using precision engineering and mass production. Yet how widespread was the economic prosperity? And how secure were the foundations of the American and Western European financial boom?

The 1920s: the reality of poverty

For millions of people in America, Britain, Germany and France the reality of life in the 1920s was one of poverty and misery.

While company profits in America increased by an average of 62 per cent a year during the 1920s, wages rose by an average of only seven per cent. While the top six per cent in the country owned 26 per cent of the nation's wealth, over 60 per cent of Americans in the 'prosperous' 1920s lived just above the poverty line. Many Americans at the bottom of the pile had no experience of the 'roaring twenties'.

For American farmers, for example, this was a period of poverty and hardship. During the First World War, farmers had been encouraged to produce as much cotton and wheat as possible, in order to help the war-torn countries of Europe. When the War ended in 1918,

SOURCE 6
Unemployed families housed in Tent Creek, near Washington, USA (1922).

America's farmers maintained their old levels of production. Eventually they were producing far more than they could possibly sell. This meant that farm produce had to be sold at prices way below the cost of production. Many small farmers lived in makeshift shacks with tin roofs, no electricity, no running water and no toilets.

Black Americans had a similar experience. The poverty was most severe for the three million blacks who farmed in the south. In their primitive shacks, these people were highly vulnerable to starvation, disease and death. The grim reality of poverty also extended into the lives of many other large groups such as coal miners and textile workers. Yet the experience of poverty has tended to receive little attention from those who have dwelt on the image of the roaring twenties.

Britain in the 1920s

While those who lived in the south-east may have found the 1920s to be a successful decade, elsewhere there was considerable poverty and distress. Throughout the so-called 'boom' decade, unemployment in Britain never fell below one million. The people who suffered most were those connected with the 'ailing giants' – the older staple industries such as coal mining, textiles, shipbuilding, and iron and steel. In large areas such as the north-west, north-east, Yorkshire, Scotland and Wales, the reality of life in the 1920s was of poor housing conditions, a declining standard of living, disease, unemployment and depression. For those who prospered in the 1920s, the Crash of 1929 would mark a dramatic turning point between prosperity and poverty. However, for those large groups who were already used to poverty, the year 1929 and the depression years which followed were not very different to the life they had known in the 1920s.

Germany in the 1920s

In Germany, too, the 1920s were only a time of prosperity for certain groups. The economic fortunes of Germany at this time illustrate the shaky and uncertain nature of the economic recovery. Defeat in the First World War had left Germany saddled with a high debt. In addition, Germany had to give up important industrial territories such as the Saar and Upper Silesia.

In 1923, the vital coal region of the Ruhr was occupied by French and Belgian troops. This devastated the German economy and sparked off the most catastrophic inflation in its history. Early in 1923 the US dollar was worth 18,000 marks, but by August it was worth 4,600,000 marks and by November it had reached 4,000,000,000 marks. However, the German economy did recover from this, and traditionally the period 1925–29 has been portrayed as a period of 'economic boom'.

Many historians now feel that this 'boom' has been exaggerated. Agriculture and small industry, in particular, did not enjoy a period of growth and prosperity. During the 1920s many small farmers and fishermen living in North Bavaria, the North German Plain and Schleswig-Holstein faced high taxes, foreign competition, bad weather and mounting debts. Once again, the reality of the 1920s seems far removed from the popular image once favoured by historians. The events of 1929 were a turning point in the sense that the depression which followed blurred the distinction between the prosperous groups of the 1920s and those who had already experienced the harsher realities of life in the post-war decade.

Knowledge and understanding

Use the material on pages 60 to 64 to investigate the following questions.

1 Write a paragraph to describe the 1920s in support of the idea that it was a boom period, justifiably known as the 'Roaring Twenties'

2 Write a paragraph explaining whether you feel that the 'Roaring Twenties' really is an accurate description for this decade.

3 What reasons can you give to explain why the prosperous side of this decade has received more attention than its negative aspects?

SOURCE 7

Crowds wait in disbelief as their life savings turn into worthless pieces of paper.

These people have gathered on the steps of the US sub-treasury opposite the Wall Street stock exchange during the Crash of October 1929.

The Great Depression

1929: The Crash

The impact of the Great Depression was made even worse because of its sudden and unexpected nature. In 1928 in an election speech, the next US President, Herbert Hoover, had confidently predicted that the country was close to the 'final triumph over poverty'. In October 1928 the President of General Motors declared his conviction that 'our general economic and industrial situation is thoroughly sound'. Yet within twelve months the world economy had plunged into a downward spiral from which it did not fully recover until the outbreak of the Second World War. The event which symbolised the onset of the Depression was the Wall Street Crash of October 1929 (**Sources 7 and 8**).

Historians are in agreement that the crisis started in the USA, the industrial centre of the world economy, and had its greatest impact there. The shock waves of this crisis were then felt around the world. Economic historian, Sidney Pollard states that the 'avalanche' began in the United States and 'with increasing

SOURCE 8

Thursday, October 24, is the first of the days which history identifies with the panic of 1929. Measured by disorder, fright and confusion, it deserves to be so regarded. That day 12,894,650 shares changed hands, many of them at prices which shattered the dreams and the hopes of those who had owned them. By eleven o'clock the market had degenerated into a wild, mad scramble to sell. The uncertainty led more and more people to try to sell. By eleven-thirty the market had surrendered to blind, relentless fear, this indeed, was panic.

Outside the Exchange in Broad Street a weird roar could be heard. A crowd gathered. Police Commissioner Grover Whalen became aware that something was happening and dispatched a special police detail to Wall Street to ensure the peace. A workman appeared atop one of the high buildings to accomplish some repairs, and the multitude assumed he was a would-be suicide and waited impatiently for him to jump. Rumour after rumour swept Wall Street. Stocks were now selling for nothing. The Chicago and Buffalo Exchanges had closed. A suicide wave was in progress, and eleven well-known speculators had already killed themselves. Tuesday, October 29 was the most devastating day in the history of the markets. It combined all of the bad features of all of the bad days before. Volume was immensely greater than on Black Thursday. Selling began again as soon as the market opened and in huge volume. Great blocks of stock were offered for what they would bring; in the first half hour sales were at a 33,000,000-a-day rate.

The worst day on Wall Street came eventually to an end. Once again the lights blazed all night. Members of the Exchange, their employees, and the employees of the Stock Exchange by now were reaching the breaking point from the strain and fatigue. In this condition they faced the task of recording and handling the greatest volume of transactions ever. In one house an employee fainted from exhaustion, was revived and put back to work again.

J. K. Galbraith, *The Great Crash 1929*, 1955.

speed it took more and more economies into the abyss' (**Source 9**). It can now be seen that the Depression had a range of causes, some of which were already apparent before the stock market collapse of 1929.

Causes of the Great Depression

It is today accepted that the prosperity of the 1920s was built on shaky foundations.

- As early as 1926, there were signs that all was not well with the American economy. Up to that point property prices had soared as part of the general financial boom. In America the Florida land boom saw house prices in the state rise to unprecedented heights. In 1926 the housing market suddenly collapsed, leaving people who had recently bought houses with property which was wildly overpriced.

- The biggest single problem was that in the 1920s industrial production of consumer goods reached too high a level. There was a high level of investment in industry from people putting money into the stock market but workers' wages stayed low, so the market for consumer goods remained small. Thus, the supply of goods eventually outstripped the demand. For example, there were too many motor cars being made and not enough people who could afford to buy them.

- The problem of overproduction also affected agriculture. Farmers had produced too much food in the 1920s so that prices for their produce became steadily lower.

- In America, and to an extent elsewhere, there were far too many small banks. These banks did not have sufficient funds to cope with the sudden rush to withdraw savings which took place in the autumn of 1929. The small banks were simply unable to return the money because much of it had been invested elsewhere, particularly on the stock market.

- During the 1920s speculation on the stock market became a middle class pastime. People eventually paid ludicrous sums of money for pieces of paper which were of no real value. Even worse, many people of limited financial means bought shares recklessly with borrowed money or 'on

SOURCE 9

The collapse of the New York Stock Exchange in October 1929 has become a symbol of the beginning of the Great Depression. This is to exaggerate its importance, but its consequences should not be underestimated. Before the crash, the sale of shares was often financed by credit. When foreign investors, as well as American banks and institutions outside New York, withdrew their money from the New York market, the crash was triggered. Firms which financed their investments through share issues had to cut back expenditure, production declined and stocks were reduced. And it was not only the professional speculators who took part in share trading; a considerable part of the American middle class had speculated with shares in order to participate in the buoyant market. When the loans with which the shares had been bought could no longer be paid back through the sale of shares, ruin was not an infrequent consequence. The general reduction in consumption caused demand within the United States to fall sharply, along with imports.

The Great Depression was the biggest crisis ever experienced by the world economy. It hit almost every country: the highly developed countries of western Europe and the United States; the less developed ones like Canada, Australia, Japan and Argentina; and the underdeveloped countries of Latin America, Asia and Africa just as soon as they became involved in the world market. Many countries experienced the catastrophic breakdown of their national economies and only a few came through without major damage.

Statistics cannot convey the extent of the effects of the Depression. In 1932, 30 million people were unemployed. While millions suffered from short hours and extremely low wages, the consequences were hunger, higher mortality, apathy and hopelessness, as well as an increase in crime.

Sydney Pollard, *Wealth and Poverty*, 1990.

the margin', which meant paying only a fraction of the full price at the time of purchase with the intention of selling them on before the rest of the payment became due.

- Events such as the Wall Street Crash and the collapse in 1931 of the great Austrian bank the Kreditanstalt produced a world financial crisis and a collapse in confidence in the international banking system.

- During the 1920s America leant huge sums of money to countries including Great Britain and Germany. Eventually this resulted in a situation in which American goods were being purchased in Western Europe with borrowed American money. The near collapse of the American banking system led to the sudden recall of these loans – and this had a devastating impact on the economies of Western Europe.

The Great Depression had begun. Yet, just as the image of the 'roaring twenties' can be questioned, there is also more than one story to tell of the 1930s (see **Investigation: Britain in the 1930s** on pages 71–3).

DATAPOINT

The impact of the Great Depression, 1929–1932

- The Gross National Product (GNP) of the 16 leading industrial nations fell by 17 per cent
- American industrial production fell by 45 per cent
- Western European industrial production fell by 30 per cent
- The volume of imports of the 16 leading nations declined by 25 per cent
- Creation of mass unemployment and poverty
- Many farmers abandoned their land, for example in Oklahoma and Arkansas in the USA
- The breakdown of the US economy
- World-wide political instability
- A general loss of confidence in the capitalist system and the international 'market' economy.

SOURCES 10 AND 11

The Great Depression in the USA (above) and Britain (left). These images reflect the everyday lives of millions in a period when unemployment soared and welfare benefits were limited or non-existent.

Knowledge and understanding

Use the material on pages 66 to 67 to investigate the following questions.

1 Summarise in a few words each of the causes of the Depression shown on this page spread.

2 Place the factors into what you consider to be their order of importance. Begin with the most important factor.

3 Now try to place the factors into some kind of sequence. When did the problems begin? What were the long term causes? What were the short term causes? Produce a flow chart to explain your answer.

4 Why was the Depression of 1929 so sudden and so severe?

The road to recovery?

The economic depression of the 1930s demanded political solutions. In this section we will explore the very different ways in which the USA, Britain and Germany dealt with the problems they faced.

The United States of America

By 1932 the USA was in the middle of the worst depression in its history. Almost 13 million people were unemployed. Since 1929, five thousand banks had gone out of business and nine million people had lost their savings. In 1933, newly elected President Franklin D. Roosevelt launched a massive programme of public spending and job creation which became known as the New Deal. Some of its key agencies are listed below.

SOURCE 12
Boys joining the Civilian Conservation Corps queue to be measured for shoes at a camp in New Jersey, USA.

The first New Deal, 1933

Tennessee Valley Authority (TVA)
A huge programme involving flood control, building dams and reservoirs, building new towns and preventing soil erosion.

Civil Works Administration (CWA)
This agency provided work for more than four million people, building roads, schools, airports and other public buildings.

Public Works Administration (PWA)
Built hospitals, libraries, schools and town halls.

Civilian Conservation Corps (CCC)
Concerned with soil conservation and reforestation. By 1935 over 500,000 young men were employed by the CCC.

Agricultural Adjustment Agency (AAA)
This agency tried to raise prices for farming produce by destroying surplus crops and livestock.

The second New Deal, 1935

The Works Progress Administration (WPA)
This was the new name for the Public Works Administration.

The Rural Electrification Administration
This project aimed at bringing electricity to America's farms. Before the project began, nine out of ten American farms had no electricity supply. By 1941, four out of ten American farmers had electricity. Ten years later the figure had fallen to under one in ten.

Further information

- The second New Deal cost a record amount for a government spending programme, a projected $4800 billion.
- The New Deal failed to solve America's unemployment problem. In 1938, after five years of heavy spending and government controls, over ten million people were still without work.
- Although the government programmes created work for the unemployed, they also created cheap labour which threatened the pay levels and working conditions of those in jobs. Strikes and industrial unrest were a major problem in the period 1934-35.
- Roosevelt was criticised by some politicians for not spending enough money and by others for spending too much.

Great Britain

In the late 1930s, the politically dominant Conservative Party showed little faith in public spending as a cure for unemployment and viewed public works (Roosevelt's strategy) as a solution that had already been tried in Britain by the Labour Party – and had failed. While the Conservatives took a cautious approach to solving the economic and social problems of the 1930s, support for the political extremes increased. However, the Fascist parties never got into Parliament, while the Communists only had one or two MPs. Despite the social unrest of this period, democracy in Britain was not seriously under threat.

SOURCE 13

The world-wide depression following the Wall Street Crash in New York in 1929 raised the level of unemployment in Britain. In 1932, the worst of the inter-war years, 13 per cent of the workforce was unemployed. By 1938 the figure had fallen to 8 per cent...

The social and political effects were less startling than in the USA or Germany, since Britain's unemployment level in the 1920s (about 6.5 per cent on average) had been already unusually high.

Martin Roberts, *Britain and Europe 1848–1980*, 1987.

SOURCE 14

The Jarrow Crusade of 1936 is the best known of the 1930s 'hunger marches' which brought home the reality of poverty and unemployment to the towns and villages they marched through – and took their message, on foot, to Westminster. The Crusade owed its success to the town's new Labour MP, Ellen Wilkinson (*second row*).

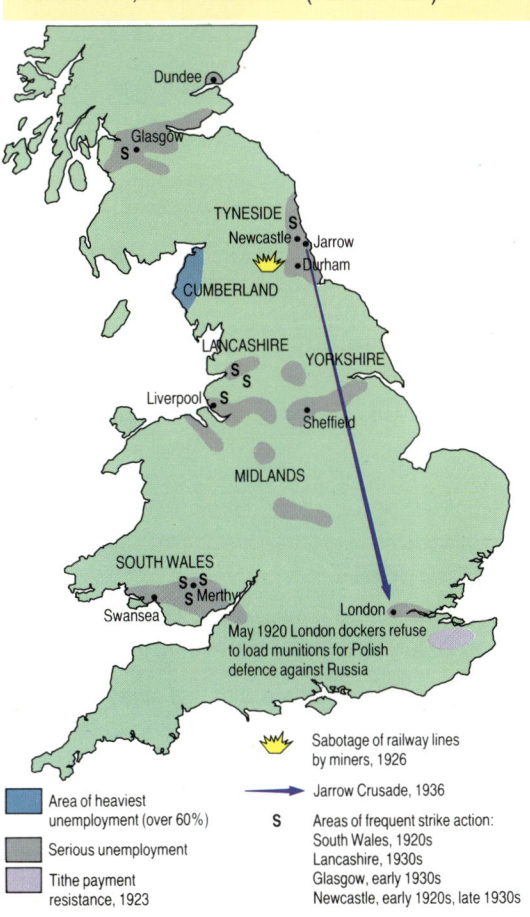

Some investment was made to boost the economy and combat unemployment. However, these provisions were on a small scale, especially when compared to the USA. Measures included:

1934 The Special Areas Act
Attended to the special problems of southern Scotland, the north-east, west Cumberland and South Wales. Commissioners appointed to spend up to £2 million per year. Had little impact.

1937 The Special Areas (Amendment) Act
Offered rent and tax incentives to firms moving to the 'special areas'.

1934 North Atlantic Shipping Act
Lent £9.5 million to the Cunard Shipping line for the building of the liners *Queen Mary* and *Queen Elizabeth*.

There were also reforms made to the benefit system aimed at saving the government money:

1931 Means Test
Very unpopular. Households were scrutinised and the earnings, savings and any extra income of all members of the family were taken into account. For example, a family would receive less money if old people (e.g. grandparents) had their own savings, or a child earned money from a paper round.

1934 Unemployment Act
Simplified the unemployment benefit system, set national scales of contributions and benefits.

Germany

> It is inconceivable that Hitler could ever have come to power had not the Weimar republic been subjected to the unprecedented strain of a world economic crisis.
>
> William Carr, *A History of Germany 1815–1985*.

By the summer of 1932 there were approximately six million people unemployed in Germany. As the country came to the brink of economic collapse, political support moved to the extremes of Communism and Fascism. There was a clear connection between rising unemployment and the growth of Adolf Hitler's Nazi party. In January 1933 Hitler became Chancellor of Germany. The measures he took to combat the depression are set out in the panel below.

Nazi economic policy

- Rearmament – more than any other nation, Hitler's Germany brought about economic recovery by launching a massive programme to build up its war machine.
- Many men were taken from the ranks of the unemployed into the rapidly growing German Army.
- The German Navy and Air Force also created a huge number of jobs.
- Many people found employment in munitions factories making arms, tanks and aeroplanes.
- Rearmament was complemented by a huge road-building programme – motorway (*Autobahn*) construction had a positive impact on the economy in general.
- Immense public building programmes took place. For example, the Nazis constructed many government buildings in the capital, Berlin.
- Generally the Nazis advocated much greater levels of intervention by the state in the economy, particularly through their major programme of public works.
- The whole economy was placed on a war footing, gearing up for the eventual outbreak of war.
- The Nazis tried to develop a programme of economic self-sufficiency in major raw materials such as oil and rubber.

SOURCE 15
The Krupps works mass-producing tanks for the German war machine.

The Nazis did not really have enough money to pay for all of this at the time, so a lot of work was paid for by government credit notes called Mefo bills.

Hitler's programmes had the combined effect of sharply reducing unemployment. However, in the War Germany would pay a terrible price for these short-term benefits.

Knowledge and understanding

Use the material on pages 68 to 70 to investigate the following questions.

1 Compare the reaction to the Depression in Britain with that of (a) Germany, (b) The USA.
  i Outline any similarities you can see.
  ii What do you regard as the key differences?

2 Which country would you say dealt with the depression (a) most effectively, (b) least effectively? Explain your answer.

Investigation

Britain in the 1930s: was it really so bad?

SOURCE A

It is now customary among economists to judge the health of an economy by applying to it four criteria; the rate of inflation, the rate of economic growth, the state of the trade balance and the rate of unemployment. In all four respects, the 1930s showed an improvement after the crisis years of 1931–1932.

W. O. Simpson, *Changing Horizons: Britain 1914–80*, 1990.

SOURCE B

Of all periods in recent British History, the thirties have had the worst press; it retains the image of the 'wasted years' and the 'low dishonest decade'. Even for those who did not live through them, the 1930s are haunted by the spectres of mass unemployment, hunger marches…

The popular image of the 1930s is that of the decade blighted by economic depression – the years of mass unemployment, dole queues, the means test and the hunger marches. Indeed this is an image securely based upon reality for the many thousands of families who suffered the miseries of mass unemployment. But as well as being the years of the slump, they also saw a remarkable degree of economic and social advance with new industries, economic growth, prosperous suburbs and a rising standard of living for those in work.

For those in work, the 1930s were a period of rising living standards and new levels of consumption, upon which a considerable degree of the industrial growth was based; most people in Britain were better off by 1939 than they had been ten years earlier.

John Stevenson and Chris Cook, *The Slump*, 1979.

SOURCE C

1931 was one of the 'crisis years' of the depression, but it also saw the construction of the huge Ford works at Dagenham, near London.

SOURCE D

Most English people were enjoying a richer life than any previously known in the history of the world: longer holidays, shorter hours, higher real wages. They had motor cars, cinemas, radio sets, electrical appliances.

A.J.P. Taylor.

SOURCE E

House building boomed. Many new private estates and urban developments appeared, especially in the south-east. New industries – motor vehicles, electrical, radios, chemical – appeared, again chiefly in the south-east. If Newcastle and Bradford were comparatively depressed, Oxford, Slough and Coventry were comparatively prosperous.

For the majority of Britons the standard of living rose and, with developments like electricity, the radio and the spread of high street shops like Marks and Spencer, the quality of life improved too.

Martin Roberts, *Britain and Europe 1848–1980*, 1987.

SOURCE F

This poster from the early 1930s is a reminder that the way of life of the wealthy classes remained one of privilege and leisure.

SOURCE G

For young people with a job there was a steady increase in leisure time. Cycling became a popular pastime in the 1930s.

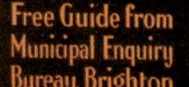

SOURCE H

On closer analysis, what was happening to the British economy in the 1930s was an intensification of the trends which had become noticeable in the 1920s. The new growth industries in the Midlands and the South East expanded faster than they had done before; contraction in the old staple industries, with some exceptions, also proceeded more rapidly. Engineering output went up by 50 per cent between 1927 and 1937. Car output reached a peak of 500,000 in 1937. The chemical industry opened new plants on Teeside and in North Wales. But four-fifths of the new factories built between 1932 and 1937 were located in the Greater London area where they provided two-fifths of the jobs.

John Stevenson and Chris Cook, *The Slump*, 1979.

SOURCE I

Single industry towns, like Jarrow might have unemployment rates over 70 per cent, Merthyr Tydfil had an unemployment rate of 61.9 per cent in 1934; In Crook, County Durham, 71 per cent of the unemployed had been without a job for five years in 1936; in the Rhondda Valley it was 45 per cent. The effect of the slump was to sharpen the differences between the prosperous Midlands and South East and the rest of the country.

W. O. Simpson, *Changing Horizons: Britain 1914–80*, 1990.

SOURCE L

[Photograph of a woman and child by a table in a poorly-lit room]

SOURCE M

The general appearance and condition of this house inside are very miserable. It is a dark house, there is no sink or tap in the house; they are in the small yard, consequently in frosty weather the family is without water. In this house live a man and wife and seven children, ranging from 15 to 1, and a large, if varying number, of rats.

Description of typical 1930s inner city housing quoted in John Stevenson and Chris Cook, *The Slump*, 1979.

SOURCE J

Unemployed as a percentage of insured workers in regions of Great Britain:

	1929	1932	1937
London and SE England	5.6	18.7	6.4
SW England	8.1	17.1	7.8
Midlands	9.3	20.1	7.2
Northern England	13.5	27.1	13.8
Wales	19.3	36.5	22.3
Scotland	12.1	27.7	15.9
Northern Ireland	15.1	27.2	23.6

SOURCE K

The cotton industry suffered a very severe contraction. Shipbuilding suffered worst of all. When Palmer's Shipyard in Jarrow closed in 1934, local unemployment rose nearly 73 per cent.

It would be true to say that in each of these four basic industries, coal, cotton, shipbuilding and iron and steel, the unemployment rate in 1938 was twice what it was in other forms of employment.

W. O. Simpson, *Changing Horizons: Britain 1914–80*, 1990.

Debate

This class supports the motion that the 1930s was a time of poverty, mass unemployment and depression for the British people.

Select two people to speak in favour of the motion and two people to speak against the motion.

Then allow for general questions and debate.

Finally put the motion to a class vote.

5 The State in Society

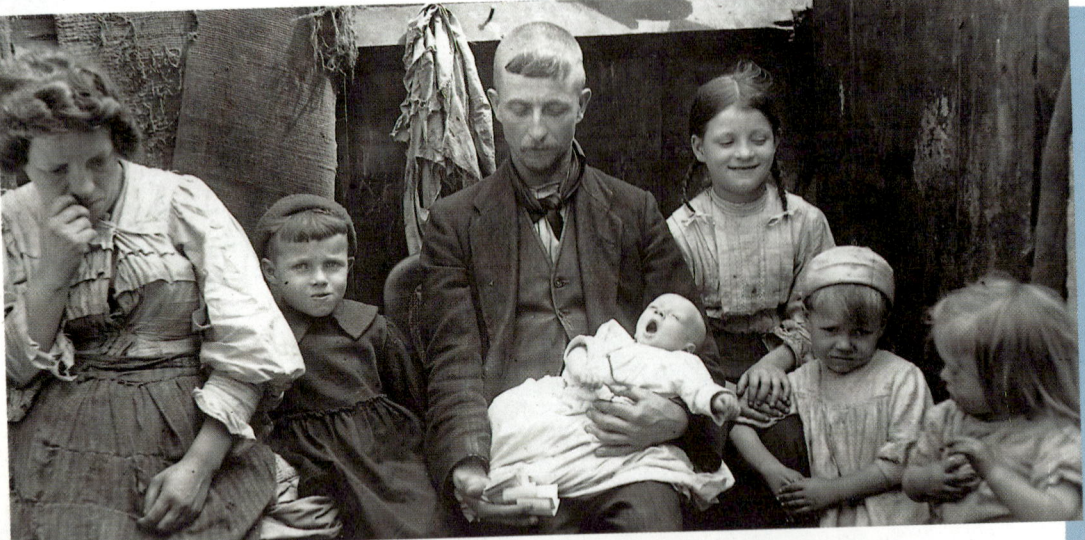

SOURCE 1
Poverty in London's East End at the beginning of the century. With contraception almost unheard of families were large and living conditions crowded. Basic hygiene was often neglected; note the filthy clothing of the two little girls in the bottom right of the photograph. Money was always short. The father holds a fistful of pawn tickets, evidence of this family's inability to make ends meet.

One third of the national income [of Britain] was enjoyed by an upper class of 1.4 million, a second third by a middle class of 4.1 million, and the remaining third by a working class of 39 million.

L.C. Money, 1911.

SOURCE 2
By contrast there was great wealth in Edwardian Britain. In this photograph the Duke and Duchess of Athlone, the Duchess of Albany and Lady May Cambridge relax on the terrace of their spacious house.

The children in these family photographs were born in the same country but grew up in circumstances which were worlds apart (**Sources 1 and 2**). Wealth and privilege ensured a good education, fine clothes, regular meals and medical care. Meanwhile, children born into the families of the lowest paid faced grinding poverty and terrible hardships. Lack of food and squalid living conditions led to ill health and early death. Families survived by making sacrifices; eating less, not heating the home and never going to the doctor. To make ends meet they pawned their clothes and the few miserable possessions they might own.

There have always been rich and poor in British society and the contrast is still evident today. However, the attitude of the state to its vulnerable groups; the old, the sick, the young and the unemployed, has undergone a fundamental change during the 20th century.

Self-help

In Victorian Britain, the state did not interfere in the lives of individual citizens to any great extent. An Edinburgh doctor called Samuel Smiles summed up the spirit of the age in his book *Self-Help* (1859). Smiles argued that hard work, careful spending and regular saving would enable a person to go through life without needing the help of the state. He preached self-reliance claiming that, 'Whatever is done *for* men ... takes away the stimulus and necessity of doing it for themselves ...' His ideas were very popular and reflected the judgement of Victorian governments that state interference was undesirable since it restricted the freedom of individuals.

By 1900, state provisions still barely scratched the surface of poverty and deprivation. For those people who became ill, unemployed or grew too old to work, the options were bleak. Many skilled workers paid subscriptions to a trade union or a Friendly Society and were entitled to receive benefits at times of need. But unskilled workers were rarely able to spare the weekly subscription out of their meagre wages. Such people were therefore forced to rely on private charity (**Source 3**). When all else failed, the last resort was to enter the workhouse (**Source 4**).

By the late 19th century people were beginning to challenge the attitude of Victorian governments towards the welfare of individuals. Self-help was clearly not the answer to the problems of millions of people who simply did not possess the means to help themselves. When the Liberals took office in 1906, they introduced reforms which began to shift responsibility for welfare from the individual to the state. What caused this change of approach?

Cause 1: Revelations of poverty

Towards the end of the 19th century dozens of investigations into the nature

SOURCE 3

Cocoa is served to destitute men at the Field Lane refuge in London. Charity of this kind was often the only source of comfort and nourishment for thousands of people who did not possess the means to support themselves. Not all Victorians liked the idea of charity, seeing it as an artificial means of prolonging the lives of the weak:

Many thousands of pounds [are spent to support] the unfit, the criminal, the unwashed; the very scum and dregs of the race whom merciless Nature, cruel to be kind, had doomed to an early extinction. The depraved and ineffectual are helped to a longer term of existence, that they may transmit their bodily and mental diseases to another generation, and so foul the blood and stunt the growth of the nation in years to come.

Charles G. Harper, 1894.

SOURCE 4

Dinner time at the St. Pancras workhouse in London. Notice how many of these women are elderly. In the days before pensions, old people without savings or generous relatives were often forced to spend their final days in these hated institutions.

and extent of poverty were carried out. The results were shocking and revealed poverty on a scale never before imagined. The most widely known surveys of town poverty were those by Charles Booth and Seebohm Rowntree.

> ### SOURCE 5
> Rowntree's 'poverty line' was designed to cover only the most basic needs. Here he describes what life on 21s 8d would mean.
>
> A family living upon the scale allowed for must never spend a penny on a railway fare or an omnibus. They must never go into the country unless they walk. They must never purchase a newspaper or spend a penny to buy a ticket for a concert. They must write no letters to absent children, for they cannot afford to pay the postage. The children must have no pocket money for dolls, marbles or sweets. The father must smoke no tobacco and drink no beer. The mother must never buy herself pretty clothes. Should a child fall ill it must be attended by the Poor Law doctor; should it die it must be buried by the parish. Finally, the wage earner must never be absent from his work for a single day.
>
> Seebohm Rowntree, *Poverty, A Study of Town Life*, 1901.

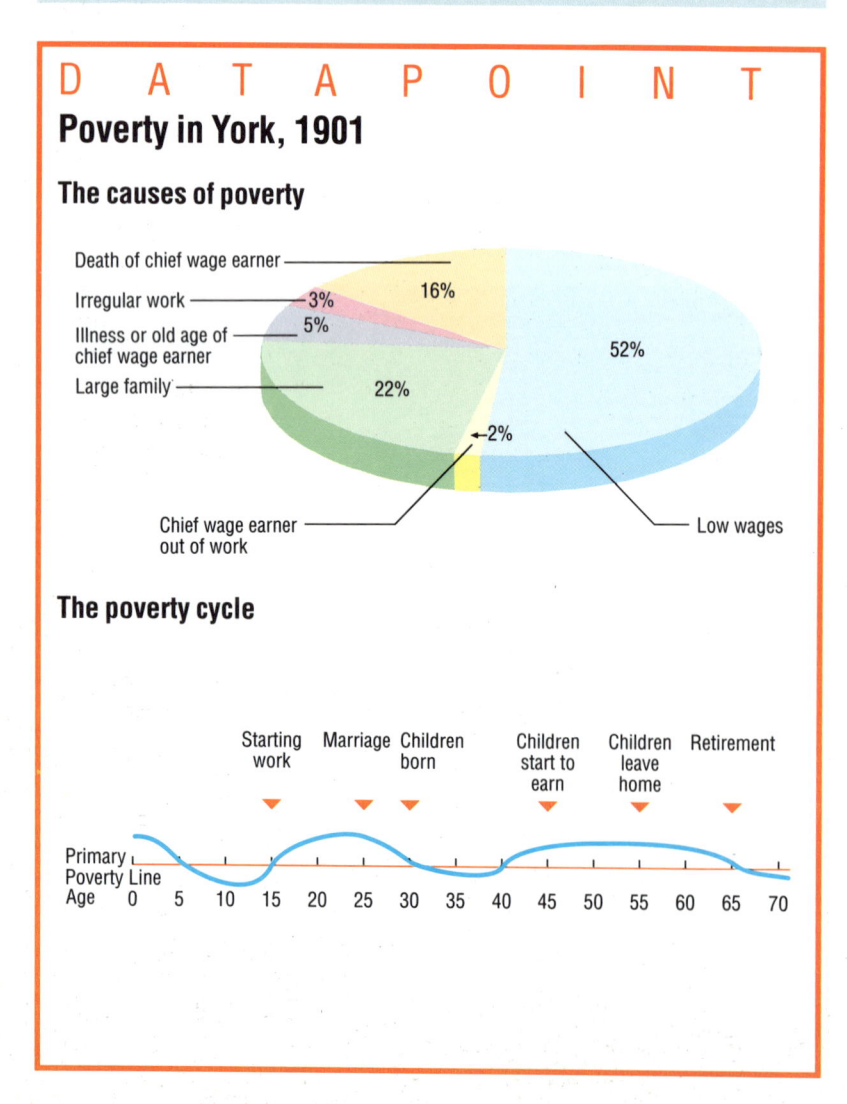

DATAPOINT
Poverty in York, 1901

The causes of poverty

- Death of chief wage earner — 16%
- Irregular work — 3%
- Illness or old age of chief wage earner — 5%
- Large family — 22%
- Chief wage earner out of work — 2%
- Low wages — 52%

The poverty cycle

[Graph showing primary poverty line across ages 0–70, with markers at: Starting work (~15), Marriage (~25), Children born (~30), Children start to earn (~45), Children leave home (~55), Retirement (~65)]

Between 1889 and 1903 Charles Booth published 17 volumes in his monumental work titled *Life and Labour of the People in London*. This huge investigation revealed that 30 per cent of the population of London were living in poverty. Seebohm Rowntree was so impressed by Booth's work in London that he decided to carry out his own research in York. He hired dieticians to determine the precise nutritional needs of the human body. Then he calculated the exact sum of money required each week to allow a family to meet its basic physical needs. His figure of 21s 8d for a family of five represented the 'poverty line'. To his dismay Rowntree found that 28 per cent of the population of York, almost half of the wage-earning class, were living below the poverty line (**Source 5**).

Rowntree published his findings in 1901 in a book called *Poverty, A Study of Town Life*. Here, he outlined the main causes of poverty and identified a 'poverty cycle' (see **Datapoint: Poverty in York, 1901**, left). The surveys of London and York made a deep impression on people at the time. It seemed a shameful fact that in one of the richest countries in the world, the income of over a quarter of the population could be insufficient to cover their basic needs.

Cause 2: National efficiency

During the 19th century Britain had developed into a hugely powerful nation. Its industrial economy made it the 'workshop of the world' and it had built an enormous overseas empire. However, by the turn of the century Britain was beginning to show signs of decline. The appearance of new industrial powers such as Germany and the USA threatened Britain's economic supremacy and the strain of defending such a far-flung empire was beginning to tell. Some politicians and businessmen believed that poverty was the cause of Britain's declining national efficiency (**Source 6**). During the second Boer War (1899–1902) an alarming discovery was made to support this view. Thousands of army recruits were rejected as medically unfit

SOURCE 6

I have been reading a book by Mr Rowntree called *Poverty*, which has impressed me very much ... It is quite evident from the figures which he (presents) that the American labourer is a stronger, larger, healthier, better fed, and consequently more efficient animal than a large proportion of our own population, and this is surely a fact which our unbridled Imperialists who have no thought but to pile up armaments, taxation and territory, should not lose sight of. For my own part, I see little glory in an empire which can rule the waves, and is unable to flush its sewers.

Winston Churchill in a letter to a leading Birmingham Conservative, 23 December 1901.

SOURCE 7

No country, however rich, can permanently hold its own in the race of international competition if hampered by an increasing load of this dead weight (the effects of poverty) or can successfully perform the role of sovereignty beyond the seas if a portion of its own folk at home are sinking below the civilisation of its subject races abroad.

Extract from the report of the Committee on Physical Deterioration, 1905.

for service. In 1903 it was revealed that 34.6 per cent of army recruits between 1893 and 1902 had been rejected following medical examinations. In the same year a Royal Commission in Scotland on Physical Training reported a national decline in standards of fitness among schoolchildren. Campaigners began to argue that the government should introduce national policies to tackle poverty in order to maintain the nation's security and commercial prosperity (**Source 7**).

Cause 3: The challenge of Labour

One of the most significant political features of the late 19th century was the development of the Labour movement. Trade Unionists, socialists and activists in the new Labour Party (formed in 1900) were united by a common ambition to drive poverty out of Britain. They argued that the only force powerful enough to accomplish this task was parliamentary legislation. The state had therefore to take a much greater responsibility for the individual. In the general election of 1906 the Liberals won 401 seats and secured a very large majority. The Labour Party, still in its infancy, won an impressive 29 seats (they had won just two seats in the election of 1900). The increasing popularity of the Labour Party worried some Liberals. They argued that if the Liberal Party failed to tackle the problems of poverty, the voting public might begin to support their political rivals (**Source 8**).

SOURCE 8

If at the end of an average term of office it was found that a Liberal Parliament had done nothing to cope seriously with the social condition of the people, to remove the national [shame] of slums and widespread poverty and destitution in a land glittering with wealth, that they had shrunk from attacking boldly the causes of this wretchedness...that they had not arrested the waste of our national resources in armaments, nor provided an honourable sustenance for deserving old age...then would a real cry arise in this land for a new party, and many of us here in this room would join in that cry.

Lloyd George speaking at a meeting in Cardiff, 11 October 1906.

SOURCE 9

David Lloyd George speaking to a crowd in his native Wales. His controversial 'People's Budget' of 1909 raised the money to pay for old age pensions. His commitment to driving poverty out of Britain can be seen in his speeches in defence of the budget.

I cannot help hoping and believing that before this generation has passed away we shall have advanced a great step towards that good time when poverty and wretchedness shall be as remote to the people of this country as the wolves that once infested its forests.

Lloyd George, 1909.

The State in Society

DATAPOINT

The Liberal Foundations

State intervention in the lives of British citizens began with a package of reforms delivered by the Liberal Government between 1906 and 1914. The main reforms targeted three vulnerable groups:

Children

1906

Education (Provision of Meals) Act: Enabled local authorities to provide free school meals for needy children. By 1914 150,000 nutritious meals a day were being served.

1907

Education (Administrative Provisions) Act: Made it the duty of local education authorities to provide regular medical inspections for the children in their schools.

1908

Children's Act (sometimes called the Children's Charter): Aimed at protecting the children from adults and their vices. It was now a criminal offence for parents to neglect their children. It became illegal for children under 16 to be sold cigarettes and for them to enter public houses. Children under 14 were no longer to be sent to prison and Juvenile Courts were set up to deal with young offenders.

The Elderly

1908

Old Age Pensions Act: Single men and women over 70 were entitled to a pension of five shillings a week, provided that they received less than £21 per year from other sources. The weekly amount was scaled down for those whose income exceeded £21 per year. Married couples were given a pension of seven shillings and sixpence per week. The scheme began on 1 January 1909 and was non-contributory. The money to pay for the new scheme came from taxes.

Workers

1909

Trade Boards Act: This measure established minimum wage rates in the 'sweated industries'. The Act applied initially to four trades: boxmaking, tailoring, lacemaking and chainmaking. By 1913 a further six trades had been added to this list.

1909

Labour Exchange Act: This set up a network of government offices to enable people to find work. Employers registered job vacancies with the exchanges and people looking for work could see at a glance what opportunities were available. The modern equivalent are the Job Centres found in most High Streets. By 1913 there were 430 Labour Exchanges nationwide.

1911

National Insurance Act: This Act came in two parts –
Part 1 - Sickness and medical insurance: Workers earning less than £160 per year had to pay fourpence (4d) a week into the Insurance Fund. To this, the employer added another 3d per worker and the government 2d. In return a benefit of ten shillings was paid to the insured worker during each week of illness for a maximum of 26 weeks. After this a weekly disability pension of five shillings was paid until the age of 70. The insured worker was also entitled to free medical attention under the 'panel' system. The panel was a list of insured patients for whom a doctor was given responsibility. A Sanatorium Benefit gave people suffering from tuberculosis free hospital treatment. There was also a maternity benefit of 30 shillings for each child.
Part 2 - Unemployment insurance: This covered about two million workers in seven trades vulnerable to seasonal unemployment such as the construction industry, engineering and shipbuilding. The worker paid a contribution of 2d per week, the employer paid 1d and the government also 1d. The benefit was six shillings a week for a maximum of 15 weeks. The measure was intended to provide short-term assistance only.

SOURCE 10

Arrangements for the payment of the first pensions appeared in post offices across the country in 1908. The first pensions were paid out in January 1909.

> **E. R.**
> **OLD AGE PENSIONS**
>
> On and after the 1st January, 1909, Old Age Pensions will be payable under the provisions of the Old Age Pensions Act, 1908, to qualified persons who have attained the age of 70 years.
>
> The forms for making claims for Old Age Pensions can be obtained gratis on and after the 24th September upon application at any Post Office in the United Kingdom. Any assistance that may be required in filling up the form will be given by the Postmaster.
>
> The name of the Post Office at which payment of the Pension is desired must be stated on the Claim Form, and the Office selected should as far as possible be the Office nearest to the applicant's home address.
>
> By Command of the Postmaster General.

The State in Society 79

SOURCE 11

When Old Age Pensions began, life was transformed for [the elderly] ... They were relieved of anxiety ... At first when they went to the Post Office to draw it, tears of gratitude would run down the cheeks of some, and they would say as they picked up their money, 'God bless that *Lord* George' ... and 'God bless you Miss!', and there were flowers from their gardens and apples from their trees for the girl who merely handed them their money.

Flora Thompson, *Lark Rise to Candleford*, 1939.

Cause 4: 'New Liberalism'

During the 19th century, the Liberal Party had stuck to the philosophy of laissez-faire which argued that people should be left to lead their own lives. The responsibility for securing an acceptable standard of living was placed squarely on the individual. Towards the end of the 19th century younger politicians sought to challenge the old ideas and 'New Liberalism' was born. The Liberal government of 1906 included 'New Liberals' like H.H. Asquith, Lloyd George and Winston Churchill. They had a genuine commitment to establishing a minimum standard of living through state intervention. The stage was set for a programme of social reform which would lay the foundations for Britain's modern Welfare State (see **Datapoint: The Liberal Foundations** opposite).

SOURCE 12

Camberwell Green labour exchange 1910.

The limitations of the Liberal reforms

Old age pensions, panel doctors, sickness benefit and unemployment insurance were a far cry from the Victorian values of self-help and laissez-faire. These reforms placed Britain firmly on the path towards the modern Welfare State.

However, the provision of state help for all those in need was by no means complete. The Liberal measures of 1906-11 had severe limitations:

- Unemployment insurance covered only two million workers. Many millions more were left out of this scheme.

- Unemployment insurance provided short-term benefits only. The long-term unemployed continued to face the prospect of the workhouse.

- Medical care provided by the 'panel' doctor was for the insured worker only, not for the family of that worker.

- Hospital treatment was not free (except for the treatment of tuberculosis).

- Dental treatment and specialist eye care at opticians were not covered under the National Insurance scheme.

- No assistance for widows and orphans was available through the new schemes.

- The age qualification for a pension (70 years) was high and meant that many thousands of elderly people still had to live below the 'poverty line'.

- Benefits paid to the sick and the unemployed were not enough to live on. They were described as 'lifebelts', keeping people afloat at times of emergency.

In the years which followed, successive governments took steps to extend the scope of the Liberal measures and to plug some of the gaps.

Knowledge and understanding

Use the information on pages 75 to 79 to investigate the following questions.

1 Examine Source 3. What was life like for families who existed on the 'poverty line'?

2 Look at the Datapoint: Poverty in York, 1901 on page 76.
a Believers in the ideas of self-help argued that the main causes of poverty were idleness and drink. How does Rowntree's analysis of poverty in York challenge this view?
b Look at the diagram showing the 'poverty cycle'. According to Rowntree what events in a person's life might cause them to fall below the poverty line? Suggest ways in which the state could intervene at each of these times to keep that person above the poverty line.

3 The Old Age Pension scheme was 'non-contributory'. The National Insurance scheme was 'contributory'. How was the money raised to provide these benefits?

4 What motivated the Liberal governments to introduce welfare reforms in the years 1906–14?

5 Make a simple chart to show (a) the benefits and (b) the limitations, of the Liberal welfare reforms.

Developments between the wars

In 1920 the Unemployment Insurance Act added ten million workers to those already covered by the 1911 Act. All workers earning less than £250 per year, with the exception of domestic and civil servants and agricultural labourers, were now protected against short-term unemployment. But a prolonged economic depression after 1920 meant that many people quickly used up their 15 weeks of benefit. Therefore, in 1921 the government was forced to begin paying extended benefits directly out of taxation. This 'uncovenanted' benefit became known as the 'dole'. The basic dole of 15 shillings a week (12 shillings for women) was supplemented with additional payments made to members of the claimant's family; five shillings a week for a wife and one shilling for each child.

In 1929 the Local Government Act ended the existing Poor Law. Its responsibilities and buildings, including the workhouses, were transferred into the control of local Public Assistance Committees. In 1931 at the height of the Depression the government cut unemployment benefits by ten per cent. Benefits were paid for a maximum of 26 weeks, after which 'transitional benefit', the new name for the dole, could be claimed. To obtain dole payments, which had also been cut by ten per cent in 1931, applicants now had to undergo a means test (see page 69). This was administered by the Public Assistance Committees and varied from region to region. The means test was bitterly resented as it involved a detailed check on the income and savings of all members of the household. The means test added insult to the injury of unemployment and sometimes had a devastating effect on family life (**Source 13**). In 1934 responsibility for means testing was transferred to an Unemployment Assistance Board.

SOURCE 13

In the meantime my wife decided to try and earn a little money... She obtained a job as a house-to-house saleswoman, and was able to earn a few shillings to supplement our dole income... Life became more and more strained... The final straw came when the Means Test was put into operation. I realised that if I told the Exchange that my wife was earning a little they might reduce my benefit. If that happened home life would become impossible... I was sent a form on which to give details of our total income, I neglected to fill it up. For this I was suspended benefit for six weeks... Quarrels broke out anew and bitter things were said. Eventually... both my wife and my son, who has just commenced to earn a few shillings, told me to get out, as I was living on them and taking the food they needed.

H.L Beales and R.S Lambert, *Memoirs of the Unemployed*, 1934.

In 1925 the Conservative government introduced a contributory pension scheme for people over 65. The pension could be claimed by anyone who had paid health insurance contributions for at least five years. At the age of 70 the original non-contributory system took over. The government also took the opportunity to introduce benefits to provide for widows over 60 (ten shillings a week) and orphans (7s 6d a week).

There were some advances in healthcare during this time. In 1918 the Maternity and Child Welfare Act allowed local authorities to set up ante-natal and children's clinics. In 1936 the Midwives Act required local authorities to provide properly trained midwives. These measures made a significant contribution to the improvement of women's health.

> **SOURCE 14**
>
> Within the present century the development of the Social Services...has been rapid and extensive. There is a system of unemployment insurance, of unemployment assistance for those who have exhausted their right to insurance, and a system of provision for the elderly or invalid poor; there is a National Health Insurance scheme and a variety of other health services; there are free old age pensions at 70, besides pensions for the widows and orphans of insured workers; there is an education system which provides for every child up to the age of 14 and for many beyond; and there are subsidies in aid of working class housing... the total expenditure on the Social Services has risen in 25 years from £63 millions to £443 millions... and the National Health Insurance scheme embraces nearly 19 million people.
>
> Next Five Years Group, *The Next Five Years*, 1935.

The Welfare State

Between 1945 and 1948 the Labour government passed laws which established the main features and institutions of Britain's Welfare State. These included a free National Health Service, comprehensive insurance for workers and a safety net for those without insurance (see **Datapoint: Labour's Welfare State** on page 85). In this way Britain's modern Welfare State was born. You can investigate the reasons behind the creation of the Welfare State in the section which follows.

Limited provision

By 1935 it was clear that much progress had been made towards the provision of welfare services (**Source 14**). In spite of this the system remained patchy and poorly co-ordinated. The various measures had been introduced at different times with no coherent plan in mind. Separate departments of state operated different parts of the system which was both inefficient and costly. Welfare provision was still limited in scope. Free medical services were denied to large sections of the population, particularly women and children. Millions of people had poor teeth and bad eyesight because a visit to the dentist or optician was too expensive. No provision was made for the dependants of sick or disabled workers and pensions at 65 were still paid only to those who had made contributions. These and other limitations showed clearly that there was considerable room for improvement in the existing system.

Ideas and attitudes

During the 1930s pressure mounted on the government to improve and expand the provision of welfare services. The writers and thinkers who pressed for change argued that society as a whole would benefit from greater state involvement. Many took their lead from the economist John Maynard Keynes. He argued that to achieve a healthy economy, governments should borrow money and invest in such things as roads, schools, houses and hospitals. To achieve this, state planning would be essential. To many people the idea of planning seemed a good way of ensuring that all citizens shared the benefits of society.

The Next Five Years Group, a non-political group of writers and thinkers, was formed in 1934 and worked to promote the case for the wider involvement of the state in society. Writers like J.B.

Priestley and George Orwell also jabbed at the conscience of Britain through books which revealed the divisions and inequalities of society. Priestley's tour of Britain in 1934 showed a country of great contrasts: prosperity and wealth in some areas, neglect and despair in others. The image of Britain in **Source 15** was not shared by the unemployed workers Priestley found in Stockton-on-Tees:

> excellent skilled workmen, who have been unemployed not merely this year and last year but for seven or eight years, who might as well be crossbow-men or armourers, for all the demand there is for their services.

Social investigators like Seebohm Rowntree and members of the Pilgrim Trust continued to draw the plight of the poverty-stricken to public attention. In his second survey of York in 1936, Rowntree found that although the numbers living in poverty had been reduced, around 18 per cent of the population were still below the poverty line. He claimed that 47 per cent of all working-class children would spend the first five years of their lives in poverty and almost a third of these would continue to do so for ten years or more. The damage done to the physical development of such children threatened to have a major impact on the labour force of the future. Similar surveys in Bristol and Merseyside told the same story.

Feminist activists like Eleanor Rathbone worked hard to persuade the government to take more notice of women's needs. As early as 1917 she had established a pressure group to secure family allowances. The campaign continued for the next 28 years before being won. The suffering of the 1930s made a long-lasting impression on many young politicians from all the main parties (**Source 16**). This helped to ensure broad support for change in the years after 1945.

Although the public's awareness of poverty and inequality had been raised in the 1930s, governments failed to make significant improvements. It required the emergency of the Second World War to mobilise the resources of the state and to show what could be achieved in the interest of the common good.

SOURCE 15

This is the writer J.B. Priestley's view of the more prosperous face of England in the 1930s.

The England of arterial and by-pass roads, filling stations and factories that look like exhibition buildings, of giant cinemas and dance-halls and cafes, bungalows with tiny garages, cocktail bars, Woolworths, motor coaches, wireless, hiking, factory girls looking like actresses, greyhound racing and dirt tracks, swimming pools, and everything given away for cigarette coupons.

J.B. Priestley, *English Journey*, 1934.

SOURCE 16

I shall never forget those despairing faces, as the men tramped up and down the High Street in Stockton... Nor can any tribute be too great to the loyal, unflinching courage of the wives and mothers, who somehow continued, often on a bare pittance, to provide for husband and children and keep a decent home in being. Even in the South of England, the sight of wounded or unemployed ex-servicemen begging in the street was now too common to be remarkable. Sometimes these demonstrations of misery took a more organised but none the less distressing form, such as the 'hunger marches' as they came to be called. Of these, the march of the Jarrow unemployed was the most poignant; for with the closing of Palmer's shipyard, almost the sole means of employment in the town had come to an end.

Harold Macmillan, *Winds of Change, 1914–39*, 1966.

The experience of war

The Second World War brought huge disruption to everyday life and united the British people through their shared experience (**Source 17**). The War brought people together in a common purpose and exposed the better-off classes to the sometimes shocking condition of people from poor backgrounds. The evacuation of thousands of children from cities vulnerable to enemy attack brought the prosperous middle class of rural Britain into direct contact with the meaning of poverty.

SOURCE 17

The armed forces gathered together men from different classes; bombs fell on the rich as well as the poor; wartime industry attracted into it women who in peacetime might never have considered such work. Government controls affected the whole of the population. The rationing of food and clothing was soon in force and the government also standardised the quality and design of many goods to avoid waste.

S. Wood, *The British Welfare State, 1900–50*, 1982.

The evacuated children were often dirty, undernourished, illiterate and in poor health. It was an eye-opening experience for the people who took the children into their homes (**Source 18**). Few had imagined that such poverty could exist in Britain. The shock helped to create a determination to improve the conditions which produced these children.

People experienced terrible hardships during the War. The weekly ration of food did not go far and it was a constant struggle to feed a family. During the blitz people living in the major cities and ports were subject to the nightly terror of air-raids. Bombs caused massive destruction and killed thousands of civilians. Mass conscription took loved-ones away to the battlefields, and many never returned home. Amidst all of this could be heard the question 'what are we fighting for?' To the people who experienced these times the answer was clear; they were fighting for a better world and a fairer society. An expectation was created that when peace returned society would be reconstructed to reward all those who had won the victory.

The War encouraged the state to take on greater responsibility for its citizens. Two examples of this were rationing and evacuation. State control over the wartime economy showed that government intervention on a large scale was both possible and effective. Important developments were made in the provision of healthcare during the War. The Civil Defence Act of 1939 made the Ministry of Health responsible for all civilian casualties. This created the principle of free hospital treatment for all who needed it. A unified Emergency Hospital Service was established to provide this treatment, creating a solid foundation upon which the National Health Service could be built. During the War the government acknowledged the value of protecting and improving the health of its citizens (**Source 19**). The rationing scheme devised by the Ministry of Food was carefully designed to provide a healthy balance of vitamins and minerals. For many people, in spite

SOURCE 18

This source presents some reactions from middle class homes which took in children evacuated from the cities.

The state of the children was such that the school had to be fumigated after the reception. Except for a small number the children were filthy ... Their clothing was in a deplorable condition, some of the children being literally sewn into their ragged little garments.

National Federation of Women's Institutes, *Town Children Through Country Eyes*, 1940.

Each night was spent in de-lousing these two little boys, as they were infested with lice. With newspapers spread out on the table, a small-tooth comb and a good light, it was case of who could collect the most lice between my sister and me.

Ben Wicks, *No Time to Say Goodbye*, 1988.

A very common complaint ... is about the children with infectious or contagious diseases. One village to my knowledge received 600 Liverpool children, of whom no fewer than 485 had such complaints.

Kingsley Martin, *Critic's London Diary*, 1960.

SOURCE 19

The war effort depended on a healthy workforce. This Ministry of Health poster shows how the Government had begun to take responsibility for basic health education as part of its strategy for winning the War.

of the shortages, this was the healthiest diet they had ever eaten.

The War showed how the state could use its power and resources to positive effect. Soon the argument followed that it should employ these same resources to build a new society in peacetime with full employment and a minimum standard of living for all. In 1942 all these hopes were collected together in the Beveridge Report. When it was published, the Report caused huge excitement and ensured that no post-war government would be able to avoid the election promise to build a better society.

SOURCE 20
Sir William Beveridge

SOURCE 21
This comment on the Beveridge Report by the cartoonist David Low was published in 1942.

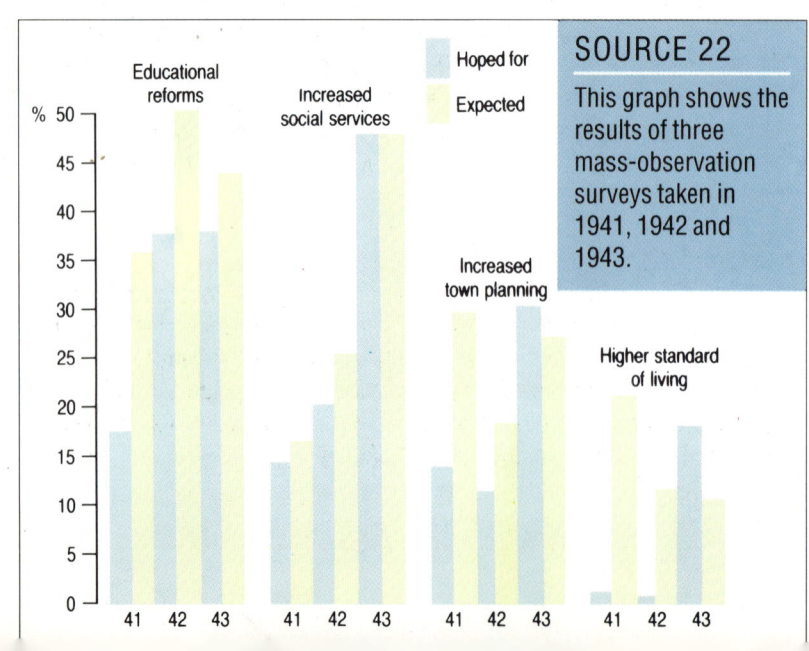

SOURCE 22
This graph shows the results of three mass-observation surveys taken in 1941, 1942 and 1943.

The Beveridge Report, 1942

In June 1941 Sir William Beveridge was appointed chairman of the Committee on Social Insurance and Allied Services (**Source 20**). The committee was asked to undertake a thorough review of existing welfare provisions. On 1 December 1942, the committee published its recommendations in the so-called Beveridge Report. The Report gripped the popular imagination and seemed to capture the spirit of the time. It clarified the hopes of the British people and gave purpose to the sacrifice and hardship of wartime (**Source 22**). Within one year 635,000 copies of the report had been sold. A Gallup poll revealed that 95 per cent of the population had heard of the report and 86 per cent were in favour of its recommendations.

Beveridge identified five 'giants' which would have to be overcome if Britain were to be re-built as a better society - Want, Disease, Squalor, Ignorance and Idleness. His report suggested a number of far-reaching proposals to slay these giants:

- A new insurance scheme to cover all people against unemployment and sickness, and for old age
- A standard insurance contribution which all would pay and a standard benefit which all could claim
- The payment of benefits to the unemployed without time limit
- The payment of a family allowance for each child
- The creation of a free national health service

At the centre of the Report were two important principles. The first was the proposal to establish a 'National Minimum', a standard below which no one should be allowed to fall regardless of their circumstances. To achieve this, subsistence benefits would have to be paid. These were payments large enough to meet all the necessities of life in all circumstances. The second principle was that of 'universality'. Before 1940 state help was only available to certain groups. Beveridge proposed to apply his welfare schemes to everyone, regardless of wealth or social status.

The panoramic vision of the Beveridge Report and the huge public attention it received made social welfare a high profile issue and demanded a response from the nation's political leaders. A great deal of support for the Report was voiced by MPs, particularly those in the Labour camp. But Churchill was not so enthusiastic (**Source 23**). He warned of a 'dangerous optimism' which was developing in the country and was concerned about the cost of implementing the proposals. Above all he did not wish attention to be diverted from the main business of winning the War. What he failed to acknowledge was that the Report, in raising public morale, was part of that very process. By the time the War ended the Report had been watered down by the Phillips Committee. The Labour Party won power in the election of July 1945 on a promise to implement the Beveridge Report. In fact, parts of the new social legislation introduced by Labour (see **Datapoint: Labour's Welfare State**, right) fell short of what Beveridge had proposed:

- Family allowances were fixed below subsistence levels and were not paid for the first child.
- Sickness benefits were paid for an unlimited time but unemployment benefit was limited to 180 days.
- Unemployment and sickness benefits and old age pensions were too low to achieve a 'national minimum' standard. They were fixed below the lowest pay level and did not increase at the same rate as the cost of living. The aim to provide benefits at subsistence levels was not achieved.
- A means test was revived to assess people who applied to the National Assistance Board.

DATAPOINT

Labour's Welfare State

When the Second World War ended the new Labour government passed a series of laws which created the modern Welfare State.

Family Allowance Act, 1945

These proposals had been agreed by the wartime coalition government but the first payments were not made until August 1946. The Act gave a weekly allowance for every child after the first. The benefit was five shillings a week and was paid regardless of the income of the family. The allowance was funded out of national taxation. Books of coupons were issued to be cashed each week at local post offices.

National Insurance Act, 1946

All workers were now required to be insured against loss of earnings. All workers paid a flat-rate contribution into the National Insurance fund. The benefit paid out was the same for everyone and could be claimed for whatever reason – sickness, unemployment, pregnancy, widowhood or old age. Sickness benefit was allowed for an unlimited time up to the age of retirement. Unemployment benefit however was only payable for 180 days. The Old Age Pension was now to be paid to men at the age of 65 and women at the age of 60. The Act also provided a single-payment maternity benefit at the birth of a child and an allowance for 13 weeks afterwards. A funeral allowance provided a lump sum to cover the cost of burial. The benefits granted by this Act were not means tested.

National Health Service Act, 1946

This Act set up the National Health Service which became operational on the 'Appointed Day', 5 July 1948. It established comprehensive and free healthcare for all citizens. All hospitals were taken under state control and organised into 20 regional Hospital Boards. 'Primary' care was provided by local doctors (GPs), dentists and opticians. Local authorities provided medical services such as health visitors, vaccination, maternity and child care, district nurses and ambulance services. All citizens were now entitled to free hospital treatment and medicine and the services of specialists in every area of medicine and healthcare. The Act was the work of the Minister of Health, Aneurin Bevan.

National Assistance Act, 1948

People who had not paid contributions into the National Insurance fund were not entitled to its benefits. The National Assistance Board was set up to provide help for these people. Benefits provided by the National Assistance Board were funded out of general taxation. People claiming National Assistance were assessed in an interview but there was no means test on other members of the claimant's family.

Although the Beveridge Report was modified, some of its more important features remained intact. The principle of universality, for example, was at the heart of the new National Insurance arrangements with the same contributions and benefits for everyone. Above all, the National Health Service, for which Labour had campaigned since 1931, became a reality. The Labour reforms were hugely popular throughout the country and enjoyed cross-party support in Parliament. The new measures were not without their critics, however, and the fiercest opposition came from the medical profession itself.

SOURCE 23

Ministers should, in my view, be careful not to raise false hopes, as was done last time [during the First World War] by speeches about 'homes fit for heroes', etc. The broad masses of the people face the hardships of life undaunted, but they are liable to get very angry if they feel they have been ... cheated. We must all do our best to win the war, and we shall do it much better if we are not hindered by a cloud of promises which have no connection with reality.

Winston Churchill from a letter to the Cabinet, January 1943. Published in Churchill's book *The Second World War*, 1951.

SOURCE 24

The experiences of the two people described in this source show how far people were forced to neglect their health before free treatment was available to all.

People always managed to find the money to bring their children [to the doctor's surgery]. But the mothers would go without. When the NHS came in, all that emerged. Within six months I had 30 or 40 women come in who had been suffering gynaecological problems, many of them for years - women with a complete prolapse of the uterus who'd been wearing nappies and towels to hide the problem.

Dr Alastair Clarke, quoted in *The Independent*, 4 July 1988.

Dad ... had a small wage, and thought with a family of four children to bring up, it was too much for him to be able to go to the doctor ... He used to buy some concoction from the chemist at sixpence a bottle, that eased his pains in his stomach. But when he went on the National Health Service, this was thoroughly investigated, and they found out that Dad hadn't a stomach upset, Dad had cancer. Had it been treated earlier, [it] could have been cured but unfortunately, due to the expensive doctors, Dad had not had this looked into before, and we lost Dad, Dad died of cancer.

Mrs Clare Bond, quoted in Paul Addison, *Now the War is Over*, 1985.

Bevan and the doctors

In 1946 a poll showed that 64 per cent of all General Practitioners (GPs) were against Bevan's proposals. Doctors had always made their living by charging fees for the services they provided. A visit to the doctor and a prescription for medicine could be a very costly business, especially for the poor. As a result many thousands of people neglected their health, sometimes with dreadful consequences (**Source 24**). Bevan wanted to scrap doctors' fees and instead to pay them a fixed salary. His proposals caused an uproar (**Source 25**). Doctors argued that they would become little more than civil servants and would lose professional status and respect.

Opposition to Bevan's proposals was voiced through the British Medical Association (BMA) and organised by two prominent medical men, Dr Guy Dain and Dr Charles Hill. Some opponents went to extreme lengths when attacking the Health Service Bill (**Source 26**). The BMA represented GPs and hospital doctors who were the main groups threatening to boycott the NHS if Bevan's proposals were accepted.

Bevan worked closely with Lord Moran, President of the Royal College of Physicians, to find ways of overcoming the opposition of the BMA. The other great ally of Bevan was public opinion. The press reported the growing impatience of the country at the attitude of the doctors who seemed intent on protecting their own interests at the expense of the nation.

Gradually the doctors began to give way. When Bevan assured them that they could keep some private patients and withdrew plans for a fixed salary their opposition evaporated. Between February and May 1948, 7000 GPs abandoned their resistance and accepted Bevan's plans.

Doctors would now be paid a fee for each patient registered at their practice. The tradition of selling practices was

The State in Society

SOURCE 25

A cartoon comment on the attitude of some doctors to Bevan's proposals. Harley Street is a famous centre for private medical treatment. The doctors in the cartoon are waiting to hijack Bevan as he strides into their territory.

HERE HE COMES, BOYS!

SOURCE 26

Dr Alfred Cox was a staunch opponent of Bevan's plans. In this letter to the *British Medical Journal* he made his views known.

I have examined the Bill [the National Health Service Bill] and it looks uncommonly like the first step, and a big one, towards National Socialism [Nazism] as practised in Germany. The medical service there was early put under the dictatorship of a 'Medical Fuehrer'. This Bill will establish the Minister of Health in that capacity.

stopped but Bevan set aside a pension fund to compensate doctors and provide them with a comfortable retirement. By the Appointed Day 90 per cent of doctors had joined the NHS.

Knowledge and understanding

Use the information on pages 80 to 87 to investigate the following questions.

1 Summarise the extent of welfare provision by 1939.

2 The following points could be used to explain why the Labour government of 1945–51 carried out its welfare reforms:
- The experience of the Depression in the 1930s
- The work of pressure groups and individual campaigners
- The experience of the Second World War
- The introduction of state controls during the War
- The socialist policies of the Labour Party

a Which of these reasons could be described as long-term and which are short-term?

b Place the five reasons listed above into what you consider to be their order of importance (most important first, least important last)

c Now explain why you decided upon this order.

d Choose any one reason from the list and show how this helps to explain why the Labour government carried out its welfare reforms.

e Now choose two other reasons from the list and explain how they can be linked together with your choice from question **d** to create a fuller explanation for the Labour reforms.

3 To what extent did the Labour reforms of 1945–51 make use of the proposals made in the Beveridge Report?

4 Explain why thousands of doctors in the BMA were opposed to the creation of the National Health Service.

5 How did Bevan secure the support of the doctors for his proposals?

88 The State in Society

DATAPOINT

A healthier nation

Infectious diseases – notifications

Diptheria (000's): 1951, 1953, 1956
Tuberculosis (000's): 1951, 1956, 1961, 1966, 1971

Infant mortality

Deaths (under 1 year) per 1000 born:
- 1951: ~32
- 1956: ~25
- 1961: ~22
- 1966: ~18
- 1971: ~17
- 1977: ~15

Expectation of life

Years: 1931, 1951, 1961, 1971, 1977

Death rate per 1000 of population
- 1901: 17.2
- 1911: 13.8
- 1921: 12.4
- 1931: 11.9
- 1941: 14.0
- 1951: 11.5
- 1961: 11.3

SOURCE 27

An NHS doctor listens to his patient as she describes her symptoms. His pen is poised ready to write the prescription for free medicine. What might have prevented this lady from seeing a doctor in the days before the NHS?

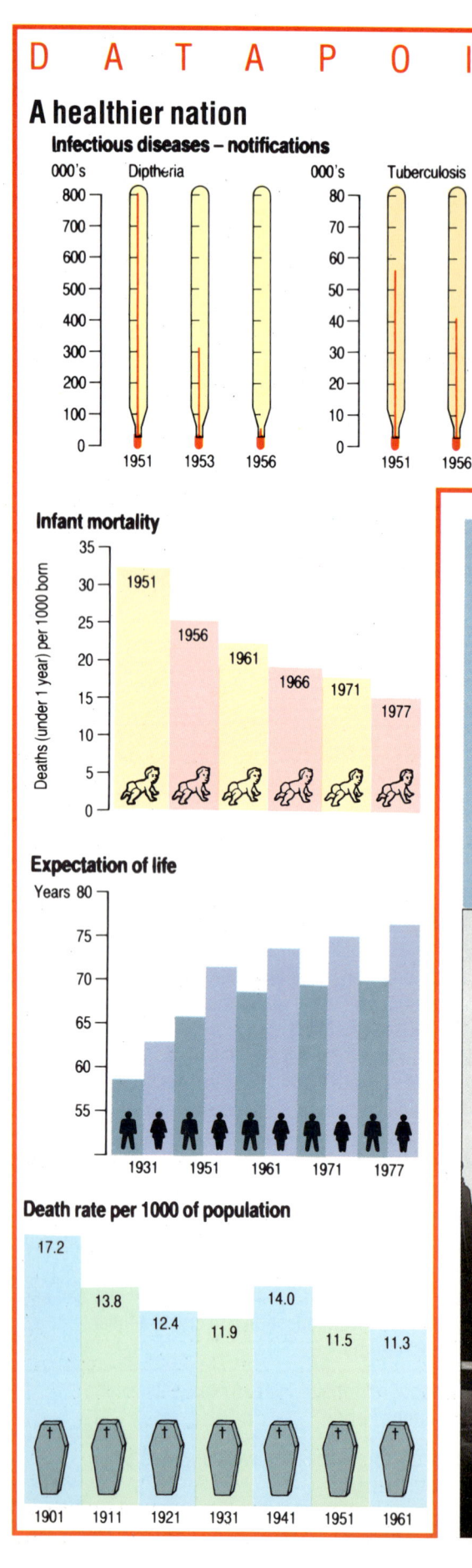

Benefits and problems

In the short term the reforms of the Labour government brought great benefits to the majority of the population. The National Health Service and the National Insurance system ignored differences of wealth, class or social background. They encouraged all people to feel part of the nation and gave everyone a stake in its future.

The most important short term effect of the reforms was to provide a much needed overhaul of the nation's health. Before the Second World War only half of Britain's population was entitled to state medical care. Doctors fees prevented the poorer classes from seeking medical attention. Large sections of the population went about their daily lives half-blind, in pain, with bad teeth or hiding serious illnesses. The free National Health Service took away the need to suffer in silence. The rush for treatment became a stampede (**Source 28**). Within six months of its launch, 21 million people had received medical attention

SOURCE 28

Within a year... 41,200,000 people – ninety-five per cent of the eligible population – were covered by it (the National Health Service). In the first year 8,500,000 dental patients were treated and 5,250,000 pairs of spectacles dispensed, illustrating the pent-up demand for the dental and ophthalmic services, which had never been part of the old insurance system. Working people no longer had to test their own eyes at Woolworths. In the first year 187,000,000 prescriptions were written out by more than 18,000 general practitioners. 'I shudder to think,' said Bevan as the statistics soared, 'of the ceaseless cascade of medicine which is pouring down British throats at the present time.' The National Health Service employed 34,000 people, and cost nearly £400,000,000 a year. In terms of money and manpower it became the second largest undertaking in the country – second to the armed forces. It was the largest single item in the civilian budget, and accounted for about 3 per cent of the national product.

Peter Jenkins, 'Bevan's Fight with the BMA'.

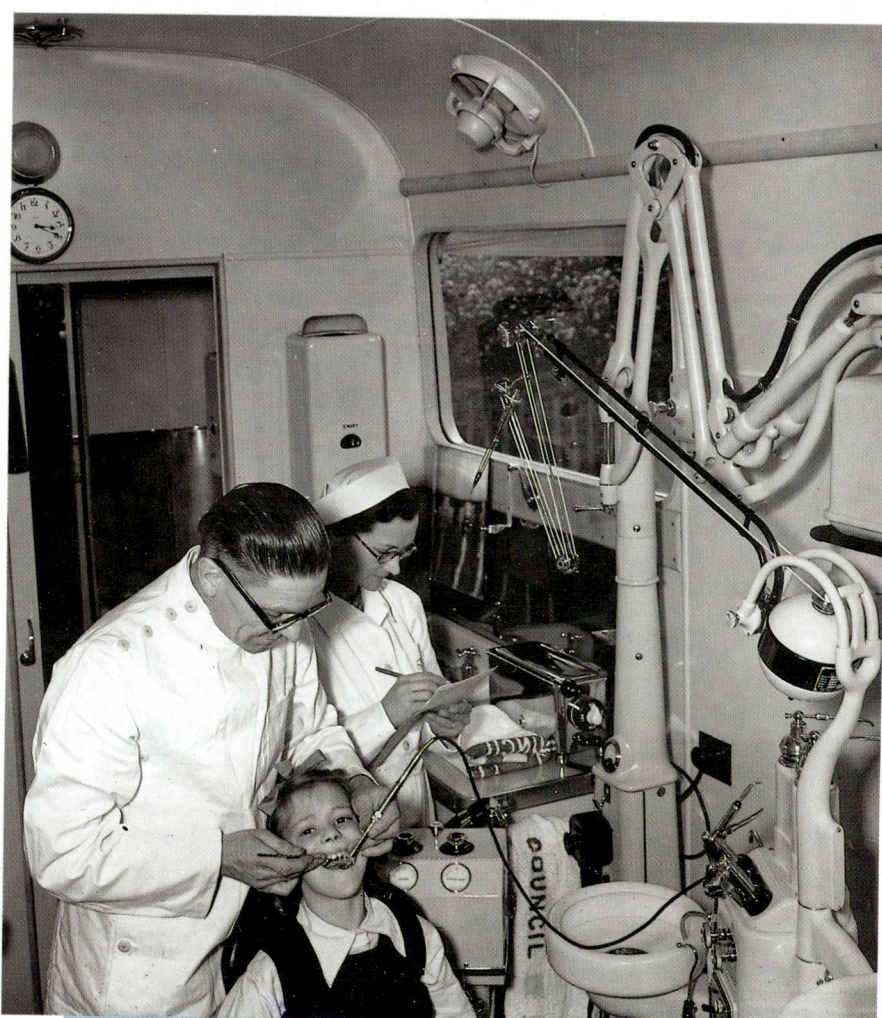

SOURCE 29

A mobile dental surgery enables schoolchildren in Kent to receive check-ups and treatment. Mobile medical facilities, which also included X-ray units to help in the fight against tuberculosis, were part of the NHS effort to provide comprehensive medical care for people in all parts of the country.

---

through the NHS. The development of vaccines and mass immunisation programmes through the NHS has virtually eliminated dangerous diseases such as diphtheria, whooping cough, scarlet fever and measles (see **Datapoint: A healthier nation** opposite).

In the longer term, however, the Welfare State has experienced problems. Within a few years the strains on the NHS began to show. The costs of restoring and maintaining the nation's health started to mount and governments found it difficult to continue providing all services free of charge. In 1951 the Labour government introduced charges to help pay for the work done by opticians and dentists. Bevan resigned in protest. The following year the new Conservative government introduced prescription charges. The principle of an entirely free health service had lasted just three years.

The cost of maintaining all aspects of the Welfare State has grown dramatically (see **Datapoint: The cost of welfare, 1900–1969** on page 90). This has been caused particularly by a change in Britain's population structure. Advances in medicine in the 20th century have meant that more people live longer. The result has been a much greater number of people reaching retirement age (**Source 30**).

Problems have also been caused by the failure to provide subsistence benefits. As pensions, and sickness and unemployment benefits lagged behind the cost of living, large numbers of people were forced to resort to the National Assistance Board for extra help. As early as 1953 a quarter of widows and pensioners were applying for assistance. This was a far cry from Beveridge's intention of eliminating poverty. In 1954 it was estimated that eight per cent of the population were living in poverty. By 1960 the figure had almost doubled.

Faced with these rising costs, the Conservative governments of the 1950s questioned the principle of 'universality'. Critics claimed that it was a waste of resources to continue paying the same

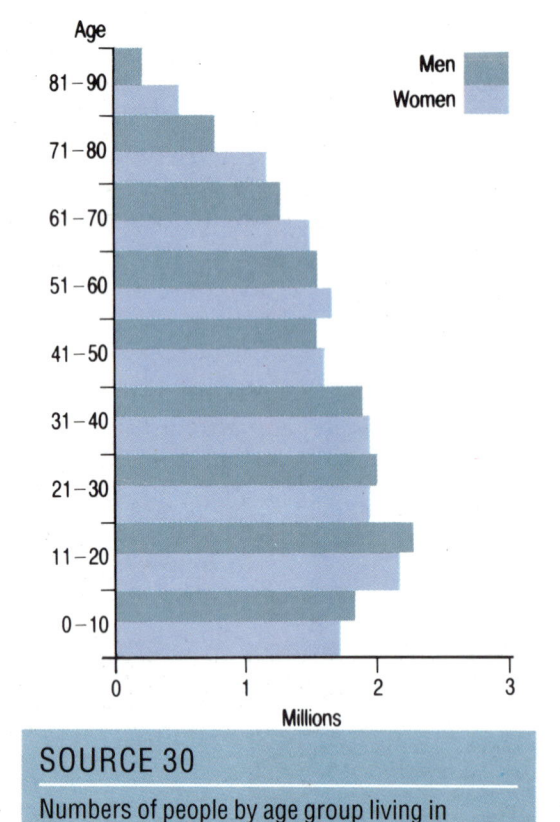

SOURCE 30

Numbers of people by age group living in Britain in 1981.

benefits to all when some people could clearly manage with less. As a result the principle of 'selectivity' was re-born. This attempted to target those in need of assistance and required those with greater resources to make larger contributions. In 1961 the government introduced a graduated insurance scheme which scrapped flat-rate contributions and required workers to pay contributions according to the size of their income. In 1966 the National Assistance Board was closed down. National Assistance was replaced with Supplementary Benefit. In 1968 responsibility for this and all other state benefits was taken over by the new Department of Health and Social Security (DHSS). Supplementary Benefit was intended for those people who were not in full-time employment and designed to ensure that no-one fell below a minimum level of income. By 1980 there were 3.3 million people receiving Supplementary Benefit.

D A T A P O I N T

The cost of welfare, 1900–1969

Social security expenditure in millions of pounds

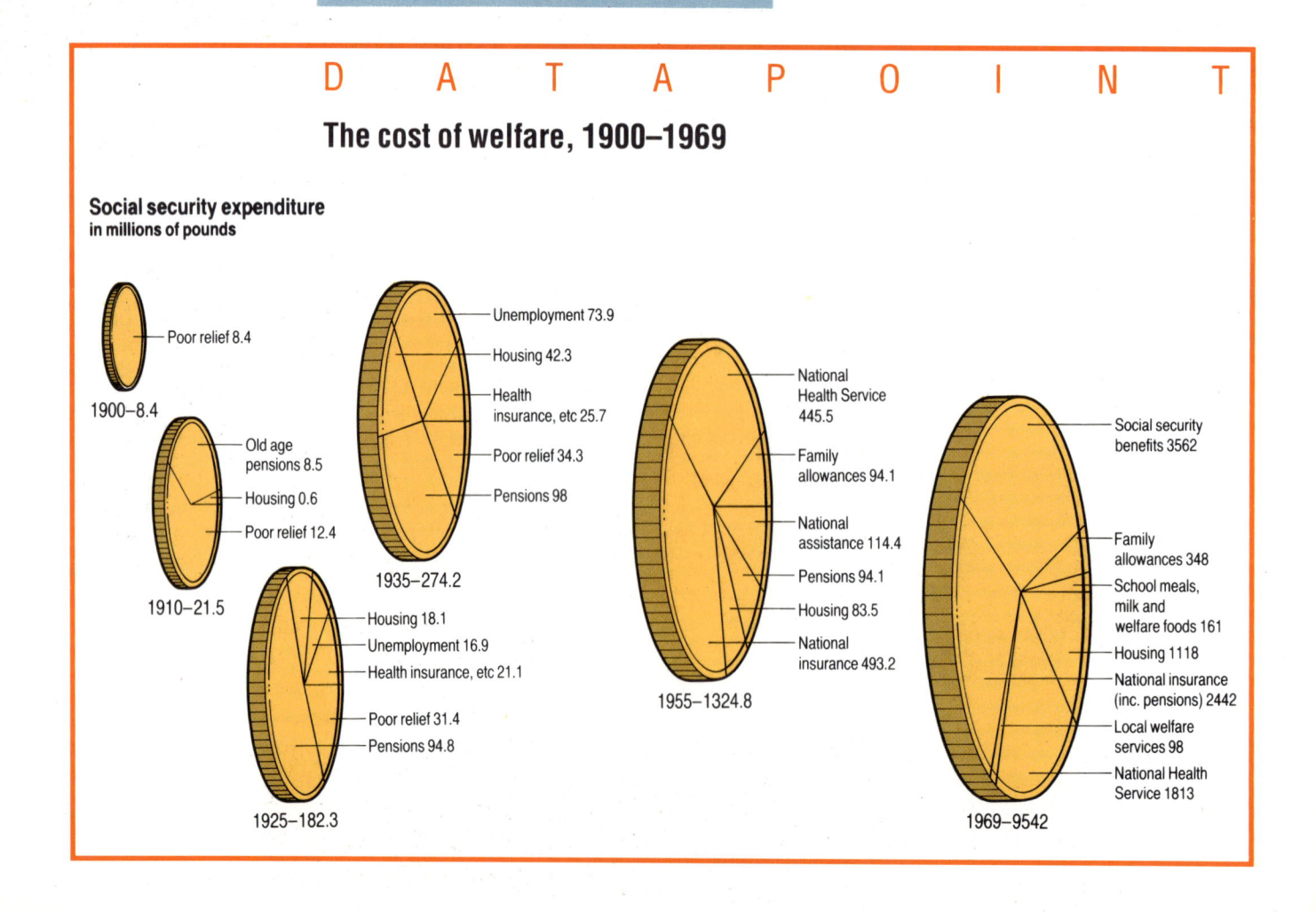

1900 – 8.4
- Poor relief 8.4

1910 – 21.5
- Old age pensions 8.5
- Housing 0.6
- Poor relief 12.4

1925 – 182.3
- Housing 18.1
- Unemployment 16.9
- Health insurance, etc 21.1
- Poor relief 31.4
- Pensions 94.8

1935 – 274.2
- Unemployment 73.9
- Housing 42.3
- Health insurance, etc 25.7
- Poor relief 34.3
- Pensions 98

1955 – 1324.8
- National Health Service 445.5
- Family allowances 94.1
- National assistance 114.4
- Pensions 94.1
- Housing 83.5
- National insurance 493.2

1969 – 9542
- Social security benefits 3562
- Family allowances 348
- School meals, milk and welfare foods 161
- Housing 1118
- National insurance (inc. pensions) 2442
- Local welfare services 98
- National Health Service 1813

Housing and education

One of the 'giants' identified by Beveridge was Ignorance. To combat this an Education Act was passed in 1944. The Act provided free, compulsory education for all children up to the age of 15. The Act was the work of the Conservative minister R.A. Butler. Children were selected to attend different types of schools through an examination taken at the age of eleven. The eleven-plus examination was supposed to identify the most academic children. They were sent to grammar schools where the education they received was considered a preparation for university. The children who failed the 11+ went to secondary modern schools.

In the 1950s criticism of this selective education system led to the introduction of comprehensive schools. These were schools for all children regardless of their abilities. After the Labour victory in the 1974 election, local authorities were required by law to adopt the comprehensive system. By 1980 more than 90 per cent of secondary schools in England and Wales had been reorganised in this way.

SOURCE 32

The Health Minister Aneurin Bevan (*second from the left*) visits a new council estate in Lewisham, South London. Flats like these were seen as the answer to the massive housing shortage caused by the War.

SOURCE 31

Prefabricated housing under construction. These rapidly constructed homes provided much-needed accommodation for thousands of people made homeless during the War.

92 The State in Society

To tackle the 'giant' which Beveridge called Squalor required a huge house building programme. Millions of houses had been damaged or destroyed during the bombing raids of the Second World War. Of those that remained intact, many were slums and in need of demolition. Within a short time 157,000 temporary prefabricated houses had been assembled (**Source 31**). These 'prefabs' were gratefully occupied by people made homeless in the War, and some are still in use today! At the Ministry of Health Bevan was responsible for housing. He announced an ambitious building programme to construct 240,000 new council houses every year (**Source 32**). A shortage of construction materials meant that this target was not achieved. However, by 1951 about 900,000 new houses had been built. In 1946 the government announced the New Towns Act. This was designed to take the pressure off the major cities through the building of twelve 'new towns'. Later other new towns such as Milton Keynes and Telford began to be developed (**Source 33**). In spite of these measures many people in the late 1960s lived in housing which fell below acceptable standards (**Source 34**).

SOURCE 33

This map shows Britain's new towns built since 1946.

SOURCE 34

Out of a total stock of 17,300,000 houses in England, Wales and Scotland, less than ten million according to government standards are fit and have basic sanitary amenities. Of the remainder over two million are 'unfit' and must be demolished, 2,500,000 are sub-standard and not worth improving and, according to the Ministry of Housing, will also have to be demolished; a further 2,500,000 are sub-standard and require improvements and repairs.

Winston Churchill, *The Times*, October 1969.

Knowledge and understanding

Use the information on pages 88 to 92 to investigate the following questions.

1 Look at the text and the Datapoint: A healthier nation. What effects did the Labour welfare reforms have on British Society?

2 What changes had been made to the Welfare State by 1968?

3 Look at the Datapoint: The cost of welfare, 1900–1969. Does this information show that during the 20th century British governments changed their attitude towards the welfare of the British people?

4 Use the following points to describe the changing attitude of the state towards the welfare of its citizens in the 20th century:
- The policy of laissez-faire
- The National Insurance Act 1911
- The National Health Service Act 1946

5 'Change and progress are not the same'. Show how this is true with reference to the means test (1931) and prescription charges (1952).

Investigation

Did everyone welcome the Liberal Reforms?

SOURCE A

We have already made a serious inroad upon personal independence by relieving parents of the duty of educating their children. That is now used as an argument for relieving them of their duty of feeding their children. When we have done that, the argument will be stronger than ever for relieving them of the duty of clothing their children. It will be said that we pay vast sums for teaching and feeding, but that the money is wasted if the children are not properly clad … From that it is an easy step to paying for their proper housing, for what, it will be asked, is the use of feeding, clothing and teaching children, if they come to school from … insanitary bedrooms … What are we to expect from the present children when they in turn become parents? The habit of looking to the state for their maintenance would be ingrained in them; everything we now give would be to them a matter of course; and they would … make new demands of their own.

The Times, 2 January 1905.

SOURCE B

Punch cartoon 1912, 'Oliver asks for less'.

Questions

1 Examine Sources A, B and E. Describe the opposition to the Liberal reforms.

2 Suggest reasons why the Friendly Societies and insurance companies were so opposed to the new National Insurance and pension schemes.

3 Consider Sources C(i) and (ii). Crosthwaite and Cadbury have different views on the effect of pensions. Does this mean that these sources are of no use to a historian?

4 Examine Source D. Labour Party members were committed to achieving social improvement through the intervention of the state in society. Why then did they oppose the Liberal National Health Insurance proposals?

5 Look at all the Sources. 'Opposition to the Liberal reforms was widespread amongst the British public.' Why would a historian reject this view on the evidence of these sources?

SOURCE C

i The strength of this kingdom … has been its great reserve of wealth and the sturdy independent character of its people. [Pensions] will destroy both sources. It will extort the wealth from its possessors by unjust taxation … and will sap the character of the people by teaching them to rely, not on their own exertions, but on the State.

Part of a letter to *The Times* by C.H.T. Crosthwaite, 1908.

ii I think old age pensions would promote thrift [saving]. It is now hopeless for a man earning 20s to 25s per week if he does his duty to his family, to provide for the future, whereas if he was sure of 7s per week there would be an inducement to add a trifle to it, either by joining a Friendly Society, by insurance or savings.

George Cadbury writing in 1899.

SOURCE D

We have opposed the Bill [to introduce National Health Insurance], first because of its contributory character … The contributory plan … is an … unjust and wasteful method of financing a great national scheme … It will encourage the displacement of labour by machinery; it will add to the cost of commodities … and it will be an excuse for resisting demands for the advance of wages. We object to the Bill, also, because it does not give relief to those who stand most in need of it and who are least able to help themselves. A contributory scheme can give … benefits only to those who contribute and a vast number of the poorer workers will never be able to fulfil the conditions laid down in this Bill.

Statement by six Labour Party members printed in *The Times*, December 1911.

SOURCE E

Health Insurance … was … introduced only after a struggle with powerful pressure groups. The Friendly Societies and the insurance companies had to be placated, for Lloyd George knew that their armies of door-to-door collectors would exert great influence … The … press, and opposition extremists, encouraged a short-lived but noisy agitation against the sticking of stamps upon insurance cards, especially by the mistresses on behalf of domestic servants. More seriously, the scheme was presented to the working classes as an oppressive system of deduction from wages … extreme opinion tried to exploit the fears of the doctors … Lloyd George was described by the President of the British Medical Association as a 'natural calamity'.

Donald Read, *England 1868–1914*, 1979.

6 Superpower Relations since 1945

SOURCE 1

The 'Big Three': Churchill, Roosevelt and Stalin at Yalta. Roosevelt was sympathetic towards the Soviet Union and, despite Churchill's distrust of Stalin, the wartime leaders of the Allied countries remained friendly as their forces secured victory over Hitler.

Yalta, February 1945

SOURCE 2

Only five months later Roosevelt had died and Churchill had been voted out of office. Here, pictured at the Potsdam conference, the 'Big Three' are Attlee, Truman and Stalin.

By now the war in Europe was over and already the Allied leaders were taking sides for the Cold War.

Potsdam, July 1945

From friendship to fear

Flashback! Superpower friendship: Yalta, February 1945

President Roosevelt's plane was the first to touch down. The most powerful man in the world had arrived in the Soviet Union. On board, the Presidential aides prepared to lift their crippled leader down the steps to the frosty runway at Saki airport in the Crimea. Meanwhile, a second plane arrived, carrying Winston Churchill, Prime Minister of Britain and the British Empire, to the superpower summit. Churchill watched as Roosevelt was carried out of the plane in a wheelchair. He was shocked by the President's drawn and haggard appearance. Later Churchill's doctor confided to the Prime Minister that he thought Roosevelt had only months to live.

Churchill and Roosevelt now embarked on a long car journey to Yalta. The leaders were able to look out of the window and witness at first hand the devastation which the Second World War had brought to the Soviet Union. Churchill was also able to think about his objectives for the meeting. Those were: to continue into the post-war world Britain's 'special relationship' with the United States, and to encourage the Americans to maintain their involvement in Europe's affairs.

The host for the summit was the last to arrive. Josef Stalin had refused to leave the USSR on the dubious grounds of 'medical advice' and 'special diet'. For nine days, in the ballroom of the former palace of the Russian Tsars, the three leaders discussed the post-war future of the world. With Soviet troops only 48 miles east of Berlin and Allied troops closing in from the other direction, it was clear to all three men that an Allied victory was now assured. Unconditional surrender was being demanded. During the War, the desperate need to defeat Germany and Japan had served to unite Britain, America and the Soviet Union, despite their obvious differences, into what became known as the 'Grand Alliance'. Yalta marked the high point of the Grand Alliance. In the evenings, over dinner, the three leaders laughed and joked together, smoking cigars and toasting their great victory. Yet it was the last time the three would meet.

Fast forward! Superpower rivalry: The 1980s

SOURCE 3

The world's first nuclear bomb exploding in New Mexico on 16 July 1945. This test detonation was followed by the dropping of the bombs on Hiroshima and Nagasaki. These are still the only nuclear bombs to have been used in war but as the arms race of the Cold War escalated, the image of the mushroom cloud and the fear of nuclear war became part of everyday life.

SOURCE 4

This is the nightmare. At 0700 hours GMT a fleet of 2000 rockets rise from their silos in the Soviet Union. Four minutes later the ICBMs (intercontinental ballistic missiles) are out in space, above the earth's atmosphere, heading for the United States. Their paths curve. Suddenly each rocket drops away leaving a 'bus' – a container loaded with warheads and decoys. The bus is left just above the North Pole. At 0711 the bus unloads.

The warheads, each carrying a computer that directs it to its own target, are released. So are a much larger number of decoys. All are still travelling in space. Three minutes later they aren't. The decoys are doing whatever they will and the warheads are falling through the earth's atmosphere to their targets. We are now in the 'terminal phase'. The entire process, the first half of a nuclear war, has taken 29 minutes, a breakfast time for man but at 0729 the beginning of the end for mankind.

Tony Osman, *The Sunday Times*, 17 November 1985.

Why did the wartime alliance break down?

In his major biography, *Hitler and Stalin: Parallel Lives*, leading historian Alan Bullock highlights the tragedy of the fact that the wartime alliance broke down and was replaced by the terrible fear and rivalry of the Cold War:

> It was the great missed opportunity of the post-war period that the condition of Europe, instead of uniting the wartime Allies in a common effort to relieve it, became the issue around which their most bitter quarrels developed.

Problems at Yalta

Behind the apparent friendship at Yalta, these 'bitter quarrels' were already emerging.

SOURCE 5

Britain went to war so 'that Poland should be free and sovereign' said Churchill. Britain's only interest, he assured the other leaders, was 'one of honour because we drew the sword for Poland against Hitler's brutal attack' … Stalin [said] … 'For Russia it is not only a question of honour but security … Not only because we are on Poland's frontier but also because throughout history Poland has always been a corridor for attack on Russia'. Twice in the last thirty years 'our German enemy has passed through this corridor' … 'Admittedly', a British diplomat commented, 'Uncle Joe … sounded sincere, and as always was hyper-realistic.'

Daniel Yergin, *Shattered Peace*, 1977.

- Russia wanted up to £20 million compensation for its losses in the Second World War. Britain and America thought this was too high.
- It was agreed that Germany would be divided up but the details were complex and needed further planning.
- The Russians were worried that they would be isolated in President Roosevelt's proposed new peacekeeping organisation, the United Nations.
- Above all, the issue of Poland dominated Yalta (**Source 5**).

The disagreements over Poland included:

- The future government of Poland: whether the pre-war government should be restored and free elections held, or whether Poland should become a Communist state.
- The post-war frontier between Poland and Russia.
- Stalin's belief that the future security of the USSR depended on the Polish question being resolved to his satisfaction.

Behind these complex issues was a basic problem. The Allies did not really trust each other at all. Privately, Stalin had still not ruled out the possibility that Britain and the USA might suddenly withdraw from the War. This would allow Hitler to move his forces on, defeating Russia, but also bringing Germany to a standstill. Meanwhile, Churchill was extremely worried about the extent of Russian ambitions. And while publicly Roosevelt often referred to his 'gallant Russian ally', privately he shared some of Churchill's concerns. To add to the general lack of trust, Roosevelt was in the habit of criticising Churchill behind his back in private conversations with Stalin! Despite these differences, none of the leaders were in disagreement about the terrible extent of Russian suffering in the Second World War.

Knowledge and understanding

Use pages 94 to 97 to investigate the following questions.

1. Who were the 'Big Three' in February 1945?

2. Read the text from pages 94 to 95. What evidence is there of friendly relations between the Big Three?

3. What reasons can you give to suggest why relations between the Big Three appeared to be good at this time?

4. Read over the text from pages 96 to 97. What evidence is there of tension and suspicion in the relations of the Big Three?

5. 'Superficial friendship; deep suspicion.' How far would you agree with this verdict on superpower relations at Yalta?

Superpower Relations since 1945

For the West, there were two ways of looking at the Soviet Union:

Hostile view

- The Russians under Stalin had an appalling record on human rights. Inside Russia millions of innocent people had been killed.
- The people of Eastern Europe were as fearful of the Russians as they had been of the Germans.
- Stalin had established a ruthless totalitarian dictatorship.
- It was felt by some that the Russians were engaged in a plan to take complete control of Eastern Europe.

Sympathetic view

- No country had given more in the Allied war effort.
- The Soviets had liberated the people of Eastern Europe from the Nazi terror.
- The Russians had not provoked the war with Hitler and had often been the victims of invasion in the past.
- The Russians were expanding into Eastern Europe in order to protect themselves from future invasion with a ring of friendly 'buffer' states.
- They were acting as they did mainly out of fear rather than aggression.

Knowledge and understanding

Use the information on this page to investigate the following questions.

1 Many Western observers felt that Stalin demanded too much at Yalta. Considering the information presented in the Datapoint below, how far would you agree with this point of view?

2 Look at the Datapoint and the 'sympathetic' view of the Soviet Union. Write a paragraph (approximately 10-15 lines) to support the argument that the way to explain Russia's conduct is to understand the extent of its suffering.

3 Now look at the 'hostile' view. Write a paragraph setting out the reasons why you feel that in 1945 the Soviet Union should have been treated with suspicion and hostility.

DATAPOINT

Russian losses in the Second World War

Approximately 20 million Russians had been killed:
10 million died in military action on land, air and sea.
3 million died in prisoner of war camps.
7 million civilians were killed.

Many more lost their homes and livelihoods:
1710 towns and 70,000 villages were virtually destroyed.
25 million people were made homeless.

Russian industry and agriculture had been devastated:
65,000 kilometres of railway track were destroyed.
428,000 freight trucks and 15,800 locomotives were demolished or damaged.
20 million out of 23 million pigs were killed.
7 million horses died.

SOURCE 6

This is Fascism

This harrowing photograph shows the suffering of the Russian people at the hands of the Germans in the Second World War. When the Russians released the photo at the end of the War, they issued it with the above caption.

The extent of Russian suffering during the Second World War made an immense impact on Roosevelt and Churchill, as they travelled to Yalta. During what the Russians called the Great Patriotic War (1941–45) approximately 20 million Russians had been killed.

98 Superpower Relations since 1945

SOURCE 7

The funeral procession of President Franklin D. Roosevelt in April 1945. Observe the flag at half-mast and the Stars and Stripes covering the funeral casket. The crowds were immense. In this scene, outside the White House, some members of the crowd who could not see properly are using mirrors to try to get a better view. Roosevelt is still regarded as having been one of the most successful US Presidents of all time.

The break-up of the Alliance

Although the Americans left Yalta feeling that Allied unity had been preserved, Russian actions in the Spring of 1945, provided ammunition for those who took a hostile view of the Soviet Union. In March a Soviet-controlled government was installed in Romania, and this was followed by a failure to organise free elections in Poland and the arrest of Polish democrats visiting Moscow in April 1945. However, the question of how to deal with the Russians was about to pass out of the hands of Roosevelt. On 12 April the President suffered a massive brain haemorrhage and died (**Source 7**). This was a critical turning point in superpower relations. Roosevelt had developed a fairly good relationship with Stalin. He had sympathised with the suffering of the Russian people and did not take as critical a view as Churchill of their intentions in Eastern Europe. Now that link of friendship was gone.

Before April was over, Hitler had killed himself in Berlin. The Grand Alliance had achieved its purpose. Hitler's suicide removed the single most important factor holding the fragile Alliance together.

President Truman, the atomic bomb and the Potsdam conference

Power now passed to Harry S. Truman, who had been Roosevelt's Vice-president. It was decided that the new President would meet with Stalin and Churchill in July 1945. This time the conference would take place in the suburb of

SOURCE 8

US President Harry S. Truman prsenting General Dwight D. Eisenhower with the Distinguished Service Medal for his role in the Second World War.

Eisenhower succeeded Truman as US President in 1953.

Superpower Relations since 1945 99

On 24 July at Potsdam, Truman casually walked up to Stalin and told him that the United States now had 'a big bomb'. 'Good,' replied Stalin, 'I hope you will use it.' Stalin's offhand response led the Americans to believe that he had not grasped the importance of the President's remark. The opposite was true. What Truman did not know was that the Russians were already being passed atomic secrets through their spy network. The Russians were now determined to speed up their own atomic programme. The rivalry between Russia and America which seemed to be increasing all the time had now been given a new and potentially catastrophic dimension.

Now the conference took another dramatic turn. On 25 July, Prime Minister Winston Churchill and his Foreign Secretary, Anthony Eden, flew to London to await the outcome of the general election. On his last night in Potsdam, Churchill dreamt that the saw himself under a white sheet, his feet sticking out, dead. He told his physician, 'perhaps this is the end'. He was right.

The Conservatives lost in a landslide, with a swing of about 12 per cent to the Labour Party. Churchill was replaced as Prime Minister by Clement Attlee (**Source 10**). Attlee, as a member of the

SOURCE 9

The 'Big Three' at Potsdam in July 1945. Truman had now succeeded Roosevelt and Churchill would soon be replaced by Attlee. What impression of superpower relations would you say is created by this photograph?

Design a caption which could be used to give a positive image of the Potsdam Conference. How did this differ from the reality?

Potsdam, just outside the shattered city of Berlin. The extent to which the relationship with Russia was cooling off was vividly demonstrated when Truman decided to make it clear to the Russians that he would take a much tougher line than Roosevelt because 'force is the only thing the Russians understand'. The first successful testing of the atomic bomb on 16 July 1945 dramatically strengthened Truman's hand.

SOURCE 10

26 July 1945. The new Labour Prime Minister, Clement Attlee, celebrating the Labour Party's landslide victory over the Conservatives. Here Attlee is shown with his wife outside the Labour Party headquarters at Transport House in London. He immediately returned to Potsdam, now as one of the 'Big Three'.

coalition government, had originally attended Potsdam as part of Churchill's delegation. On 28 July he returned as Prime Minister, with his new Foreign Secretary, Ernest Bevin. Within a few months, Roosevelt had died and Churchill had been replaced. The Grand Alliance was breaking up.

In principle, all three of the Allied leaders were still in favour of keeping the Alliance in being. However, Truman and Attlee had less in common than Roosevelt and Churchill, and as the world moved from war to peace they did not have the degree of personal power to act without consultation at home, which their predecessors had enjoyed.

Despite all of this, it was also clear that the Labour Government's view of the Russians was very similar to that of Truman. Attlee observed of Stalin:

> no principles, any methods, but no flowery language – always Yes or No, though you could count on him if it was No.

Bevin felt even more strongly than Attlee about the threat of Soviet expansion.

Britain and the Cold War

The Iron Curtain

Churchill had been shattered by his election defeat. At the very moment of triumph, with Hitler vanquished, the British electorate had rejected him. Arriving in the United States in January 1946, Churchill spent several months basking in the sun in Florida. However, Churchill was brooding over his personal nightmare which was that one by one, the capital cities of Eastern Europe were falling under the domination of Russia. A chance for him to escape from his depression came when he was invited to speak at Westminster College in Fulton, Missouri (**Sources 11 and 12**).

SOURCE 11

This photograph was taken when Churchill was in the USA for his famous 'Iron Curtain' speech. Here he is shown in distinctive 'V for victory' pose alongside US President, Harry Truman.

Most historians now agree that Britain took the lead in alerting world opinion to Soviet ambitions. The USA had taken a more positive line until Truman replaced Roosevelt and adopted a 'get tough' policy towards the Soviets.

SOURCE 12

A shadow has fallen upon the scenes so lately lighted by the Allied victory. Nobody knows what Soviet Russia and its Communist International organisation intends to do in the immediate future, or what are the limits, if any, to their expansive ... tendencies ... We understand the Russians' need to be secure on their western frontiers from all renewal of German aggression ... We welcome her [Russia] to her rightful place among the leading nations of the world ... It is my duty, however, to place before you certain facts about the present situation in Europe.

From Stettin, in the Baltic, to Trieste, in the Adriatic, an iron curtain has descended across the continent. Behind that line lie all the capitals of the ancient states of Central and Eastern Europe – Warsaw, Berlin, Prague, Vienna, Budapest, Belgrade, Bucharest, and Sofia. All these famous cities ... are subject ... to a very high and increasing measure of control from Moscow ... this is certainly not the liberated Europe we fought to build up. Nor is it one which contains the essentials of permanent peace.

Winston Churchill speaking at Westminster College, Fulton, Missouri, 5 March 1946.

SOURCE 13

A significant new departure in recent discussions of the Cold War has been the close attention given to British policy. A number of historians ... have suggested that in the decisive period from mid 1945 to early 1946 Britain's contribution was to awaken the United States to the reality of the Soviet Union and that the United States had to be coaxed into its role of Western leadership. From this perspective the central theme of the early Cold War was Anglo-Soviet conflict, in which the United States sought initially to play a mediating role.

Richard Crockatt, *The United States and the Cold War, 1941–1953*, 1989.

SOURCE 14

The Cold War has been defined as a state of extreme tension between the superpowers, stopping short of all-out war but characterised by mutual hostility ... The Cold War remained 'cold' because the development of nuclear weapons had made resort to war a suicidal enterprise: both sides would be totally devastated.

M Dockrill, *The Cold War, 1945–1953*, 1988.

Churchill proposed that the only way forward was to set up a permanent military alliance between the British Commonwealth and the United States. Some observers thanked Churchill for 'exposing ... the gravity of the peril Russia is presenting to the world' and 'putting into words what was gravely in the minds of many Americans.' Others denounced the speech and advised President Truman to seek co-operation rather than conflict with Stalin. **Source 13** provides a recent view of Churchill's role at this stage.

There is no doubt that Churchill's speech helped to win approval in Congress for a massive loan from the US to Great Britain. Britain benefited from a payment of $3.75 billion, but some observers felt that the economy was now completely subordinate to the USA. The American historian Daniel Yergin says that Churchill had come to understand, long before the War had ended, that the only way for a drastically weakened Britain to hang on to its former status was for it to become, in effect, a junior partner of the United States. This coming together was made easier by Truman's increasing antagonism towards the Soviet Union:

> Unless Russia is faced with an iron fist and strong language, another war is in the making. Only one language do they understand – 'How many divisions have you?' ... I'm tired babying the Soviets.

Significantly, the line taken by Churchill was not criticised by Attlee or Bevin. By the end of 1946, the most important features of Labour's foreign policy were very clear. Any further move made by Russia to extend its influence would be vigorously opposed, hopefully in agreement with the Americans. By 1946 the following trends were clear:

- Britain was relying heavily on American financial support to maintain its status as world power.
- The basis of British and American foreign policy was to resist Soviet expansion.
- Anglo-American relations with the Soviet Union had deteriorated dramatically.

The Cold War had begun.

Knowledge and understanding

Use pages 98 to 100 to investigate the following questions.

1 In what ways did superpower relations deteriorate between Yalta and Potsdam?

2 How and why had the individuals who made up the 'Big Three' changed by July 1945?

3 What impact did these changes in personnel have upon the development of the Cold War?

4 Make a list of other factors apart from changes in leadership which contributed to the development of the Cold War.

5 Place these factors in their relative order of importance (most important first).

6 None of these factors on their own are sufficient to explain why superpower relations took a turn for the worse. Show how each factor is directly linked to other factors on your list to explain why superpower relations deteriorated so quickly between Yalta and Potsdam.

DATAPOINT

Cold War diary, 1945–1979

Winston Churchill, British Prime Minister 1939–45, 1951–55.

February 1945
Yalta Conference
Disagreements on the future of Europe begin to emerge in discussions about the post-war constitution of Poland.

July–August 1945
Potsdam Conference
Disagreements about Eastern Europe intensified by new US President, Harry Truman's distrust of Stalin's motives. Potsdam Conference abandoned without an agreement being reached.

6 August
USA drops atomic bomb on Hiroshima in Japan.

9 August
USA drops atomic bomb on Nagasaki.

6 March 1946
Churchill makes his famous 'Iron Curtain' speech in Fulton, Missouri, warning the USA of the Soviet threat.

1946–1948
USSR consolidates control of the countries of Eastern Europe.

March 1947
President Truman sets out the 'Truman Doctrine' that the USA should use armed force to prevent the spread of Communism.

June 1947
The Marshall Plan is announced, to provide US aid throughout Western Europe.

June 1948–May 1949
Berlin blockade by Soviet forces, Berlin airlift provides supplies from US and British zones of West Germany.

April 1949
North Atlantic Treaty Organisation (NATO) established as a pro-USA military alliance.

July 1949
USSR completes its first successful test of a nuclear bomb.

August 1949
Federal Republic of Germany (West Germany) established as an independent nation, uniting the Western zones of Germany.

October 1949
German Democratic Republic (East Germany) established in Soviet zone of Germany with East Berlin as its capital.

October 1949
China goes Communist: Peoples Republic of China declared by Mao Zedong.

June 1950–July 1953
Korean war.

March 1953
Death of Stalin

1954
South East Asian Treaty Organisation (SEATO) set up by the USA along the lines of NATO.

Mao Zedong, Chinese leader 1949–76.

November 1956
Soviet troops enter Hungary to remove Imre Nagy's government by force, resulting in the loss of over 30,000 lives.

1960
Increasing US involvement in Vietnam - Kennedy sends in 'military advisers'.

May 1960
International tension rises following the bringing down of an American U2 spy plane over the Soviet Union.

August 1961
Soviet troops build the Berlin Wall.

October 1962
Cuban Missile Crisis brings the superpowers to the verge of war.

June 1963
President Kennedy uses a visit to the Berlin Wall as an opportunity to denounce Communism, declaring: 'Ich bin ein Berliner'.

late 1964
US Congress approves President Johnson's plans to use American troops in Vietnam.

1968
Soviet troops enter Czechoslovakia to crush Alexander Dubček's more liberal version of Communism.

1970–72
West Germany develops 'Ostpolitik': extending trade and investment links with East Germany.

Lyndon B. Johnson, US President 1963–69.

1971–73
President Nixon pursues a policy of 'détente' – calming international relations. This results in improved relations with China and successful arms control talks with the Soviet Union.

September 1973
USA involved in the assassination of the socialist President Allende of Chile. Allende is replaced by the pro-USA military dictator, General Pinochet.

October 1973
The Yom Kippur Arab-Israeli war leads to high tension between the USA and Soviet Union.

1973
US withdrawal from Vietnam completed.

1979
The USA gives increased support to the Contras – right wing guerrilla forces involved in trying to bring down Nicaragua's democratically elected socialist Sandinista government.

1979
The Soviet Union invades Afghanistan, setting up a pro-Soviet regime. The limitations of détente are revealed, and the tensions of the Cold War are seen to be as high as ever.

Leonid Brezhnev, Soviet leader 1964–82.

Superpower Relations since 1945

British foreign policy in the era of the Cold War

Although Britain was proud of the fact that it had neither been invaded nor defeated in the War, and the threat from Germany had gone, the end of the War presented policy makers with a new set of problems:

- What to do about Britain's many and varied commitments in Europe?
- To what extent Britain should move towards closer co-operation with its European neighbours.
- How to cope with the huge commitments of the British Empire and Commonwealth, and with the increasing pressure to grant independence to the colonies.
- How best to deal with a new and potentially highly destructive enemy, the Soviet Union.
- Where to find the resources to do all of this.

Foreign Secretary Ernest Bevin stressed the Labour Government's concern about Soviet expansion. Labour ensured that Britain's defences were kept in a good state of repair. They also took the critical decision to develop Britain's own nuclear weapons (see **Datapoint: The development of Britain's independent nuclear force** on page 104). Attlee's reasoning was as follows:

> if we had decided not to have it, we would have put ourselves directly in the hands of the Americans. That would have been a risk a British Government should not take ... For a power of our size and with our responsibilities to turn its back on the bomb did not make sense.

Britain's European commitments

Bevin felt that Britain had little choice but to make a long-standing, extensive and costly commitment to running its occupation zone in Germany. He hoped that the Russians might be persuaded to agree to free elections in Eastern Europe. Some observers believed that a left-wing Labour government might be well placed to reach some kind of understanding with the Communists in the Kremlin. This did not happen, however. Meanwhile, Bevin feared that America might withdraw many of its forces from Europe and place the onus on Britain to preserve European peace. Evidence that some of Britain's overseas commitments would have to be scaled down came in February 1947, as domestic economic problems came to a head. In the words of historian Alan Bullock, Britain had to admit that 'it could no longer play the world role to which it had been accustomed since the 18th Century'. It was announced that British troops would have to be withdrawn from Greece despite the political instability that remained there.

The Truman Doctrine

Bevin was soon reassured by President Truman's announcement of the 'Truman Doctrine' which underlined America's commitment to defending 'free peoples' of the world from Communist pressure (**Source 15**).

On 22 May, the US Congress put the words of the Truman Doctrine into action when it approved a massive aid programme for Greece and Turkey. Although some observers felt that Truman had simply heightened the divisions of the Cold War, the response of Attlee and Bevin was one of 'warm enthusiasm'.

SOURCE 15

I am fully aware of the broad implications involved if the United States extends assistance to Greece and Turkey ... At the present moment in world history nearly every nation must choose between alternative ways of life. The choice is too often not a free one. One way of life is based upon the will of the majority and is distinguished by free institutions, representative government, free elections, guarantees of individual liberty, freedom of speech and religion, and freedom of oppression. The second way of life is based upon the will of a minority forcibly imposed upon the majority. It relies upon terror and oppression, a controlled press and radio, fixed elections, and suppression of personal freedoms. I believe that it must be the policy of the United States to support free peoples who are resisting attempted subjugation by armed minorities or by outside pressures.

President Harry S. Truman, 12 March 1947.

DATAPOINT

The development of Britain's independent nuclear force

1940
Otto Frisch and Rudolph Peierls, refugees from Hitler's Germany working in Britain, made a scientific breakthrough which indicated that a small quantity of uranium could be used to make an enormous explosion.

1941
The Maud Report informed the British government that Frisch and Peierls were right, and that an atomic bomb was feasible.

Aware that Hitler could not be allowed to develop the first atomic bomb at any cost, the British government made the findings of the Maud Report available to the USA.

1943
Churchill and Roosevelt met in Quebec to discuss nuclear weapons research. At this stage, Britain was ahead of the USA in nuclear research. The two leaders agreed on full Anglo–American co-operation and as a result, British scientists travelled to the USA to work on the development of the Bomb.

1945
USA dropped nuclear bombs on Hiroshima and Nagasaki.

Truman, the new American President, showed himself less keen than Roosevelt to share US nuclear technology with Britain. As a result, Attlee's Labour government launched Britain's own nuclear weapons programme.

The Windscale (Sellafield) reactor was planned as a source of the plutonium needed for nuclear weapons, and the RAF began to develop V-Bombers to carry nuclear bombs.

1946
President Truman passed the McMahon Act which prevented US nuclear collaboration with any other nation, including Britain. This ban lasted for two years.

1947
On 8 January 1947, a Cabinet Committee took the formal decision to make the atomic bomb, but this was not announced to Parliament until 12 May 1948.

1951
A new Conservative government was elected and Churchill became Prime Minister again. By now, the nuclear weapons programme was well advanced, with £100 million having already been spent. These facts had been concealed from Parliament.

1952
The first British device was successfully tested on the Monte Bello Island off the north west coast of Australia.

1954
Churchill's Cabinet took the decision to develop the powerful hydrogen bomb (H-bomb).

1957
In May 1957, on Christmas Island in the Pacific, the British H-bomb was tested, this led to restored collaboration between Britain and America.

1969
The USA offered Britain the Polaris nuclear missile system.

This system was still in service in 1993, although now being replaced by US-produced Trident missiles.

SOURCE 16

In 1957 the Campaign for Nuclear Disarmament (CND) was formed with the aim of persuading the government to abandon nuclear weapons. Although this aim has not been achieved, CND is still campaigning today, and has done much to raise public awareness of the horrifying nature of nuclear weapons and the moral and political issues surrounding them. This photograph shows an early CND march to the nuclear weapons research establishment at Aldermaston (April 1958).

Marshall Aid

In addition, the Americans now announced plans for the Marshall Aid programme of economic support for Western economic recovery (**Sources 17 and 18**).

Bevin was very quick to appreciate that Europe needed to respond to this offer of help in a co-ordinated way. He contacted all of the major European leaders including the Russians – although in the negotiations that followed, the USSR made it clear that it would not co-operate with the United States and would not accept any American aid. Bevin's efforts led to the formation in April 1948 of the Organisation for European Economic Co-operation (OEEC). Between 1948 and 1951 a total of $12 billion in Marshall Aid was provided for Europe, of which Britain's share was $2.6 billion. While Britain was grateful for this support, there was some public resentment that British power and status was rapidly diminishing.

SOURCE 17

Our policy is directed not against any country or doctrine but against hunger, poverty, desperation and chaos. Its purpose should be the revival of a working economy in the world so as to permit the emergence of political and social conditions in which free institutions can exist.

George C. Marshall speaking at Harvard University, 5 June 1947.

SOURCE 18

This photograph shows Britain signing up for Marshall Aid. In July 1948 Ernest Bevin, the British Foreign Minister (*seated, second from left*) and Lewis Douglas, the American Ambassador to Britain (*seated, second from right*), signed the Anglo-American Marshall Aid Pact. Standing on the left hand side is Harold Wilson, at that time President of the Board of Trade, but a future Prime Minister.

Knowledge and understanding

Use pages 100 to 105 to investigate the following questions.

1 Where and when did Churchill make the 'Iron Curtain' speech?

2 What do you consider to be the main points of his speech?

3 What was the reaction to Churchill's speech in the United States?
Try to answer this question in some detail. In what ways, for example, did Churchill and Attlee have similar ideas about the Soviet Union? Consider also the change in American leadership.

4 According to recent historians' accounts, such as Source 13, what role did Britain play in the early part of the Cold War?

5 How far would you agree that this shows that Britain was the dominant partner in the relationship with the United States? Give reasons for your answer.

Post-War Germany

Once-great cities were in ruins. A proud people had been reduced to a mass of shocked, hungry and worn-out refugees. *The Guardian* reported on the hopeless journeys of refugees to their capital city:

> Millions of Germans are on the move. Groups trek hundreds of miles and lose half their numbers through disease and exhaustion. Children have arrived in Berlin looking like the emaciated creatures of Belsen.

In the words of historian Daniel Yergin:

> Most of Berlin was a city of rubble, bombed-out buildings, and broken sewers, wandering women, children and old men – a city of the dead.

The division of Germany

The fate of Germany was determined by the Allies. In 1945 they divided the defeated country into four zones, with Britain, France and America occupying areas in the west, and a Russian zone in the east, where Soviet soldiers had been since the spring of 1945. Within the Russian zone was the vitally important city of Berlin. The Allies agreed that this city would also be divided into four zones, as shown on the map below. Germany would be run by an Allied Control Council until the day came when it could safely be reunited as a single democratic country. However, as relations between the Allies deteriorated, Germany became the focus of a series of bitter disputes, which seemed to symbolise the Cold War itself. Although the former Allies did not actually go to war against each other, the coming years were characterised by mutual suspicion, fear, hostility and threats.

The reparations issue

At Yalta, Russia had demanded that Germany should compensate them for their massive losses in the War. The Allies felt that the figures Stalin demanded were too high and proposed an alternative. Russia would provide food and coal from the Soviet zone in return for a quarter of the industrial goods made in the Western zones. It was also agreed that Russia could take industrial goods and machinery from the Soviet zone and send them to Russia.

By the summer of 1946 the agreement was breaking down. In retaliation for the Russians failing to send the promised food and coal, Britain and America ended their deliveries of industrial goods to the Russian zone. The Western Allies now decided to develop the western zone and restore its economy and output. On 1 January 1947 Britain and America merged their zones. A year later, the French zone also joined, creating a single western zone. Russia reacted to these developments by extending even further its military, economic and political control over East Germany and the rest of Eastern Europe. The future of Berlin, which was still divided into its original four zones, was now of critical importance.

The Berlin blockade

After 1945, the political and physical position of Berlin was unique. The three Western sectors of the city were isolated more than 100 miles inside the Soviet

The partition of Germany, 1945

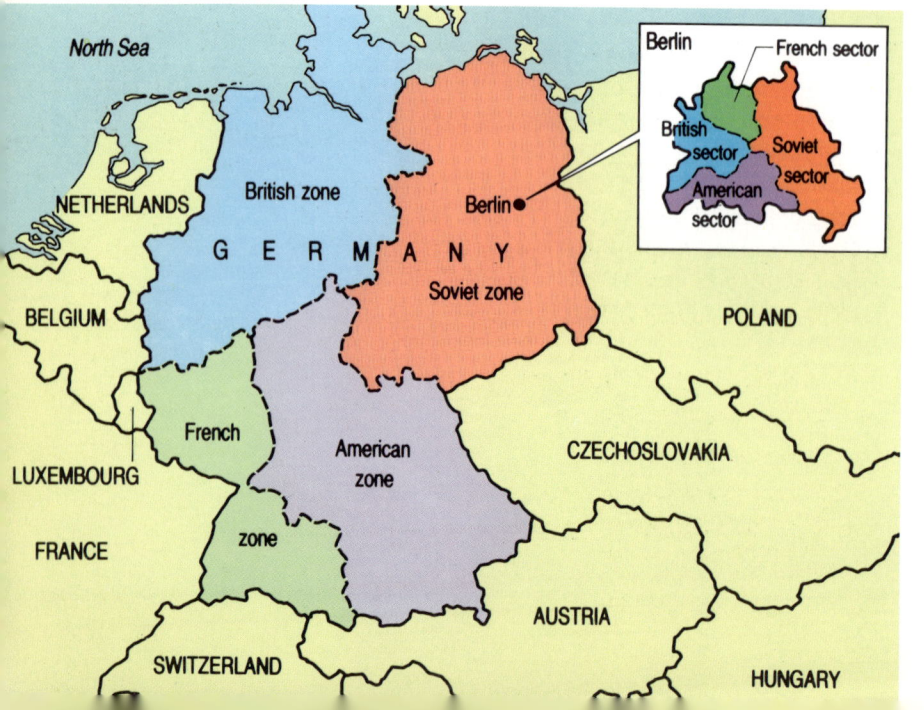

zone of Germany. The Allies relied on long road and rail links to maintain communications between the western zones of Berlin and the western zones of the rest of Germany. In the summer of 1948, these links were subject to a growing amount of Russian interference, culminating in this Soviet press announcement on 23 June:

> **The Soviet administration is compelled to halt all traffic to and from Berlin from tomorrow at 0600 hours because of technical difficulties.**

This dramatic Russian move was a direct response to the West's decision to introduce a new West German currency as part of their plans to stimulate the West German economy. The Russians disagreed with the West over whether this new currency should be allowed to circulate in Berlin. Most of all, the Russians were concerned that as they brought Eastern Europe under their control the contrast between the bleak economic prospects of the people living under Communism and the relative prosperity in the West would become a source of great embarrassment. Berlin was now effectively cut off from the West. The Russians shut down all railways, roads and canals between Berlin and West Germany. It was estimated that the 2.5 million German inhabitants in West Berlin probably had enough food to last them for 36 days and enough coal for 45 days. The aim of the Soviet blockade was clear. In order to prevent the West Berliners facing starvation, the West would have to allow West Berlin to become part of the Soviet zone. The West would then lose its only foothold in the whole of Eastern Europe and the division of the continent would be complete.

The Berlin airlift, June 1948–May 1949

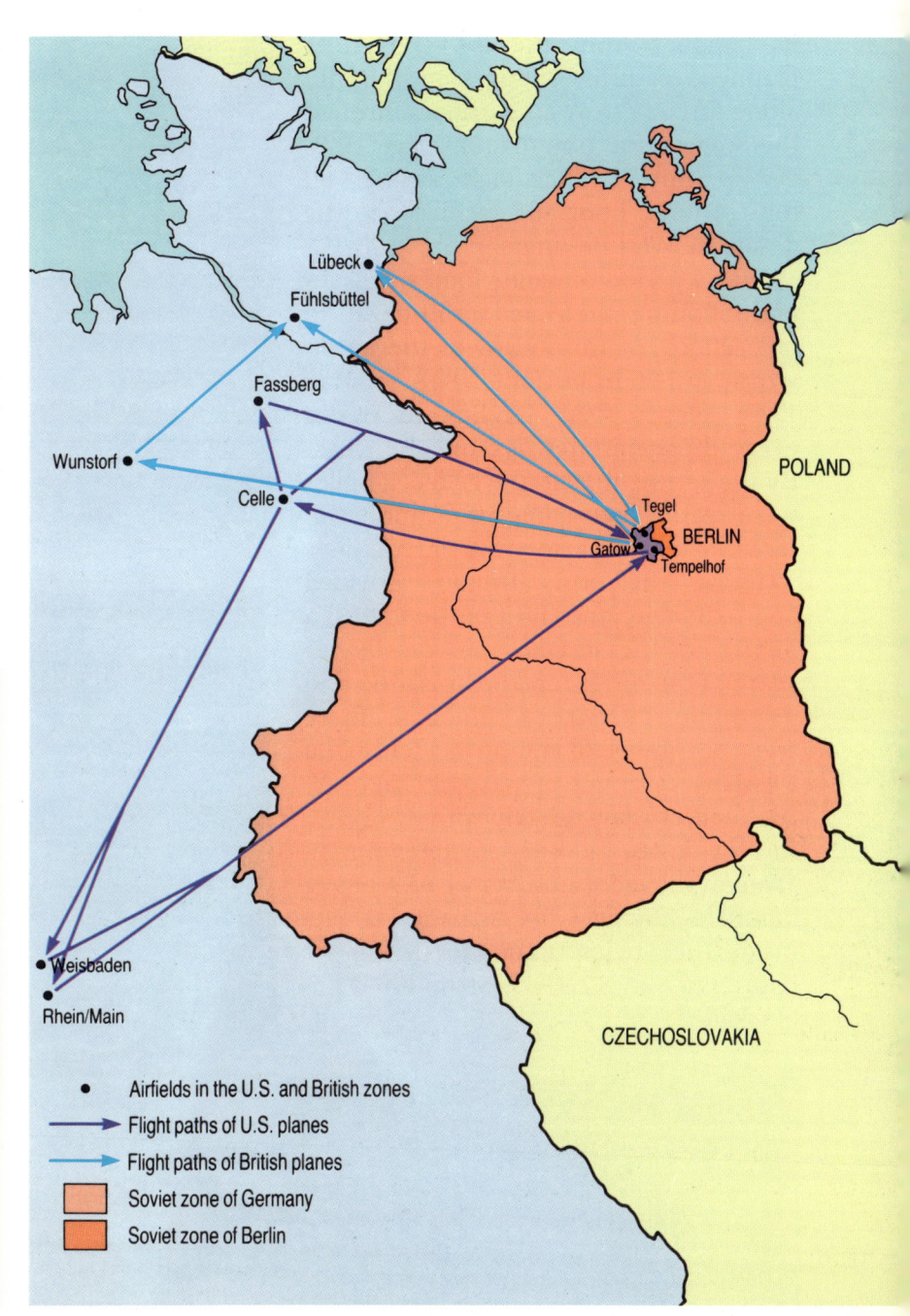

SOURCE 19

While in theory Germany was to be treated as a single unit, both economically and politically, as each country now began to extract reparations from its own zone this meant that the economic division of Germany began from the first days of the Allied occupation. Because most of Germany's agriculture was located in the Russian zone, Britain and the United States were soon faced with the task of feeding much of the German population in their zones and they thus had every incentive to get the German economy going again. Russia, who had suffered much more severely, was anxious to extract whatever she could from her zone... the prospects of a united Germany steadily receded.

W.O. Simpson, *Changing Horizons: Britain 1914–1980*, 1986.

108 Superpower Relations since 1945

The option of giving in to the Russians was immediately dismissed. In Washington and London it was felt that if Berlin was lost, western Germany would probably follow. A second option, to use force to smash the blockade, was also ruled out, because of the obvious risks of a major war. The third, and chosen, solution was put forward by a British RAF officer, Air Commodore Waite, who persuaded the British and American Commanders in Berlin, General Robertson and General Clay that he had a workable plan. It was decided that the beleaguered western zone would receive its supplies from the air, the Allies planned to airlift supplies into Berlin along three narrow air corridors through the Soviet zone (see map on page 107). On 26 June, the first flight airlifted 80 tons of milk, flour and medicine to the desperate West Berliners.

After a period of panic, food shortages and rationing, the Allied airlift began to take effect. At the height of the airlift, which lasted from June 1948 to May 1949, planes were landing in Berlin every three minutes, around the clock. By the spring of 1949 the Allied supplies were easily exceeding the minimum required for people to avoid starvation.

During the crisis Britain provided approximately one third of the flights, a quarter of the supplies and the largest share of the on-ground organisation and distribution services. Although there were a number of minor incidents, the Russians were not prepared to take the risk of interfering directly with the airlift. In July 1948, in order to deter Stalin, Truman moved a number of B29 heavy bombers, capable of striking targets inside the Soviet Union, to British air bases. On May 12 1949, Stalin lifted the blockade.

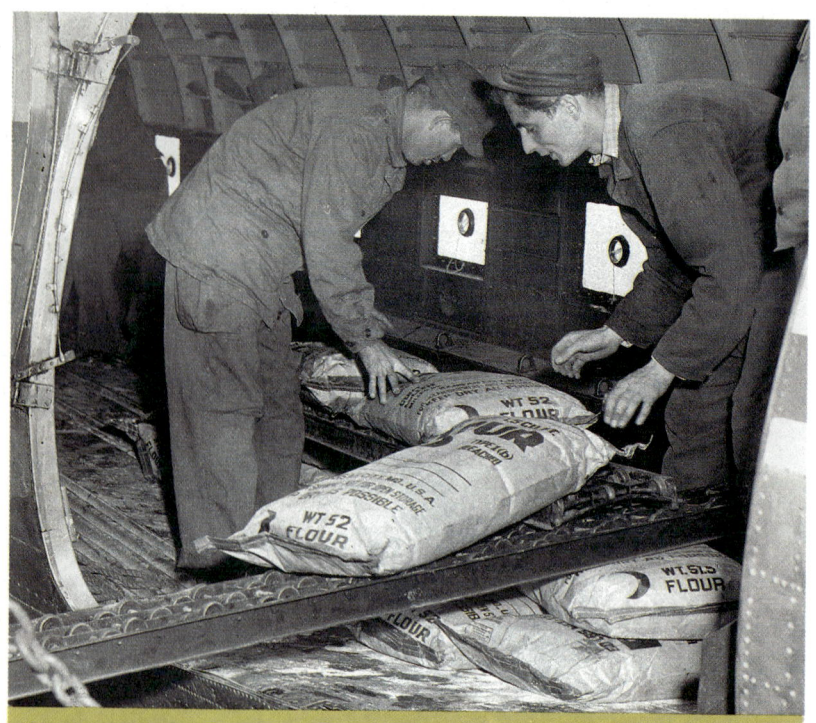

SOURCE 20

This photograph shows American food-aid brought into Berlin to beat the Russian blockade. American and German personnel are seen unloading bags of flour at Templehof airfield from an American transport plane. When this photograph was taken, flour was arriving in Berlin at the rate of a tonne a minute, with one plane landing every three minutes and discharging its cargo of 2000 kilograms of flour in just under four minutes.

Devise two captions, for and against the Allied action, which could be used to accompany this sort of photograph.

SOURCE 21

This image graphically illustrates the impact of the blockade on the people of Berlin. Can you work out what has taken place in this photograph and why? Try to guess the time of year when the photograph might have been taken.

SOURCE 22

Signing up for NATO.

US Secretary of State Dean Acheson asks dignitaries to witness the signing of the North Atlantic Defence Treaty, 4 April 1949.

The North Atlantic Treaty Organisation (NATO)

Amid concern about the Soviet Union and the future of Germany, Britain decided to sign a Fifty Year Alliance with France, concluded, symbolically at Dunkirk, in March 1947. A year later in March 1948 Britain, France, Belgium, the Netherlands and Luxembourg signed the Brussels Pact, which resolved the signatories to take mutual action in the event of outside aggression.

These moves reflected British anxiety about how long America would sustain its commitment to Europe. However, these fears were reduced with the setting up of the North Atlantic Treaty Organisation (NATO) in April 1949 (**Source 22**). The countries which had signed the Brussels Pact were now joined by Denmark, Iceland, Italy, Portugal, Norway, Canada and, most important of all, the United States. The Americans, convinced that the Soviet Union was a major threat to world peace, were now making a massive military and political comment to the defence of Western Europe. The critical clause of the NATO agreement was Article 5, which established the principle of collective self-defence (**Source 23**).

Historian Alan Bullock has described the securing of an American commitment to NATO as:

> the peak of Bevin's achievement as Foreign Secretary ... and one which for over 30 years, has provided the security and confidence which Bevin sought for Western Europe.

SOURCE 23

Within NATO, all member states are bound to protect any member against attack.

Article 5
The parties agree that an armed attack against one or more of them occurring within the area defined below shall be considered an attack against them all; and consequently that if such an armed attack occurs, each of them in exercise of the right of individual or collective self-defence recognised by Article 51 of the UN Charter, will assist the party or parties so attacked by taking forthwith such military or other action, individually and in concert with the other parties, as may be necessary to restore and assure the security of the North Atlantic area.

Britain's relationship with the USA in the Cold War

Britain has generally followed a foreign policy which has tied in closely with that of the USA (**Source 24**). This was the case in 1950 when America became involved in the Korean War (**Source 25**). However, despite Britain's steady support for the USA there have been occasions when the 'special relationship' between the two nations has come close to breaking down.

SOURCE 24

Since 1949 British membership of NATO has been the fundamental influence on British foreign policy. Britain's armed forces are at NATO's disposal, her diplomacy has been conducted with a careful regard to the views of her partners in the alliance. As the United States is by far the most powerful member of the organisation, her influence has been the greatest. Whereas up to 1949 it was arguable that Britain played a genuinely independent role in international affairs, since that date, with rare exceptions, her policies have generally been aligned with those of the United States.

W.O. Simpson, *Changing Horizons: Britain 1941–80*, 1986.

SOURCE 25

The British government, both as a loyal ally of the United States and as a dutiful member of the UN had no hesitation in endorsing Truman's actions. Attlee, in a broadcast to the country, compared the North Korean invasion to the aggression which had led to the Second World War. He warned his audience: 'The fire which has started in distant Korea may burn down your home.' Britain did what she could to assist. Rearmament was accelerated, conscription extended to two years and a Commonwealth Brigade was sent out to Korea where it gave distinguished service.

W.O. Simpson, *Changing Horizons: Britain 1941–80*, 1986.

SOURCE 26

General Nasser can be seen, second from the left in this photograph. It was taken in August 1953 at a press conference to celebrate a first anniversary of the revolution which deposed King Farouk.

The Suez Crisis

Britain had stationed troops in Egypt and the Suez Canal zone since the 19th century. Even after Egyptian independence was proclaimed in 1936, the British military presence there remained substantial. Things began to change in 1952. In that year Egypt came under the control of a group of nationalist army officers led by Colonel Abdul Gamel Nasser (**Source 26**). The generals overthrew the Egyptian monarch, King Farouk and were now determined to force out the British.

Britain still regarded the area in general, and the Suez Canal in particular, as vital to its interests. Anthony Eden, who became Prime Minister in 1955, was deeply suspicious of Nasser and feared that he was being backed up by the Soviet Union. Eden was determined to safeguard the security of Britain's vital oil supplies through the Suez Canal. In 1955, in an attempt to strengthen its position in the Middle East, Britain signed a defence agreement with Turkey, Iran, Iraq and Pakistan, known as the 'Baghdad Pact'. Nasser denounced this move and urged all Arabs to stand against it.

Britain and the USA now tried to win Nasser's favour by promising him a major loan to be spent on the Aswan Dam on the Lower Nile. This project was a vital part of Nasser's economic strategy, as it was designed to improve irrigation and provide electricity. However, Nasser's continued hostility and his contact with the Soviet Union angered Eden and the US Foreign Secretary, John Foster Dulles, and on 26 July 1956 they cancelled their offer of a loan. On the same day, President Nasser announced that he was nationalising the British and French owned and operated Suez Canal Company. Nasser said that shareholders would be offered compensation and the new revenue raised by the canal would be spent on the Aswan Dam.

The British were horrified. Nasser's move effected British business interests in the Suez Canal Company and threatened access to a vital communications link. Also, within the delicate political balance of the Middle East this increased Nasser's power and prestige and dealt a serious blow to Britain's status. The British government decided that Nasser, an 'outspoken dictator', had gone too far.

It was at this stage that Britain and America parted company. Dulles, acting for the USA, tried to find a compromise by setting up a committee to look at the issues of compensation and future management of the canal. This was not enough for Britain.

The British now entered into highly secret talks with France and Israel, designed to find a more forceful solution to their problems. At this time Israel had its own dispute with Egypt over Nasser's blockade of the Straits of Tiran. The three nations quickly agreed a plan. It amounted to a three-fold invasion of Egypt, designed to humiliate Nasser and lead to his downfall. However, the participants knew that an open act of aggression would be condemned so they agreed on an elaborate cover-up:

- Israel would invade Egypt first.
- An 'impartial' France and Britain would then call for the withdrawal of both sides ten miles either side of the Suez Canal.
- Egypt would certainly refuse while Israel would comply.
- Britain and France would then move in against Egypt.

SOURCE 27

As the Suez Crisis developed, Britain and France came under intense pressure from the United States. This photograph was taken in August 1956 and shows, from left to right, M. Pineau (French Foreign Minister), Sir Anthony Eden (British Prime Minister) and Mr John Foster Dulles (the US Secretary of State).

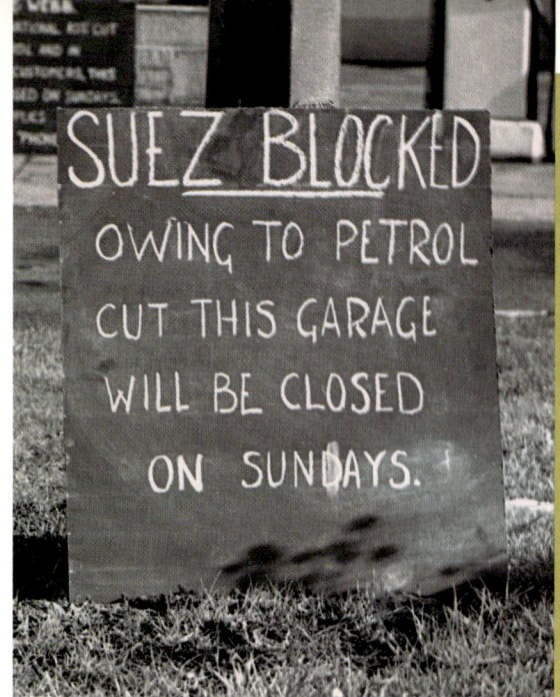

SOURCE 28

In November 1956 the government reduced petrol supplies by 10 per cent. Consequently many garages introduced their own rules to 'ration' petrol. Some country garages, like this one in Gloucestershire, reserved their supplies for their regular weekday customers and closed at the weekend.

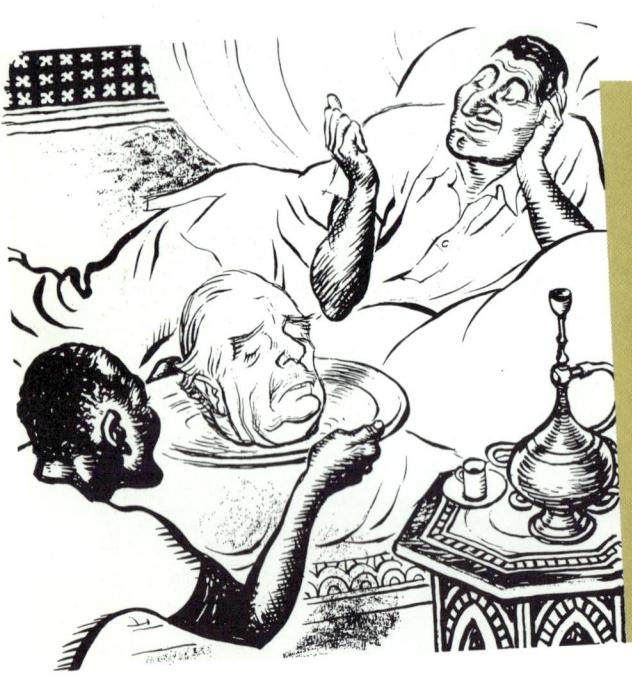

SOURCE 29

Britain's humiliating withdrawal from Egypt was an important symbolic victory for Nasser over Egypt's former colonial masters. As this cartoon indicates, the victory was also a personal one, which gained Nasser much prestige in the Arab world and forced Eden to resign as Prime Minister.

SOURCE 30

The Suez affair disclosed that the British government did not now have the power, militarily or economically, to mount an overseas expedition if the United States disapproved... what had happened was gross miscalculation of Britain's power and capacity. Even if the actual invasion force had been mounted more swiftly and effectively, the political ramifications had not been properly assessed... Britain could no longer suppose that the United Nations would invariably find British policy congenial; the United States would, in the last resort, always look after its own interests; the commonwealth was not likely to expand its ranks yet maintain the similarity of outlook and interest which had hitherto characterised it. After 1956, apprehensively, uncomfortably and uncertainly, the United Kingdom began to enter the post-colonial world.

Keith Robbins, *The Eclipse of a Great Power: Modern Britain, 1870–1975*, 1992.

At first things went according to plan. On 25 October the Israelis launched an attack on Egypt. Five days later Britain and France called for a withdrawal. Egypt immediately refused. However, whereas the Israeli attack had been successful, Anglo-French forces took until 4 November to reach Alexandria. By now, world opinion had turned decisively against Britain. On 2 November, the United Nations General Assembly condemned Britain and France. To make matters worse, the United States made it clear that they were strongly opposed to Britain's action. Meanwhile, the Soviet leader, Khrushchev, warned on 5 November, Guy Fawkes night, that the British people might see more fireworks and rockets in the sky than they had bargained for.

Eden had kept his plans from Washington in the hope that the US would stand behind Britain as events unfolded. However, US President Eisenhower made clear that he would not support what he considered to be a reckless act of aggression. America now sponsored a UN call for the removal of Anglo-French troops and their replacement by a UN peacekeeping force. Britain now found itself isolated and with possible US oil sanctions threatening to intensify the problems caused by Nasser blocking the Suez Canal. Even Britain's partners in the Commonwealth refused to support the UK. On 22 December 1956, in the most humiliating circumstances, the Anglo-French forces withdrew.

The Suez Crisis marked a bitter blow to British prestige (**Source 30**). Britain's position in the Middle East was fatally damaged. In January 1957, Eden, who had come under a relentless barrage of criticism both at home and abroad, resigned on grounds of ill health.

Case study: the Cuban Missile Crisis

A nuclear holocaust?

In October 1962 the world came the closest it had ever been to the point of nuclear oblivion. At the height of the Cuban Missile Crisis many people, from heads of state to ordinary citizens, believed that humanity was on the brink of extinction. In America, people moved out of the big cities on the East Coast which would be the prime 'targets' for the Soviet Union. At high schools across the nation students were put through a drill in which a siren was sounded and they had to scramble under their desks, with their hands on their heads. At the White House, President Kennedy called home his wife and children, who had been travelling, so that they could be ready to be moved into the Presidential bunker. Even America's favourite cartoon characters responded to the crisis: Bert the Turtle signed off by pulling into his shell with the slogan 'Duck and Cover'.

The Pentagon, the centre of US defence operations, ordered the priming of 140 Titan and Atlas nuclear missiles, in addition to mobilising 600 aircraft with a nuclear capability. In the Soviet Union, all armed forces were on full combat alert. With the possibility that the first nuclear exchange between the superpowers was at hand, the world held its breath.

How was it possible for the superpowers to get themselves into such a dangerous position? Why was Cuba at the centre of superpower rivalry at this time?

Cuba and the Castro revolution

Until 1959 Cuba, a Caribbean island only 90 miles from Florida, had been very much under the control of the USA. Since 1930, the White House had supported Cuba's corrupt dictator, Fulgencio Batista. The capital, Havana, was a popular tourist destination for American citizens. The Mafia made huge profits from the vice operations which it ran there. The island's main crop was sugar, grown for money rather than food, with the largest plantations owned by US business interests. Yet, after a seven year struggle, Batista was deposed by a charismatic, popular leader named Fidel Castro.

Castro's slogans about 'freedom' and 'national pride', combined with his policy of nationalising Cuba's land and industry, alarmed American politicians and businessmen. When Castro visited America in April 1959 he was treated with hostility (**Source 31**). After being offered a series of favourable trade agreements and receiving a warm welcome from Soviet President Khrushchev, Castro decided that it was better to gravitate towards the Soviet Union and Marxism than the USA and Capitalism.

SOURCE 31

Dr. Fidel Castro, the new leader of Cuba, meets Vice President Nixon in Washington, April 1959.

Castro was told that President Eisenhower was 'too busy' to meet him, and the Vice President gave him a frosty reception. The Americans had already decided that Castro was a Communist.

The Cuban premier had been prepared to co-operate with his powerful neighbour, but when the US leadership snubbed him, an alliance with the Soviet Union seemed increasingly attractive.

President John F. Kennedy

In 1960 the American presidential elections saw John F. Kennedy, the Democrat candidate, narrowly defeat his Republican rival, Richard Nixon. During the election campaign, Kennedy had portrayed himself as a man who would be prepared to make tough decisions on foreign policy and take a hard line against the spread of Communism (**Source 32**).

Nikita Khrushchev

Meanwhile, in the Soviet Union, premier Khrushchev was just as determined as Kennedy to take a firm line. Khrushchev presented an image of a tough, brash, outspoken, and uncompromising leader. In addition, Khrushchev was also surrounded by many hardline Communists and generals who expected to see their leader stand up to America. The future of Cuba therefore presented itself as an issue over which neither power could afford to be seen to back down or lose face.

Khrushchev made his position clear when he spoke of Cuba as a 'beacon for revolutionary struggle', and openly threatened the USA with speeches such as:

> They'd soon realise what a couple of nuclear bursts over New York could do ... A million tons of explosive could do a lot more than the 20,000 tons dropped on Hiroshima.

Yet in America, the US leadership was already planning to extinguish the 'beacon' of Communism in Cuba.

The CIA

In 1959, undercover agents passed weapons and supplies to Castro's enemies and set fire to a number of factories, power stations and sugar plantations. More bizarrely, the CIA even concocted plans to take advantage of Castro's well known liking for cigars. Three plans seriously discussed were:

- To fill a cigar with explosive material and blow Castro's head off!

SOURCE 33

Kennedy and Khrushchev meet face to face at the Vienna Summit in 1961.

The meeting was not a success. Khrushchev came away convinced that the young American President was naive and weak. Bitter exchanges between the two leaders as the summit broke up summed up the tension and hostility of the Cold War.

SOURCE 32

I have strong ideas about the United States playing a great role in a historic moment, when the cause of freedom is endangered all over the world. When the Unites States stands as the only sentry at the gate. When we can see the camp fires of the enemy burning on distant hills.

John F. Kennedy, extract from a presidential campaign speech.

- To fill a cigar with chemicals which would cause his beard to fall out and subject him to ridicule!
- To impregnate a cigar with the powerful drug LSD, ideally to be smoked while Castro was conducting a television interview!

Meanwhile the Soviet Union had counteracted American trade sanctions by providing Russian supplies, technicians and arms. In effect, an island only 90 miles from the American mainland was receiving Soviet sponsorship.

The Bay of Pigs

Kennedy was determined to be seen as a man of action and he therefore gave approval to a CIA plan, initiated under Eisenhower, to invade Cuba. The plan was to train and equip Anti-Castro exiles at secret camps in Central America. On 20 January 1961 a force of approximately 500 men landed on Cuban soil, at the sandy beach known as the Bay of Pigs.

Although the attack was unexpected, Castro was quick to mobilise his forces. More importantly, the Americans had completely underestimated the extent of popular support which the charismatic Castro had built up in Cuba. Castro used the invasion to arouse patriotic feeling and the exiles were met with massive resistance. As the invasion crumbled, a furious Kennedy refused to go any further with a plan which was going disastrously wrong.

With the exiles trapped and the US refusing to provide further assistance, the Americans tried to deny any involvement. At the United Nations, American representative Adlai Stevenson stated that 'the United States has committed no aggression against Cuba. No offensive has been launched.' Meanwhile, more than 100 exiles had died and over 1200 were taken prisoner. Castro called the Bay of Pigs a great triumph and declared that he was now, officially, a Marxist-Leninist. For Kennedy, the Bay of Pigs was a humiliation.

The Missile Crisis looms

In the wake of the Bay of Pigs fiasco, Kennedy and Khrushchev came face to face, for the first time, at the superpower summit held in Vienna in June 1961 (**Source 33**). Khrushchev told Kennedy that if the West did not give up its hold on Berlin, he would cut the city off and there might even be war. Kennedy's parting remark was that they could both anticipate 'a very cold winter'.

Kennedy returned to Washington more determined than ever to remove Castro from Cuba. 'Operation Mongoose', a plot to oust Castro, was funded with $50 million of government money. Meanwhile, Khrushchev, boosted by his performance at Vienna, came to the decision to deter an American move against Cuba by installing Soviet nuclear missiles there.

It was well known that the USA already had Jupiter nuclear missiles based in Turkey as well as warheads in Italy and Britain. Khrushchev felt that this established a precedent for the stationing of nuclear missiles abroad. In the summer of 1962, Soviet nuclear missiles were secretly moved to a number of Russian ports. Before long, the Soviet Union would be in a position to hit some of the major cities of the United States with a nuclear strike, with only a few minutes warning.

Knowledge and understanding

Use the material on pages 113 to 115 to investigate the following questions.

1 What signs are there that the world came to the brink of nuclear war in 1962?

2 Explain why Cuba was such an important issue to:
a The USA;
b the Soviet Union.

3 Summarise the importance of Fidel Castro in the development of the Cuban Missile Crisis.

4 Why was the Bay of Pigs invasion such a disaster for the United States?

5 Khrushchev obviously took a considerable risk in locating nuclear weapons in Cuba. Try to explain why he was prepared to do this.

Anatomy of a crisis

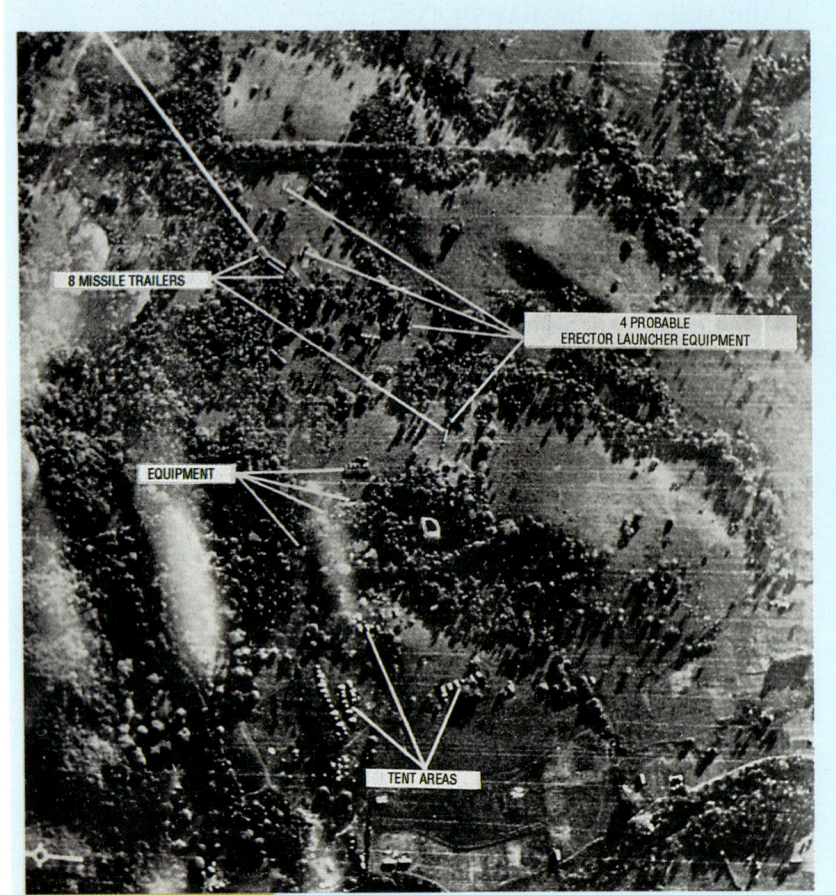

Sunday 14 October 1962
An American U2 aircraft flew from Edwards Air Force Base in California to a position twelve miles above Cuba and took a series of reconnaissance photographs (**Source 34**).

Monday 15 October
Analysis of the reconnaissance photographs showed a great deal of activity in fields near the village of San Christobel in western Cuba. They established without doubt, that a site was being prepared for a number of ten-metre-long, medium-range ballistic missiles. Defence experts predicted that the site would soon be operational. New York City and Washington DC would easily be within range.

Tuesday 16 October
Alarmed by the intelligence reports, Kennedy hastily called an emergency meeting of a group of high-level advisers which included his brother Robert Kennedy (the Attorney General), as well as the Military Chiefs of Staff. This group, which met regularly as the crisis developed, became known as the Executive Committee.

Friday 19 October
A further reconnaissance mission at a lower level revealed more Soviet missiles, this time with a

SOURCE 34

This photograph sparked off a crisis which nearly led to the Third World War. What can you actually see in the photograph which might have caused concern to the Americans?

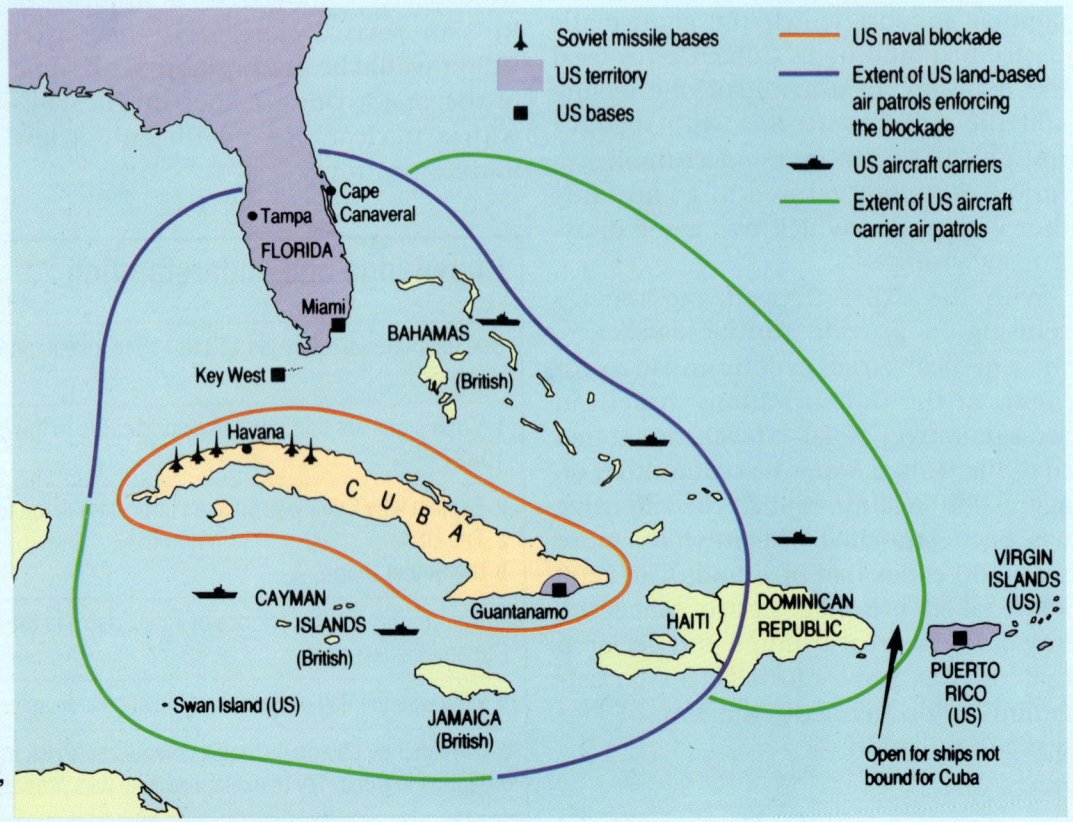

The Cuban Missile Crisis, October 1962

SOURCE 35

Dialogue from President Kennedy's taped record of a confidential meeting. The President's contribution is marked JFK, his brother Robert's RFK.

We've never really believed that Khrushchev would take on a general nuclear war over Cuba.

JFK: He's initiated the danger really hasn't he? He's the one playing God ... not us ...

We're impressed, Mr President, with the great importance of getting a strike in, with all the benefits of surprise ...

RFK: Then we're going to have to sink Russian ships. Then we're going to have to sink Russian submarines.

Or, are we going to decide that this is the time to eliminate the Cuban problem by actually eliminating the island?

longer range. Intelligence suggested that the Russians were working flat out and that the missiles were almost ready.

Monday 22 October

The President asked the Joint Chiefs of Staff if it would be possible to guarantee taking out all the Soviet missiles in a single attack. They told Kennedy that they could not guarantee that there were not undetected missile bases which could retaliate against the USA. Kennedy therefore ruled out a 'first strike', but he went on television that evening to warn the US people about the grave situation (**Source 35**).

Meanwhile, Khrushchev placed all Soviet forces on maximum alert. A number of Soviet ships were already on their way across the Atlantic to Havana, where they would meet the US blockade.

Wednesday 24 October

At 10.25 am President Kennedy received the most important message in his political career. The Soviet ships had stopped dead in the mid-Atlantic. Then, increasing grounds for optimism, Kennedy received a personal message from Khrushchev implying that he was ready for some sort of political settlement.

This was followed by a broadcast on Radio Moscow suggesting that the Russian missiles might be removed from Cuba if the US made an undertaking not to invade the island and promised to withdraw its nuclear missiles from Turkey.

Khrushchev appeared to be looking for a way out of the crisis. However, Castro's troops in Cuba were unaware of this dialogue and at the worst possible moment, they shot down a U2 spy plane, killing its American pilot. Kennedy was stunned. He had no way of knowing that the shoot-down was contrary to Khrushchev's wishes. Perhaps Khrushchev had tricked him. The 'hawks' among the President's advisers urged their leader to give the military the go-ahead. Yet still Kennedy resisted the growing military pressure to invade Cuba.

Friday 26 October

The President was dismayed when he then received a second, more aggressive, message from Khrushchev.

It was Robert Kennedy who saw his way to a solution: he proposed that they should ignore the aggressive message and reply to the first, more friendly one.

The President's reply said that the US would undertake not to invade Cuba, but could not make a decision about Turkey without consulting its NATO allies. In return for the Cuban guarantee, America demanded withdrawal of Soviet missiles from Cuba. The Russians replied immediately, saying they would accept these terms.

Sunday 28 October

Radio Moscow announced that the weapons would be dismantled. Privately the powers agreed to resolve the Turkey issue, provided that the Russians did not discuss it publicly. Six months later, the American missiles were removed.

SOURCE 36

This government ... has maintained the closest surveillance of the Soviet military build up on the island of Cuba ... Unmistakeable evidence has established the fact that a series of offensive missile sites is now in preparation ... To halt this offensive build up, a strict quarantine on all ... military equipment under shipment to Cuba is being initiated ... I have directed the Armed Forces to prepare for any eventualities. Any missile launched from Cuba against any nation in this hemisphere would bring a full retaliatory response upon the Soviet Union.

President Kennedy, 22 October 1962.

SOURCE 37

At the height of the Cuban Missile Crisis anti-war demonstrations took place throughout western Europe. These demonstrators can be seen in Whitehall, with the Houses of Parliament in the background. How much impact do you believe demonstrations such as this had on the decisions made by the superpower leaders?

Investigation

The Role of Britain in the Cuban Missile Crisis

SOURCE A

The British had received their first notification on Saturday, October 20. At Sunday noon Kennedy called David Ormsby-Gore to the White House and outlined the alternatives. Ormsby-Gore expressed strong support for the quarantine and, with his knowledge of Macmillan, assured the President of a sympathetic British reaction. Late the same day Kennedy explained directly to Macmillan that he found it essential in the interests of security and speed to make his first decision on his own responsibility, but that from now on he expected to keep in closest touch.

A. Schlesinger, *A Thousand Days*, 1965.

SOURCE B

We were 'in on' and took full part in (and almost responsibility for) every American move. Our complete calm helped keep the Europeans calm.

Harold Macmillan.

SOURCE C

Kennedy ... telephoned Macmillan every night throughout the crisis, both to keep the Prime Minister informed and to seek his advice ...

There was nothing Britain could have done to prevent the United States from unleashing a nuclear war over the Cuban issue, had they chosen to do so.

W.O. Simpson, *Changing Horizons*, 1990.

Questions

1. Use evidence from Sources A and B to support the argument that Britain was closely consulted by the USA during the missile crisis.

2. To what extent is this argument supported by the evidence in Source C?

3. Look at Source D. Why might Macmillan have been anxious to claim that Britain was being kept in touch with events by the Americans?

4. How far does Source E agree with the viewpoint in Source D?

SOURCE D

Top secret official papers released today reveal that the solidarity shown in public by Harold Macmillan and John F Kennedy during the Cuban Missile Crisis of October 1962 masked the grave doubts in the British government about the US military response.

Macmillan ... was in constant telephone contact with the President between October 22, when the Prime Minister first learnt that U-2 flights had identified Soviet missiles on Cuba, and October 28, when Khrushchev yielded to the US naval blockade and overwhelming international pressure. Yet classified documents kept secret for 30 years now show that British ministers and officials had serious reservations about Kennedy's brinkmanship.

In a cabinet memorandum dated October 25, Lord Dilhorne, the Lord Chancellor, doubted the legality of Kennedy's tactics, 'In our view the imposition of the "quarantine" cannot be justified as a "pacific blockade" under international law.' It might be argued that the United States was in immediate military danger, 'but we doubt that can be established, as the United States' action appears to be designed to prevent that threat being imminent.' Two days earlier, a telegram from the Foreign Office to the British officials at the UN questioned Kennedy's claim that the presence of the missiles so close to American soil was a 'secret disturbance' of the balance of power. 'We see considerable difficulty in [this] claim ... while the presence of Soviet missiles in Cuba no doubt greatly increases Soviet striking power, it could still be argued that total American nuclear strength was still ahead of Soviet nuclear strength' ...

On October 23, in the heat of the crisis, Macmillan rallied his colleagues to the US standard. But Home [Sir Alec Douglas Home, a member of Macmillan's Cabinet] insisted that Khrushchev had merely been forced into a 'military gamble' by the Soviet agricultural crisis, and that 'it was unlikely that [he] wanted to start a war ...' Macmillan later wrote a glowing preface to Robert Kennedy's account of the crisis, *13 Days*, praising the President's performance in the days that led to 'Black Saturday'. Yet letters between the Prime Minister and Sir David Ormsby-Gore, the Ambassador to Washington, reveal that even Macmillan was unsure 'what it is that the President is really trying to do.'

The Times, 1 January 1993.

SOURCE E

Tuesday 22nd October, the American Ambassador called at Number 10 to present 'evidence of the Soviet build-up in Cuba', and in a cable to President Kennedy at 9.35 pm that day, Macmillan promised British support and sympathy, while expressing reservations about the legality of the action and concern that Russian retaliation might be provoked against Berlin.

But in a separate cable to Sir David Ormsby-Gore, the British Ambassador to Washington, sent at 9.42 pm, Macmillan asked 'what it is the President is really trying to do?' He said, 'Since it seemed impossible to stop his action, I did not make the effort, although in the course of the day I was in a mind to do so.

'You will realise, for your personal information only, that I could not allow a situation in Europe or in the world to develop which looks like escalating into war without trying some action by calling a conference of my own, or something of the kind, to stop it.'

The Independent, 2 January 1993.

Case study: the United States and the war in Vietnam

On a crisp autumn weekend in 1982, thousands of Americans travelled to the nation's beautiful capital city, Washington DC. In the centre of the city, near the memorial to Abraham Lincoln, a huge wall had been erected. It was made of highly polished black granite and listed the names of 58,132 Americans who died or were still 'missing in action', in the Vietnam War. When the memorial was opened in November 1982 the President, thousands of Vietnam veterans, their families and members of the public came to pay their respects. There was a tremendous outpouring of grief.

Even though the war ended in 1975, the memory of the Vietnam war, the only major military defeat in their history, still haunts the American people today. Meanwhile, in Vietnam the devastating impact of the war there remains very apparent. Approximately four million Vietnamese soldiers and civilians, in North and South Vietnam, lost their lives. In South Vietnam the villages and countryside are filled with large plots containing whole families, including children and old people, who perished in this terrible conflict. In the North, neat rows of white stones mark the deaths of the people there. They contain the simple inscription, *Liet Si*: hero.

The origins of America's war in Vietnam

Between 1945 and 1954, France, the colonial ruler of Vietnam, had fought desperately to hold on to their prized possession in Indo-China. Yet by 1954 they faced a humiliating military defeat. On 7 May the French army at Dien Bien Phu surrendered to the Vietnamese nationalist army, known as the Vietminh and led by Ho Chi Minh.

The Vietminh and France called an armistice and agreed a temporary partition of Vietnam along the 17th parallel. It was planned that the Vietminh would control the north and the French the south until 1956. Then, elections would be held which would unify the country – probably under the Communist leader, Ho Chi Minh.

However, the United States and South Vietnam refused to recognise this agreement. In America, President Eisenhower and his advisers were convinced that if Vietnam was allowed to fall to the Communists then it would be the first of many countries to fall. This view became knows as the 'Domino Theory' (**Source 39**).

The Americans, desperate to prevent Communism taking hold in the South, now placed their support firmly behind the South Vietnamese government led by an anti-Communist named Ngo Dinh Diem. The United States began to provide arms and military 'advisers' to the South, while Ho Chi Minh and his Communist forces consolidated their

SOURCE 38

The Vietnam war memorial, Washington DC.

SOURCE 39

To justify his support for South Vietnam, Eisenhower put forward the 'domino theory' – if the first domino is knocked over then the rest topple in turn. Applying this to South-east Asia he argued that if South Vietnam were allowed to be taken by any group of communists, then the other countries in the region, Laos, Cambodia, Thailand, Burma, Malaysia and Indonesia would be taken in turn.

J. Simkin, *American Foreign Policy 1945–80*, 1986.

hold on the North and gathered strength for another war with an overseas power. This decision by President Eisenhower in effect committed the next three US Presidents to the struggle in Indo-China. Vietnam was now set to become the centre-piece in the struggle between Communism and capitalism.

President Kennedy and the Vietnam war: 1960–63

To many observers Kennedy's intelligence, youth and vigour seemed to hold out the promise that America was about to embark on a new era of military strength, economic growth and political decisiveness. Kennedy promised:

> We shall pay any price, bear any burden, meet any hardship, support any friend, oppose any foe to assure the survival and success of liberty.

However, in Vietnam Kennedy had inherited an appalling problem which he would prove unable to resolve. When he came into office, Kennedy continued Eisenhower's strategy of maintaining the Diem government with military and financial aid. However, in the early 1960s the situation in Vietnam quickly began to deteriorate. Increasingly, Ho Chi Minh used his guerrilla forces (known as the Vietcong or 'VC') to carry out actions against the South Vietnamese army. Kennedy now felt obliged to increase the level of military support provided by the US.

While Kennedy was in office, the number of US military advisers rose from 500 to 10,000. Meanwhile, the ruthless policies of Diem increasingly turned the people of South Vietnam against him. At times the show of anti-Diem feeling came close to outright rebellion.

The protest, led by the Buddhists, brought home to everyone the nature of Diem's cruel, corrupt and repressive regime (**Source 42**). Diem was increasingly becoming a political embarassment for the White House. Backed by the CIA, and with Kennedy's knowledge, the South Vietnamese army carried out a coup and executed Diem in November 1962.

The Vietnam war, 1968

- Areas of Vietcong activity
- Principal US bases by 1968
- Extent of US naval control, 1968
- US air attacks
- Vietcong supply routes

SOURCE 40

South Vietnam, covering an area of some 66,200 square miles and with a population of some 16 million in 1965, presented a wide variety of terrain and climatic conditions. Stretched like a bow from the Demilitarised Zone (DMZ) on the 17th Parallel in the north to the low-lying Mekong Delta in the south, the country was hot and humid, with average temperatures of 27°C and a heavy annual rainfall, produced by monsoons which came from the south in the summer and the north in the winter. In the south was the Mekong Delta, interlaced with a myriad of unmapped waterways. The ricebowl of the country and heavily populated, it had always been a hotbed of communist activity. No central government forces had ever been able to assert themselves fully in the region, although President Diem had done his best to root out those members of the Viet Minh who had remained there after the partition of Vietnam in 1954.

Further north, lay the capital Saigon, with 1.5 million inhabitants.

The Vietnam Experience 1965-75, Vol 1, 1990.

President Lyndon B. Johnson and the Vietnam war: 1963–68

Johnson was determined to halt the spread of Communism at all costs. 'I am not going to be the President who saw South East Asia go the way China went', he said. By the winter of 1965 President Johnson was ready to step up the American campaign in Vietnam. In February 1965 Vietcong units attacked a US army barracks, killing nine Americans and destroying five aircraft. Johnson's response was typically direct:

> We have kept our guns over the mantel and our shells in the cupboard for a long time now ... I can't ask our American soldiers out there to continue to fight with one hand behind their backs.

By July 1965 Johnson had set the US on a course of action which would lead to seven years of bloody conflict. In the words of Johnson, the objective was to apply enough force against the North Vietnamese and Vietcong until the enemy 'sobers up and unloads his pistol'. However, like his successor Richard Nixon, President Johnson made the assumption that the increased use of force would be enough to force the Vietcong into submission (**Source 43**).

1968: A turning point

On 30 January 1968, the North Vietnamese launched a massive assault mobilising 84,000 troops against major urban centres in South Vietnam. The Tet offensive, launched on the Vietnamese New Year, cost the Vietcong dearly in casualties, but they had struck a massive psychological blow against the US government and people. Even after all of Johnson's bombing campaigns, the Vietcong only seemed stronger than ever. No matter how much force America exerted, the VC seemed unbeatable.

It was against this background of increasing frustration that one of the darkest days in American military history took place.

SOURCE 41

Guerilla warfare was the key strategy of the Vietcong, whose equipment could not compare with high-tech resources of the US army. They made the most of their knowledge of the countryside in what was a hostile environment for the Americans.

This VC propaganda poster proclaims the defeat of the US military by the elusive guerillas.

SOURCE 42

Then, on 11 June, an aged Buddhist priest, Thich Quang Duc, sat down at a major intersection, poured gasoline on himself, took the cross-legged 'Buddha' posture and struck a match. He burned to death without moving and without saying a word. Thich Quang Duc became a hero to the Buddhists in Vietnam, and he dramatised their cause for the rest of the world.

J. Simkin, *American Foreign Policy 1945–80*, 1986.

SOURCE 43

While visiting the aircraft carrier 'Ranger' off the coast of Vietnam in 1965, Robert Shaplen overheard a fellow journalist remark: 'They just ought to show this ship to the Vietcong – that would make them give up. 'From Lyndon Johnson in the White House to the GI in the field, the United States went to war in 1965 in much this frame of mind. The President staked everything on the casual assumption that the enemy could be quickly brought to bay by the application of American military might ...

The United States never developed a strategy appropriate for the war it was fighting, in part because it was assumed that the mere application of its vast military power would be sufficient. The failure of one level of forced led quickly to the next and then the next, until the war attained a degree of destructiveness no-one would have thought possible in 1965.

George C. Herring, *America's Longest War*, 1979.

The My Lai massacre: 16 March 1968

In the aftermath of the Tet offensive, all American soldiers were told to take the fight to the enemy, confront the VC and show more aggression. At a briefing meeting in March 1968, the men of Charlie Company (1st Platoon) were told that the time for revenge was at hand (**Source 44**). Their search for the 48th Vietcong Local Force Battalion centred on the area known as My Lai 4. Because the area had been shaded in pink on their military maps, the troops called it 'Pinkville' – 'pinks' being US slang for Communists. What happened next became a symbol of all the horror stories that were emerging from Vietnam, although a cover-up operation concealed the story from the American public for a year (**Source 45**).

SOURCE 44

Prior to My Lai we had a briefing. This was supposed to be our first real chance to come face to face with the enemy, one to one. This was our chance to get even. Our instructions were that it was an enemy strong point. Anybody or anything that was left in the village was considered to be VC or a VC sympathiser and we were to obliterate the village ... It didn't turn out to be the way we thought. There was no enemy ... I witnessed things I had never seen before – people being executed.

Fred Widmer quoted in *The Sunday Times Magazine*, 23 April 1987.

SOURCE 45

Early on March 16, 1968, a company of American Division soldiers was dropped in by helicopter for an assault against a hamlet known as My Lai 4, located in the bitterly contested province of Quang Ngai, on the north-eastern coast of South Vietnam. The one hundred GIs and officers stormed the hamlet in military-textbook style, advancing by platoons; the men expected to engage the 48th Vietcong Battalion there, one of the enemy's most successful units, but instead found women, children and old men – many of them still cooking their breakfast rice over outdoor fires. During the next few hours the civilians were ruthlessly murdered. Many were rounded up in small groups and shot; others were flung into a drainage ditch at one edge of the hamlet and shot; and many more were shot at random in and about their homes. Some of the younger women and girls were raped, and then murdered. After the shootings the GIs systematically burned each home, destroyed livestock and food, and fouled the area's drinking supplies.

Seymour Hersh, *Cover Up*, 1969.

SOURCE 46

Bodies of women and children slaughtered by American soldiers litter the road from My Lai (March 1968).

The collapse of domestic support for the Vietnam war

From 1966 onwards the American people went through a series of traumatic events which all served to reduce public support for the continuing war in Vietnam.

- Rumours of atrocities committed by the US troops in Vietnam began to circulate.
- Horrifying television pictures of the war brought the conflict into people's living rooms and stunned the American public.
- All Americans were horrified by the continuing high levels of US casualties and many wanted an end to the war at all costs.
- Many Americans were shocked by the TV pictures of children suffering in napalm attacks and forests and farm land being defoliated with chemicals such as Agent Orange.
- On 21 October 1967, 50,000 anti-war protesters demonstrated outside the Pentagon, the headquarters of the US military establishment.
- In 1970 demonstrations against the war, and its extension under Nixon into Cambodia, culminated in clashes between students and the US National Guard which led to the deaths of six students at Kent State University and Jackson State College.

SOURCE 47
Children fleeing from a US napalm attack on their village (1972).

SOURCE 48
A girl screams before the body of a dead student lying face down on the campus of Kent State University, Ohio (4 August 1970). In violence following an anti-war demonstration, four students were shot dead by the US National Guard.

DATAPOINT

The Vietnam war

Vietnamese Soldiers and civilians killed. (in North and South Vietnam) = approx. 4 million

American forces killed or still classified as missing in action = 58,132

American forces wounded = approx. 300,000

Raids by US troops against North Vietnam

Year	Raids
1965	25,000
1966	79,000
1967	108,000

US involvement

1960–63 President Kennedy sent in 500 military advisers, this was gradually increased to 10,000, fighting alongside the South Vietnamese army.

End of 1963 Annual cost of the US assistance to South Vietnam = $400 million.

US expenditure on Vietnam 1965–1973 = more than $120 billion

Number of bombs dropped

More than the entire total dropped by the USA in all areas in the Second World War.

Tonnage of bombs dropped on North Vietnam

Year	Tonnage
1965	63,000
1966	136,000
1967	226,000

President Nixon and the end of the Vietnam war: 1968–75

President Nixon came into the White House determined to get the United States out of Vietnam. However, he was just as determined not to be the first American President to lose a war. Consequently, over the next four years Nixon followed a policy of trying to achieve 'peace with honour'. Nixon and his Foreign Secretary Henry Kissinger believed that the most effective way of getting the North Vietnamese to agree terms dictated by the United States was to use more force against them than ever before. In Nixon's words, 'The bastards have never been bombed like they're going to be bombed this time.'

Nixon now gave instructions to the military to unleash a new level of bombing against North Vietnam and its capital Hanoi. Then, frustrated by the evasive tactics of the Vietcong, he authorised the use of force against the neutral neighbouring country of Cambodia, on the grounds that it was being used by the Vietcong as a supply base and a safe haven.

However, Nixon slowly began to realise that no amount of force would compel the Communist government in Hanoi to agree to his terms. Instead, the Vietcong seemed content to allow the growing domestic hostility towards the war in America take its toll. By 1970, Nixon was withdrawing troops from Vietnam at the same time as increasing the pressure of the bombing raids. At home, unhappiness with the war continued. In 1971 a military court found Lieutenant William Calley guilty of 'at least twenty-two murders' in the My Lai massacre of 1968 and sentenced him to life imprisonment. Once again, the Vietnam war dominated the news and calls for peace escalated.

Negotiations for peace

The peace negotiations were by no means straightforward:

- America maintained its tactic of trying to bomb the Vietcong (eg the massive bombing raids of Christmas 1972) until they accepted US terms.

- Hanoi demanded the complete withdrawal of US troops.

- Hanoi refused to release American Prisoners of War (POWs) until their terms were met.

However, after months of secret and difficult negotiations, a treaty was finally signed in January 1973 at the Hotel Majestic in Paris. Kissinger for the Americans and Le Duc Tho for the North Vietnamese agreed that:

- American soldiers would leave Vietnam

- American Prisoners of War would be returned

- North Vietnamese troops would stay in the South

- The political future of South Vietnam would be resolved later

Two years after the treaty, North Vietnam launched a major offensive. In the spring of 1975, South Vietnam collapsed with little resistance. The war in Vietnam was finally over.

Knowledge and understanding

Use pages 120 to 125 to investigate the following questions.

1 Explain in detail why it was that America became more and more involved in Vietnam between 1945 and 1963.

2 What problems were faced by President Kennedy in offering support to the South Vietnamese under the leadership of Ngo Dinh Diem?

3 What policy was adopted by President Johnson in trying to deal with the Vietnam War?

4 What went wrong with the policy which he introduced?

5 Read the material on the My Lai Massacre (page 123). Try to explain why the massacre happened. Many historians would say that it would not be fair to only blame the actual soldiers involved. What other reasons can you think of for why My Lai took place?

6 Explain why President Nixon decided to withdraw America from the Vietnam war. What problems were faced before the war could be brought to an end?

Investigation

Why did America lose the Vietnam war?

SOURCE A

American troops fought well, despite the miserable conditions under which the war was waged – dense jungles and deep swamps, fire ants and leeches, booby traps and ambushes, an elusive but deadly enemy.

George C. Herring, *America's Longest War, The United States and Vietnam 1950–1975*, 1979.

SOURCE B

North Vietnam demonstrated great ingenuity and dogged perseverance in coping with the bombing. Civilians were evacuated from the cities and dispersed across the countryside; industries and storage facilities were scattered and in many cases concealed in caves and under the ground. The government claimed to have dug over 30,000 miles of tunnels, and in heavily bombed areas the people spent much of their lives underground. An estimated 90,000 North Vietnamese, many of them women and children, worked full-time keeping transportation routes open, and piles of gravel were kept along the major roadways, enabling 'Youth Shock Brigades' to fill craters within hours after the bombs fell ... B-52s devastated the narrow roads through the Mu Gia Pass leading to the Ho Chi Minh Trail, but, to the amazement of the Americans, trucks moved back through the pass within several days.

George C. Herring, *America's Longest War, The United States and Vietnam 1950–1975*, 1979.

SOURCE C

[North Vietnamese] Losses in military equipment, raw materials, and vehicles were more than offset by increased aid from the Soviet Union and China. Until 1965, Russia had remained detached from the conflict, but American escalation presented opportunities and challenges the Soviet leadership could not pass up ... The Chinese continued to supply large quantities of rice, small arms and vehicles. Soviet aid increased dramatically after 1965, and included such modern weaponry as fighter planes, surface-to-air missiles, and tanks ... Total assistance from Russia and China has been estimated in excess of $2 billion between 1965 and 1968.

George C. Herring, *America's Longest War, The United States and Vietnam 1950–1975*, 1979.

SOURCE D

The average age of the American soldier in Vietnam was nineteen ... which made him vulnerable to the psychological strains of the struggle – strains that were aggravated by the special tension of Vietnam, where every peasant might be a Vietcong terrorist.

Stanley Karnow, *Vietnam*, 1983.

SOURCE E

'Every minute, hundreds of thousands of people die on this earth,' General Vo Nguyen Giap, the Communist commander once said, and he discounted 'the life or death of a hundred, a thousand, tens of thousands of human beings, even our compatriots.' During the war against the Americans, he spoke of fighting ten, fifteen, twenty, fifty years, regardless of the cost, until 'final victory'.

American strategist ... Westmoreland ... reckoned that he knew the threshold of [North Vietnamese and Vietcong] endurance: ... he would awaken their leaders to the realisation that they were draining their population 'to the point of national disaster for generations,' and thus compel them to sue for peace. Even after the war, he still seemed to have misunderstood the phenomenal discipline and determination of the North Vietnamese. 'Any American commander who took the same vast losses as General Giap', he said, 'would have been sacked overnight'

Stanley Karnow, *Vietnam*, 1983.

SOURCE F

The US army in Vietnam was a shambles as the war drew to a close in the early 1970s. With President Nixon then repatriating the Americans, nobody wanted to be the last to perish for a cause that had clearly lost its meaning, and the name of the game for those awaiting withdrawal was survival. Antiwar protests at home had by now spread to the men in the field, many of whom wore peace symbols and refused to go into combat ... nearly one third of the troops were addicted to opium or heroin, and marijuana smoking had become routine. Soldiers not only disobeyed their superiors but, in an alarming number of incidents, actually murdered them with fragmentation grenades.

Stanley Karnow, *Vietnam*, 1983.

Questions

Imagine for this exercise that a commission of inquiry has been set up in America to try to explain why America lost the Vietnam war.

The following viewpoints are being considered:

1 It was the fault of the American government and successive Presidents.

2 It was the fault of the American soldiers.

3 It was down to the skill and endurance of the Vietnamese army.

In each case:

a Write a detailed paragraph in support of the point of view.

b Then write a paragraph opposing the viewpoint.

4 Explain which interpretation you feel is closest to the truth. You may wish to indicate that your explanation would involve aspects of all three ideas.

7 The United Nations

SOURCE 1

The headquarters of the United Nations Organisation on the East River in Manhattan, New York. The location of the UN in the United States was important, representing the shift away from the domination of Europe over the rest of the world. The League of Nations had been located in Europe.

The impact of war and the origins of the United Nations

The United Nations was devised and created, above all, because none of the victorious states ever wanted to experience anything like the Second World War again. The War convinced those countries which emerged victorious that there was an urgent need for 'an organisation of peace-loving states', to maintain international peace and security and to work together for the future progress of the world community.

The League of Nations

Attempts at international peacekeeping were not new. In the aftermath of the First World War, the League of Nations was set up (1919) as an attempt to preserve future peace. However, the League was ultimately seen as a weak, toothless organisation. In particular, it was widely felt that America's failure to join the League and the organisation's lack of its own armed forces to enforce its decisions were critical weaknesses. In addition, it was clear with hindsight that the League of Nations had been dominated by Britain and France and did not have a sufficiently worldwide membership. These weaknesses would have to be remedied if a new peacekeeping organisation was to have any credibility.

SOURCE 2

One of the major differences between the United Nations and the League of Nations was the UN's ability to use military force. When US President Truman rushed the UN into war with Korea, however, many felt that things had gone from one extreme to the other.

HISTORY DOESN'T REPEAT ITSELF

The formation of the United Nations

Roosevelt, bearing in mind the failure of the League to live up to its idealistic aims, originally discouraged talk of a new organisation along similar lines. Instead, he put forward the idea of 'Four Policemen' – the United States, Great Britain, the Soviet Union and China, who together would maintain world peace and deter aggression. Many observers rightly noted that this would amount to a world dominated by four big, powerful countries who, deep down, would always have their own interests at heart. It was only when it became clear to Roosevelt that people were looking for a broader, fairer and more principled organisation, that he moved towards the new concept of the United Nations. The name 'United Nations' was suggested by Roosevelt and was first used officially in 1942, when representatives of 26 countries signed the Declaration by United Nations, pledging their co-operation in the 'struggle for victory over Hitlerism'. Roosevelt was now fully committed to the new organisation and was determined to convince the American people that they had no choice but to support US membership of the United Nations (**Source 3**).

SOURCE 3

In our disillusionment after the last War we gave up hope of achieving a better peace because we had not the courage to fulfil our responsibilities in an admittedly imperfect world. We must not let it happen again, or we shall follow the same tragic road again – the road to a Third World War.

President Roosevelt, State of the Union Address, January 1945.

SOURCE 4

More than anyone else, Roosevelt was responsible for the creation of the United Nations. He was very aware that the weakness of the League had largely been caused by America's failure to join it. He was therefore determined that the USA would be at the centre of the new peacekeeping organisation. Yet before the war was over, it was clear that Roosevelt did not have long to live. This close-up photograph of him at the Yalta Conference of February 1945 shows how ill he looked.

The principal institutions of the UN

The General Assembly

This is the main representative body of the UN. All members of the United Nations are members of the General Assembly. Each has one vote. When the UN was founded there were 51 members. By June 1985 this had reached 159. Therefore, the General Assembly has been described as the first 'town meeting' to involve the entire world. Membership of the UN, and thus the General Assembly, is open to all 'peace-loving countries' that accept the obligations of the UN Charter, or rule book. Although the General Assembly has no power to compel any government to take any action, it can sometimes carry considerable weight and influence as an expression of world opinion. The main function of the General Assembly is to act as a forum for debate and discussion; a strength of the General Assembly is that all nations, big and small, have the same rights within it. A criticism has been that its growing size has made it unwieldy. Such a range of interests and countries are represented here that it tends to be divided more often that it is united. The General Assembly meets every year in regular session from September to December. In emergencies it can be called together within 24 hours.

The Security Council

In many respects the most powerful and important element of the UN, the Security Council consists of 15 countries, five of these are permanent members: China, France, the Soviet Union, the United Kingdom and the United States. The remaining ten are non-permanent members, elected by the General Assembly for two-year terms. Countries cannot immediately serve a further term. Originally the number of non-permanent members was six but this was increased to ten in 1965.

Whilst other organs of the UN, such as the General Assembly, can make recommendations to governments, the Security Council alone has the power to take decisions which all member states are obliged under the Charter to carry out.

The Security Council, as its name suggests, concentrates its work on the maintenance or restoration of international peace and security. It can compel all member states to apply economic and other sanctions against an aggressor. If this is inadequate, the Security Council can call for military action. Under the Charter all members undertake to make available armed forces and other resources necessary for maintaining international peace and security.

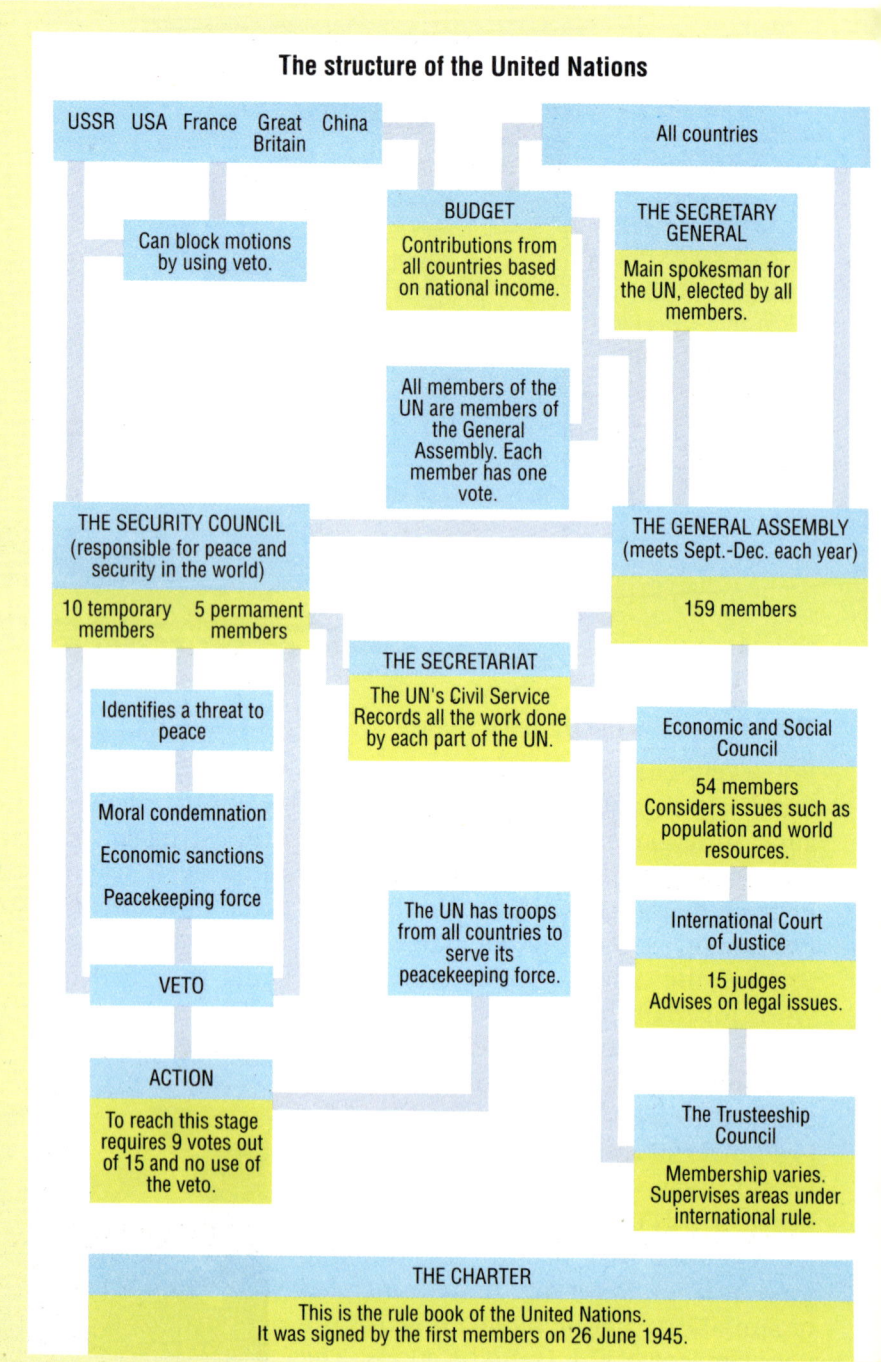

The structure of the United Nations

- **USSR USA France Great Britain China** — Can block motions by using veto.
- **All countries**
- **BUDGET** — Contributions from all countries based on national income.
- **THE SECRETARY GENERAL** — Main spokesman for the UN, elected by all members.
- All members of the UN are members of the General Assembly. Each member has one vote.
- **THE SECURITY COUNCIL** (responsible for peace and security in the world) — 10 temporary members, 5 permanent members
  - Identifies a threat to peace
  - Moral condemnation
  - Economic sanctions
  - Peacekeeping force
  - VETO
  - ACTION — To reach this stage requires 9 votes out of 15 and no use of the veto.
- **THE SECRETARIAT** — The UN's Civil Service Records all the work done by each part of the UN.
- The UN has troops from all countries to serve its peacekeeping force.
- **THE GENERAL ASSEMBLY** (meets Sept.–Dec. each year) — 159 members
- **Economic and Social Council** — 54 members. Considers issues such as population and world resources.
- **International Court of Justice** — 15 judges. Advises on legal issues.
- **The Trusteeship Council** — Membership varies. Supervises areas under international rule.
- **THE CHARTER** — This is the rule book of the United Nations. It was signed by the first members on 26 June 1945.

Voting procedures and the veto

Each member of the Security Council has one vote. For standard procedures and basic decisions to be approved, at least nine out of 15 votes have to be cast in favour.

More important matters have to receive at least nine votes, including the support of all five permanent members. Thus, on important issues, each of the five permanent members has the right to veto (reject) the proposal – even if all the other members are in agreement. This is known as the rule of 'great power unanimity'. All of five permanent members have used their right of veto at one time or another.

If a permanent member does not support a decision, but has no desire to block it, it may abstain. An abstention is not the same as a veto and does not mean that a proposal has to be rejected. The Security Council can meet at any time. A representative of each member state must be present at all times at the UN headquarters in New York.

The Economic and Social Council

This body, which acts under the authority of the General Assembly, co-ordinates the economic and social functions of the UN and its various agencies. The Council concerns itself with issues such as human rights, the status of women, world trade, education and science.

Related agencies

These agencies have considerable independence but work with the UN through the co-ordination of the Economic and Social Council. Important agencies include:
- United Nations Educational, Scientific and Cultural Organisation (UNESCO)
- World Health Organisation (WHO)
- International Monetary Fund (IMF)
- International Labour Organisation (ILO)

Other UN bodies include:

- **The United Nations International Children's Emergency Fund (UNICEF)**
  In 1953 when this organisation was made permanent, the words International and Emergency were dropped, so it is now sometimes referred to simply as the Children's Fund.
- **International Atomic Energy Agency (IAEA)**
- **The General Agreement on Tariffs and Trade (GATT)**
- **Trusteeship Council**
  This body was set up under the UN Charter to provide international supervision for the world's 'non-self-governing territories'. There were originally 11 areas represented; by 1977 all bar one had gained self-government.
- **The International Court of Justice**
  The International Court of Justice, based at The Hague in the Netherlands, is the main legal and judicial organ of the United Nations. The Court has the authority to take legal decisions in cases referred to it by member states. The Court of Justice concerns itself with the application of international laws and treaties. It has 15 judges of different nationalities, elected by the General Assembly and the Security Council.

Secretary Generals of the UN since 1945

Name	Country	Period of office
Trygve Lie	Norway	1945–53
Dag Hammarskjöld	Sweden	1953–61
U Thant	Burma	1961–72
Kurt Waldheim	Austria	1972–76
		1976–81 *(re-elected)*
Javier Perez de Cuellar	Peru	1982–86
		1986–91 *(re-elected)*
Boutros Boutros-Ghali	Egypt	1991–

- **The Secretariat**
  The Secretariat is the international staff of the United Nations, based at the UN Headquarters in New York. By 1985, the UN employed over 25,000 staff from more than 145 countries. The senior member of staff is the Secretary General, the chief administrative officer of the United Nations. The Secretary General is appointed by the General Assembly, on the recommendation of the Security Council.

SOURCE 5

This photograph shows a meeting of the Security Council at UN headquarters in New York on 22 August 1968. The motion before the 15 members on this occasion concerned a condemnation of the Soviet Union's invasion of Czechoslovakia in 1968. You can see the Soviet delegate is voting against the motion, whereas the UK and USA had supported it. In this case then, the power of the veto had been used by the USSR to block a motion.

Between 1941 and 1945 a series of meetings took place to determine the precise nature and organisation of the new body. Britain's commitment began with the signing of the Declaration of the United Nations in January 1942 and was maintained throughout the long discussions which came to a conclusion in San Francisco in 1945.

The Charter of the United Nations was signed on 26 June 1945 in San Francisco. It expressed the determination of the members of the UN 'to save humanity from the scourge of war' and to promote 'international justice, progress and freedom'. The purposes of the United Nations are set out in Article 1 of the Charter. They are:

- To maintain international peace and security
- To develop friendly relations among nations
- To co-operate in solving international economic, social, cultural and humanitarian problems and in promoting respect for human rights.
- To be a centre for harmonising the actions of nations towards these common goals.

SOURCE 6

'As a matter of fact the UN now is not so much a worldwide organisation as an organisation for the Americans acting for the needs of American aggression.' Stalin.

The quotation inspired this cartoon about the UN (OOH).

The role of Britain in the United Nations

From the creation of the UN up to the present day, Britain has retained its permanent seat on the Security Council of the United Nations. It could be argued that by remaining on the Security Council Britain's leaders have held onto an illusion of their country as a major power, while in fact Britain's importance in the world has greatly declined. Nevertheless, no British leader has been prepared to give up this position of power.

Weaknesses of the UN

Criticisms of the UN were soon forthcoming. It was widely felt that too much of the power of the UN rested with the five permanent members of the Security Council. The increasingly acute rivalry of the Soviet Union and the United States, the two key members of the Council, made many question how 'united' the UN could be. The fact that any permanent member could use its power of veto to block proposals raised the dismal prospect that America and Russia would simply cancel out each other's initiatives and prevent important decisions from being taken.

Knowledge and understanding

Use pages 128 to 132 to investigate the following questions.

1 What were the main weaknesses of the League of Nations?

2 What motives did Roosevelt have in setting up the United Nations?

3 What role was played by Britain in the development of the UN?

4 Explain in your own words, the function of the General Assembly.

5 Why has the security Council been described as the most important agency of the UN?

6 In what ways has the voting procedure of the Security Council shown that the UN has not always been a united organisation?

7 'Britain is no longer entitled to a seat on the Security Council.' Would you support or disagree with this statement? Give detailed reasons for your answer.

The United Nations in action: The Middle East

Rival claims for the same land

The Holy Land is claimed as home by the Jews and the Palestinians. For both groups it is the Holy Land, with great significance in the Jewish, Moslem and Christian religions. Before the expulsion of the Jews by the ancient Romans, this land was known as Judea. The Arabs know the land as Palestine, its official name up to 1948. Today it is the state of Israel – a name with religious significance for the Jews.

The Jews

- For hundreds of years before the birth of Christ, the Jews had lived in Judea.
- The Jews regarded Israel as the Promised Land which God had given to his chosen people. It was also part of their faith that the Jews would eventually return to Israel.
- Despite being exiled from the Holy Land by the Romans, the Jewish people maintained a distinctive religion and culture.
- Following their terrible suffering in the pogroms of Eastern Europe and in Hitler's Holocaust (see pages 180–81), the Jews longed to establish their own homeland.

The Arabs

- The Arabs had lived in Palestine since before the Jews or Romans.
- Since the expulsion of the Jews from the area around 135AD the Arabs had been the majority in Palestine.
- Following hundreds of years of Turkish rule and a short period as a British mandate, the Palestinian Arabs had strong aspirations to govern their own land.
- In 1917 the population of Palestine was 700,000 Arabs and 56,000 Jews.
- Palestine was a Holy Land for the Arabs, with the mighty Dome of the Rock mosque situated in Jerusalem.

SOURCE 8

Two thousand seven hundred refugees on board the *Theodor Herzl*. After the War, the British forces controlling the mandate of Palestine continued to restrict Jewish immigration into the area. The message on the side of the boat represents the feelings of the vast number of Jews who no longer wanted to live in Central and Eastern Europe.

The Middle East since 1945

At the centre of the complex and drawn-out problems of the Middle East is the issue of Palestine. Between 1917 and 1947 Palestine was administered by the United Kingdom, under a mandate from the League of Nations after 1922. By the end of the Second World War, Palestine had a population of approximately two million, two thirds Arabs and one third Jews. Both sides have consistently stressed their rights to control and live in Palestine, at the expense of the other.

In 1947 the United Kingdom raised the issue of Palestine at the UN and the General Assembly established the United Nations Special Committee on Palestine to examine the issue in depth. In November of that year the UN put forward a

SOURCE 7

The search for a just and lasting peace in the Middle East has occupied the United Nations since its early years. For more than three and a half decades the Organisation has, in response to hostilities that have broken out at various times, sent impartial observers or peace-keeping forces to the region and it has formulated principles for solving the underlying political problems.

The UN Handbook

partition plan which recommended the co-existence of an Arab state and a Jewish state, with the key city of Jerusalem given special international status (see map). This plan was basically approved by the Jews and rejected by the Arabs – to the Arabs this would have meant losing part of the country; to the Jews it would have been the first step to nationhood.

Proclamation of the state of Israel

On 14 May 1948, the United Kingdom ended its mandate over Palestine and the Jewish Agency proclaimed the State of Israel. The next day, fighting erupted as the Palestinian Arabs, supported by the Arab states, launched hostilities against Israel. Within a year, Israel had gained more land in the north, part of the West Bank, part of the Gaza Strip and half of Jerusalem (see map). Many Arabs were now forced to live in refugee camps in neighbouring Arab states. The children born in these squalid conditions were destined to become bitter enemies of Israel in adult life. After several weeks' fighting the UN, through the Security Council, managed to secure a truce, supervised by United Nations military observers. However, this early success was soon marred when the United Nations Mediator for Palestine, Count Bernadotte of Sweden, was assassinated in the Israeli-held sector of Jerusalem on 17 September 1948.

UN Conciliation: 1948–49

In December 1948 the General Assembly called for the demilitarisation of Jerusalem and its establishment as an international zone. It called for the return of those refugees who wished to return to their homes and live peacefully alongside their neighbours, while offering compensation for those who chose to re-settle outside the area. Although the UN has repeatedly called for these proposals to be implemented, the parties involved have failed to act upon its suggestions.

On 11 May 1949, Israel's status was formally recognised when the new state was admitted as a member of the General Assembly. Through a UN mediator separate armistice agreements were reached in early 1949 between Israel and her neighbours, Egypt, Jordan, Lebanon and Syria. However, tension in the area remained high and came to a head in the Suez Crisis of 1956 (see page 110).

1967: The Six Day War

Conflict erupted in the Middle East with the third Arab-Israeli war in the summer of 1967. By then, talk of liberating Palestine from the Jews was rife. Much of the hostility towards Israel stemmed from the Egyptian leader, Nasser. However, other Arab states were jealous of Nasser's powerful position and eager to demonstrate their own hatred of Israel. As tension mounted, an attack from Syria and Jordan seemed imminent. However, on 5 June 1967 the Israelis surprised everyone when they struck first. The Egyptian air force was destroyed before it left the ground. The

The state of Israel, 1948–67

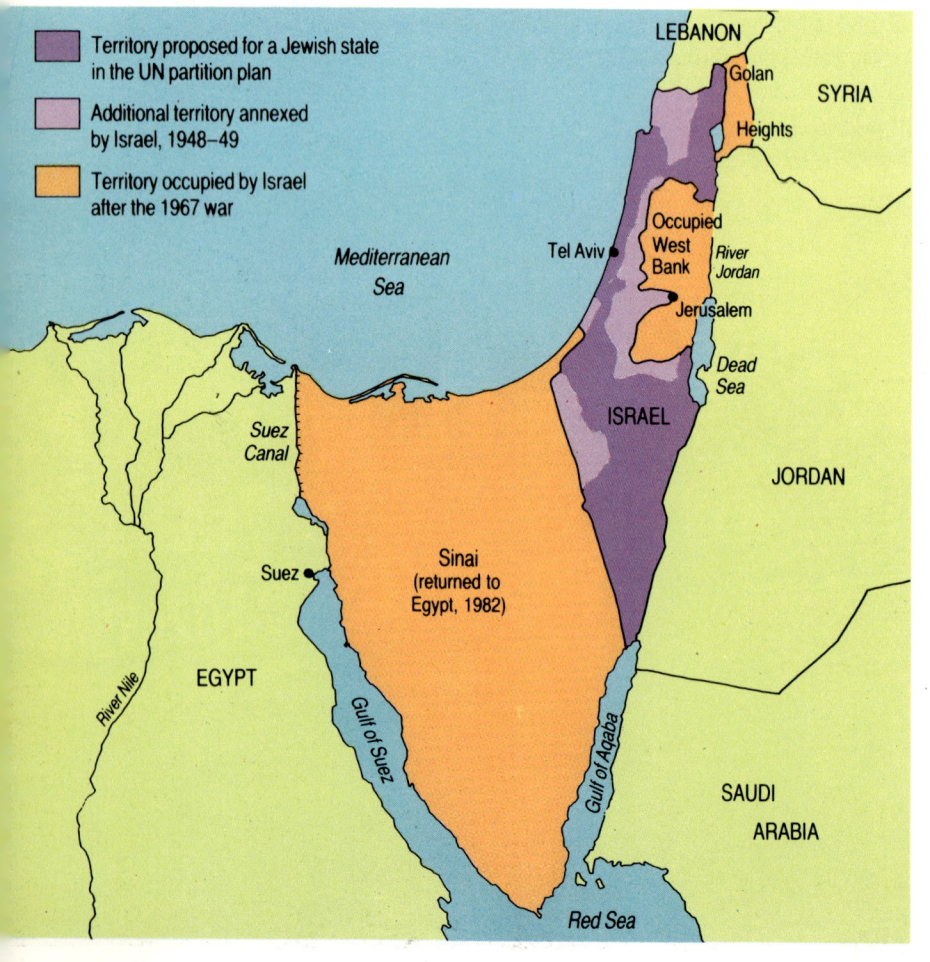

Egyptian army was soundly beaten. The West Bank was taken from Jordan and part of the Syrian Golan Heights was captured. The Israelis now annexed all of Jerusalem, including the holy places of the Moslems, Christians and Jews. Israel had more than doubled its size and secured its frontiers (see map) but at enormous cost to the native population of the annexed areas.

After six days of conflict a cease-fire called for by the Security Council came into effect. The Security Council acted again in November 1967 when its Resolution 242 called for 'withdrawal of Israeli armed forces from territories occupied in the recent conflict' and for 'political independence of every state in the area... free from the threats and acts of force.' Finally, the resolution called for a 'just settlement of the refugee problem.'

However, the Arabs and Israelis could not agree on implementation of the resolution and the problem remained acute. The differences between the parties became so intense that the UN was unable to make much progress. For example, a General Assembly Special Committee investigating Israel's conduct concerning human rights in the Occupied Territories was denied access by Israel and had to base its work on visits to the neighbouring Arab states.

The Palestinians

As a result of the Six Day War there were now 250,000 Palestinian refugees and Israel ruled approximately one million Palestinians in Jerusalem and the Occupied Territories. The Arabs in these areas were denied the vote and did not have the same rights as their Jewish neighbours. In the face of these difficulties some of the Arab States began to train guerillas who could offer armed resistance to Israel. The most significant Arab resistance movement was the Palestine Liberation Organisation (PLO) set up in 1964 by Yasser Arafat (**Source 9**). The PLO argued that Israel was an illegal occupying force. They swore that Palestine would be liberated by an armed struggle.

Jordan and armed resistance

The majority of Palestinian refugees lived in Jordan and so it was in this country that the PLO attracted most support and grew most powerful. However, the power of the PLO grew to such an extent that it seemed to King Hussein of Jordan to represent a threat to his authority. Meanwhile, the PLO carried out acts of international terrorism which

SOURCE 9

Yasser Arafat, leader of the Palestine Liberation Organisation (PLO).

SOURCE 10

The Palestinian struggle has been brought to the world's attention by terrorist actions such as the hijacking of aircraft. Here we see jubilant Palestinians on the wreckage of a British VC10. Their hostages had been released before the plane was destroyed.

commanded world attention and, in many quarters, condemnation. International airlines were particularly vulnerable to determined terrorists. Planes were hijacked, passengers taken hostage and often executed. In particular, the USA, which had given Israel political and financial support, faced repeated attacks upon its citizens and passenger aircraft. Suddenly King Hussein of Jordan, concerned at the continued activities of the PLO, used his own troops to drive the Arab activists out of Jordan and into the Lebanon.

October 1973: The Yom Kippur War

Meanwhile in Egypt a new President, Anwar Sadat, had come to power. His objective was to regain the Sinai peninsula and his method was to wage war. On Yom Kippur, an important Jewish religious festival when normal life grinds to a halt, Egypt and Syria launched a sudden invasion. On 6 October 1973, Israeli positions were attacked by Syria in the Golan Heights and by the Egyptian forces in the Suez Canal Sector. At first Israel suffered heavy losses but gradually the Arabs were driven back.

As the Israelis, backed by the West, began to repel the Arabs, the Arab oil-producing states responded by dramatically reducing their oil supplies to the West. The Western nations now urgently needed a cease-fire, as their vital oil supplies were seriously threatened. They persuaded Israel to negotiate.

On 22 October the Security Council unanimously passed Resolution 338 urging the parties to cease fire. In December 1973 the UN organised an International Peace Conference, after which all sides disengaged their military forces.

Although the territorial situation had not substantially changed, the Arabs felt that they had shown that militarily they could still be effective against Israel.

Diplomatic advances

In 1974 the PLO embarked upon a radical change in policy. Arafat launched a major diplomatic campaign aimed at convincing the Arab States that the PLO was the only true representative of the Palestinian people. This was followed by official UN recognition of the Palestinians' right to self-rule. Force seemed to be giving way to diplomacy.

In 1977 the Egyptian President, Anwar Sadat, took the unprecedented step of visiting Israel to attempt reconciliation. US President Jimmy Carter built on this by bringing together Sadat and the Israeli leader, Menachem Begin, at the Camp David summit in the USA in 1978. The outcome was that in return for Arab recognition of Israel's right to exist, the Egyptians were given back Sinai.

The Lebanon

The diplomacy between Israel and Egypt only paved the way for fresh conflict elsewhere. After they had been driven out of Jordan, the PLO had established itself in Lebanon, from where they had

SOURCE 11
These men were taken prisoner by Israeli troops advancing towards the Syrian capital of Damascus during the Yom Kippur War (12 October 1973).

launched regular attacks against Israel. The Israelis, having concluded peace with Egypt, now felt they had a freer hand to tackle the PLO.

Meanwhile, political and religious turmoil in Lebanon had reduced the country to civil war. In 1982, the Israelis, determined to smash the PLO, launched a massive invasion force against Lebanon. The capital city, Beirut, was bombarded, and the PLO-controlled south came under sustained attack. Amid enormous casualties, the PLO were driven out of Lebanon, but the Israelis remained. Israel's brutal treatment of the Palestinians in Lebanon now aroused concern amongst their own people. Yet at the same time, within Israel the government had moved to the right and become increasingly hard-line towards the Arabs. Although the Israelis withdrew some of their forces, their presence in Lebanon continued.

Recent developments

Arabs in the Occupied Territories have faced poor housing conditions, the worst-paid jobs, detention without charge and compulsory ID passes. By 1987 tension in the area had erupted. The Palestinians launched the *Intifada*, an uprising against the Israelis. The Israelis responded with brutal attacks, such as blowing up the houses of people suspected of helping in the uprising.

The violent events of the late 1980s seemed to put an end to the hope raised by earlier diplomatic advances. However, in 1993 an agreement was signed which offered a new chance for peace, with the Jews and Arabs recognising for the first time each other's right to exist within the land of Israel / Palestine.

SOURCE 12

This photograph, taken in Rahallah on the occupied West Bank, shows Israeli soldiers beating a Palestinian youth (April 1986). Scenes like this provoked outrage round the world and also influenced Israeli public opinion about the brutality being used to keep control in the Occupied Territories.

Knowledge and understanding

Use pages 133 to 137 to investigate the following questions.

1 Set out the origins of the Arab – Israeli conflict:
a from the Arab viewpoint;
b from the Israeli viewpoint.

2 What role did Britain play in the Middle East crisis between 1914–47?

3 Why was Palestine such a vital issue to both sides?

4 Evaluate the success of the UN in the Middle East between 1948–66.

5 Why was there a fresh crisis in the Middle East in 1967?

6 To what extent was the UN able to resolve this conflict?

7 What problems were faced by the Palestinian people after the Six Day War?

8 Explain the role of the PLO in the Middle East crisis.

9 Summarise the build up to and the events of the Yom Kippur war.

10 Was the Yom Kippur war a victory for the Jews or the Arabs?

11 Why does the West desire a peaceful resolution to the Arab – Israeli conflict?

12 How successful were diplomatic methods in resolving the problems of the Middle East between 1974–77?

13 Why did the Arab – Israeli conflict reach such a bitter level in the Lebanon?

14 How far would you regard the Middle East as a successful area for the UN since 1945?

The United Nations in action: Korea

The background to the Korean war

The events of 1949 greatly heightened fears of Communist expansion in the United States. The American public had been shocked by the revelation that the USSR had successfully tested an atomic bomb, and then further dismayed when Mao Zedong and the Communist Party took control in China.

The United Nations refused to recognise Mao as the legitimate ruler of China and carried on supporting the defeated nationalist government. Russia was angered by this anti-Communist decision, and in a show of support for China, the Russians announced that they would boycott the meetings of the Security Council. Meanwhile, in the United States, the government was coming under increasing pressure to take a firm stand against the spread of Communism. The test of President Truman's resolve came in the summer of 1950.

In the aftermath of the Second World War the UN had tried to bring about a unified independent Korean State through nation-wide elections, but this was unsuccessful. In 1948, separate Governments came into being in the north and in the south.

On 25 June 1950 Communist troops from North Korea, armed with Russian-made weapons, poured over the border into South Korea.

The significance of the Korean war

Before the war was over, Korea would become the only battlefield since the Second World War in which troops of two great powers, in this case the USA and China, would clash. Only in the case of the Cuban Missile Crisis has America come closer to using its nuclear weapons. The British army would fight its biggest battles since 1945.

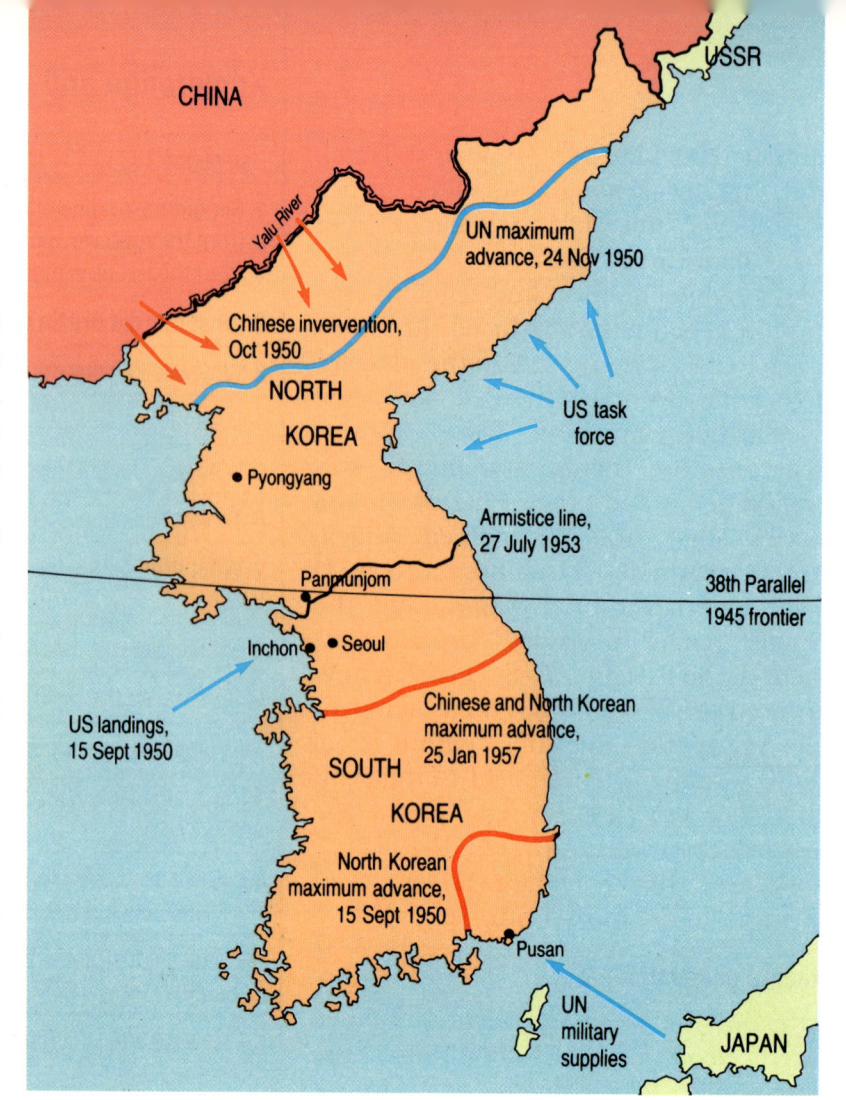

The Korean war

DATAPOINT

The Korean war, 1950–1953

Casualties

North Korea
At least one million

China
Uncertain, but probably hundreds of thousands

South Korea
415,000 killed
429,000 wounded

United Nations
Total UN casualties: 135,000

USA
33,629 killed
105,785 wounded

Commonwealth (Britain, Canada, Australia and New Zealand)
1,263 killed
4,817 wounded

Belgium, Colombia, Ethiopia, France, Greece, Netherlands, Turkey, Phillippines, Thailand
1,800 killed
7,000 wounded

Countries who contributed to the UN action
Australia, Belgium, Canada, Colombia, Cuba, Ethiopia, France, Greece, Luxembourg, the Netherlands, New Zealand, Philippines, Thailand, Turkey, UK, USA (16 in total).

Principle British regiments deployed
The Gloucesters,
The Ulsters,

The Korean war, 1950–51

June 1950
When the Communists crossed the 38th Parallel, the border between North and South Korea, they met little resistance. In America, many observers assumed that the invasion was backed by Russia. If firm action was not taken, some Americans feared that it could eventually lead to a Russian invasion of Japan.

On the day of the invasion the United Nations Security Council, during the period of Soviet non-attendance, adopted a resolution calling for the withdrawal of North Korean forces to above the 38th Parallel. On 27 June President Truman instructed American forces to support South Korea.

July 1950
On 7 July General Douglas MacArthur was named as Supreme UN Commander. On the same day the Security Council asked all member states to make available forces which would then be brought under the unified command of the United States. This command was authorised to fly the United Nations flag. In total, sixteen nations sent troops and five others supplied medical units. In addition, the forces of South Korea were placed under the control of what was known as the United Nations Command. However, the *UN Handbook* makes the following vital point:

> The international force in Korea ... was not a United Nations peace-keeping operation. The force was not under the authority of the Secretary General but under the unified command of the United States. Reports on the operation during the period of fighting were not submitted to any United Nations organ.

The Soviet Union and the People's Republic of China declared the Security Council's actions to be illegal.

August 1950
In August the Soviet Union returned its delegate to the UN and took over the presidency of the Security Council. On 15 September the US 10th Corps launched a massive assault on Inchon, enabling UN forces to push towards the 38th Parallel. By the end of the month General MacArthur was able to retake Seoul.

October 1950
On 1 October 1950 South Korean troops crossed over the 38th Parallel into North Korea. On 7 October the UN passed a Resolution that 'all appropriate steps be taken to ensure conditions of stability throughout Korea.' The vital issue which this raised was that now UN troops were not just restoring South Korean independence but were actually going beyond that. Forces under US command were advancing into North Korea. Any idea that the control of Korea was now passing into the hands of the UN was shaken when, in October 1950, the Chinese leader Mao Zedong ordered Chinese 'volunteers' into Korea to resist the US forces. At the end of October the 8th Army (US/UN forces) was halted by the Chinese.

November–December 1950
By November, the number of Chinese forces in action was of immense proportions. In December the 8th Army was forced to withdraw after a massive Chinese offensive. A cease-fire proposal later that month was rejected by China because it did not mention China's demands for removal of foreign troops from Korea and for a Chinese seat at the UN.

On Christmas day 1950 Chinese troops crossed the 38th Parallel into South Korea, and by 4 January 1951 US/UN forces had to evacuate Seoul. Western concern at these developments was reflected in a UN resolution of 1 February which declared China to be the aggressor. The tide turned back in favour of America, and after months of heavy fighting the 8th Army once again crossed the 38th Parallel as the Communists were obliged to withdraw. At huge cost, both in lives and money, China and America seemed to be locked into a terrible deadlock.

Events then took a dramatic turn when the US Commander General MacArthur publicly criticised President Truman's tactics and the idea of a limited war. MacArthur wanted to be given the resources and permission to drive the Communists as far back as possible regardless of the original position. Within days, MacArthur was replaced as UN Commander by General Ridgway.

By the summer, a military solution to the problem of Korea seemed no nearer, while casualties steadily mounted. In June the Soviet Ambassador to the UN called for a cease-fire which, two days later, received some support from the Chinese.

July–December 1951
Between July and December 1951, armistice talks took place on an irregular basis, although the fighting continued. The move towards peace was interrupted at the start of 1952 when a major dispute over the exchange of prisoners of war held up the peace talks. America responded to this deadlock in the summer of 1952 by carrying out a major bombing raid. During June fresh Chinese military moves took place, but on 17 June a revised demarcation line (border) agreement was signed. The way was now clear for the end of the war and on 27 July 1953 an armistice was signed at Panmunjom.

SOURCE 13

The following excerpts came from a book by Max Hastings, a British journalist who observed the Korean war at first-hand.

This passage reveals the contrast between America's perceived military might and the reality of the 'under-strength infantry battalion' he was travelling with as they faced Communist forces for the first time.

In the early hours of 5 July 1950, 403 bewildered, damp, disorientated Americans sat in their hastily dug foxholes on three Korean hills, looking down upon the main road between Suwon and Osan. The men of 1/21st Infantry had been in the country just four days ... Ever since, they had been moving north in fits and starts – by train and truck, sleeping in sidings and schoolhouses, amid great throngs of refugees crowding roads and stations. Some men were sick from the local water ... All of them were savaged by mosquitoes. They learnt that Korea stank literally of the human manure with which the nation's farmers fertilised their rice paddies ... They knew that the communist North Koreans had invaded the anti-communist South on 25 June, and had been striking ruthlessly southwards ever since, meeting little opposition from Syngman Rhee's shattered army. They were told that they themselves would be taking up defensive positions somewhere in the path of the enemy, as far north as possible ...

This was 1950, when vast economic wealth, possession of the atomic bomb and the legacy of victory in the Second World War caused America to be perceived as the greatest power the world had ever seen, mightier than the Roman Empire at its zenith, or the British a century before. Yet now, on a hill in Korea, the first representatives of United States military power to meet communist aggression on the battlefield were the men of a mere under-strength infantry battalion which faced annihilation as a military unit ... The Americans were softened by years of inadequate training and military neglect, bewildered by the shock of combat, dismayed by the readiness with which the communists had overwhelmed them, and the isolation in which they found themselves. As men saw others leaving the hills, they hastened to join them fearful of being left behind. 'It was every man for himself', said Lieutenant Day. 'When we moved out, we began taking more and more casualties ... Guys fell around me. Mortar rounds hit here and there. One of my young guys got it in the middle. My platoon sergeant, Harvey Vann, ran over to him. I followed. "No way he's gonna live, Lieutenant." Oh, Jesus, the guy was moaning and groaning. There wasn't much I could do but pat him on the head and say, "Hang in there." Another of the platoon sergeants got it in the throat. He began spitting blood ... For the rest of the day he held his throat together with his hands. He survived, too.' The retreating Americans abandoned arms, equipment; sometimes even helmets, boots, personal weapons. Cohesion quickly vanished ... They reached American positions on 10 July, five days after the battle of Osan, utterly exhausted, their feet agonisingly swollen. By the time they returned, they discovered that any shortcomings in their own unit's performance on 5 July had already been outstripped by far less honourable, indeed positively shameful, humiliations suffered by the other elements of the American 24th Division in its first days of the war, as the North Korean invaders swept all before them on their bloody procession south down the peninsula. And all this flowed, inexorably, from the sudden decision of the United States to commit itself to the least expected of wars, in the least predicted of places, under the most unfavourable possible military conditions.

In October 1950, Chinese forces began to pour into North Korea. Here Max Hastings records the reaction of one American unit facing an attack by the Chinese.

On the evening of 1 November 1950, Private Carl Simon of G Company, 8th Cavalry, lay in the company position with his comrades, speculating nervously about the fate of a patrol of F Company, which had reported itself in trouble, 'under attack by unidentified troops'. As the darkness closed in,

SOURCE 14

Max Hastings' accounts of the 8th US Cavalry's encounters with Communist forces tell a different story to this newspaper photograph, originally published with the following caption:

'Going quietly – Chum?'

The scene as a member of the United States 8th Cavalry Regiment takes a Communist prisoner during a recent assault on an enemy hill position in Korea – where the battle for freedom continues against the aggression of the North Korean and Chinese reds.

they heard firing, bugles and shouting. Their accompanying Koreans could not identify the language, but said that it must be Chinese. When a wave of yelling enemy charged the Americans out of the gloom, firing and grenading as they came, no effective resistance was offered. 'There was just mass hysteria on the position,' said Simon. 'It was every man for himself. The shooting was terrific, there were Chinese shouting everywhere, I didn't know which way to go. In the end, I just ran with the crowd. We just ran and ran until the bugles grew fainter.'

The following analysis of the United Nations' role in the Korean War reveals the unique circumstances in which the UN banner came to be used in a war 'in pursuit of [the] ideological and political objectives of the USA'.

Yet it was also self-evident that for the United Nations, the Korean commitment was an experience that would never be repeated. UN forces might be granted an international mandate to carry out policing and peace-keeping tasks around the world. But never again was it conceivable that such a mandate would be granted for a military commitment, in pursuit of ideological and political objectives. Even in the summer of 1950, it was only the accident of the Soviet boycott that made the UN vote possible, sending troops into Korea. The relatively small number of countries which then possessed UN membership, most of them sympathetic towards the United States, accepted American leadership in going to war for Korea. But only sixteen members provided any measure of military support, none of whom could properly be called non-aligned. The Korean War was fought by the United States, with token support from her allies in the capitalist world. Within months of the outbreak, these allies were displaying their dismay at the economic and military cost, and uncertainty about the merits of the regime they were committed to defend ... It is a measure of the desperate economic plight of Britain, in contrast to booming post World War II America, that the Korean War and the rearmament programme that it provoked drove the country to the brink of financial crisis.

The Korean War, Max Hastings, 1987.

SOURCE 15

This photograph was taken at the height of the Korean War in the winter of 1951.

The explosion in the background has been caused by an air attack, the soldiers in the front of the picture are now moving in on the target. The photograph was released by the Americans to show the close co-ordination between air and ground units of the US Marines.

Knowledge and understanding

Use pages 138 to 141 to investigate the following questions.

1 Explain the importance of the 38th Parallel in the Korean war.

2 Why did President Truman decide to become involved in the UN?

3 What factors made it possible for the USA to secure the UN Security Council's condemnation of North Korea's aggression?

4 In what ways did the internal war in Korea become an international conflict?

5 Was the Western opposition to the Communists in Korea being led by the UN or the USA?

6 Explain why the events of October 1940 were of such importance in the Korean war.

7 Why did the Chinese enter the Korean war and what impact did their intervention have?

8 Explain why General MacArthur and President Truman were in such disagreement over the Korean war.

9 Why was the peace process for bringing the Korean war to an end so difficult?

10 To what extent was the Korean war a successful operation for the UN?

The United Nations in action: The Congo

Between 1960 and 1964 the UN became involved in by far the biggest and most expensive operation it had ever undertaken. At the peak of its involvement it had stationed 20,000 troops in the former Belgian colony of the Congo (now Zaire).

The crisis flared up in the summer of 1960. On 30 June the Congo became independent from Belgium. However, four days later a mutiny in the ranks of the Congolese army (the Force Publique) led to a total breakdown of law and order. Many Belgians who had remained in the Congo were now subjected to violent attacks. The Belgian government announced that in order to protect its people it would send troops into the Congo. The crisis intensified with the announcement on 11 July that the wealthiest part of the Congo, Katanga province led by Moise Tshombe, wanted to be independent from the rest of the Congo.

On 12 July Joseph Kasa-Vubu, the President of the Congo, and Patrice Lumumba, the Prime Minister, made a joint request to the Secretary General of the United Nations for a military force to remove Belgian troops and restore Katanga province to the rest of the Congo. The Security Council responded by calling for Belgium to withdraw its troops, and by sending in its own peace-keeping force to supervise this operation. The UN also performed a major role in providing emergency relief and medical care through its agency, the World Health Organisation.

The Belgians quickly withdrew and it seemed that the UN force had secured a major victory. However, the restoration of Katanga to the remainder of the Congo turned out to be much less straightforward. The Katangese authorities were desperate to hold on to their independence and hired foreign mercenaries to support them in their struggle. These paid soldiers now subjected the UN forces to a sustained attack, lasting for almost a week. Finally, the Security Council took the unprecedented step of authorising UN soldiers to use force and to eliminate the mercenaries.

Although the UN eventually achieved its objective, the UN's actions produced bloodshed which shocked and antagonised those who thought that a peace force should achieve peace without using force.

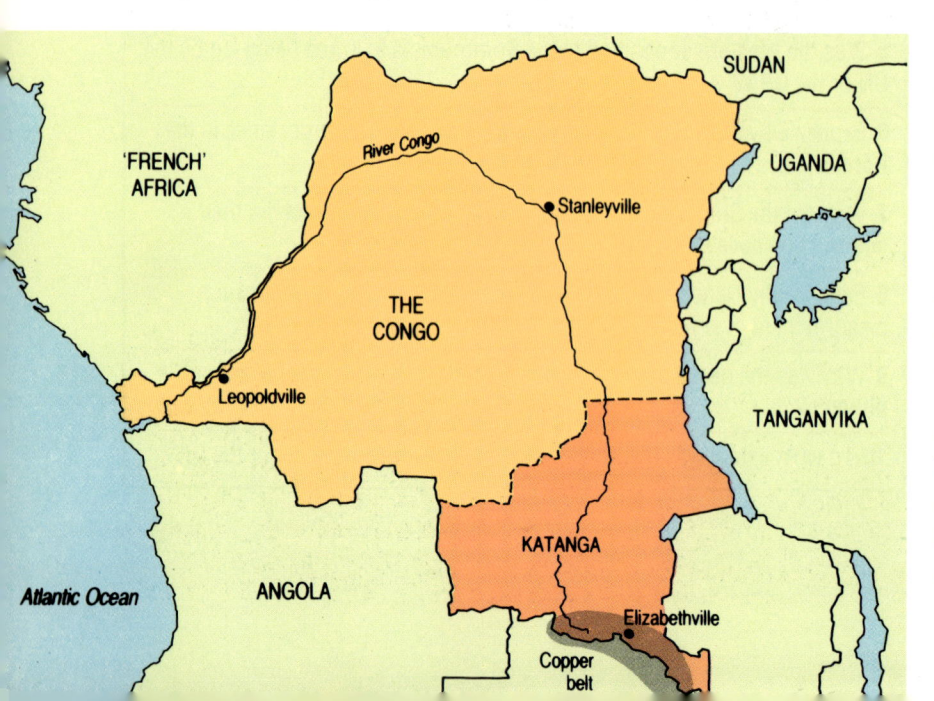

SOURCE 16

This photograph shows Swedish members of the UN peacekeeping operation in action in Elizabethville in the Congo in East Africa. The picture gives some idea of the scale of the relief operation which the UN faced in the Congo from 1960 onwards.

The United Nations and disarmament

Since the destruction of Hiroshima in 1945, the spiralling arms race has presented the UN with massive problems. Between 1945 and 1985 governments spent more money on arms than at any time in history. At the same time, the massive increase in the world's population has meant that well over a quarter of the world's population are close to starvation. The line taken by the United Nations is that the shortage of food and resources in developing countries has been caused by the overspending of the superpowers on weapons.

The competition between the Soviet Union and the United States has been by far the most important part of the arms race. The weapons have improved dramatically in terms of power, reliability and accuracy. So within forty years of the first atomic explosion, the world was awash with weapons of mass destruction. In 1984, for example, the United Nations estimated the world stockpile of nuclear weapons to be equivalent to around 15 billion tons (1,500 megatons) of TNT. It was calculated that this provided the superpowers with an explosive capacity estimated to be 5,000 times greater than that used during the entire Second World War. By 1984 it was estimated that Russia and America possessed around 16,000 missile carrying warheads in addition to a vast number of shorter-range and tactical nuclear weapons situated in areas of potential conflict. Ironically then, it has been the two most powerful members of the United Nations which have contributed most to the arms race which the UN itself condemns.

On 9 December 1981 the General Assembly declared that the first use of nuclear weapons would be the gravest crime against humanity, for which there could be no possible justification or pardon. The UN has used its agencies to alert nations to the potential impact of a nuclear war (**Source 18**).

In 1984, the WHO (World Health Organisation) carried out a major study

SOURCE 17

The arms race between the USSR and the USA was characterised by suspicion and distrust.

In this Soviet cartoon the barrels of the missile launcher are labelled: The Plague, Cholera and Typhus. Meanwhile, at the front of the vehicle the US Secretary of State, Dean Acheson, alongside the UN Secretary General Trygve Lie, is saying: 'The USA does not use chemical weapons'. The Soviets in particular were suspicious of UN disarmament initiatives, which they often felt to be pro-US propaganda.

SOURCE 18

The civilian casualties would outnumber the military ones: millions could die and a similar number be subjected to severe biological, physical and psychological damage which may make those surviving envy the dead. A one megaton nuclear explosion on a city with a population of one million could kill over 300,000 and leave another 380,000 in need of medical aid.

The Economic and Social Consequences of the Arms Race, United Nations, 1983.

on the catastrophic consequences of the use of nuclear weapons, not just on the Soviet Union and America but for the entire planet. The report concluded that in all-out nuclear war, it was possible that as many as 1,000 megatons of nuclear weapons could be exploded globally. Ninety per cent of this explosive would be detonated in Europe, Asia and North America, with the remainder in Africa, Latin America and Oceania. It was likely that half of the world's population would instantly become victims. It was estimated that 1.5 billion could die and 1.1 billion could be injured. The survivors would face a future of radiation sickness, disease, plummeting global temperatures, contamination of food and livestock and starvation.

The UN has also committed itself to persuading countries to slow down and ultimately reverse the arms race. However, as the UN itself acknowledges, it has had limited success in this area: The pace of technological innovation and the resulting improvement and sophistication of nuclear weapons systems have occurred much faster than the achievements of disarmament efforts.

UN Handbook

SOURCE 19

In 1986 the Secretary General of the UN, Perez de Cuellar, pointed out some of the problems which the UN has faced.

Certainly the United Nations system for ensuring international peace and security suffers from several shortcomings. There is a lack of unanimity among Governments, especially among the permanent members of the Security Council, and a lack of respect for, and a failure to co-operate with, its decisions.

UN Handbook

Limiting the arms race

Although the UN has always regarded nuclear disarmament as a priority, it has often found the arms race beyond its immediate control. As the arms race gathered pace, the UN took the step of declaring the 1960s, and then the 1970s, to be 'disarmament decade'. However, gestures such as this made little impact and the words often sounded rather hollow (**Source 19**).

DATAPOINT

Nuclear disarmament and arms limitation

1963 Partial Test Ban Treaty
Prohibited nuclear testing in the atmosphere. Signed by the Soviet Union, the United States and Great Britain.

1968 Nuclear Non-Proliferation Treaty
An agreement signed by countries with nuclear weapons agreeing not to assist other countries in developing them, and by countries without nuclear weapons pledging not to develop them. Countries refusing to sign included France, China, Israel, South Africa, West Germany, Japan.

1973 SALT 1 (Strategic Arms Limitation Treaty)
This was the result of bilateral talks between the two superpowers. The treaty was aimed at slowing down the arms race.

1979 SALT 2
Signed by Soviet leader Leonid Brezhnev and US President Jimmy Carter, this treaty was not ratified by the US Congress. However, most of its provisions were followed by the superpowers.

1982 START (Strategic Arms Limitation Talks)
These talks lead to the first agreements to make serious cuts in the superpowers' nuclear arsenals.

The SALT treaties and the policies of *détente* ('relaxing' of the Cold War) were mostly political gestures by the superpowers. Meanwhile, the arms race went on:

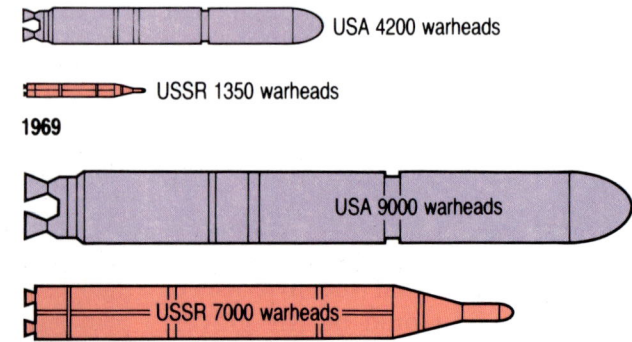

USA 4200 warheads
USSR 1350 warheads
1969

USA 9000 warheads
USSR 7000 warheads
1981

Despite the UN's diplomatic efforts to encourage nuclear disarmament, most arms control agreements have taken place directly between the countries possessing nuclear weapons (see **Datapoint: Nuclear disarmament and arms limitation treaties** opposite). However, despite the signing of numerous treaties, the Cold War nuclear arms race continued, with the superpowers developing new weapons systems as quickly as they agreed to dismantle existing ones. The multilateral agreements were weakened by France and China refusing to sign the Partial Test Ban and the Non-Proliferation Treaty, and by the fact that countries such as Israel and South Africa possessed nuclear arms technology 'in secret' and therefore were not included in the negotiation process.

In addition to the limitation of nuclear testing there has also been some progress in the limiting of chemical and biological weapons and nerve gas. Generally though, the lack of trust and co-operation between the superpowers meant that progress was slow and the UN proved completely unable to break into this cycle of superpower rivalry. Although the superpowers both made much of *calling* for peace in speeches and propaganda, they continued to pour money into developing new arms systems. Meanwhile, the UN contended that as long as weapons of mass destruction existed, there was a chance that they would be used – either in war, or by accident!

The economic and social programmes of the UN

There can be no doubt that the cost of the arms race has had a heavy impact on the people of the developing world. The United Nations has always placed a great emphasis on economic and social conditions. In the immediate aftermath of the Second World War the people of post-war Europe experienced terrible hardship. In particular the UN provided aid for the thousands of European refugees who were without homes and means of support. The UN helped to reconstruct war-torn areas and provide help for the welfare of children in devastated countries. The United Nations International Children's Emergency Fund (UNICEF) was created by the General Assembly in 1946 to provide relief for suffering children in the aftermath of the War.

The World Bank, the UN's most important financial agency, has also played a vital role in the United Nations' various programmes of social development. From 1945, the World Bank was heavily involved in helping developing countries, concentrating at first on the construction of roads, railways and power facilities (**Source 20**). Education has also been a priority so that between 1960 and 1982, school enrolment in the developing world doubled, with almost 400 million new places being added, thanks to UN involvement. In Africa, the UN has invested huge sums on tree planting programmes, fertilisation schemes and combating the spread of the continent's deserts.

SOURCE 20

The World Bank in action: a road building programme in Kano State, Nigeria.

More recently the World Bank has adjusted its role by trying to involve the poorer people of the world more closely in their own programmes, providing them with funds to develop their own agricultural techniques, water and sewerage facilities, and low-cost housing. By the 1980s, average annual World Bank expenditure in this area reached over £10 billion, bringing the UN's total spending on economic aid to more than £100 billion.

The UN has also raised public and governmental awareness of issues such as famine, human rights, deforestation and the rights of women in work. In addition, it has examined the political causes of these problems, and highlighted the connection between the arms race and global poverty (**Source 21**). However, the UN as a whole has shown a greater desire to take action on these issues than its most powerful member nations.

SOURCE 21

Over 1,200 million people all over the world ... remain undernourished; yet less than one half of one per cent of the global military spending in 1980 alone would have been sufficient to pay for all the equipment needed to increase food production and approach self-sufficiency in food-deficient, low-income countries by 1990. An additional allocation of a mere $200 million – the price of two strategic bombers of the latest type – to the annual budget of the United Nations Educational, Scientific and Cultural Organisation (UNESCO) would enable it to free the world from illiteracy in less than a decade.

The Economic and Social Consequences of the Arms Race, United Nations, 1983.

Knowledge and understanding
Debate

The two most important members of the UN Security Council have been the USA and the USSR. They have spent immense amounts of money on the arms race. Much less money has been spent on the aid to the Third World. The motion you have to debate is therefore:

The UN is morally responsible for the problems faced by the developing countries

a Choose two people to speak for the motion.
b Choose two people to speak against the motion.
c The rest of the class are to ask questions and raise points with the four main speakers.
d A vote should be taken at the end of the debate to decide whether the class agrees or disagrees with the motion.

The UN and decolonisation

Colonies: A change in world opinion

The Second World War had a tremendous impact in terms of the attitude of the major powers towards colonialism. The War had been fought to preserve political freedom. It was obviously wrong for Germany to invade and take control of other countries, such as Poland. Yet at the end of the War virtually a third of the world's population, mainly in Africa and Asia, lived under foreign rule.

The British, French and Dutch empires spanned the globe. How could it be right for this to continue? Surely the native peoples of Asia and Africa were now entitled to independence and self-rule? The UN Charter firmly committed the world's new peacekeeping organisation to support decolonisation (**Source 22**).

The Charter stated that one purpose of the UN was:

> To reaffirm faith in fundamental human rights, in the dignity and worth of the human person, in the equal rights of men and women and of nations large and small ... [and to] ... Develop friendly relations among nations based on respect for the principle of equal rights and self-determination of peoples, and to take other appropriate measures to strengthen universal peace.

SOURCE 22

When the United Nations was established in 1945, 750 million people – almost a third of the world's population – lived in Territories that were non self-governing, dependent on colonial Powers. Forty years later, fewer than 3 million people have yet to achieve political self-determination or independence, and more than 80 Territories, former dependent colonies, have gained their independence, and joined the membership of the United Nations.

Everyone's United Nations: A Handbook on the work of the UN, 1986.

The UN and decolonisation: Rhodesia / Zimbabwe

The colony of Rhodesia

Towards the end of the 19th century the continent of Africa was carved up by the European colonial powers, each seeking the profit and political prestige of running an empire (see page 164). The greatest empire builder in British history was called Cecil Rhodes. He had travelled to southern Africa with the objective of bringing as much of the continent into the British Empire as possible. Attracted by the prospect of finding huge diamond deposits, Rhodes travelled into the area which Africans knew as Zimbabwe.

With an armed group of pioneers Rhodes brutally crushed an uprising by the Shona tribe who already inhabited Zimbabwe. Even though the Shona people had an important history and culture they were regarded by the European settlers as savages.

In 1889 Southern Rhodesia, a landlocked territory of 389,115 square kilometres in south-central Africa, came under the control of the British South Africa Company under a royal charter. In 1923 the United Kingdom Government annexed Southern Rhodesia to the Crown and granted the settlers internal self-government. The country, named after Cecil Rhodes, was a white man's country in which discrimination ran through every aspect of life:

- The Land Apportionment Act took the fertile land from the blacks and gave it to the whites.
- Towns and cities were exclusively for whites. Blacks had to live on reserves or in African Workers' Compounds.
- When they were employed in a town, black people were not even allowed to walk on the pavement.
- Black workers were paid exceptionally low wages.

The Second World War and its aftermath

Despite their lack of rights and the discrimination against them, thousands of black Africans fought and died for the Commonwealth in the Second World War. Those who returned home in 1945 found that nothing had changed. Post-war Rhodesia experienced a period of booming business and great prosperity for the whites. Encouraged by the wealthy lifestyle, more than 50,000 white immigrants moved to Rhodesia after the War. Yet all of this wealth rested with a tiny minority of the population. Blacks outnumbered the whites by a ratio of 12 to 1.

The growth of black resistance

During the 1950s segregation remained complete. In shops, whites were always served first. Segregation applied to public transport and lavatories and blacks were excluded completely from most bars and restaurants. If a black person said a word of criticism they could be arrested and held without trial.

The white community, however, was governed by fear as well as prejudice. As black consciousness began to grow, the whites' fear was that concessions would

SOURCE 23
The parliament house in Salisbury (now Harare), capital of Rhodesia. This building was put up by black people, but it was an all-white parliament that sat here until Zimbabwe gained majority rule in 1980.

lead to more and greater black rights. This would eventually lead to equality and the end of white rule.

A black nationalist movement was now emerging which was determined to put an end to the discrimination. The Zimbabwe African Peoples Union (ZAPU) came to prominence with the slogan, 'one man one vote'. The Government's response came in 1962 when ZAPU was declared illegal.

Black resistance had been driven underground but it could not now be extinguished. It was now that the UN began to focus increasing attention on the struggle in Rhodesia. In 1961, the almost completely European electorate of Southern Rhodesia approved a new constitution, which was agreed to by the United Kingdom. Black people were almost completely without the vote. In 1962 the UN General Assembly declared that Southern Rhodesia was a non-self-governing territory under the Charter. The UK now tried to bring about the independence of the territory. The UN asked the UK to suspend the 1961 constitution, to draft a new constitution based on one person, one vote, and not to grant independence until this had been done.

Meanwhile, in Rhodesia events were escalating. The white clamp-down on ZAPU, in which thousands were held without trial, inflamed black opinion. In 1963, a new organisation, the Zimbabwe African National Union (ZANU) emerged. At first, it took a non-violent approach with strikes and demonstrations. Then, under the influence of black nationalists like Robert Mugabe, ZANU's tactics changed. Large white farms and factories were petrol bombed. Soldiers were trained in secret locations. African nationalism was growing in strength and determination.

However, the white leadership, headed by Ian Smith, was just as determined to hang on to white rule. Smith's tactic was for Rhodesia to break away from UK authority so that white rule could be preserved. Smith declared that blacks would not rule Rhodesia in a thousand years. Events took a dramatic turn when on 11 November 1965, the white minority regime made a unilateral declaration of independence (UDI).

The UDI was immediately condemned by the United Nations and the United Kingdom. A week later the Security Council called on the UK to 'quell this rebellion of the racist minority'. In addition, the UN called on all states to ban the supply of arms and military equipment, and to do their utmost to cut off trade with Rhodesia, including an embargo on oil and petrol. For the first time in the history of the UN the Security Council now imposed selective mandatory sanctions. This meant that all members were obliged to take part. Although Rhodesia was land-locked and heavily dependent on foreign trade and oil, the sanctions did not break Smith's resistance. The whites would not give in and were still provided with many essential supplies by South Africa and Portugal.

In May 1968 the Security Council stepped up the pressure, extending the sanctions to include all exports and

SOURCE 24

White security forces survey the charred remains of a pregnant woman and five of her children. They have been burnt alive in their mud hut by an attacker who locked them inside the hut and set the thatch alight.

Such scenes of brutality became commonplace in Rhodesia with a white army trying to contain black freedom-fighters and increasing violence between rival guerilla groups.

imports with the exception of medical and educational supplies and, in special cases, foodstuffs. Yet the real battle for the future was taking place in the jungle, bush and towns of Rhodesia. The armed struggle of the black people took the form of guerilla warfare, with the first reported clash between them and the regime's security forces taking place in April 1968. The UN now called on all its member states and agencies to give all their assistance to the freedom fighters. From 1976 the war intensified. The white government imposed harsh penalties on anyone suspected of offering support to the guerillas and sometimes whole villages were destroyed. The fighting lasted for 13 years, during which time at least 30,000 people were killed and up to a million made homeless.

From 1970 onwards the UN General Assembly frequently condemned the UK's failure to take steps against Smith's illegal regime. In November 1975 the UN demanded that the white regime stop executing freedom fighters and release all political prisoners. In addition, the UN condemned Rhodesia's recruitment of mercenaries and urged members to prevent this taking place in their countries. In April 1976 the Security Council called for the further expansion and tightening of sanctions.

It was a combination of the black guerilla resistance, UN sanctions and world opinion, in that order, which finally brought the white government to the conference table.

The Lancaster House Agreement

On 10 September 1979 the UK informed the General Assembly that it had successfully called a Constitutional Conference at Lancaster House in London to negotiate the introduction of majority rule in Rhodesia. On 21 December the Lancaster House Agreement was signed. It led to:

- An immediate cease-fire
- The drafting of a new constitution which would establish genuine majority rule
- Free elections
- The end of sanctions

In February 1980, elections, supervised by the UN and conforming to the Lancaster House Agreement, took place, resulting in Robert Mugabe becoming President (**Source 25**). On 18 April Zimbabwe became independent and on 25 August it became a member of the United Nations.

Knowledge and understanding

Use pages 147 to 149 to investigate the following questions.

1 Explain why Rhodesia was regarded by white Europeans as such a valuable colonial possession.

2 What problems did black people in Rhodesia face during the period of colonial rule?

3 Write a speech to be made by a nationalist in the 1960s describing the injustices faced by the black people of Rhodesia and explaining why you feel that freedom and independence will eventually come.

4 Summarise the role played by the UN in helping to bring independence to Zimbabwe. To what extent could this be described as a success for the UN?

SOURCE 25

Robert Mugabe, President of Zimbabwe since it gained full independence in 1980.

8 European Unity: 1945–1975

'Do you think that the United Kingdom should stay in the European Community?'

On 1 January 1973 Britain joined the EEC. Just over two years later in June 1975 the people of the United Kingdom were asked to vote in a referendum, which would decide whether or not they stayed in Europe.

They voted as follows:

Yes   17,378,000   67.2%
No   8,470,000   32.8%

How would you vote on this issue?

Perhaps you feel strongly that the UK's future belongs at the centre of Europe. On the other hand you may take the view that the UK's independence and unique character is under threat from closer ties within the European Union (the new name for the EEC). Or it may be that you have no idea how you would answer this question and have little knowledge of European issues. Regardless of your answer it is a fact that our membership of the European Union affects each and every one of us.

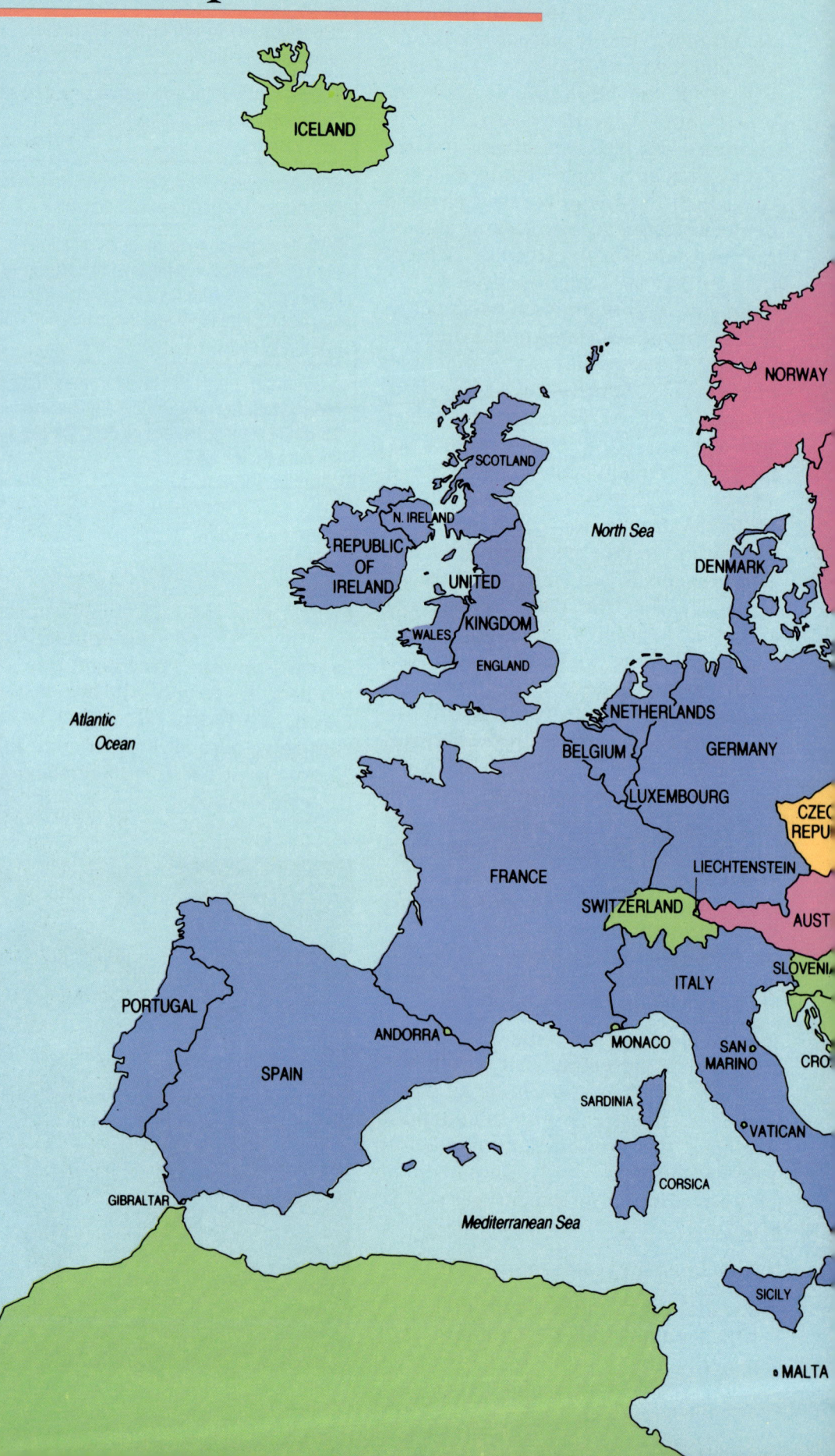

Europe, early 1994

- ■ European Union (EU member state)
- ■ Application to join EU under consideration
- ■ Association agreement with EU

The New Europe

Before we examine the background to the moves towards European unity, it is vital to be familiar with the political map of Europe in the late twentieth century.

This map was drawn after the revolutions in Eastern Europe and the collapse of the Soviet Union. But the map of Europe is always changing. For instance, on this map the borders within what used to be Yugoslavia (which included Bosnia-Herzegovina, Croatia and Macedonia) were changing as the map was being drawn, due to the civil war in that area.

Activities

- Familiarise yourself with this map.
- Test your knowledge of exactly where countries are.
- Work with a friend, by covering up names of certain countries and seeing if your friend can identify them.
- Do you know which countries were part of the Soviet Union and the Communist-controlled 'Eastern bloc'?

Europe: divided or united?

In 1989, the Berlin Wall, the most powerful symbol of division in Europe, was torn down (**Sources 3 and 4**). Since 1961 the people of Berlin had been physically divided between East and West. One side of the Wall had seen firm Communist control, a low standard of living and a lack of freedom. On the Western side, as far as the East Berliners were concerned, there was a very high standard of living and personal and political freedom. So when the Wall came down, the move was greeted with great optimism. It seemed to be the end of the division which for so long had split the people of Europe into two.

Just as important, the old division of Europe into two massive power blocs of East and West also began to crumble. The Soviet Union, which had seemed to exercise permanent control over Eastern Europe, rapidly disintegrated into separate states.

But when had the division between East and West begun? The division of Berlin and Europe was, in many respects, a consequence of the Second World War.

SOURCE 1

Britain before decimalisation and before entry into the EEC.

This market stall in Camden Town, London is showing the old prices which were used in Britain.

The old currency used: **£** pounds; **s** (or **/-**) shillings; **d** pence.

In the photograph 1/6 means 1 shilling and 6 pence.

The old currency was quite complicated:

£1 = 20 shillings
1 shilling = 12 pence
(so £1 = 240 pence)

However, people who had used this system all their lives coped very well with its complexities and found it very difficult to make the change, even though the decimal system was simpler.

DECIMAL CURRENCY BOARD

When you go decimal shopping, remember

10/- = 50p
2/- = 10p
1/- = 5p

So sixpence equals 2½p

SOURCE 2

When it was first introduced, decimal currency had to be carefully explained to the British public. One old penny was not worth the same as a new penny. People wanted to be able to compare the new prices to the old. There were only 100 pence in a pound now, compared to 240 pence in the pound before. The pound was still worth the same.

In this poster people are told that:
1/- (1 shilling) = 5p (5 new pence)

The division of Europe

Even before the defeat of Hitler, new lines of division began to be marked on the map of Europe. The Soviet Union soon took control of the Baltic states of Latvia, Lithuania and Estonia and parts of Germany. Poland was extended at the expense of Germany. Germany and Austria were divided into occupied zones by Britain, the USA, the USSR and France. Berlin, the former German capital, was similarly divided (see page 106).

American involvement in Europe

In 1946 the Americans offered to provide Europe with a huge programme of aid, based on money, food and medicine. This was known as the Marshall Plan.

By 1948 the massive injection of US aid had begun to make its mark (**Sources 3 and 4**). America continued its efforts to revive the German economy, believing that stability and democracy would result. However, when the Western zone of Germany introduced a new strong currency, Stalin responded with a blockade of Berlin. By the time Stalin abandoned the blockade, the division of Germany had become a reality. In September 1949 West Germany formally became a separate state called the Federal Republic of Germany. East Germany also became a state in its own right as the German Democratic Republic, but it remained under close Soviet control. At the same time, Poland, Czechoslovakia, Hungary, Romania, Albania and Bulgaria were also effectively under the control of the Soviet Union. The division of Europe into two power blocs was virtually complete.

SOURCES 3 AND 4

Marshall Aid in action.

This picture shows new construction taking place in Berlin, using money from the Marshall Aid programme. The project being developed here is an office building and shopping centre on Berlin's main high street, the Kurfürstendamm.

The emblem of the European Recovery Programme paid for by Marshall Aid shows the Stars and Stripes, and was stamped on every relief package sent abroad under the ERP so that Europeans would know where the help was coming from.

DATAPOINT

Berlin, symbol of a divided Europe

1945
At the end of the Second World War the Allies agree to treat Berlin as a separate entity within the Reich. The city is divided into four sectors and governed jointly by America, the Soviet Union, Great Britain and France.

1948
East-West tension flares up over Berlin.

24 June 1948
The Soviets respond to currency reform in the Western zones by imposing a blockade which cuts off land routes through East Germany to West Berlin.

1948-49
The Allies mount an 11 month airlift during which the city's population of around two million survive solely through supplies brought in by air.

12 May 1949
The Soviets lift the Berlin blockade.

1953
Stalin's death is followed by a popular uprising in Berlin against Soviet rule, which is quickly crushed.

SOURCE 5
Measures have been taken ... in the interests of peace in Europe and security of the GDR [East Germany] and other socialist states.

Broadcast by East German radio on 13 August 1961.

SOURCE 6
The day after the East-West Berlin border was closed: *The Daily Telegraph*, 14 August 1961.

SOURCE 7
Two thousand years ago the proudest boast in the world was *Civis Romanus sum*. Today, in the world of freedom, the proudest boast is *Ich bin ein Berliner*. There are many people in the world who do not understand what is the great issue between the free world and Communism. Let them come to Berlin, and there are some who say in Europe and elsewhere that we can work with the Communists. Let them come to Berlin.

President Kennedy in Berlin, June 1963.

European Unity: 1945–1975 **155**

1955
The Federal Republic of Germany (West Germany) becomes a fully independent state, but the Allies retain special rights in Berlin.

January 1949 – June 1961
Approximately 2.6 million refugees flee from East to West Germany.

July – August 1961
Around 45,000 people cross from East to West.

13 August 1961
The border between East and West Berlin and between West Berlin and the surrounding East German territory is closed, leaving 13 controlled crossing points.

14 August 1961
The Brandenburg Gate is closed on a 'temporary' basis.

17 August 1961
Communist workers put up a two metre high concrete barrier across the Potsdamer Platz and at other key crossing points.

22 August 1961
Crossing points now down to six, with a 100 metre wide 'no man's land'. The Wall now surrounds West Berlin.

Knowledge and understanding

Use pages 152 to 155 to investigate the following questions.

1 Explain in your own words why the Berlin Wall has been described as a symbol of the division of Europe?

2 Discussion: What practical problems do you think were created when the Wall which had divided East Berlin from the West was suddenly removed?

3 Consider the material concerning the development of NATO and the Warsaw Pact. Work in pairs for this exercise. The first person has to describe these developments from the Western point of view, and the second person has to take the Soviet view. Therefore, the first account might describe the formation of NATO as an understandable security measure, whereas the second version might portray it as an act of aggression.

SOURCE 8

For most west Europeans now alive, the world has always ended at the East German border and the wall; beyond lay darkness ... The opening of the frontiers declares that the world has no edge any more. Europe is becoming whole ... When the Berlin Wall was built in 1961, the East Germans claimed that by sealing the Berlin border they had saved the peace. Then as now, the outrush of people to the West was threatening to bring about the collapse of the East German state, but in an utterly different world, it was the world of Nikita Khrushchev and that collapse would have brought the two superpowers into violent collision.

Neal Ascherson, *The Independent*, 10 November 1989.

SOURCE 9

Berlin, November 1989. The Wall comes down after dividing the city for 28 years. The demolition of the Wall by the people of Berlin marked the end of the Cold War. Millions hoped that it heralded a new era of co-operation.

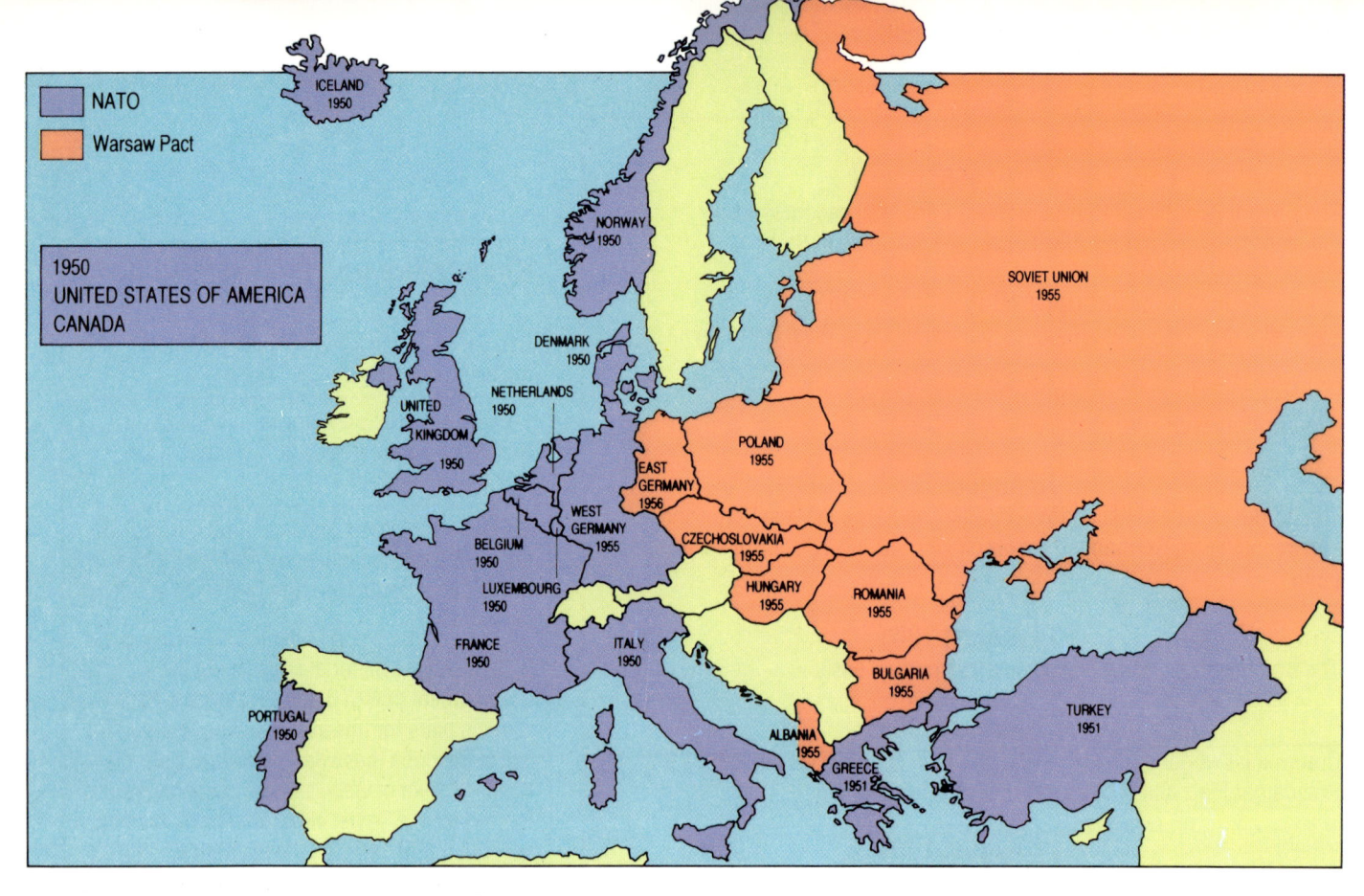

Membership of NATO and the Warsaw Pact by 1956

West versus East: NATO and the Warsaw Pact

Clearly the impact of war on Western Europe was a vital factor in the subsequent moves towards some degree of European unity. The countries of Western Europe had been brought together in their resistance to Hitler. Perhaps their future security and defence would be best served by them coming together more formally in the post-war years.

In March 1949 Britain, France, Belgium, the Netherlands and Luxembourg signed a defence pact, known as the Treaty of Brussels. A year later, the need for defence and security felt by the Western European nations led to the formation of the North Atlantic Treaty Organisation (NATO).

Because NATO appeared to put the people of Western Europe under the protection of the military might of the USA, this Treaty was warmly welcomed by most people in the West. Yet in the East, the Soviet Union saw the new group as a major threat. One of the side effects of NATO was to make the Eastern bloc even more tightly knit.

The Soviets responded to NATO with the establishment of COMECON, the Communist economic co-operation organisation, set up in January 1949. The Eastern bloc also organised a military alliance, signing the Warsaw Pact in May 1955 (**Source 10**).

With the establishment of the two power blocs, the chances of Europe ever being united seemed virtually over. The 'Cold War' between East and West looked set to last for a very long time.

SOURCE 10

The Warsaw Pact has been a crucial instrument of Soviet domination. The ostensible reason for its formation was West Germany's entry into NATO, but it was superimposed on a series of bilateral agreements between the Soviet Union and the relevant states which already tied them to the Moscow line. The treaty helped to legitimise the stationing of Soviet forces outside Soviet territory and provided a framework through which pressure – and in notorious cases force – could be used to prevent deviations from the socialist path. Stalin recreated Eastern Europe in a Soviet image (and many of its leaders in his own).

Lawrence Freedman, *The Independent*, 15 December 1989.

European Unity: 1945–1975 **157**

The European Coal and Steel Community

Whilst the main motive behind NATO was military security, the tendency towards general co-operation extended to areas such as industry, trade and the economy. As early as 1946, Churchill had put forward the idea of a more unified Europe. In a famous speech in Zurich, Churchill spoke of a United States of Europe. However, for Churchill European unity was a way of bringing France and Germany closer together to prevent future antagonism which could lead to another war. Britain was not part of his vision of Europe as he held the traditional view that Britain's future lay more with the Commonwealth and Empire.

Benelux

On 1 January 1948 Europe's first free-trade market, known as Benelux, was established between Belgium, the Netherlands and Luxembourg. With standardised prices, welfare, wages and taxes, and, later, free immigration and movement of labour, this agreement represented closer co-operation than the EEC. In 1960 the Benelux states entered into full Economic Union. These agreements meant that in many ways Benelux could be considered as a single unit within the European Community.

Robert Schuman

Of all the speeches made on the theme of European unity, Robert Schuman's speech of 9 May 1950 was perhaps the most important of all. The French Foreign Minister proposed pooling the production and consumption of steel and coal and setting up a European

SOURCE 12

The Common Market opened for coal and iron ore in February 1953, and for steel in May. Here a train, bearing flags of the member states, carries the first load of coal across the border between France and Luxembourg.

SOURCE 11

Robert Schuman (*standing*) presents his plan to pool Western Europe's coal and steel resources to delegates from six nations: France, Belgium, Italy, Luxembourg, the Netherlands and West Germany. Seated is Jean Monnet, who helped devise the ECSC and became its first president.

The European Coal and Steel Community (ECSC) – The first European Community

The ECSC included the following institutions:
- The High Authority: to take decisions on behalf of ECSC members
- A Council of Ministers: representatives of the member states
- A Court of Justice: to settle any disputes between members
- A Parliamentary Assembly: to give advice but without legislative powers.

This structure was, in many respects, to be followed by the statesmen who devised the EEC.

The benefits of co-operation in the ECSC

- For the post-war rebuilding of industry and housing, steel was of vital importance, from building machinery to the construction of blocks of flats.
- The ingredients of steel are coal and iron ore. As Germany had massive coal reserves and France had major iron ore deposits, this co-operation would be of great benefit to both nations.
- The ECSC removed the costs and complications of tariffs and customs regulations.
- The new institutions of the ECSC were European rather than national, and so represented a major step towards political co-operation in Europe.
- Some authority had been passed from state governments to a European body (the High Authority of the ECSC).
- The ECSC provided the foundations for the European Economic Community.
- The ECSC aided the recovery of the German economy after the War.
- Germany and France were co-operating with each other rather than engaging in hostilities.

Knowledge and understanding

Use pages 157 to 158 to investigate the following questions.

1 Explain how Winston Churchill's experience as Britain's Prime Minister during the Second World War might have led him to become an advocate of a united Europe?

2 What advantages of increased European unity were put forward by Robert Schuman?

3 Why do you think the European Coal and Steel Community was of such great importance for the future development of Europe?

4 Explain why it was that Britain did not join the European community at this stage.

5 What were the disadvantages to Britain of the decision not to join the ECSC?

organisation for this purpose. This economic move would also bring France and the Federal Republic of Germany together politically. Schuman had lived in the Lorraine region of France and had witnessed the horrors of warfare between France and Germany. It was his vision of future co-operation which led to this fundamental step towards a united Europe.

The detailed plan for the European Coal and Steel Community was drawn up by Schuman and Jean Monnet, who became the president of the ECSC High Authority. The Federal Republic of Germany, Italy and the Benelux countries supported the French plan. So the ECSC came into being in April 1951 with the signing of the Paris Treaty.

Britain and the ECSC

Great Britain was invited to join the ECSC but chose not to become so closely involved with the economies of its European neighbours. The Labour Prime Minister, Clement Attlee, did not even feel that the issue was of sufficient importance to consult his Cabinet. In June 1950 he confirmed that the UK's other interests meant that membership could not be contemplated. These 'other interests' consisted of Britain's continuing commitment to the Commonwealth and close relationship with the USA. The Conservatives criticised the decision but were themselves divided. As historian Keith Robbins puts it:

> Both parties looked on ... as the initiative in Western Europe slipped steadily away from London.

Meanwhile, the ECSC nations flourished, benefiting from increases in trade in general, and steel in particular. The miracle of West German economic recovery had begun.

The European Defence Community (EDC)

Encouraged by the success of the ECSC, the members began to look for new ways of working together. As with the ECSC, the development of the EDC was closely linked to Western fears of Communism.

The birth of the Common Market

The Messina Conference 1955

Meeting at Messina in June 1955, the foreign Ministers of the Six (Germany, France, Italy, Belgium, the Netherlands and Luxembourg) looked at what further steps to a united Europe might be taken. The Belgian Foreign Minister, Paul Henri Spaak, an ardent supporter of the European movement, was asked to chair a committee which looked at proposals for a common market in all commodities traded between the Six, and the possibility of close co-operation in the field of atomic energy. The general approval given to the Spaak Report led to the drawing up of the Treaty of Rome, signed by the Six on 22 March 1957 (**Source 14**). This established:

- The European Economic Community (the EEC, also known as the Common Market)
- The European Atomic Energy Committee (Euratom)

In effect, all customs controls and barriers to trade within the Community were removed. Each member state could buy and sell freely to a potential market, at that time, of 170 million customers. It was envisaged that eventually people would be completely free to travel and work within the Common Market. This economic union might then ultimately lead to political union.

SOURCE 13

A turning point in the history of Western Europe. On 25 March 1957 Ministers from six nations signed the Treaty of Rome, which established the EEC.

The EDC's ultimate aim was to be the integration of the armed forces of Europe. This dramatic move would also have necessitated an unprecedented level of political co-operation and so it was proposed to move quickly towards a political community as well. The Europeans were moving too rapidly and too ambitiously and by the summer of 1954 these far-reaching plans were rejected. However, this did not mean that plans for closer economic integration were to be abandoned.

Key elements of the Treaty of Rome

The main themes in the 248 articles of the Treaty of Rome were:
- A desire to harmonise the members' economic and social policies to promote stability, a better standard of living and economic growth.
- Removal of all barriers to the free movement of goods, labour and capital within the Community.
- Ultimately, common policies for agriculture and transport.
- Fifteen years to be allowed for harmonisation to take place.
- EEC-wide institutions to be developed such as the European Commission, the Council of Ministers, the European Assembly and the Court of Justice.

Britain refuses to join the Common Market

In 1957 Britain was given a second opportunity to join the Six, this time as a member of the EEC, but once again the offer was turned down.

Several factors contributed to this decision:

- Britain was an island, not part of the European mainland, and its people and leaders had a very strong sense of their unique history, culture and customs. Many felt this national pride was threatened by the European movement.

- Britain was more closely tied to the USA, through language and history, than Europe.

- Britain was still the head of the Commonwealth and the Dominions and as such was clinging on to memories of the British Empire. To fall in with the rest of Europe, it seemed to some, would imply reduced status.

- Britain still had strong economic ties with its colonies and former colonies. These trade links would be damaged if Britain moved towards Europe.

- Britain had not been invaded during the two World Wars and so was less concerned about organisations designed to break down nationalism and reduce the risk of another war.

By now, Britain was under the leadership of a Conservative Prime Minister, Harold Macmillan. In 1957 he made it clear that, like Attlee before him, he would not take the UK into the Common Market. Instead, Britain came up with an alternative proposal.

The European Free Trade Association (EFTA)

The signing of the Treaty of Rome obviously raised the prospect that Britain could be excluded from a huge tariff-free area. Through the Organisation for European Economic Co-operation (the OEEC) Britain now tried to devise an alternative to the Common Market. The outcome was the European Free Trade Association (EFTA), set up by the Stockholm Agreement of January 1960 – a simple trading partnership, between Britain, Austria, Denmark, Sweden, Switzerland and Portugal. Yet, while the Common Market had grown to more than 200 million, the population of EFTA only amounted to 90 million.

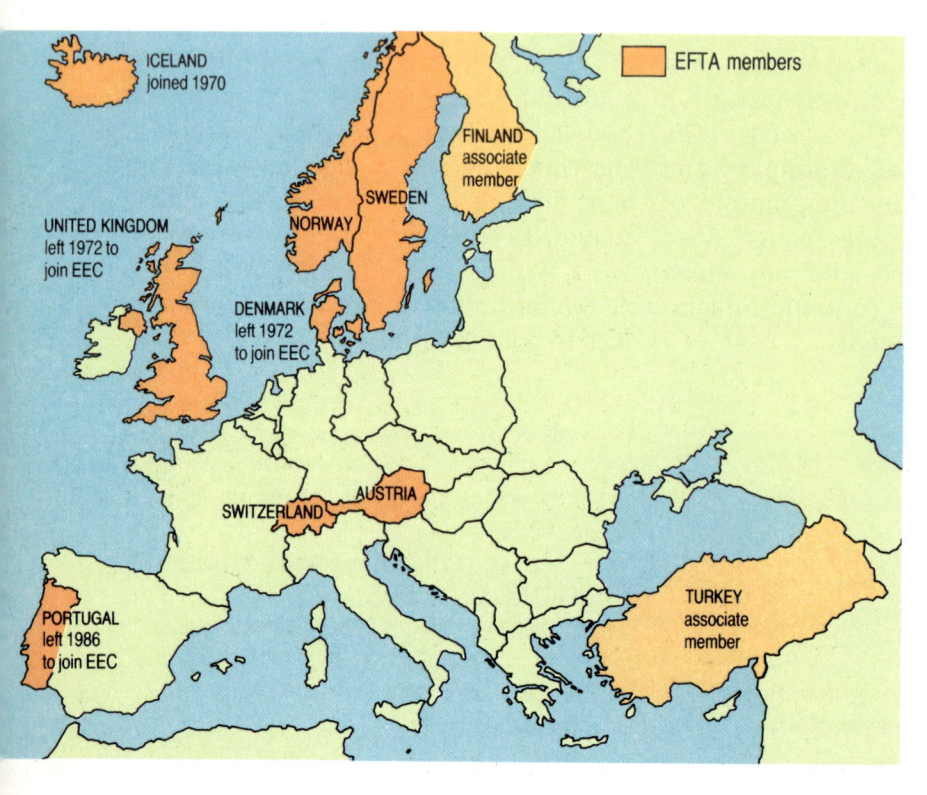

SOURCE 14

The attitude in London varied between open scepticism about the European efforts and frank hostility to them.

A major reason for this detachment was that British Ministers persisted in seeing the United Kingdom as one of the Big Three, automatically entitled to a leading role in any international conference. Britain retained its permanent seat on the Security Council of the United Nations.

Keith Robbins, *The Eclipse of a Great Power: Britain 1870–1975.*

Membership of the European Free Trade Association (EFTA)

Eastern Europe

Meanwhile, the economic growth spurred by the Common Market contrasted with the inefficiency and stagnation of the Communist regimes. The emphasis which Stalin placed on defence spending meant that the people of Eastern Europe faced the continuing prospect of food shortages, long waiting lists for consumer goods, poor quality manufactured products and excessive bureaucracy. While Stalin lived, no protest could be voiced.

Stalin's death in 1953, and the subsequent criticism of his regime by Khrushchev, seemed to herald better things. For the first time, people in East Germany and Poland violently protested about their poor standard of living.

In Hungary, protests for democracy led to a new government being set up by Imre Nagy in 1956. Nagy took moves to end the one party system and, on 31 October, announced his intention to withdraw from the Warsaw Pact. In response, the Russians and their allies in Hungary denounced Nagy's government as 'fascist counter-revolutionaries' and sent in tanks to restore Communist rule.

However, it was more difficult to control the less obvious protest which was taking place in East Germany. There, people were streaming across the border from East Berlin to the West in search of political freedom and decent living standards. In 1961, the Communists erected the Berlin Wall (see **Datapoint: Berlin, symbol of a divided Europe** on page 154).

The sense that Europe was more divided than ever was confirmed when the so-called 'Prague Spring' of 1968 was throttled by a Soviet invasion. The Czech leader, Alexander Dubček had tried to set out his vision of 'socialism with a human face'. The Soviet leader Leonid Brezhnev was not prepared to allow this to develop and Dubček was quickly replaced by a hard-line Communist. The East-West division of Europe was still firmly in place.

SOURCE 15

Czechoslovakia: 5 Soviet Union: 4

Meeting in the wake of the Soviet armed repression of Dubček's 'Prague Spring', tempers frayed in this tightly fought ice hockey match in February 1969. But the Czechs were able to gain a momentary victory over their Warsaw Pact 'allies'.

A change of direction

The Suez Crisis of 1956 (see page 110) marked a crisis of confidence in Britain's position as an international power. The decline of Britain's international status was also marked by economic problems. Gradually, politicians began to realise that Britain should shift its focus from the Empire and Commonwealth, and that it would be better off within the Common Market than outside it.

Britain's first application to join the Common Market

Towards the end of 1960 Prime Minister Macmillan informed the Cabinet of a new British drive towards increased unity with Europe. In February 1961 Edward Heath, a senior government minister, was sent to discuss the issues with the European Council of Ministers. In July the Cabinet unanimously agreed to seek British membership of the EEC. In August of that year Britain made a formal application to join the EEC, and in October the complex negotiations between Britain and the Six began. Heath, as leader of the British delegation, promised that Britain was now ready to become a 'full, whole-hearted and active

European Unity: 1945–1975

member of the European Community' because,

> faced with the threats which we can all see, Europe must unite or perish. The United Kingdom, being part of Europe, must not stand aside.

Despite this change of heart, Britain's application was to be completely derailed. Just as Britain thought that it was about to be accepted, its application received a stunning blow.

At a press conference in Paris on 14 January 1963, the powerful French President, Charles de Gaulle, remarked that Britain's ties with the Commonwealth and the USA meant that it was not ready to join the Community. He declared that regardless of what the British Government said, the British people as a whole were not 'European' in their outlook. While there was some truth in de Gaulle's remarks, it is probable that his objection was based more on concern that France's position in the Community would suffer with British membership.

SOURCE 16

Here the British cartoonist Vicky satirises Macmillan's attempt to join the EEC in 1963.

The figures in the cartoon are (*from left to right*) Charles de Gaulle, Konrad Adenauer (the German premier) and Harold Macmillan.

Consider how the view put forward by this cartoon differs from the view that de Gaulle vetoed (rejected) Britain's application for purely selfish reasons.

"HE SAYS HE WANTS TO JOIN – ON HIS OWN TERMS..."

1967: The second British application to join the EEC

In April 1966 the British government, now led by Labour Prime Minister Harold Wilson, announced that it intended to apply for a negotiated entry to the European Community. During the winter of 1966 and the spring of 1967, Wilson and his Foreign Secretary George Brown toured the capitals of Western Europe trying to build up support for their application. Once again, though, the French President stood in the way. This time, de Gaulle ruled out Britain's application because of the financial and economic problems which it faced at this time. He contrasted the favourable economic performance of the Six with the poor state of the British economy. What was to be gained for the Six by accepting British membership?

The third and successful application

In 1970 Edward Heath became Prime Minister. The Conservative leader, who had already proved himself to be a committed European, was determined to finally secure British membership of the Community. Meanwhile, de Gaulle had been replaced with the more amenable figure of Georges Pompidou (de Gaulle died in 1970). Heath's chief negotiator, Geoffrey Rippon, was an effective operator and Heath himself established a good relationship with President Pompidou. The outcome was Britain's entry into the EEC, along with Ireland and Denmark, being fixed for 1 January 1973 (**Sources 17 and 18**). It was agreed that a transitional period of four years would be needed, which would enable Britain to come to terms with the Common Agricultural Policy and to negotiate with its Commonwealth partners. In addition, a detailed formula was devised to eventually settle the level of Britain's contribution to the Community budget.

The move towards European unity was increased when Greece joined the European Community in 1981, to be followed by Spain and Portugal in 1986.

Knowledge and understanding

Use pages 159 to 163 to answer the following questions.

1 Imagine that it is March 1957 and the Treaty of Rome has just been signed. You have to prepare a radio news report to sum up this key event. You need to devise:
a A news headline
b A summary of the key points
c An explanation of why the Treaty of Rome is of such great importance

2 Look at the reasons why Britain chose not to join the European Economic Community in 1957. Working on your own at first, place these factors in what you consider to be their order of importance. Begin with what you think is the most important point.
Next, compare your list with a partner and then with the rest of the class. To what extent is there agreement?

3 Would you agree that these factors show that Britain's leaders made the right decision in not joining the European Community at this time?

4 Explain the importance and aims of the European Free Trade Association.

5 To what extent did membership of EFTA successfully compensate for Britain not joining the EEC?

6 Explain why it was that Britain refused to join the EEC in 1957 but then tried to join only three years later.

7 What factors led to the first British application to join being rejected in 1963?

8 What differences can you see between the first British application to join and the second one in 1967?

9 To what extent were the reasons why the second application was rejected the same as those given for the first rejection?

10 Why was it that the third application was successful after the first two had been so completely rejected?

SOURCE 17

This photograph taken in 1972 shows a landmark in British history in the 20th century:

Edward Heath signs for Britain to join the European Economic Community. On the left is Foreign Secretary Sir Alec Douglas Home, and on the right is Britain's chief negotiator, Geoffrey Rippon.

SOURCE 18

Following Edward Heath's signing to join the EEC, Britain's membership commenced on 1 January 1973.

With the start of the New Year, Britain became part of an enlarged Common Market. This is how the national newspapers announced Britain's entry that morning.

9 The End of the European Empires

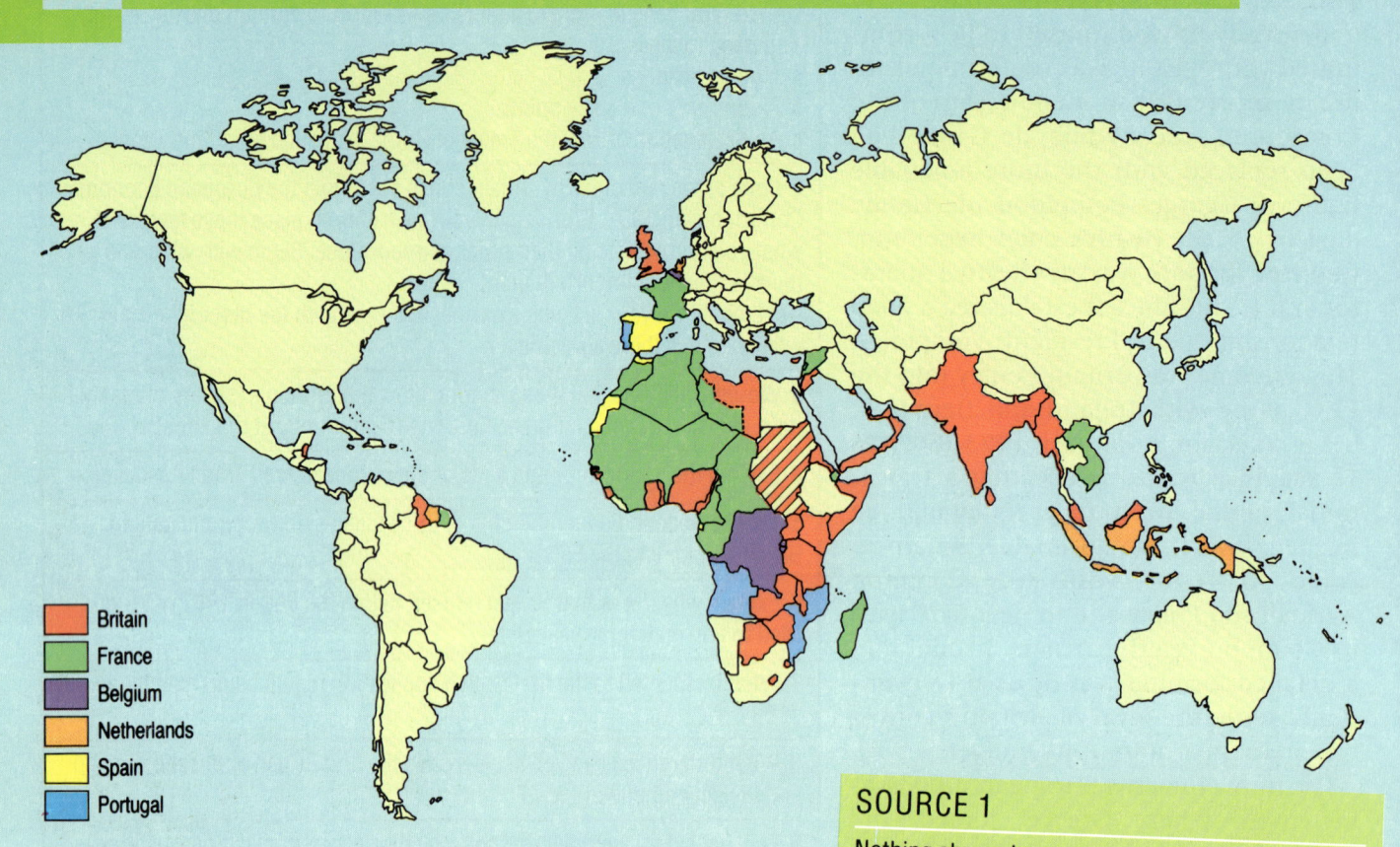

Map legend:
- Britain
- France
- Belgium
- Netherlands
- Spain
- Portugal

The European Empires

As the map above shows, before the Second World War the globe was dominated by the colonial empires of the nations of Europe. These empires had been built up through the 19th Century for a number of reasons:

Resources
- Mineral wealth, such as gold and diamonds in South Africa
- Agricultural land suitable for growing 'cash crops' – coffee, tobacco, sugar cane, etc.
- Cheap labour for manufacturing industry, especially textiles and clothing

Profit
The colonies' resources meant:
- Many opportunities for European investors to make their fortune
- A flow of cash into the economies of the colonial rulers
- Trade on terms dictated by the colonialists

Politics
- Colonies were regarded as a sign of power and prestige
- The lack of arms amongst the native peoples made them vulnerable to Western invaders
- The Europeans claimed that white people were fundamentally superior to the native Africans and often justified their colonial conquests as missions to 'help' native peoples to become 'civilised'

SOURCE 1

Nothing showed more clearly the reduction in Europe's power in the world than the swift disappearance of European empires after 1945. At the beginning of the Second World War virtually all Africa and much of the Middle East and Asia were directly or indirectly controlled by Europeans. Forty years later the only remnant of these empires of any size still under European control was South Africa.

Martin Roberts, *Britain and Europe 1848-1980*, 1986.

This chapter is about the break up of the European Empires after the Second World War

- Why did these empires collapse so suddenly after 1945?
- What differences were there between the British decolonisation and the French experience?

To answer these questions, we shall focus on the British withdrawal from India and the war between France and Algeria. The British experience is also covered in the section on Zimbabwe in Chapter 7 (pages 147–9).

The British Empire

The impact of the Second World War

At first it seemed that the British Empire had survived the Second World War intact. If you compare the map on page 182 with the one opposite, you will see that in 1945 the Empire covered as large a part of the world as it had ever done. Yet it was on the brink of collapse. The reality was that the Second World War had a massive impact on the imperial powers.

Firstly, the Second World War dramatically changed attitudes towards colonialism. The War had been fought against Italy, Germany and Japan. These countries had attacked political freedom and invaded other countries in the name of racial supremacy. Yet the European empires had been founded on the rule of small white minorities over much larger numbers of non-white people. In 1945 virtually a third of the world's population, mainly in Africa and Asia lived under foreign rule. Millions of people in the colonies were denied political rights. By the end of the War many politicians and ordinary people felt that the colonial system was no longer acceptable.

Within the colonies, a small but rapidly growing number of non-Europeans were beginning to question the existence of the empires. These people took encouragement from the military defeats such as those inflicted by Japan upon the British and Dutch during the Second World War, which had shown that the colonial powers could be defeated. The massive cost of the War had drained European economies and would make any attempt to hold on to the colonies very difficult.

Meanwhile, the USA, Britain's major wartime and post-war ally, made clear that it disapproved of the empires. In addition, the Soviet Union was strongly opposed to Western colonialism. The scene was therefore set for the collapse of the European empires.

SOURCE 2

This painting shows the sheer scale of the British Empire in the early 20th Century. Under the Union Jack flag are a range of people from round the world ruled by Britain. The artist was reflecting the British view of the time that the colonies were fortunate to live under the 'civilising' influence of the British Empire.

SOURCE 3

Strange though it may seem, in 1870 a small group of islands off the mainland of Europe dominated a large part of the world. The 'British' were established in Newfoundland and New Zealand, Cape Colony and Calcutta, Nova Scotia and New South Wales, to name but a few ... A century later, with a few small exceptions, the British were confined to their islands. No other people in the modern world has experienced such a dramatic change.

Keith Robbins, *The Eclipse of a Great Power*, 1992.

THE PRINCE OF WALES HUNTING IN THE NEPAL TERAI – THE FIRST DAY'S SPORT: THE PRINCE'S BAG

SOURCE 4

Read the caption on this drawing from 1876. The Prince of Wales later became King Edward VII. In those days the British aristocracy took great pride in displaying the animals they had killed. How do you feel about this?

This 'sport of kings' continues today in the form of fox hunting.

India and Pakistan

The Republic of India is one of the great nations of the world. It covers a land area the size of Europe and, with more than 500 million people, its population is second in size only to China. Its three main regions, the Himalayas, the Northern Plain and the Peninsula, contain peoples with a wide range of languages, cultures, customs and beliefs. Its major cities include Calcutta, Madras, Bombay and Delhi. Although these cities contain some of the poorest areas on earth, India is of great significance in terms of agriculture and industry. Religion is of profound importance to the people of India. The vast majority follow the Hindu religion but there are also important minority groups of Muslims, Sikhs, Buddhists and Christians.

In the north-west corner of the Indian sub-continent is the Republic of Pakistan. This state has a population of more than 60 million people. The majority of these people are Muslims although there are sizeable minorities of Hindus, Buddhists and Christians. Important cities include Karachi, Lahore, Hyderabad and the capital, Islamabad. Key areas include the north-west frontier and the provinces of Sind and Punjab. To the north-east lies the disputed province of Jammu and Kashmir.

Today, relations between India and Pakistan are poor. Indeed, in 1971 when a war erupted between East and West Pakistan, India helped the East to break away from the rest of the country, creating the new nation of Bangladesh. Yet the fact that the name India is derived from the name of the River Indus, which flows through Pakistan, serves as a reminder that before independence, India and Pakistan were part of a single huge country. Until 1947 this was the India that was part of the British Empire.

On 15 August 1947, India was granted freedom from British rule and the two independent states of India and Pakistan were born. How did this move to independence come about, and what were its consequences?

The Jewel in the Crown

Historically, the Indian sub-continent was of enormous importance to the British. For over 300 years British merchants and traders had exploited the country's cheap labour, natural resources and mineral wealth. By 1850 the British East India Company was the dominant force in the Indian sub-continent. Following a series of wars, repressed mutinies and conquests, the government of India was taken over by Britain in 1858. The British government appointed a Viceroy to rule the country on behalf of the monarch. During the period of the British Raj (a word of Hindi origin meaning reign) the British ruled India with great pomp and splendour. For the British aristocracy, India was a land of beauty, mystery and riches. India was, in many respects, the most important part of the British Empire and became known as the 'Jewel in the Crown'.

Yet the wealth of the British rulers contrasted sharply with the urban deprivation and rural famines suffered by the ordinary people of India. Despite this, the British put forward the argument that the people of India were better off under their 'civilising' influence.

Certainly western technology and communications had a major impact on India. The British way of life also moulded the Indian education system and its civil service.

However, not all Indians were prepared to accept British rule. As early as 1857 the British had put down a major uprising which became known as the Indian Mutiny. In 1885 the British Government made a small concession by allowing the Indians to organise their first National Congress, which met in Bombay. At first this group was no more than a polite annual gathering, limited to a tiny minority of wealthy and well-educated middle class people.

The Indian nationalist movement grew in strength when more than a million Indians who had fought for Britain in the First World War returned home to find that they still had virtually no say in the way their own country was run. While Britain claimed to be fighting for democracy in Europe, it was clearly unwilling to extend these rights to the people of its own colonies.

Indian nationalism

Within the Congress Party a figure was emerging who would do more than anyone else to raise awareness of national Indian consciousness and highlight the injustices of British rule. He was Mohandas Gandhi.

Gandhi's objective sounded simple and yet it was of massive importance: he wanted to persuade the British to leave India. He aimed to turn the Congress Party from a small, well-educated elite into an organisation of mass resistance. Gandhi had set in motion an independence movement for all Indians. Central to Gandhi's beliefs was the idea that resistance had to be non-violent. The sheer power and moral force of his argument was only increased by actions such as the massacre of nearly four hundred peaceful Indian demonstrators by the British army at Amritsar in 1919. Gandhi was supported in his actions by the Congress leader, Motilal Nehru and his radical son, Jawaharlal. The struggle was to be a long and difficult one.

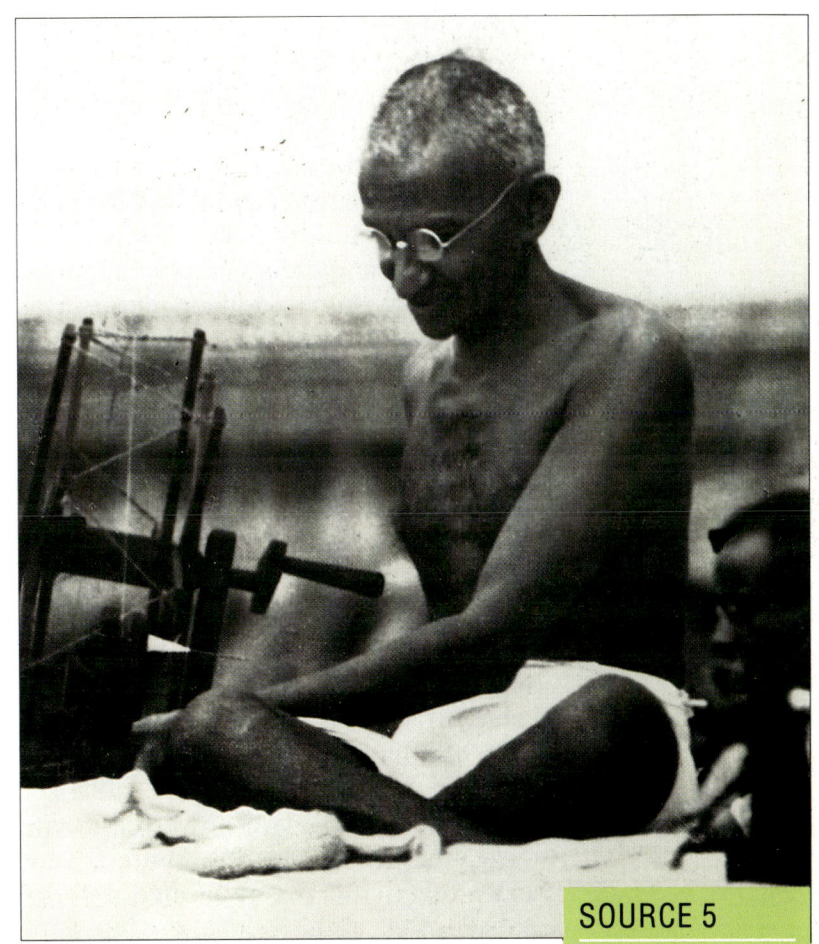

Despite British resistance and repression, Gandhi relaunched his campaign in 1930 with renewed vigour. In that year Gandhi staged a dramatic demonstration against the British government's unjust and unpopular monopoly of salt production. In a highly publicised move, Gandhi walked more than 200 miles to the sea, where he showed his defiance of the government by making salt. Not for the first time, Gandhi and other nationalists like J. Nehru were imprisoned. But by now it was clear that acts of repression could not damp down the flames of Indian nationalism. The British Government recognised this to some extent and changed tactics in 1935 by passing the Government of India Act. This allowed for new levels of participation by Indians in their own government and elections, particularly at a local level. To radicals such as the younger Nehru, however, this was simply too little too late.

SOURCE 5

Mohandas Gandhi, 1869–1948.

Gandhi believed passionately in the traditional way of life. He wore a home-spun *dhoti* (loincloth), and he can be seen here spinning thread to encourage fellow Indians to use home-made cloth.

SOURCE 6

Jawaharlal Nehru, became the first Prime Minister of India. This photograph was taken in 1956, it shows the Indian statesman with his daughter Mrs Indira Gandhi driving through the city of London in an open carriage. Indira Gandhi, in turn became the Prime Minister of India following her father's death in 1966. Mrs Gandhi was assassinated in 1984 and succeeded as Prime Minister by her son Rajiv Gandhi, but he too was assassinated during an election campaign in 1991.

In 1939 Britain entered the Second World War. So did India. Yet it was the British Viceroy who decided, without consulting the Indian people, that the Indian Army would support Britain and join the War. The Second World War was to have a profound impact; in this case, its outbreak and India's involvement had shown that Indian independence was still a long way off. Yet in other ways the War would serve to help the cause of Indian nationalism.

The role of religion in Indian politics

It is vital to bear in mind that not all Indian people shared the same religious beliefs. When war broke out in 1939 there were approximately 225 million Hindus in India, forming by far the biggest group and exercising control over large parts of India. However, there were also 92 million Muslims, who were particularly strong in the north of India. On many issues these two powerful groups were completely opposed. Matters were made even more complicated by the existence of a third, smaller, but very important group – the Sikhs, who lived mainly in the Punjab.

Gandhi and Nehru were both Hindus, but claimed that the Congress Party which they had developed could represent the views of all Indians, regardless of their religion or class. When Congress was not consulted about entering the War its members refused to support the British war effort. Instead Congress now launched the 'Quit India' campaign designed to force the British out. Millions of Hindus joined in the disobedience campaign which culminated in the 'Congress Rising' of 1942. With Britain already under severe military pressure from the Germans and the Japanese, the Indian uprising was stretching its resources to the limit. The revolt was costing millions of pounds in terms of physical damage and the massive expense of containing the uprising. At its height, 60,000 people were under arrest.

Britain was desperate for some kind of support in India. With the Hindus completely hostile, the answer seemed to lie with the Muslims. Led by Muhammed Ali Jinnah, the Muslim League announced from the start that it was fully prepared to support the British war effort. But the Muslims wanted something in return for this show of loyalty. Jinnah told Britain that the price of Muslim co-operation would be a British commitment to set up a completely separate Muslim state when the War was over, to be known as Pakistan. Jinnah knew that the British did not have much choice. His slogan was 'Pakistan or perish'.

When the War ended in 1945, a momentous change was at hand. The Conservative government which had led Britain through the War had always resisted colonial independence. In November 1942 Prime Minister Winston Churchill made his views clear:

> We mean to hold our own. I have not become the King's First Minister in order to preside over the liquidation of the British Empire.

However, in July 1945 the Conservatives were voted out of office. The election of a Labour government in Britain at last brought with it the prospect of independence for India.

Independence and partition

The replacement of the Conservatives by a Labour government under Prime Minister Clement Attlee paved the way for Indian independence. The issue now became not whether Britain would withdraw, but how and when. In March 1946 Labour sent a Cabinet mission to India to try to resolve these issues. Once again, the problem was that the Indian nationalists were still divided between the Hindu-dominated Congress and the Muslim League. The British met leaders from each of the groups and then proposed a new constitution to establish a free India. Its proposals were as follows:

- To preserve a united India
- To set up a central government with responsibility for major issues such as defence and foreign affairs
- To set up across India a network of provincial governments which would take all of the local decisions

It was obvious that the central government would be dominated by the Hindus but the local governments would represent the different groups in each area (eg Muslims in the north and Sikhs in the Punjab). The question was whether each of these groups would find these proposals acceptable. Many observers later concluded that it was Jinnah who did more to split India than anyone else. However, it is important to remember that to begin with Jinnah made it clear that he would accept the British proposals including a united India. Indeed, Jinnah announced that the Muslims demands had been met. British optimism that the plan would be unanimously accepted received a further boost when Jawaharal Nehru said that he would also accept the terms despite the fact that Congress would not control the areas with a Muslim majority. However, the plans were plunged into disarray by a press conference held by Nehru on 10 July 1946. In reply to a question, Nehru implied that he would accept the plan but also wanted to modify it. The Muslims reacted with alarm and suspicion to Nehru's statement, worrying about what changes a Hindu-dominated government might make to any constitution they agreed to.

Jinnah now decided upon a radical change in tactics. Previously he had co-operated with the British. He now feared that the British might underestimate how strongly the Muslim people felt about their own independence. In August 1946 the Muslims responded fervently to Jinnah's call for 'direct action'. Violence flared up in the communal areas where Muslims and Hindus lived close together. The worst outbreak was in Calcutta (**Source 7**).

In London, Attlee now feared that Britain was going to be caught up in the middle of a frenzied civil war. What had once been a marked reluctance to withdraw now turned into a headlong rush to get out. In September 1946 the Viceroy was authorised to set up an interim government, which he would lead, as a half way point to complete independence. By now, the Muslims were in no mood for what they regarded as an empty gesture. They refused to take part. The fact that the Hindus agreed to the new proposal only highlighted the divisions which now existed.

SOURCE 7

Calcutta police using teargas bombs during an attempt to set fire to a Hindu temple (24 August 1946). Five days' rioting left over 2,000 dead and 4,000 injured.

The End of the European Empires

SOURCE 8

The first meeting between Lord Mountbatten, 29th Viceroy of India (*left*) and Muhammad Ali Jinnah, leader of the Muslim League (5 April 1947).

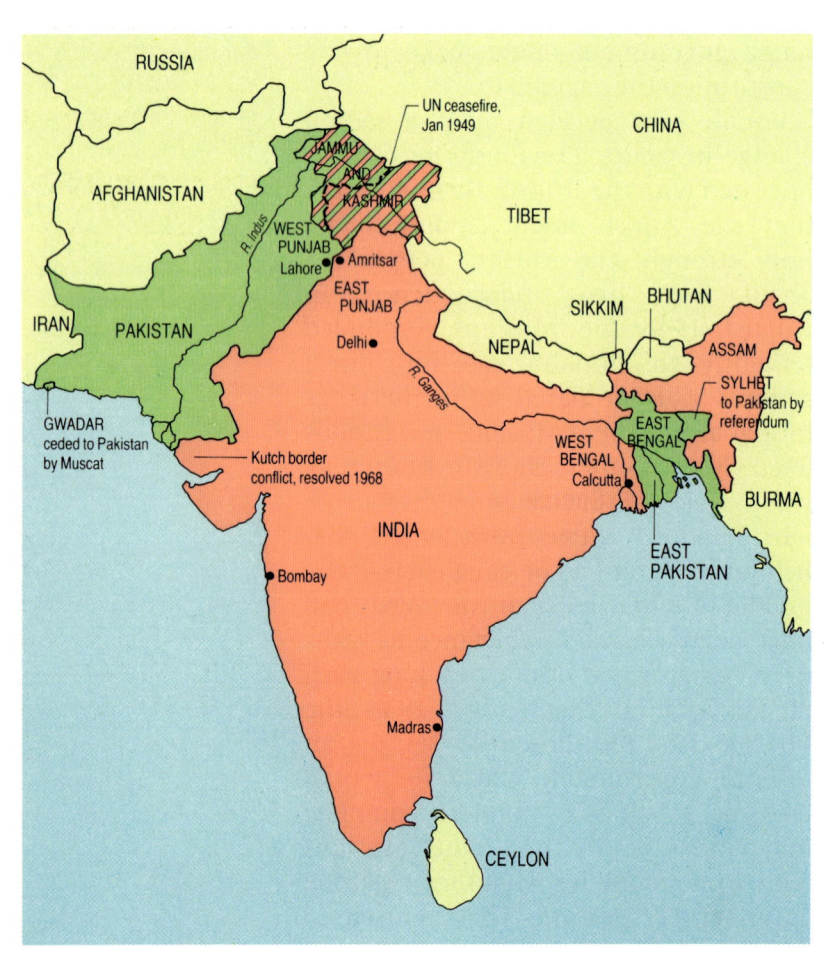

For tactical reasons the Muslims then announced that they would join after all. It was soon clear to all that the Muslims had simply decided that it would be easier to wreck this organisation from the inside than the outside.

In these difficult circumstances Britain now tried to regain the initiative. The old Viceroy was replaced by a new, dynamic figure, Lord Louis Mountbatten, who became the 29th Viceroy in India's history. He was destined to be the last Viceroy. When he arrived in Delhi to take up his new post this grandson of Queen Victoria was 47 years old and a skilled and experienced diplomat. Mountbatten immediately set to work and quickly struck up a good working relationship with Nehru. However, their co-operation only made Jinnah even more suspicious. He made it clear to Mountbatten that he did not trust him and the two men failed to get on. Jinnah now stated that nothing less than a separate Muslim state of Pakistan would be enough to protect his people from the dangers of a Hindu-dominated India. In February 1947 Attlee announced that by June 1948 Britain would be ready to withdraw from India and hand over power to a responsible body. However, the atmosphere of violence and tension soon led Lord Mountbatten to the conclusion that a united India would be impossible. He advised the government that British withdrawal would have to be accompanied by the division or partition of India. In addition, Mountbatten now persuaded the British government to bring the date of partition forward to August 1947. When this was accepted it left only 72 days to arrange for the division of an entire sub-continent. Even in a peaceful country it would have been hard to fairly divide up the finances, factories, armed forces, farm land and other resources in such a short time. In a country already torn apart by religious conflict it was virtually impossible.

The partition of India, 1947

The Punjab and Bengal

In most parts of the Indian sub-continent, a clear Hindu or Muslim majority determined whether they joined India or Pakistan. However, the provinces of the Punjab and Bengal contained large numbers of both Muslims and Hindus. It was in these two regions that the partition of India had its most violent consequences. In the Punjab a line of partition divided the state in two. Millions of Muslims now found themselves on the wrong side of the dividing line. Some six million Muslims migrated west from India to the new Pakistan. Meanwhile, 4.5 million Sikhs and Hindus fled to the east from what had now become Pakistan. Well over ten million people had been forced to leave their homes. As this two-way movement took place, violence erupted. This violence was particularly intense in cities such as Lahore, Delhi and Amritsar In Delhi, the victims of violence included Gandhi, who was shot while walking to his prayer ground on the lawn of his home.

In the first nine months after partition, more than 50,000 people were killed in the Punjab. Events in Bengal followed a similar pattern. Some Indians have estimated that the final death toll as a direct result of partition was approximately half a million. Mountbatten's estimate was that, of the total population of 400 million, probably 200,000 were killed.

On one issue there is widespread agreement: it was the haste with which the partition plan was introduced and carried out which was largely to blame for the level of suffering. To the British government, however, the main feeling was a sense of relief that the withdrawal from India had been achieved so quickly and that direct British responsibility for the Indian sub-continent was over.

SOURCE 9

On 15 August 1947, the flag of the Raj was hauled down forever from the viceroy's residence in New Delhi, less than six months after Mountbatten began his frantic period of summit diplomacy. India and Pakistan became independent states and full members of the Commonwealth. Earlier Burma had received its independence in late 1946, while Ceylon (later named Sri Lanka) also became a self-governing member of the Commonwealth in 1949. Britain's historic domain in south Asia had been abruptly liquidated. The withdrawal from India might well have been regarded as a national retreat, even a humiliation, after the lengthy three-hundred-year-old presence of the British in India, going back to the days of the old East India Company... In fact, the British reacted to the transfer of power in an almost matter-of-fact way... Indian civil servants and judges came quietly home ... Most tea planters stayed on after 1947... The explanation can only be that the processes of withdrawal from India had been long under way... and had been long anticipated. In practical terms, the advantages of the imperial connection for Britain remained, as indeed the Labour government had carefully planned. The defence ties continued... In financial terms, India remained a vital member of the sterling area.

Kenneth D. Morgan, *The People's Peace*, 1992.

Knowledge and understanding

Use pages 164 to 171 to investigate the following questions.

1 Which were the largest European empires before the Second World War?

2 Why had the powerful European countries been so attracted to the idea of building up empires?

3 To what extent and why was the appeal of the empires damaged by the impact of the Second World War?

4 Summarise the main historic and geographical features of
a India;
b Pakistan.

5 Explain in your own words:
a how these countries were once united;
b the partition of India.

6 Why was India of such great value and importance to the British?

7 Imagine that you are a British Civil servant in India. You have been asked to write a brief report:
a explaining what the nationalist leader Gandhi stands for;
b setting out the actions which Gandhi has taken;
c recommending what you consider to be the best tactics for dealing with the Indian nationalists.

Investigation

Why did Britain grant India independence?

SOURCE A

We have something more important than guns. We have truth and justice – and time on our side. You cannot hold down much longer three hundred and fifty million people who are determined to be free.

Mohandas Gandhi.

SOURCE B

The idea of a great country like India being treated as a chattel and her people utterly and contemptuously ignored was bitterly resented … one man, the Viceroy, and he a foreigner, could plunge 400 millions of human beings into a war without the slightest reference to them. There was something fundamentally wrong and rotten in a system under which the fate of millions could be decided in this way.

Jawaharlal Nehru, *An Autobiography*, 1962.

SOURCE C

There are only two links between the Muslims and the Hindus: British rule – and the common desire to get rid of it.

Muhammad Ali Jinnah.

SOURCE D

During the War, Winston Churchill, Britain's wartime Prime Minister and leader of the Conservative Party, reinforced his plans for India:

We ought to make it perfectly clear that we intend to remain rulers of India for a very long and indefinite period, and though we welcome co-operation from loyal Indians, we will have no truck with lawlessness.

SOURCE E

Stafford Cripps, the principle government negotiator in the lead-up to Indian independence, presents the options faced by the post-war Labour government:

After 1945 we were demobilising the British Armed Forces as rapidly as was possible, and that meant that the number of British troops which could be left in India and the East was being rapidly diminished.

At the same time, the Indianisation of the Indian Army was proceeding more rapidly than ever. What were the alternatives which faced us? First, we could attempt to strengthen British control in India on the basis of an expanded personnel and a considerable reinforcement of British troops. Such a policy would entail a decision that we should remain in India for at least another 15 to 20 years.

The second alternative was, we could make a further attempt to persuade the Indians to come together, while at the same time warning them that there was a limit of time during which we were prepared to maintain our responsibility while awaiting their agreement. One thing that was, I think quite obviously, impossible, was to decide to continue our responsibility indefinitely.

SOURCE G

A young Indian recalls the moment, sitting near a broken-down train in India, when he heard of the Labour victory in the British general election.

We sat there ... on this moonlit night and a radio was on. The news that the British Labour Party had won the election came. There were only two Indians and we didn't know each other – the rest were all British. we both got up and started dancing and embraced each other. These poor British ... were absolutely disgusted. They knew why we were celebrating – this meant that Britain would soon relinquish [give up control of] India.

THE ROPE TRICK

SOURCE F

Questions

Listed below are four factors which played a part in the British withdrawal from India.
- Increasing violence in India between different religious groups.
- The replacement of Churchill's wartime coalition by a Labour government.
- The activities of nationalist leaders such as Gandhi and Nehru.
- The inability of the British rulers to maintain control of India.

Place these factors in what you consider to be their order of importance, giving reasons for your decisions.

Compare your list with a partner's. How far were you in agreement?

Now discuss your findings as a group.

SOURCE H

Once talks began on the independence of India, the violence escalated. The different religious groups were all rallying for their position in the new political order and the British government became increasingly desperate to get out, rather than have this bloodbath on their hands.

A British river pilot, Radclyffe Sidebottom, witnessed these horrifying scenes on the Muslim League's 'day of direct action' of 16 August 1946.

You could see a crop of one religion or another who had been captured and tied, brought down to the river, being pushed down the bank into the river where dinghies with poles were pushing them under. You could see them being laid on their faces with their heads poking out over Howrah Bridge and being beheaded into the river, their bodies being thrown in afterwards. After the riot the river was literally choked with dead bodies which floated for a while, sank for a while and then, when the internal gases blew them up, floated again after three days. They were carried up and down the river by the tide, with vultures sitting on their bellies taking bits and leaving the rest to float ashore to be eaten by the dogs, the jackals and the vultures.

The collapse of the French Empire

War in Algeria

In 1830 French troops occupied Algiers, the capital city of Algeria, in North Africa. Forty years later they extended their control so that the whole country became a French colony. With the native Arab Muslim population conquered, more and more French people chose to settle in Algeria. By the 1950s approximately 1.25 million French settlers, or *colons* lived there. Yet the *colons* were still vastly outnumbered by 8.25 million Muslim Arabs. It was a situation which the native Algerians were no longer prepared to accept. They took encouragement from the recent experiences of some of the other countries struggling against colonialism:

- *1953*: Cambodia became independent from France.
- *1954*: The French suffered a humiliating defeat by the Vietnamese at Dien Bien Phu.
- *January 1956*: Sudan became independent (formerly under Anglo-Egyptian rule).
- *March 1956*: France recognised the independence of Morocco and Tunisia.
- *November 1956*: France and Britain were humiliated by Egypt in the Suez Crisis (see page 110).

Reasons why Algeria was different to the other colonies

Although the Arabs' desire for freedom and independence was very similar to the nationalist uprisings elsewhere in Africa, the French felt more strongly about Algeria than some of their other colonies.

SOURCE 11

Rebels in training: here we see a young Muslim woman practising with a sub-machine gun.

- The European population in Algeria had been there for a lot longer than in most other colonies.
- Algeria was physically closer to France than many other colonies.
- In the main cities the French population virtually equalled that of the Arabs.
- The French could not accept the idea of surrendering another colony after the humiliation in Vietnam.
- The senior French officers felt honour-bound to keep control of Algeria.
- Constitutionally, Algeria was regarded as part of France, voting in national elections and sending delegates to the French National Assembly in Paris.

The Revolt at Setif: 1945

On 8 May 1945, as the Europeans celebrated VE day, an Algerian uprising against the French flared up. Believing that the Second World War had been fought for political freedom, the Algerians attempted a revolt, centred on the town of Setif. However, the French reacted to the rising with great brutality and the revolt was bloodily suppressed. The nationalist leader Ferhat Abbas was arrested and the Algerian independence movement seemed to be over.

The Algerian war: 1954–62

However, on 1 November 1954 (All Saints Day) a new, much more serious, rebellion erupted. A bloody war had begun which was to last for eight years. By the time independence was granted in 1962, almost one in ten of the inhabitants of Algeria would be dead. An estimated one million Algerian Muslims lost their lives. Approximately one million European settlers were driven from their homes.

When hostilities first began in the Aures mountains in 1954 it made relatively little impact on the people of France. During the eight years of 'la guerre d'Algérie' as the French called it, or 'the Revolution' as it was known in Algeria, no declaration of hostilities was ever made.

The brutal guerilla actions of the Algerian revolutionaries, the Front de la Libération Nationale (FLN), shocked the French nation. However, the French public were equally alarmed by reports coming out of Algeria of the methods of torture used by the French army against Algerian guerillas (**Source 13**).

Political upheaval in France

As atrocities on both sides mounted, the political stakes grew higher. The government now found itself in an increasingly difficult position:

SOURCE 12

This horrifying account illustrates several aspects of the war in Algeria. First of all, look for the innocence and naiveté of the young French soldiers who at first regarded their military service in Algeria as something of an adventure. Secondly, consider the impact on the French army and the general public when they first heard details of the massacre at Palestro in 1956.

On 4 May 1956 the 9th Regiment d'Infanterie Coloniale battalion of reservists raised in the Paris region landed in Algiers. Just two weeks later one of its platoons, commanded by a thirty-year-old second lieutenant, Hervé Artur, was on Patrol at Palestro, a bare fifty miles south-east from Algiers. 'What a thrilling and marvellous life!' enthused Artur in an unfinished letter to his parents: It was a rugged, beautiful country cut by deep gorges, prompting one of the reservists to write to his parents, in a letter that was never sent: 'How good it would be to pass the holidays here!' Leaving the platoon sergeant behind at base, Second Lieutenant Artur set our for... Amal, with twenty one men. Shortly after passing through Amal the platoon ran into an ambush well prepared... evidently with the complicity of the villagers. Lying in wait behind rock, they caught the reservists at point blank range. Artur was killed immediately, and within a few minutes all but six of the platoon were wiped out. The survivors were dragged off by the FLN, but one by one the four wounded collapsed and were left by the wayside... when the patrol failed to return, the sergeant at base raised the alarm and that evening troops reached the scene of the massacre. At least two of the bodies had been atrociously mutilated; testicles cut off, disembowelled and the ventral cavities stuffed with stones. Further off one of the wounded was found, apparently despatched by the villagers, but no trace was ever found of the other three. The village itself was deserted...

The ambush of the twenty one roused a furore in France; these were the first reservists to die in the war, and it was the biggest single loss suffered by the army since the war began... it was brought home to France for the first time, and more sharply than anything else could, the cruel realities of the Algerian war, and in doing so strengthened the hand of those... arguing for a negotiated peace.

Alastair Horne, *A Savage War of Peace*, 1987.

SOURCE 13

As the following excerpts show, torture and brutality were continual features of the Algerian War.

'Often he would be confronted with a boukkara ... a Muslim with his head covered in a sack with eye-slits, who had broken under interrogation and was now acting as an informer.'

'If the suspect makes no difficulty about giving the information required, the interrogation will be over quickly, otherwise specialists must use all means available to drag his secret out of him. Like a soldier he must then face suffering and perhaps even death which he has so far avoided.'

'The most favourable method of torture was the gegene, an army signals magneto [generator] from which electrodes could be fastened to various parts of the human body ... it was simple and left no traces.'

If the one side practised unspeakable mutilations, the other tortured and, once it took hold, there seemed no halting the pitiless spread of violence ... it seemed as if events had escaped all human control.

'In Algeria ... all forms of horrible death are part of the war!'

Alastair Horne, *A Savage War of Peace*, 1987.

SOURCE 14

This street corner looks like a typical town centre anywhere in France but the large group of armed police tell us that this is Algiers.

Here we see police throwing stones which had just been thrown at them by rioters (December 1960).

- Whenever it stepped up military operations in Algeria the situation seemed to become more inflamed. A military victory against guerilla warfare seemed impossible.

- Any concession to the Algerians was immediately condemned by the French settlers (*colons*).

- The French army in Algeria became increasingly out of step with the government. They believed that their 'mission' of holding on to Algeria at all costs was not being backed up sufficiently by the government in Paris.

With no way out of the crisis, the French Fourth Republic was plunged into turmoil. A number of Prime Ministers in quick succession were forced to resign due to their inability to resolve the crisis. At times, between resignations, the country was left for days on end with no one actually in charge.

Then in May 1958, the army in Algiers itself rose up in revolt against its own government. Amid this upheaval, the former French leader, General de Gaulle, a highly respected figure, returned to lead the country out of disaster (**Source 15**). Appointed on 1 June 1958, de Gaulle had to use all of his political skill to end the crisis. He skilfully used the tactic of 'promoting' rebellious army officers away from where they could cause trouble for him in Algiers. At the same time, de Gaulle tried hard to build up a relationship with the Arabs, without offending the Europeans (**Source 16**).

Despite his political skill, de Gaulle had to face two further white revolts against him, firstly in the autumn of 1959 and secondly in April 1961. Even when these were crushed the French threat against de Gaulle remained through the secret terrorist group the 'Organisation de l'Armée Secrète' (OAS). This group aimed to kill de Gaulle and take control of Algeria. On 8 September 1961 the OAS carried out an assassination attempt against de Gaulle at Petit Clamart in France.

These acts only increased de Gaulle's

SOURCE 15

French President, Charles de Gaulle.

De Gaulle escaped to Britain after the fall of France, and in 1943 he became head of the Committee of National Liberation (the 'Free French'). He entered Paris in August 1944, and became President of the provisional government in 1945, but resigned in 1946. During the Algerian Crisis of 1958, he was asked by the National Assembly to head a temporary government. He won a referendum on setting up a new constitution, and was subsequently elected as the first President of the Fifth Republic in 1959. He was keen to work more closely with West Germany, and blocked Britain's entry to the EEC in 1962–3 and 1967 (see pages 161–62). De Gaulle was re-elected as President in 1965. He was re-elected again in 1968, but resigned in 1969 after losing a referendum on constitutional reforms.

determination to find a solution to the crisis. In the summer of 1961 peace talks between the French Government and the FLN at Evian broke down, but in March 1962, at the same location, the peace talks succeeded and an agreement was signed. It stated that French troops would gradually withdraw, although France could continue its nuclear tests in the Sahara and retain its air bases there for five years. On 3 July 1962 Algeria became an independent state for the first time in its history.

SOURCE 16

Historian Peter Calvocoressi summarises de Gaulle's role in bringing the war in Algeria to an end.

He probably saw the inevitable end. What happened was that, by a mixture of authority and ambiguity, he imposed himself upon the situation and gradually acquired the power to impose a solution upon it. This took him nearly four years. By doing enough to retain the initiative but not too much to reveal himself, he prevented potentially hostile groups from acting against him until it was too late.

Peter Calvocoressi, *World Politics since 1945*, 1968.

What was the importance of the Algerian War?

- The last of France's major colonial wars.
- The war gave birth to the new Algerian nation.
- It showed the effectiveness of guerilla warfare against a well equipped modern army. (This was to be repeated with the USA's experience in Vietnam.)

Knowledge and understanding

Produce a detailed comparison between the British withdrawal from India and the French withdrawal from Algeria. In your answer you will need to indicate similarities and differences between the two situations. Why, for example, were the French more determined to hold on to Algeria than the British were to keep control of India? Why did the war in Algeria last for so long, whereas the British withdrawal from India was relatively quick?

Why was France's loss of this colony so bitter?

- The *colons* were determined not to lose Algeria.
- The French army became obsessed with their sense of mission and honour.
- Having lost Vietnam the army was determined not to face another humiliation.
- The French government initially underestimated the depth of feeling on both sides.
- The French failed to meet, or even understand, the needs and aspirations of a Third World nation.
- The war brutalised both sides. One atrocity was followed by another. The French government lacked firm leadership until de Gaulle took over.
- France could not come to terms with the loss of its empire.
- The nature of the Algerian war made negotiations extremely difficult – the French army did not want its government to negotiate.

10 Destination Britain

DATAPOINT

People on the move, 1900–1976

Today, because of its mixture of race, colour and religion, Britain is often described as a multi-cultural society. During the 20th century people from all parts of the globe moved to Britain and made their homes in this country. At the same time, many left these shores and settled in other parts of the world. The movement of people in this way is called migration. This Datapoint shows the main immigrant groups who have made Britain their permanent home during this century.

■ 1900–39
■ 1940 and after

Ireland
During the second half of the 19th century, the largest immigrant group were the Irish. By 1901 there were 632,000 immigrant Irish resident in Britain.

Russia and Poland
Between 1880 and 1908 about 200,000 Jews from Eastern Europe settled in Britain. Most went to the East End of London, though smaller communities were established in other cities, including Liverpool, Manchester and Leeds.

The Caribbean islands
Around 15,000 West Indians stayed on after fighting in the British forces during the First World War. They joined the small black communities already established in towns such as Cardiff, Liverpool, Glasgow, London and South Shields.

Germany and Austria
About 60,000 Jews from Nazi controlled Germany and Austria entered Britain between 1933 and 1939.

Poland
The Poles were the largest group of refugees from Europe who sought sanctuary in Britain during the Second World War. In 1945 about 114,000 Poles decided to remain in Britain rather than return to Poland.

Eastern Europe
(Hungary, Poland, Ukraine, Estonia, Latvia, Lithuania) By 1950 some 100,000 people from these the countries behind the 'Iron Curtain' had emigrated to Britain.

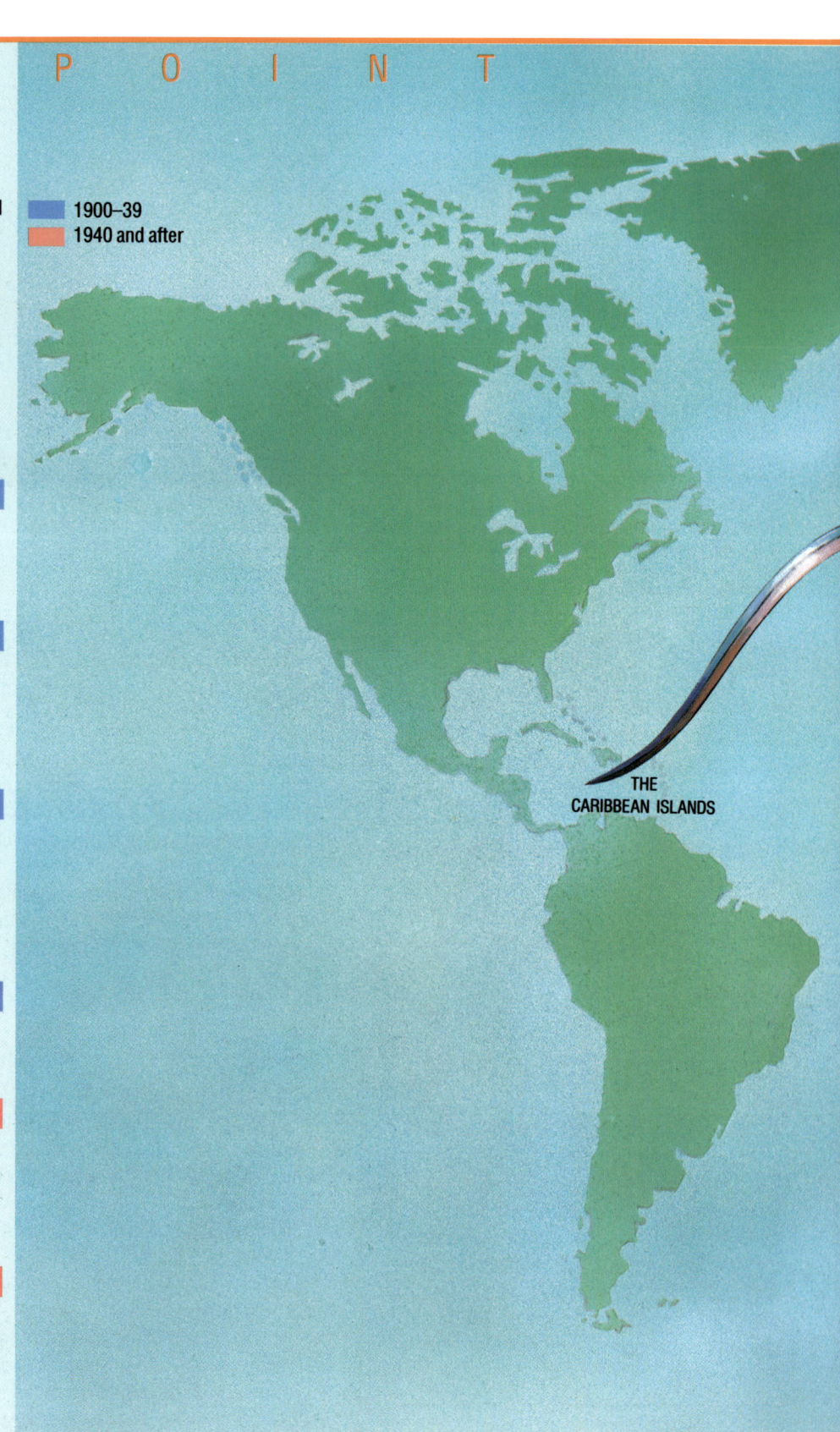

THE CARIBBEAN ISLANDS

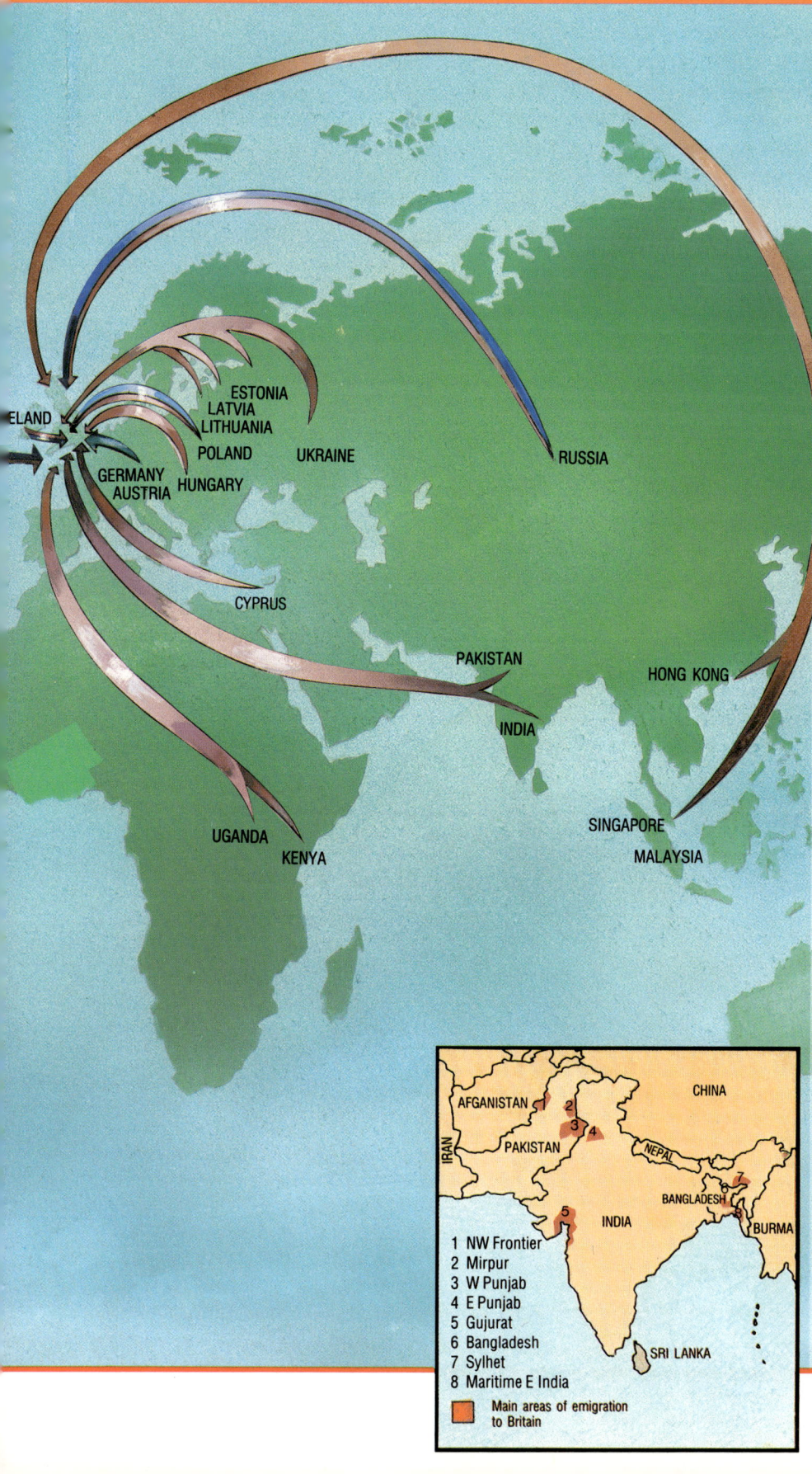

Destination Britain

Ireland
Between 1946 and 1951 an estimated 100,000 Irish people settled in Britain; by 1959 this figure had risen to 352,000. These new immigrants took the numbers of people of Irish extraction in Britain to almost one million.

The Caribbean islands
Thousands of West Indians came to Britain during the Second World War to assist with the war effort. Most returned home when the War ended. From 1948 to 1952 about 1000 per year settled in Britain. About 60 per cent came from Jamaica. After 1952 there was a sudden increase. By 1961 there were almost 172,000 West Indians in Britain.

India and Pakistan
From the end of the Second World War to the 1960s immigrants from the Indian sub-continent came to Britain. The largest numbers came after 1960. Indians and Pakistanis came from four main areas:
- Gujarat state in western India – most Gujuratis in Britain follow the Hindu religion.
- The state of Punjab in northern India – most Punjabis in Britain follow the Sikh religion.
- Pakistan – most Pakistanis in Britain are Muslims.
- Bangladesh (East Pakistan until 1971) – most Bengalis are from the area of Sylhet in central Bangladesh, the Bengalis are Muslims.

Kenya and Uganda
East African Asians entered Britain in the 1960s and 1970s. From 1963-68, 44,000 Kenyan Asians settled in Britain; 26,000 Ugandan Asians entered Britain in 1972.

Hong Kong, Malaysia, Singapore
In the late 1950s and the 1960s immigrants from the Far East arrived in Britain. The largest numbers came from the British colony of Hong Kong, mostly from the rural district surrounding the city known as the 'New Territories'. In 1951 there were 12,000 people from the Far East in Britain, by 1961 this figure had increased to 29,600.

Cyprus
Cypriot immigrants arrived from the 1950s to the 1970s. Most were Greek Cypriots but about 20 per cent were Turkish Cypriots.

Inset map key:
1 NW Frontier
2 Mirpur
3 W Punjab
4 E Punjab
5 Gujarat
6 Bangladesh
7 Sylhet
8 Maritime E India

Main areas of emigration to Britain

Why did people move to Britain?

The reasons why people settled in Britain are as varied as the places from which they came. Many had strong personal motives; to be with their families or to seek out new opportunities, for example. But three factors which caused people to migrate to Britain stand out. You can examine each in turn in the section which follows.

1 Escape from persecution

The first major group of immigrants to arrive in Britain in the 20th century were Russian and Polish Jews. About three million Jews left Eastern Europe between 1880 and 1920. Most settled in America but over 200,000 made their homes in Britain. Jews came to Britain to escape discrimination and persecution. In Russia and Poland, strict anti-Jewish laws set out where Jews could live, the sort of employment they could have and the numbers allowed to go to school. Jews were driven out of their villages in the countryside and herded into the squalid and overcrowded cities. Worse still, whenever the country experienced a major social disaster such as a famine, or a political crisis, like the 1905 revolution in Russia, pogroms were organised against Jewish communities (**Source 1**). Pogroms were vicious attacks on Jews and their property often with official government support (**Source 2**). This savage treatment caused the large scale movement of Jews from central and Eastern Europe.

In the 1930s this brutal persecution returned to haunt the Jewish people. This time it was in a different place and was to be on an even more horrific scale. Jews living in Nazi-controlled Germany and Austria, were subjected to racist laws and became the victims of Fascist violence (**Source 3**). Persecution turned thousands of Jews into *refugees*: people who flee from their homes to find shelter and safety in another place.

2 Political refugees

People become refugees for reasons other than persecution. Some are unable or unwilling to live in countries which have experienced major political changes. Since 1945 many of these political refugees have established themselves in Britain. In 1945 there were about 250,000 Polish exiles living in Britain. They had fled from Poland when Hitler's armies invaded in 1939. When the War ended about 100,000 returned home but an equal number remained in Britain. Many did so because Poland had been

SOURCE 1

The dreadful aftermath of a pogrom in 1905. Russian Jews lie in small family groups awaiting burial in a Jewish cemetery. In this incident alone, 600 Jewish communities were attacked and over 1000 Jews murdered.

SOURCE 2

... a rumour started that ... for three days you could do whatever you wanted to do to the Jews. For three days there was no check on the looting ... and all the pillage and murder went unpunished. I heard that many of the Jews who had been beaten were in the factory infirmary. I decided to go there and have a look with one of my friends, another little boy. We found a horrible scene. The corpses of Jews who had been beaten to death were lying in rows on the floor.

Nikita Khrushchev.

taken over by the Soviet Union. The Soviet authorities made it difficult for Poles who had lived in exile in the West to resume their lives in Poland.

A different type of political refugee was created in Africa. In 1967 President Kenyatta of Kenya gave all Asians living in his country two years to take up Kenyan citizenship or face expulsion. In 1972 the President of Uganda, Idi Amin, announced a similar 'africanisation' programme. However, he did not offer the alternative of citizenship. Ugandan Asians were given just three months to leave the country and 50,000 people became political refugees (**Source 4**). In all, more than 70,000 East African Asians from the two countries took up their right to British citizenship and came to Britain to begin a new life.

3 Employment and better prospects

In the early years of peace following the end of the Second World War, there was a desperate shortage of workers in Britain. Accordingly, the Ministry of Labour decided to tap into the huge reservoir of European refugees whose countries had been swallowed up by the Soviet Union. Recruitment schemes were set up to bring these 'stateless persons' to Britain to work in hospitals and factories. In this way many thousands of Poles, Ukrainians, Hungarians, Latvians and others came to Britain to assist with the vital task of reconstruction. Many moved on after a few years but some made Britain their permanent home.

The chronic labour shortage was not solved by the arrival of people from Eastern Europe. The need to attract more workers was behind a government organised recruitment campaign in Ireland. Between 1945 and 1960 a third of a million Irish citizens moved to Britain. They joined established Irish communities in the major industrial areas of London, the Midlands, the North and Scotland. In the 1950s the Irish were the largest immigrant group in Britain.

SOURCE 3

Buchenwald extermination camp today.
Hitler's massacre of 6 million Jews was the culmination of the horrific persecution of the Jewish people in central Europe. Those who escaped the Nazis sought refuge abroad. About 60,000 settled in the UK, although immigration controls kept out many more (see page 188).

SOURCE 4

September 1972: Mrs Sushila (*centre*) and her ten year old daughter Kirta (*left*) arrive at Heathrow airport after being expelled from Uganda. Thousands of Ugandan Asians were forced to leave as part of President Idi Amin's 'africanisation' programme. The expelled Asians had their wealth and property confiscated; Mrs Sushila even had her tape recorder taken from her at Entebbe airport.

DATAPOINT

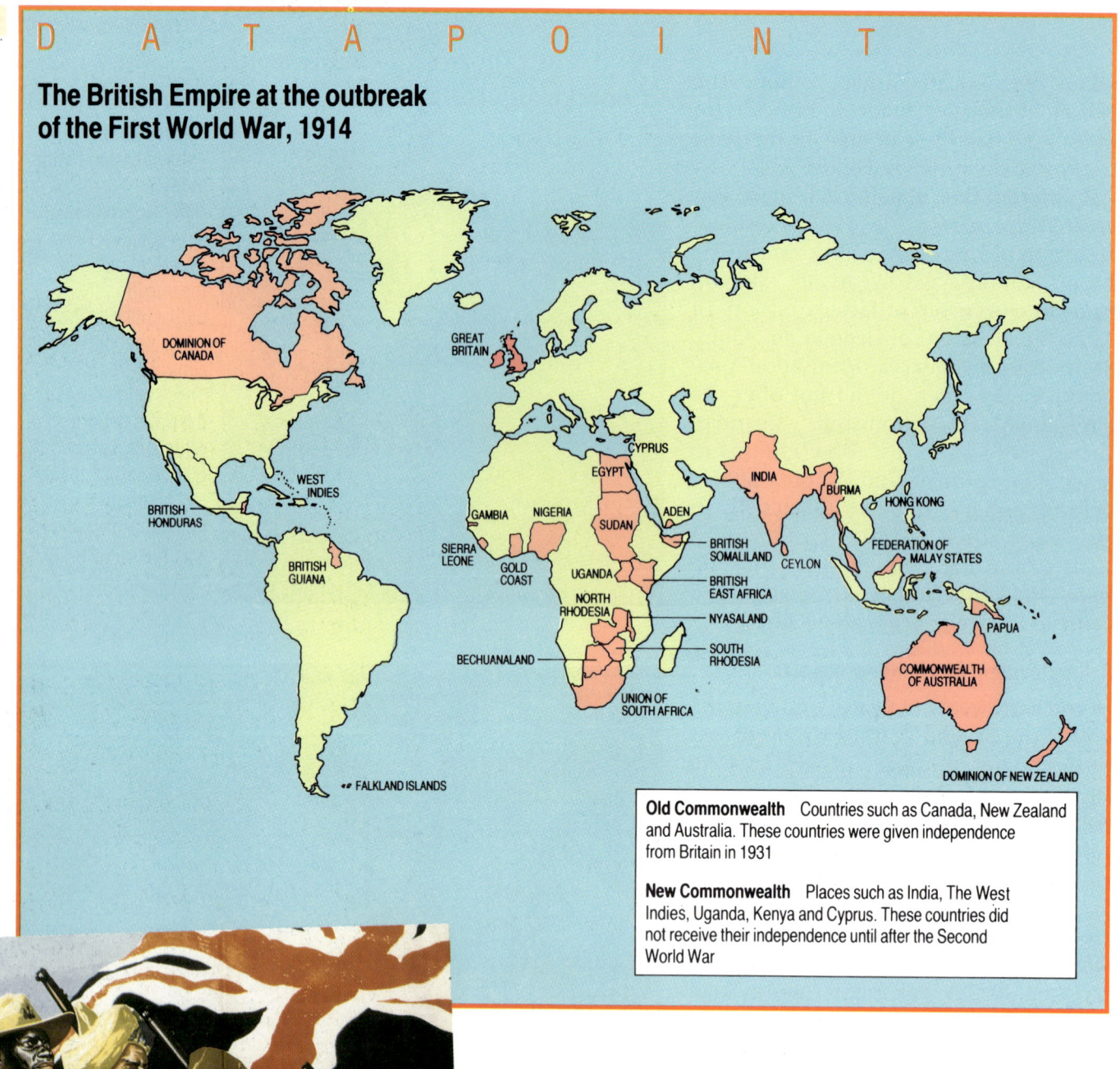

The British Empire at the outbreak of the First World War, 1914

Old Commonwealth Countries such as Canada, New Zealand and Australia. These countries were given independence from Britain in 1931

New Commonwealth Places such as India, The West Indies, Uganda, Kenya and Cyprus. These countries did not receive their independence until after the Second World War

SOURCE 5
The Second World War brought thousands of Commonwealth citizens together to help win the victory over Germany and Japan. This poster, however, is misleading. Units from different countries seldom marched or fought side by side.

Case Study: New Commonwealth immigration 1945–1976

The right to settle

During the 19th century the major European countries divided large parts of the world between them. This process of acquiring territory by force and controlling the population with the laws and systems of the conquering power is called colonialism.

Under British rule, the people of the colonies had adopted much of the language and culture of Britain and

SOURCE 6

West Indian workers in the 1950s were shocked to find how little British people knew about the Caribbean. Many did not even know where it was! West Indian people, however, had been brought up to believe that Britain was their second home.

... their ideas about Britain were largely derived from a colonial education system in which Britain was revered as the 'mother country'. They took their British citizenship seriously and many regarded themselves not as strangers, but as kinds of Englishmen. Everything taught in school ... encouraged that belief.

Peter Fryer, *Staying Power: The History of Black People in Britain*, 1984.

expressed feelings of loyalty and patriotism towards the 'mother country'. Thousands of colonial subjects fought and died for Britain in the First and Second World Wars. In their hearts they saw themselves as British citizens (**Source 6**). This belief was given legal status with the passing of the British Nationality Act in 1948 which declared all Commonwealth citizens to be 'Citizens of the United Kingdom and the Colonies'. As British passport holders, Commonwealth citizens now had the right to enter, work, and settle in Britain without restriction. This Act provided an 'open door' for Commonwealth immigration and enabled much of the immigration from the Caribbean, India and Pakistan after 1948 to take place. However, although the British Nationality Act was a very powerful incentive to migrate to Britain at this time, other factors also played their part in encouraging this mass movement of people.

SOURCE 7

22 June 1948: The arrival of the *Empire Windrush* at Tilbury Docks, London. The 492 Jamaicans on board were the first of a new wave of Commonwealth settlers to make Britain their home after the Second World War.

SOURCE 8

One of hundreds of advertisements for passage to England appearing in West Indian newspapers. This one comes from the *Barbados Advocate*, 2 January 1955.

SOURCE 9

This testimony shows how some people in the Caribbean islands became aware of the opportunities available in Britain and explains why they felt comfortable about making the decision to settle in Britain.

There were adverts everywhere: 'Come to the mother country! The mother country needs you!' That's how I learned the opportunity was here. I felt stronger loyalty towards England. There was more emphasis there than loyalty to your own island. It really was the mother country and being away from home wouldn't be that terrible because you would belong.

'Push and pull'

After 1948 thousands of New Commonwealth people responded to a persuasive advertising campaign designed to increase the size of the workforce in Britain (**Source 9**). The use of slogans and posters appealing to the loyalty of British citizens in the countries of the New Commonwealth and encouraging their movement to Britain, can be called a *pull* factor (a reason why people are attracted to another place). There were many other pull factors, but also a number of push factors (reasons why people leave a place).

Push factors

In 1938-39 the British government sent a team to investigate conditions in a number of the Caribbean islands which were under British colonial rule. The team reported 'poor housing, poor wages, chronic sickness and an education system with serious inadequacies in every respect.' Despite their status as British colonies, these islands did not share the welfare systems that the 'mother country' enjoyed. This situation was made more acute when, in August 1951, a hurricane of great force hit Jamaica killing 132 people and making many more homeless. In the face of such hardships many West Indian people were prompted to seek opportunities elsewhere. In the past they had gone mainly to the United States, as it was close by. However, in 1952 the McCarran-Walter Act in America halted this process by cutting down the numbers allowed entry from 65,000 to 800 per year. Britain, as the colonial ruler, seemed a sensible second choice.

In 1947 India regained its independence from Britain and two new states, India and Pakistan, were created out of the old Indian Empire (see page 166). The partition of India led to social and economic problems with many Sikhs and Hindus losing their land and homes in Pakistan as they were driven across the border into the Indian province of East Punjab. This area was unable to support the sudden increase in population and many Sikh and Hindu people were forced to look to Britain for work.

Pull factors

In post-war Britain a recruitment campaign aimed at the colonies was organised on a large scale. The National Health Service, London Transport, the British Hotels and Restaurants Association and the British Transport Commission actively encouraged workers from the Caribbean and the Indian sub-continent to come to Britain. The intention was to help build up the workforce in these areas of acute labour shortage. In addition, there were employment opportunities in agriculture, coal mining, engineering, building and textiles. In 1956 London Transport launched its recruitment scheme in Barbados and in the same year an estimated 26,000 West Indians entered Britain. Similarly, by the end of 1958, 55,000 Indian and Pakistani men and women had responded to the plea for workers in Britain.

By the late 1950s the demand for New Commonwealth labour had almost dried up. In spite of this, immigrants from these countries continued to enter

Number of immigrants from Commonwealth countries

Year	Number
1955	43,000
1956	47,000
1957	42,000
1958	30,000
1959	22,000
1960	58,000
1961	136,000
1962	107,000
1963	56,000
1964	53,000
1965	51,000
1966	44,000
1967	55,000
1968	46,000
1969	31,000
1970	24,000

Britain. One reason for this was that the initial settlers were now beginning to bring their families over to join them. The majority of the early settlers had been men. In Southall in the late 1950s, for example, only four per cent of Sikhs were women. It was only natural that once settled, wives, children and other dependants would be brought to Britain to be re-united with their husbands, sons and fathers.

In the early 1960s another factor encouraged large scale migration to Britain. Political pressures at home led the Government to prepare stricter controls on immigration to Britain. When this became known there was a rush to beat the new controls. In the 18 months between 1961 and 1962, the numbers entering Britain were greater than the total over the previous five years. When the Commonwealth Immigration Act was passed in 1962 this movement became increasingly restricted.

> **Knowledge and understanding**
>
> Use pages 178 to 185 to investigate the following questions
>
> 1 Look at the Datapoint: People on the move 1900–1976. From which countries did migrants to Britain come in (a) the period 1900–39, (b) the period 1940–76.
>
> 2 Give at least three reasons why people become migrants.
>
> 3 The factors which encouraged New Commonwealth immigration from the 1940s to the 1960s can be described as economic, political and social. Make a copy of the following key:
>
> Economic   Political   Social
>
> Seven causes of immigration are listed below. Copy the list out and decide which are economic, which are political and which are social. Underline each cause using the colour code in your key.
> - The British Nationality Act, 1948
> - The post-war recruitment campaign
> - The McCarran-Walter Act, 1952
> - Poor quality housing, education and healthcare
> - The threat of immigration controls
> - The partition of India
> - Family ties
>
> 4 'The British Nationality Act of 1948 was the main reason why New Commonwealth immigrants came to Britain between 1948 and 1962'. Do you agree? Explain your answer carefully.

The immigrant experience: The Jews

The Jews who came to Britain in the early part of the 20th century, settled in distinct communities, in particular in London's East End (**Source 10**).

The response of the British people to their new neighbours was often hostile and owed much to prejudice. Anti-Jewish attitudes were fuelled by articles in the press which warned that the newcomers would take jobs and houses and bring down wages. Politicians were quick to pick up on the hysteria (**Source 11**). The situation was made worse by the widespread use of Jewish labour in the so-called 'sweated trades'. These workshop-based industries which

SOURCE 10
East End Jews photographed in 1909.

SOURCE 11

At the beginning of the 20th century there was great hostility towards Jewish immigrants in Britain. Much of this was based on fear. The MP for Stepney, a major area for Jewish settlement in the East End of London, expressed one of these fears:

> There is hardly an Englishman in this room who does not live under the constant danger of being driven from his home, packed out into the streets, not by the natural increase in our own population, but by the off-scum of Europe.

produced goods such as furniture, footwear and cheap clothing, employed people prepared to work punishing hours for very low wages. Jewish workshops which specialised in tailoring accepted rock-bottom prices for their finished goods in order to win business. They were criticised for taking work away from established businesses and for depressing wages at a time when Trade Unions were trying to improve working conditions and rates of pay (**Source 12**). In fact, the Jewish tailoring industry helped the British clothing trade to fight off foreign competition and save the jobs of other clothing workers. Without the Jewish workshops the clothing trade in the East End would have almost certainly collapsed. Yet Jews were accused of being behind almost all the problems of society (**Source 13**). The areas in which they settled had severe social problems such as poor housing, unemployment, overcrowding and disease. It was convenient, therefore, to blame these problems on the newcomers with their strange habits, dress, language, religion and customs. Jews kept the Sabbath on Saturday, did not eat pork and used the Hebrew alphabet. They were accused of being dirty and clannish and were said to be behind the high crime rate and the outbreak of contagious diseases such as smallpox. However, such accusations were mostly unfounded and unfair. The East End districts into which the Jews moved were poor before they arrived, and overcrowded homes and bad sanitation were common features of London's working class districts. Contrary to popular belief Jews were not a major burden on the system of welfare relief (**Source 14**). Nor did investigations into Jewish communities support these prejudiced views about their way of life (**Source 15**).

SOURCE 12

A number of destitute men and women ... land on our wave-beaten shores in a destitute condition, and offer to do work at any price ... [This] undermines all our commercial arrangements and drives English labour out of the labour market. All the 'sweating system' in the East of London is carried on by cheap foreign labour.

The Eastern Argus newspaper, 1887.

SOURCE 13

In 1903 a Royal Commission was set up to investigate the effects of 'alien immigration'. The majority of these 'aliens' were Jews and the investigators found a number of common complaints against them:

> In respect of Alien Immigrants it is alleged:
> 1. That on their arrival they are (a) in an impoverished and destitute condition, (b) deficient in cleanliness and practice insanitary habits.
> 2. That amongst them are criminals, anarchists, prostitutes and persons of bad character.
> 3. That many of these being and becoming paupers and receiving Poor Law relief, a burden is thereby thrown upon the local Rates.

SOURCE 14

... there is very little evidence that poor Jews were a burden on the Poor Rates. Indeed, in 1901 although 15.2 per 1000 of the population were in the workhouse, the figure for European immigrants was a mere 1.7 per 1000. However [bad] their conditions the immigrant poor did not tax the English public purse with their poverty. The workshop rather than the workhouse became the natural habitat for the Eastern Europeans in London.

James Walvin, *Passage to Britain*, 1984.

SOURCE 15

When I came to examine the death rates (in the Jewish districts), which I had expected to find very high in view of the conditions of the houses and the prevailing conditions of the district, I found them very low ... the only conclusion I could come to was that the difference in the death rate was due to the better care the inhabitants took of themselves and their mode of life.

London County Council Medical Officer, quoted in the Royal Commission on Alien Immigration, 1903.

The Jewish children have proved excellent scholars, far the most regular in London, usually well fed even in poor families, and bright in school. This is due largely to the excellent domestic character of their parents, never drinking and devoted to their children.

Member of the London School Board, quoted in the Royal Commission on Alien Immigration, 1903.

SOURCE 16

The object of the League is to prevent any further incursion into this country of destitute aliens ... We ... think and believe, that this country is too small to allow any more in, that its own natural increase will be, and is, quite sufficient, therefore we say there is no room for foreigners.

Statement of the British Brothers League.

British anti-Semitism

The irrational hatred of the Jewish people and their way of life is known as anti-Semitism. At the beginning of the 20th century, British anti-Semites began to organise themselves. In 1901 the British Brothers League was formed and a campaign started to restrict the entry of immigrants into Britain (**Source 16**). The campaign was taken up by MPs and the case for immigration controls was pressed in Parliament. As a result the Aliens Act was passed in 1905. This limited the right of entry to Britain to those people with 'visible means of support'. This meant that all those who had no money and no job to go to were turned away. Since the majority of Jews attempting to enter Britain were refugees escaping a dangerous situation, few had the necessary 'qualifications' to get past the immigration officers. Jewish immigration dropped by 40 per cent.

The British Union of Fascists

During the 1930s anti-Semitism was most visible in Nazi Germany. However, Britain's anti-Semites were not idle at this time. In 1932 Oswald Mosley created the British Union of Fascists, copying much of the organisation and ideas from Mussolini's Fascists in Italy. The British Fascists wore black-shirted uniforms and spent hours in military-style training. Fascist rallies and marches were organised and there were violent clashes with left-wing opponents. Gradually the Fascists began to concentrate their efforts on attacking Jews and their property. The routes of Fascist marches were deliberately planned to pass through the Jewish communities of London's East End. The violence reached a climax in

SOURCE 17

Oswald Mosley, the leader of the British Union of Fascists.

SOURCES 18 AND 19

The face of British Fascism in the 1930s. Not Berlin or Rome but London: a rally at the Empire Pool, Wembley and Fascists taking to the streets in Bermondsey. Mosley brought his racist message to many such meetings: 'We have created the Empire without race mixture or pollution. It should only be necessary by education and propaganda to teach the British that racial mixtures are bad.'

October 1936 when anti-Fascist demonstrators barricaded Cable Street in the East End in order to force a confrontation with Mosley's supporters (**Source 20**). The police banned the Fascist march and broke up the Cable Street crowd with a baton charge. Soon afterwards the government passed the Public Order Act which banned the use of political uniforms and thus robbed Fascism of much of its appeal.

The anti-Semitism of Mosley and his supporters was unmistakable and high-profile. Rather more subtle, but ultimately more deadly, was the official reaction of the British government to the plight of Europe's Jews in the 1930s. As increasing numbers of Jewish refugees began to leave Nazi Germany, the British government refused to relax the immigration controls set up by the Alien Restriction Act of 1919. This Act specified the ports at which non-Commonwealth immigrants could land. In addition it instructed immigration officers to refuse entry to anyone who was medically unfit or who had no means of support. The numbers of Jews allowed entry to Britain in the 1930s under these rules was small. The strict enforcement of the 1919 Act trapped thousands of Jews within the Third Reich and condemned them to suffer the brutality of the Nazi regime.

SOURCE 20

The Cable Street riot, October 1936. Anti-fascist demonstrators flee as the police charge towards them. The protests against Mosley's Blackshirts were attended by 100,000 people.

SOURCE 21

West Indians arriving at Victoria station in London. The authorities made little effort to help the newcomers settle in Britain. Those with family already in the country fared best, the rest were left to their own devices.

The immigrant experience: New Commonwealth people

Migrants from New Commonwealth countries such as the Caribbean islands, India and Pakistan encountered many of the problems faced by earlier groups like the Jews. Finding a place to live was very difficult. Boarding houses offering 'Rooms to Let' often displayed accompanying signs saying 'No Coloureds' or 'No Blacks' (**Source 22**). Banks and Building Societies were at first reluctant to grant mortgage facilities to New Commonwealth applicants and local authorities applied rules which made it difficult for council properties to be let to the newcomers. Some landlords rented properties to black people but they were often charged higher rents than white people and were sometimes subject to humiliating rules such as night-time curfews. One result of the housing problem was the creation of 'black areas' in Britain's major cities (**Source 23**).

New Commonwealth immigrants frequently encountered shocking prejudice born out of the ignorance of the British people (**Source 24**). Many had no idea where the Caribbean was and could not distinguish between Asians, Africans and West Indians. Many Asian people found

SOURCE 22

A young Jamaican encounters prejudice in his search for accommodation in Britain. This kind of racism was made illegal by the 1968 Race Relations Act. However, the Act could not prevent racial discrimination from talking place. Landlords might not display such signs but they could continue to use excuses for not taking in black lodgers.

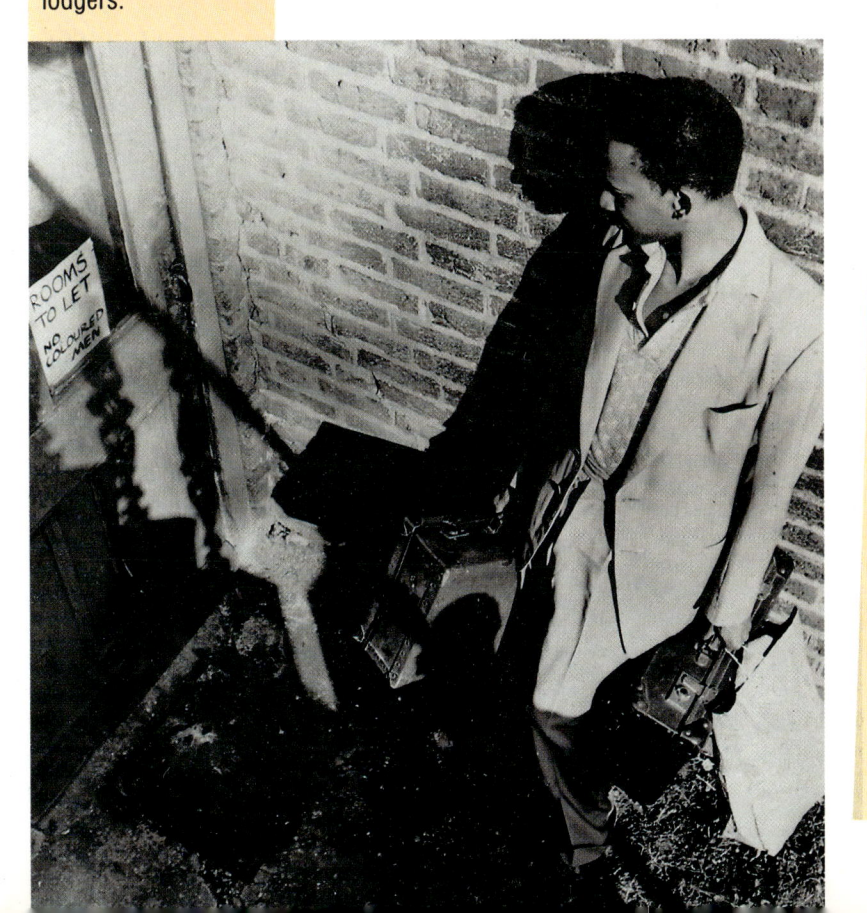

SOURCE 23

Turned away from private lodgings by an unofficial colour bar, and obliged to wait five years for low-cost council housing, many low paid Afro-Caribbeans had no choice but to rent rooms in a slum. Even then many could only afford to share one room with fellow blacks, no matter how overcrowded and stressful. If they tried to buy or rent homes in better areas, by pooling their resources with partners, some families were abused or attacked. Not trusting the police to protect them, most stayed in 'black areas' of London or other big cities, including Toxteth (Liverpool), St Paul's (Bristol), Butetown (Cardiff), Chapeltown (Leeds), Handsworth (Birmingham) and Moss Side (Manchester).

David Bygott, *Black and British*, 1992.

SOURCE 24

Though half of Britain's white population had never even met a black person ... prejudice against black people was widespread. More than two-thirds of Britain's white population, in fact, held a low opinion of black people or disapproved of them. They saw them as heathens who practised head-hunting, cannibalism, infanticide, polygamy and 'black magic'. They saw them as uncivilised, backward people, inferior to Europeans, living in primitive mud huts 'in the bush', wearing few clothes, eating strange foods, and suffering from unpleasant diseases. They saw them as ignorant and illiterate, speaking strange languages, and lacking proper education ... Half of this prejudiced two-thirds were ... only 'mildly' prejudiced. The other half were extremely so. This deeply prejudiced third of the white population strongly resisted the idea of having any contact or communication with black people; objected vehemently to mixed marriages; would not have black people in their homes as guests or lodgers; would not work with them in factory or office; and generally felt that black people should not be allowed in Britain at all.

Peter Fryer, *Staying Power: The History of Black People in Britain*, 1984.

racist attitudes towards them to be particularly aggressive. Unlike the West Indian migrant who spoke good English and followed the Christian faith, Asian people exhibited a completely different set of religious and cultural beliefs and customs. At work the discrimination and prejudice continued. It was believed that the migrants would swamp Britain, take jobs away from British people and bring down wages by accepting lower rates of pay (**Source 25**). New Commonwealth workers tended to be offered unskilled and unattractive jobs in spite of having the training and skills to perform more demanding work (**Source 26**). Promotion to positions of responsibility was difficult to achieve. In the nursing profession black nurses were often discouraged from taking the SRN qualification, which would have gained them higher professional status and better promotion prospects.

The colour bar

Black and Asian people found that prejudice and discrimination against them was widespread. The differences perceived by white communities made it convenient to blame them for social problems such as unemployment and housing shortages. They were accused of encouraging crime and carrying disease. Poor immigrants were criticised as being lazy and for living off the Welfare State.

Immigrants who did well were envied and resented. Discrimination was evident at work and in the housing market. It was also a part of everyday society. Black and Asian people were frequently barred from hotels, public houses, dance halls and restaurants. This type of discrimination, where a person is prevented from having access to public places, is called a 'colour bar'.

Race riots

Fear and prejudice mounted in the 1950s and there were a number of well publicised protests against the employment of black and Asian workers. In 1955 bus workers in Wolverhampton, West Bromwich and Bristol protested at the 'increasing numbers of coloured workers employed' by staging overtime bans and one-day strikes. In West Bromwich, the protest was over the employment of just one Indian conductor. By the late 1950s a number of right-wing groups had begun to organise a 'Keep Britain White' campaign. In 1958 the tensions spilled over into racist attacks and full-scale riots. The disturbances began in Nottingham where about 2500 West Indians and about 600 Asians were living. For months there had been a series of violent attacks upon black people carried out by groups of white youths. On Saturday 23 August fighting broke out between blacks and whites in the St Ann's Well Road area. The fighting continued for around 90 minutes with injuries on both sides caused by razors, knives and bottles. The disturbances provoked both Nottingham MPs to demand an end to black immigration and for deportation laws to be passed.

Almost immediately riots broke out in the Notting Hill area of London (**Source 27**). This district contained a mixture of

SOURCE 25

The following motion, put before the Trades Union Congress in 1958, shows white fears about blacks taking away their jobs.

It is time to put a stop to all foreign labour entering this country. In the event of a slump occurring, the market would be flooded with cheap foreign labour … a serious deterrent to trade union bargaining power.

SOURCE 26

Of the men who came here, a mere 13 per cent had no skills; of the women only 5 per cent. In fact, one in four of the men, and half of the women, were non-manual workers. And almost half the men (46 per cent) and over a quarter of the women (27 per cent) were skilled manual workers. Yet the newcomers found themselves in most cases having to settle for a lower job status than they had enjoyed at home. This indeed was their first big disappointment, for, by and large, the jobs they were offered were those the local white people did not want: sweeping the streets, general labouring, night-shift work. In the late 1950s, more than half the male West Indians in London had lower status jobs than their skill and experience fitted them for.

Peter Fryer, *Staying Power: The History of Black People in Britain*, 1984.

Destination Britain

SOURCE 27
Headline news: the Notting Hill race riots.

Daily Mirror, Mon Sept 1 1958
Police squads rush to Notting Hill
400 CLASH IN 'COLOUR' RIOT
M.P. sends SOS to Yard

races living in squalid and overcrowded conditions. Right-wing groups blamed blacks for the bad conditions, and violence against them had been growing during the summer of 1958. News of the Nottingham riots brought hundreds of white youths onto the streets. They attacked black people and threw petrol bombs at their houses. During September gangs roamed the streets armed with knives and iron pipes, attacking anyone with a coloured skin. The disturbances lasted for two weeks. Outside London in virtually every area of black settlement there were copycat attacks on black and Asian people. Pressure mounted on the government to impose immigration controls.

Immigration controls

Before 1959 pressure within Parliament for immigration controls was organised by a lone MP, Sir Cyril Osborne. He used the 'Keep Britain White' slogan of

DATAPOINT
Immigration controls 1962–1971

1962 Commonwealth Immigrants Act

This Act introduced a work voucher system which controlled the number of Commonwealth people who were able to enter. These vouchers were issued on the basis of whether Commonwealth citizens had a job to come to or a valuable skill that was in short supply in Britain. In 1965 the number of vouchers was limited to 8500 per year.

1968 Commonwealth Immigrants Act

This Act was passed in order to control the number of Kenyan Asians entering Britain following Kenyan Independence. The Act restricted work vouchers to 1500 per year. It also introduced a 'close connection' clause. This meant that entry was not allowed unless the passport holder had either been born in Britain or had a parent or grandparent who had. The purpose of the Act was to keep out non-white colonial citizens.

1971 Immigration Act

This Act gave the right of settlement to people it defined as *patrials*. These were people who had been born in Britain or who had lived in Britain for over five years or who had a parent or grandparent born in Britain. All other Commonwealth and non-EEC citizens had to apply for employment vouchers or permission to enter Britain. The Act came into effect on 1 January 1973.

SOURCE 28

A National Front march in London, August 1977.

groups like the White Defence League and encouraged the fears of many British people with outlandish claims, such as: 'If the rate of increase continues the time will come when there will be more coloured than white people in England'.

The 1959 election returned a Conservative government and a number of MPs with similar views. Soon after the election a group of Tory MPs from the Birmingham area began a campaign to force the government to introduce immigration controls. Locally organised groups such as the Birmingham Immigration Control Association added to the pressure on the government. The government did not resist for long. In 1962 they passed the Commonwealth Immigration Act which restricted the entry of Commonwealth settlers to those with employment vouchers. Subsequent laws in 1968 and 1971 meant that the British citizenship of Commonwealth people became virtually worthless (see **Datapoint: Immigration Controls 1962–1971** on page 191).

The National Front

In 1967 an openly racist political party, the National Front, was founded. The National Front objected to all 'coloured' immigration into Britain. They wanted it to be halted and for all immigrants to be repatriated (returned to their country of

SOURCE 29

The National Front, formed in 1967 from a collection of smaller racist groups, had clear aims.

To preserve our British native stock in the United Kingdom, to prevent increased strife, such as is seen in the United States, and to eradicate race hatred by terminating non-white immigration with humane and orderly repatriation of non-white immigrants.

SOURCE 30

The National Front gained widespread attention in spite of having few members and little success at elections. This source explains how they achieved their publicity.

Surrounding themselves with the trappings of British ceremonial, especially the widespread use of the Union Jack, protected by ranks of local policemen, the National Front has taunted its political and racial opponents through marches and rallies on sensitive occasions or in sensitive quarters. These were the tactics of Mosley's fascists in the 1930s. Not surprisingly, perhaps, these organised and provocative taunts have often had the result they sought: a violent retort from the left and from non-white community organisations. In the process, the anger of the newspapers is often deflected from ... the National Front to the actions of their opponents. This often has the bizarre effect of portraying the fascists as the victims of unwarranted aggression, particularly when ranks of policemen are used to safeguard the National Front's right to march or speak.

James Walvin, *Passage to Britain*, 1984.

SOURCE 31

The rise of racist groups like the National Front did not go unopposed. In the late 1970s the Anti Nazi League attracted thousands of people of all ages and racial groups to its rallies, like this Rock Against Racism event in London's Hyde Park. These people came to see bands including Aswad and Elvis Costello & The Attractions, and speakers including the Labour MP Tony Benn.

origin). They saw Britain as the natural home of the British people whom they described as a single, white race (**Source 29**). The National Front blamed Britain's economic decline on racial mixing and predicted the destruction of the British people and nation if racial interbreeding were not stopped. The National Front did badly at general elections but its performance in local or by-elections through the 1970s was much better. The Party was small but gained much publicity and even some sympathy through its manipulation of British law and the media (**Source 30**).

Enoch Powell

Judging by the results of opinion polls in the 1960s and 1970s, the British public were unhappy with the numbers of immigrants living in Britain. In polls taken in 1963, 1964 and 1966, over 80 per cent of those questioned believed that too many immigrants had been allowed into the UK. The results of polls taken in the 1970s were similar. Against this background of popular disapproval entered the Conservative MP for Wolverhampton South West, Enoch Powell. In a series of public speeches against coloured immigration, Powell captured the attention of the national press and became the hero of the anti-immigration movement. He spoke of his fears that large parts of Britain would be overrun by immigrants and claimed that this would spell disaster for the British way of life. In a speech in 1968 he shocked his audience by claiming that:

> Englishmen... found their wives unable to obtain hospital beds, their children unable to obtain school places, their neighbourhoods changed beyond all recognition, their plans and prospects for the future defeated.

In his most famous speech, before an audience at Birmingham in April 1968, he predicted increasing racial conflict and violence and claimed that the only answer was to end Commonwealth immigration immediately (**Source 33**). By 1971 he had gone even further and was demanding the creation of a Ministry of Repatriation to send 'home' Britain's immigrant population. Enoch Powell was expelled from the Conservative Shadow Cabinet but his stand on race and immigration was backed by large sections of the British public. He received over 100,000 letters of support and the

London dockers and Smithfield meat porters marched to the House of Commons to express their solidarity with his views. In Powell's wake membership of the National Front rose, there were increased attacks on blacks and Asians, and the militant Black People's Alliance (BPA) was formed to promote and defend black interests. Racial harmony in Britain seemed an unlikely possibility.

SOURCE 32

Enoch Powell addressing a meeting at Wolverhampton.

SOURCE 33

This source contains part of Enoch Powell's most famous speech. Delivered in Birmingham on 20 April 1968 it has become known as the 'rivers of blood' speech. It was carefully written by Powell to play on the fears of Britain's white majority.

In fifteen or twenty years, on present trends, there will be in this country three million Commonwealth immigrants ... Whole areas, towns and parts of towns across England will be occupied by different sections of the immigrant ... population ... The natural and rational first question for a nation confronted by such a prospect is to ask: How can its dimensions be reduced? ... The answers ... are equally simple and rational: by stopping, or virtually stopping, further inflow, and by promoting the maximum outflow ... While the immigrants' entry to this country was admission to privileges and opportunities eagerly sought, the impact upon the existing population was very different ... For reasons which they [white British people] could not comprehend ... they found themselves strangers in their own country ... The sense of being a persecuted minority which is growing among ordinary English people in the areas of the country affected is something that those without direct experience can hardly imagine ... As I look ahead I am filled with foreboding. Like the Romans I seem to see the River Tiber foaming with much blood' ...

Better relations?

Between 1965 and 1976 Parliament passed three Acts designed to improve race relations and end discrimination. In 1965 the Race Relations Act began this process. The Act made it illegal to discriminate against anyone on the grounds of race and colour in places such as restaurants, pubs and cinemas, or on public transport. The Act was a step in the right direction but it failed to combat much of the more serious discrimination, in housing and employment for example. In 1966 a Race Relations Board was established to deal with complaints but it had no authority to enforce the law. What's more it was composed almost entirely of white people which reduced its credibility within black communities.

In 1968 a second Race Relations Act widened the scope of the 1965 Act to outlaw discrimination in housing and employment. The Act also made it illegal to publish or display advertisements or notices which discriminated along racial lines. Although outright discrimination could be detected and corrected, it was not possible to get rid of more subtle forms of discrimination. Landlords advertising lodgings could easily claim that the room had just been let, and employers could use excuses such as inappropriate qualifications or lack of experience when turning down a black applicant. In 1976 the Racial Equality Act was passed in an effort to end this indirect discrimination. Anyone who felt they had been the target of such discrimination could take their case to a race relations tribunal. The Act also made it illegal to use racially offensive language in a public place or to publish written material which was threatening, abusive or insulting to a 'racial group'. At the same time the Commission for Racial Equality was established to investigate claims of discrimination. It was given the power to serve legal notices on offenders to prevent their continued discrimination. However, by 1980, of the 96 cases of incitement to racial hatred brought by the Commission, only four were successful in the courts. Laws such as these have helped to remove some of the more glaring examples of discrimination in British society. But laws by themselves do not remove prejudice. Equal rights are important but equality of opportunity is just as vital; and this has proved much more difficult to introduce into a society shaped by its colonial past.

Immigration and British society

> The arrival of migrants from the New Commonwealth countries after 1945 had a substantial impact upon British society. The enlargement of existing black and Asian communities, and the creation of new ones, was an obvious result of this migration.

This effect was not felt uniformly across the country, however (see **Datapoint: Britain's Immigrant Population** on page 196). The new arrivals settled in clearly defined areas of Britain's industrial cities. These were often decaying inner city areas which the white population was deserting and where accommodation was cheap. Such districts contained the only housing that most immigrants could afford or were allowed to rent. As such communities were established it was natural for successive waves of migrants to be attracted to them (**Source 34**). In towns such as Birmingham, Leicester and Bradford the impact of this community-building has been highly visible with shops, restaurants, banks, cinemas and places of worship reflecting the cultural and religious make-up of the local population. Many other areas of Britain have had little direct experience of the effects of immigration on this scale.

Employment

Immigrants have fulfilled an important role in the economy ever since the recruitment campaigns of the 1950s. As the taxi driver in **Source 35** points out, many areas of the British economy are dependent on the work of black and Asian people. Over a third of all UK hospital doctors were born overseas (mostly in the Indian sub-continent). Along with GPs, nurses, auxiliaries and porters, they play a vital role in keeping Britain's National Health Service going. Faced with prejudice in many areas of business, immigrants have often proved their commercial and managerial skills by setting up and operating successful businesses of their own. These provide local employment and economic stimulus, often in areas otherwise suffering from economic decline.

The British retail trade has been particularly influenced by the arrival of post-war immigrants. The decline of the 'corner shop' caused by the popularity of supermarket chains, was halted by the arrival of Asian migrants. In many British cities the great majority of small local shops are owned and run by Asian families. In London over half of the sub-post offices are owned by Indians. In fact, in virtually every field of employment, from transport to banking and finance, New Commonwealth people have made a significant contribution to

SOURCE 34

New Commonwealth immigrants ... came into a country that was not prepared to help them adjust to life in the new society except in a few isolated instances. When they arrived they were left to their own devices. This strengthened their tendency to turn to relatives or friends who had already settled there. Instead of dispersing gradually over the country, they began to concentrate on particular quarters of the industrial towns. They were forced to establish themselves in a strange environment and find employment with little help from the host society.

Gurbachan Singh, *Language, Race and Education*, 1988.

SOURCE 35

... this black minicab driver I know had a good idea the other day ... suppose all the immigrants were to strike for one day, he said. Suppose every black, every Asian, every Jew and all the others were to lay down tools for just one day? The country would grind to a halt. The hospitals, the buses, the London Underground, hotels, shops, plenty of factories, artists the whole lot – then you'd see what kind of mess there'd be. Because all these jobs, especially the menial ones, are being done by immigrants.

Miriam Karlin, quoted in *Never Again, Women Against the Nazis*.

Destination Britain

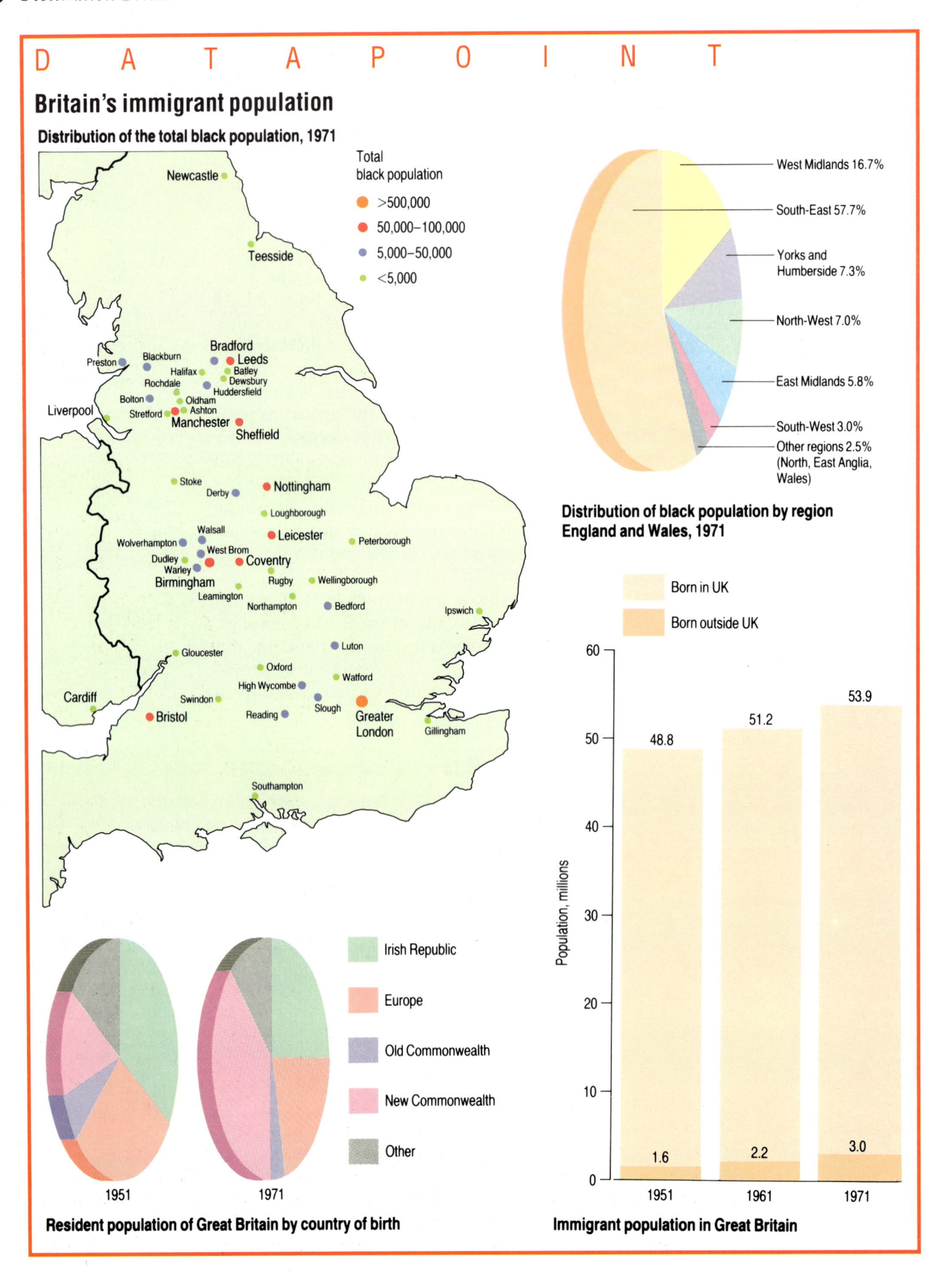

DATAPOINT

Britain's immigrant population

Distribution of the total black population, 1971

Total black population:
- >500,000 (orange)
- 50,000–100,000 (red)
- 5,000–50,000 (blue)
- <5,000 (green)

Cities shown on map: Newcastle, Teesside, Preston, Blackburn, Bradford, Leeds, Halifax, Batley, Rochdale, Dewsbury, Huddersfield, Bolton, Oldham, Liverpool, Stretford, Ashton, Manchester, Sheffield, Stoke, Derby, Nottingham, Loughborough, Wolverhampton, Walsall, Leicester, Dudley, West Brom, Peterborough, Warley, Birmingham, Coventry, Leamington, Rugby, Wellingborough, Northampton, Bedford, Ipswich, Gloucester, Luton, Oxford, Watford, Cardiff, Swindon, High Wycombe, Slough, Greater London, Bristol, Reading, Gillingham, Southampton.

Distribution of black population by region England and Wales, 1971

- West Midlands 16.7%
- South-East 57.7%
- Yorks and Humberside 7.3%
- North-West 7.0%
- East Midlands 5.8%
- South-West 3.0%
- Other regions 2.5% (North, East Anglia, Wales)

Resident population of Great Britain by country of birth (1951 and 1971 pie charts)

- Irish Republic
- Europe
- Old Commonwealth
- New Commonwealth
- Other

Immigrant population in Great Britain

Population, millions:

Year	Born in UK	Born outside UK
1951	48.8	1.6
1961	51.2	2.2
1971	53.9	3.0

SOURCE 36
A mass-meeting of Ford workers at Dagenham shows a racial mix which reflects the nature of the modern British workforce.

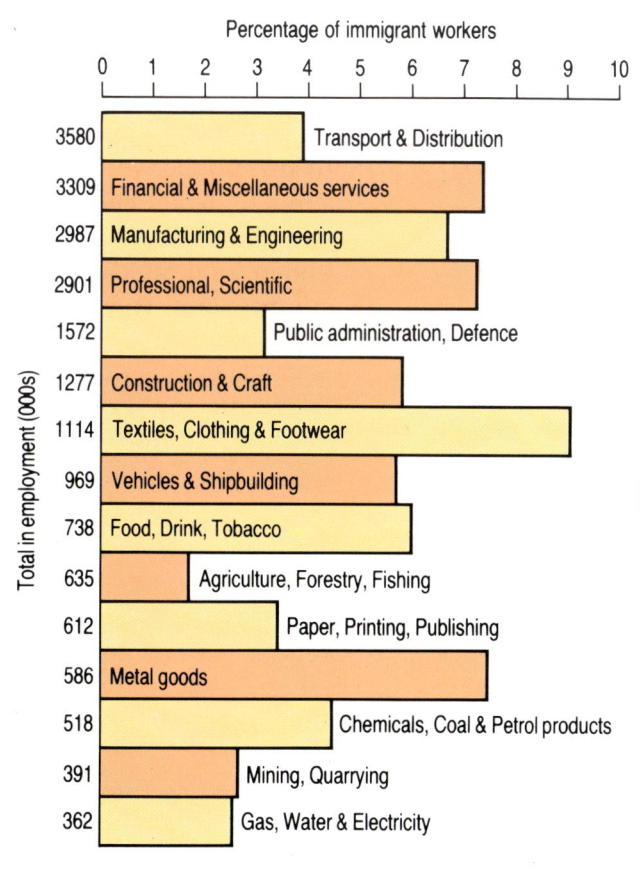

SOURCE 37
Graph to show immigrant workers from the 1971 census.

SOURCE 38
ITN newsreader Trevor McDonald at his desk.

the British economy (**Source 37**). Blacks and Asians have also played an increasing role in high-profile occupations as lawyers, trade union officials, politicians and academics. Many of Britain's sporting heroes in football, cricket, boxing, rugby league and athletics are of New Commonwealth descent. In addition, there are many black and Asian broadcasters, actors, artists and musicians.

Religion
Immigration has brought about changes in the religious make-up of Britain. Most people from the Caribbean islands were of the Christian faith, and in this respect were the same as the white majority in Britain. However, people of Asian origin had quite different religious beliefs and practices. A survey in 1977 showed that among Asians 40 per cent were Muslims, 29 per cent Hindus and 25 per cent Sikhs. The mosques and temples of these religions are now evident in cities and towns across the country. The devout practice of these religions in Britain has been an important factor in changing

SOURCE 39

The Central London Mosque in Regent's Park.

Many British cities now have examples of these spectacular buildings. They reflect the religious diversity of British society and offer visible reminders of the multicultural nature of Britain today.

British attitudes towards world faiths. Until recently many British people regarded these religions as little more than the superstitions of primitive people. In Victorian and Edwardian times missionaries travelled the globe searching out 'heathens' to convert to Christianity. The appearance of such religions in Britain's cities has gone some way towards promoting the understanding and respect of different beliefs and cultures (**Source 40**). One result of this broader awareness has been the appearance of new religious festivals on the British calendar. For instance, the celebration of Diwali – the Hindu New Year Festival of Lights, the start of Ramadan – a month of fasting from sunrise to sunset practised by Muslims, and Eid-Ul-Fitr – the Festival of Fast Breaking which ends Ramadan, are part of many school programmes. For Sikhs, November 1st is the most important day of the year. This is the birthday of Furu Nanak (1469–1539), the founder of the Sikh religion.

Religion has sometimes brought conflict between the laws and practices of the white majority and those of immigrant groups. An example of this is the problem faced by Sikh men, whose religion forbids them from cutting their hair or beards. Wearing the hair in a turban is part of this belief. However, some schools and employers have tried to insist that turbans be removed, and British law demands that Sikh motorcyclists should wear crash helmets, even though this is impossible on top of a turban.

Culture

Perhaps the most obvious cultural effect of New Commonwealth immigration on Britain has been the revolution in British eating habits. Britain ended rationing in 1953 just at the time when migrants from the West Indies and India were beginning to settle in large numbers. The British public were suddenly exposed to a much greater choice of foods than they had ever known before. The taste for Indian food rapidly caught on with restaurants and shops opening in towns across the country. Eating out became a major leisure activity and by 1976 there were almost 2000 Indian restaurants catering for this trend. Changes in the British diet are not just reflected in the popularity of Indian restaurants. The food processing industry was quick to seize upon the potential of packaged Indian foods and ingredients. Supermarkets in Britain now sell tons of frozen, canned and 'ready meal' versions of traditional Indian dishes every year.

Music and the Arts have also been influenced by the immigrant arrivals. In London and other major cities there are annual carnivals which bring music, costume and dance to the streets. The largest is the Notting Hill Carnival which began in London in 1958. Seven thousand people attended the first carnival, nowadays it lasts for two days an attracts over a million people (**Source 42**). Carnival is a tradition of Trinidad which began following the abolition of slavery. The music is mostly provided by steel bands, and reggae, which originated in Jamaica.

SOURCE 40

The presence of ethnic groups with their different religious traditions has given new breadth and generosity to our vision of the brotherhood of man and the fatherhood of God. The new arrivals from Asia, Africa and the Caribbean have sometimes been blamed for the incoherence of Britain, but in reality British society was in the process of being atomised (broken up) long before they arrived... The immigrants bring rich gifts.

Robert Runcie, Archbishop of Canterbury, speaking in 1982.

SOURCE 41

The Taj Mahal restaurant in Cambridge. Hundreds of such restaurants specialising in Indian cuisine can be found across Britain.

SOURCE 42

The annual Notting Hill Carnival in London – Europe's biggest street festival.

Reggae music has established a worldwide popularity and, in Bob Marley, produced the first 'superstar' from the Third World. In its pure Jamaican form reggae music at first had only a limited appeal beyond the West Indian communities. But when the musical structures of reggae began to be used by mainstream bands such as the Police and the Clash in the late 1970s, it became a common feature of British popular music. Reggae music had an important social side-effect in Britain. Much of the content of reggae songs deals with the oppressed past of black people and the racism and prejudice of the present. Such lyrics have been an important way of raising awareness among young white people, and reggae music has been part of initiatives such as Rock Against Racism (**Source 31**).

The appearance of different musical cultures in Britain encouraged popular musicians to experiment with 'ethnic' instruments. By the late 1960s the Beatles had incorporated Indian instruments such as the sitar into their music. More recently, bhangra has come to influence popular music. Originally a folk dance from the Punjab, bhangra has been revitalised by young Indians and there are now many thriving clubs playing bhangra in disco form.

Knowledge and understanding

Use pages 185 to 199 to investigate the following questions.

1 What problems did many New Commonwealth people encounter after arriving in Britain?

2 How are these problems (a) similar, (b) different to those faced by Jewish settlers at the turn of the century?

3 Look at Source 13. What were the principal complaints made against Jews according to this Source. How do Sources 14 and 15 challenge these allegations?

5 Why did race riots break out in Nottingham and London's Notting Hill district in 1958?

6 To what extent was the race relations legislation of the 1960s and 1970s successful?

7 Look at the Datapoint: Britain's immigrant population.
a How do Sources 23 and 34 help to explain the concentration of black and Asian people in particular parts of Britain?
b How could the material in the Datapoint be used to challenge a racists' claim that Britain is 'being taken over by black people'?

8 In what ways has British society been changed or influenced by immigration since 1945?

Investigation

The Notting Hill Riots 1958

SOURCE A

This comment by Conservative Home Secretary R. A. Butler on the cause of the Notting Hill Riots was reported in the *Daily Mirror* on 17 September 1958.

It is untrue to suggest that the trouble was caused by pure prejudices of race and colour. It is purely a question of competition breeding discontent – competition for housing and jobs and, above all, the age-old stirrer-up of strife – competition for women.

SOURCE B

[Disturbances in Nottingham] made national radio and newspaper headlines, and had an immediate effect in the poverty-stricken area of North Kensington in London [Notting Hill] where communal trouble had been brewing for some months. Right-wing organisations had been active distributing leaflets and scrawling slogans, inciting people to 'Act now to Keep Britain White'. Within hours of the news of the Nottingham riots, a gang of teddy boys went 'nigger-hunting' through the Notting Hill area, armed with iron pipes, rods, table legs and knives.

Philippa Stewart, *Immigrants*, 1976.

SOURCE C

In 1958, the year of the Notting Hill riots, Labour Party Chairman Tom Driberg made the following comments at a TUC conference.

People talk about a colour problem arising in Britain. How can there be a colour problem here? Even after all the immigration of the past few years, there are only 190,000 coloured people in our population of over 50 million – that is, only four out of every 1000. The real problem is not black skins, but white prejudice.

SOURCE D

In ... Notting Hill ... black and white working class families lived in squalid, overcrowded slums. Black and white tenants alike were exploited, bullied and harassed by racketeering slum landlords. Few landlords were willing to let to black families. One that was, the notorious Rachman, sent strong-arm men and fierce dogs to intimidate any tenant who dared to appeal to the rent tribunal. The fascists blamed black people exclusively for the overcrowding and other bad conditions that afflicted everyone.

Peter Fryer, *Staying Power: The History of Black People in Britain*, 1984.

SOURCE E

Hundreds of black people are pouring into the larger cities of Britain including Coventry and are lowering the standard of life. Many will not work. They live on public assistance. They frequently are the worse for liquor (many of them are addicted to methylated spirits) and they live in overcrowded conditions. Police Chiefs of London, Liverpool, Birmingham, Bristol and Hull are gravely concerned about the menace. Unless the situation here is checked, England's green and pleasant land will become very largely a reserve for natives.

Coventry Standard, October 1954.

SOURCE F

Estimated net inward movement of West Indians, Indians and Pakistanis

	1955	1956	1957	1958
West Indians	27,550	29,800	23,000	15,000
Indians	5,800	5,600	6,000	6,200
Pakistanis	1,850	2,050	5,200	4,700
TOTAL	35,200	37,450	34,800	25,900

SOURCE G

Who or what is behind the race riots? Ignorance is the real villain. Ignorance of how people live. Ignorance of their aims and ambitions. Ignorance of what they are actually doing. Ignorance breeds fear. Fear breeds violence.

Daily Mirror, September 1958.

Questions

1. According to Source B, what was the immediate cause of the Notting Hill race riots?

2. What reasons are given in Sources A, B and G for the outbreak of the Notting Hill riots?

3. What evidence do Sources C, D and F provide to suggest that the Notting Hill riots were racially motivated?

4. Examine Sources A and G. Which of these explanations for the Notting Hill disturbances do you think is the most reliable? Explain your answer.

5. How useful would Source E be to a historian who wanted to study the causes of the racist attacks on the black residents of Notting Hill?

6. Why would it be difficult for a historian to explain accurately why the Notting Hill riots happened?

11 Shrinking the World

Mass communications and popular culture

Since the beginning of this century the world has been shrinking at an astonishing rate! This has nothing to do with the physical size of the planet but is the result of our fascination with technology. The inventions and discoveries of science have made the great distances which separate people often seem meaningless.

When the international news agency Reuters began its news service in the 19th century, it used the latest in communications technology: carrier pigeons! In the modern world, physical distances can be overcome in a matter of seconds.

Satellites

Hundreds of satellites have been put into orbit around the Earth since 1957. Radio and television signals are beamed from broadcasting stations and 'bounced' back to receiving dishes from the satellites.
This enables 'live' events to be seen as they happen thousands of miles away. Satellites are also used to provide direct telephone links between countries.

Air travel

The rapid movement of people over long distances has been achieved by spectacular advances in aircraft technology.
The first ever powered flight was by the Wright brothers in 1903. Today, millions of people every year fly the world's air routes on business or for pleasure.

Telephones

The world's telephone network covers most of the globe. At the touch of a few buttons telephone technology allows people in Britain to make direct contact with 135 countries. A single cable beneath the Atlantic ocean is capable of handling over 4000 telephone calls at the same time. The telephone is essential to business, commerce, the emergency services and social life.

The shrinking world

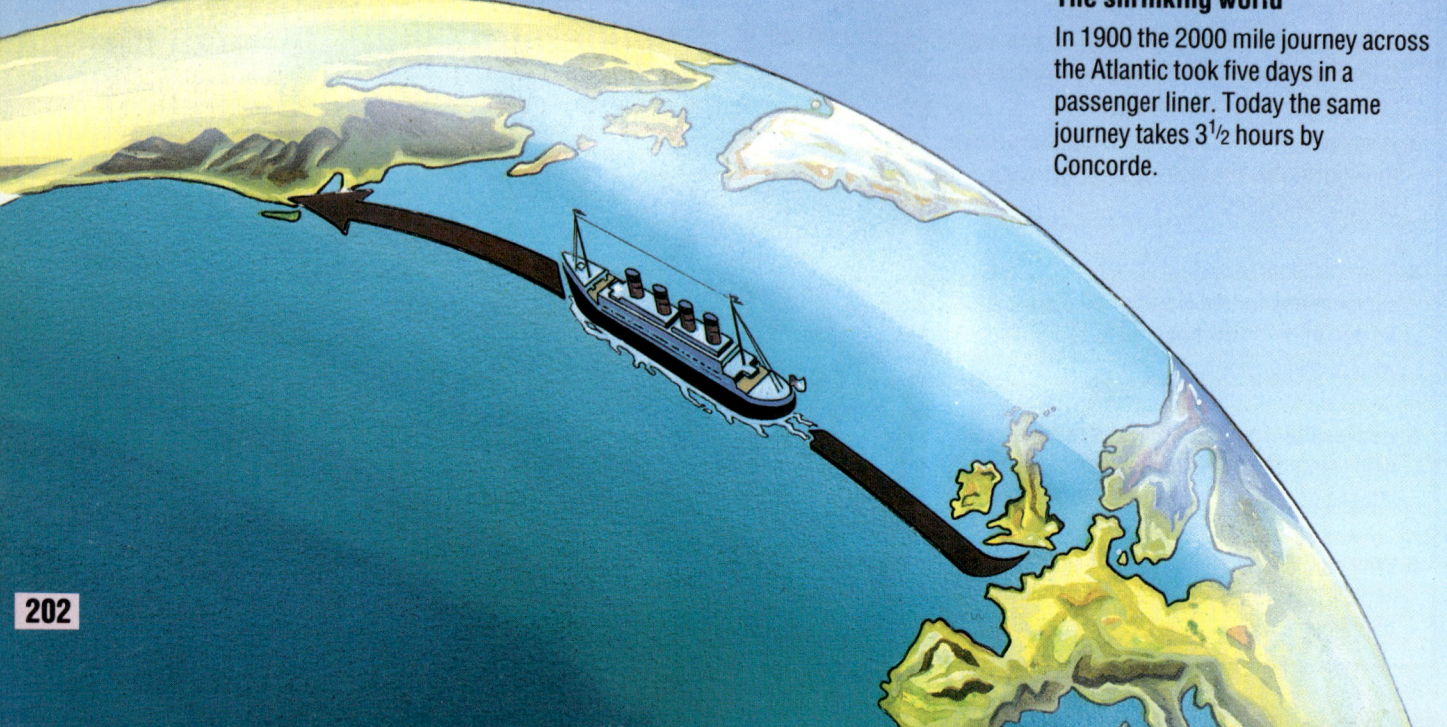

In 1900 the 2000 mile journey across the Atlantic took five days in a passenger liner. Today the same journey takes $3\frac{1}{2}$ hours by Concorde.

Shrinking the World

SOURCE 1

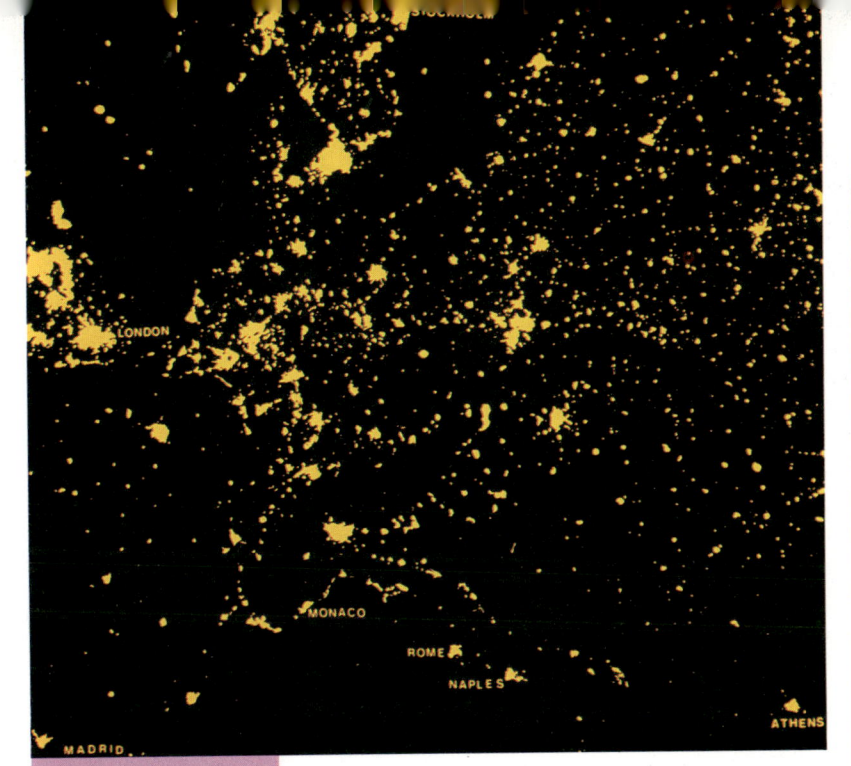

The astonishing versatility of modern satellites is revealed in this photograph of the city lights of Europe. The image was recorded by a US weather satellite in orbit 450 miles above the Earth.

Technology and mass communications

In 1896 Alfred Harmsworth founded the *Daily Mail*, the first popular national newspaper in Britain. In the same year Gugliemo Marconi demonstrated his pioneer radio apparatus which could send signals without wires for a hundred yards. A short distance away in London's West End, the first moving picture show was presented at the Regent Street Polytechnic. These exciting and pioneering developments were to have enormous impact on 20th century society and signalled the beginning of mass communications.

By this time two other inventions had already made their mark. The electric telegraph used wires to transmit morse code messages over long distances. In 1866 a telegraph cable was laid beneath the Atlantic ocean to provide a communications link between Europe and America. In 1876 Alexander Graham Bell invented the telephone and the first British telephone exchange was opened three years later. By 1900, 3000 telephones were in use in Britain. In 1978 there were 23.2 million telephones (**Sources 2 and 3**).

SOURCES 2 AND 3

A manually operated telephone switchboard of the type in use at the end of the 19th century. The women in the picture had to stand to operate the switchboard because of its large size.

British Telecom engineers run tests on the first digital international telephone exchange. These electronic exchanges are controlled by microprocessors and are amazingly fast.

Wireless communication

The next big breakthrough in communications technology came with the discovery that messages could be sent without wires using radio waves. Marconi followed up his first public demonstration of wireless communication by sending messages, first to France, and then across the Atlantic where they were picked up in Canada. The potential of radio communication was enormous.

Shrinking the World

In 1910 a radio message from a suspicious ship's captain alerted Scotland Yard to the whereabouts of the wanted murderer, Dr Crippen. Radio lengthened the long arm of the law and Crippen was arrested off the Canadian coast. Having murdered his wife and dismembered her body, Crippen became front page news in all the popular newspapers of the day. The public feasted on the grisly details of the crime and marvelled at the new wonder of technology which had led to his capture. Radio gained enormous publicity and its use spread quickly (**Source 4**).

When the *Titanic* hit an iceberg and sank in the North Atlantic in 1912, radio distress signals brought ships to the area to pick up 700 survivors. During the First World War, radio proved to be vital to the armies and navies of both sides. The wireless was soon developed to transmit the human voice and other sounds such as music. It soon became clear that the future of radio was in broadcasting.

Television

In 1924 John Logie Baird succeeded in transmitting the first television pictures. Baird's technological breakthrough was soon improved by other scientists. When British television broadcasting began in 1936 it used a technically superior method developed by Isaac Shoenberg at EMI (Electrical and Musical Industries) and based on the cathode-ray tube. By 1939 there were only about 20,000 sets in use. These were all to be found in the London area since pictures could not yet be transmitted over long distances.

However, from the 1950s the appeal of television grew at an astonishing rate. By 1977, 95 per cent of British homes had a television set. Television has become one of the most powerful and widely used inventions of the 20th century.

Satellites

The conquest of space led to a revolution in world communications. The first satellite, *Sputnik 1*, was sent into orbit by Russian scientists in 1957. Signals from the two radio transmitters on board were picked up in countries around the world as it circled the Earth every 95 minutes. In 1962 America launched the *Telstar* communications satellite which relayed the first live transatlantic television pictures. The age of round-the-world television had begun.

Satellite technology has advanced at a bewildering pace since the early days of space exploration. Satellites now form an essential part of the world's information and communications network.

SOURCE 4

The effect of the case and the part played by radio in the capture of Crippen not only captured the imagination of the world but had a tremendous effect on the use of radio in ships. In 1910 only about 100 ships in the mercantile marine used the system: within six months over 600 ships were equipped and within eighteen months radio was required by law on all ocean-going ships.

Great Newspapers Reprinted, 1972.

SOURCE 5

Final preparations being made to the *Syncom II* communications satellite before its launch into orbit in 1963. Space hardware of this sort paved the way for mass communications on a global scale.

Shrinking the World

SOURCE 6
Orville Wright makes the world's first powered flight in a craft made from wood, canvas and bicycle parts. His brother and co-inventor Wilbur runs alongside their machine to witness the historic flight.

Air travel

Another form of mass communication is air travel. This enables the rapid movement of people over long distances for business or leisure purposes. The dramatic advance of aircraft technology in the 20th century has played a major part in shrinking the world. The first powered flight took place at Kitty Hawk in North Carolina, USA in 1903. The aircraft called the *Flyer* was built by Wilbur and Orville Wright and stayed in the air for just 59 seconds (**Source 6**). It would be almost impossible to calculate how many minutes of flying time the world's aircraft have clocked up since that historic moment.

In 1919, the year in which Alcock and Brown made the first transatlantic flight, a daily air service began between London and Paris. This marked the beginning of modern civil aviation and other operators soon followed. These small companies found it difficult to make profits, so in 1924 the British government merged all existing operators into one large company called Imperial Airways. New routes were established including the first passenger service to Australia which began in 1932. By the time the Second World War broke out, there were regular passenger and freight services to most Commonwealth countries including Canada, South Africa and India.

Early passenger aircraft were small, expensive and slow. The 1938 Empire Flying Boat operated by Imperial Airways, flew at just 160 mph and carried only 17 passengers. Air travel did not yet have mass appeal although the number of travellers was increasing; 64,000 passengers were carried in 1919, twenty years later the figure had increased to 210,000 per year.

In 1935 British Airways was created to develop European routes. Five years later it merged with Imperial Airways to form the British Overseas Airways Corporation (BOAC). It was this company which put the first jet airliner, the de Havilland Comet, into service in 1952.

SOURCE 7
At one time huge airships had been regarded as the future of airborne passenger transport. However, these hydrogen-filled giants were potentially lethal. A number of the craft exploded, and the final nail in the coffin of airship travel came in May 1937 when the craft pictured here, the *Hindenburg*, burst into flames as it came in to land at Lakenhurst in New Jersey, USA. More than 30 people died in the inferno and soon after airships around the world were taken out of service.

Shrinking the World

DATAPOINT

The impact of air travel

Passenger miles flown by British airlines

- 1938: 53 (in millions)
- 1945: 302
- 1959: 3,000
- 1972: 12,000

Crossing the Atlantic
Percentage of passengers using air and sea

- 1948: sea 72%, air 28%
- 1953: sea 64%, air 36%
- 1963: sea 22%, air 78%
- 1970: sea 10%, air 90%

Number of Britons taking holidays abroad

- 1951: 2 million
- 1961: 4 million
- 1973: 8 million
- 1983: 15 million

Air travel and employment

- Pilots and stewards
- Engine manufacturers
- Travel agents
- Construction, eg airports
- Ground support staff: caterers, emergency services, security, baggage handlers
- Electronic systems manufacturers, eg for navigation equipment
- Air traffic controllers
- Aircraft builders
- Hoteliers
- Travel companies

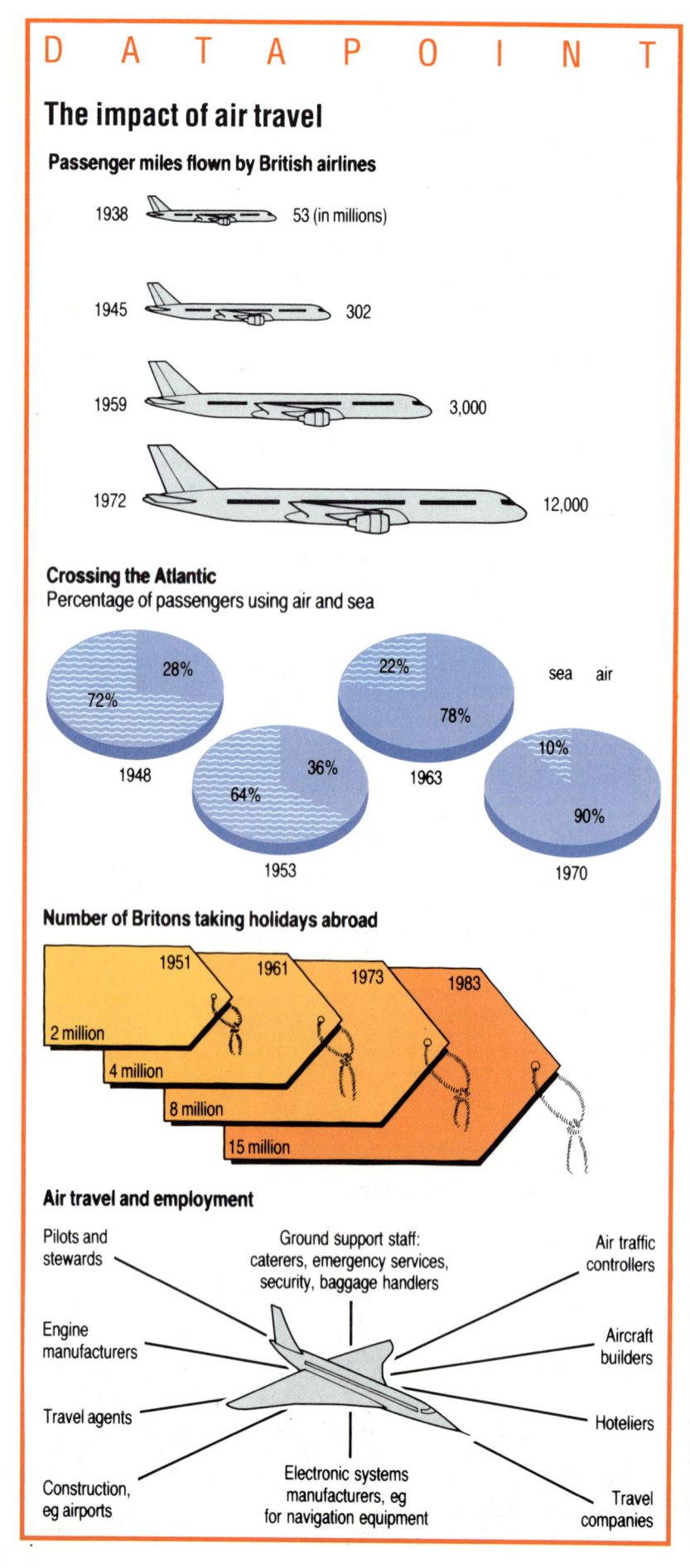

The development of the jet engine made air travel faster and more reliable. Another invention, radar, made safe navigation possible even in difficult conditions such as fog or darkness. From 1946 two state-owned companies operated Britain's air routes, British European Airways (BEA) and BOAC. Air travel now became increasingly popular. Following the introduction of the first transatlantic jet service in 1958, the number of aircraft passengers doubled every ten years. The shipping companies could not compete and the huge passenger liners which had once been the only means of crossing the Atlantic, began to be sold for scrap. In the 1960s airlines teamed up with travel companies to provide 'package holidays'. This opened the

SOURCE 8

Heathrow airport on the outskirts of London. Heathrow handles an enormous amount of air traffic, with an aeroplane landing or taking off every minute. It is one of the busiest airports in the world.

way for millions of people to take cheap holidays abroad in popular destinations such as Spain (see **Datapoint: The impact of air travel** opposite).

Between 1962 and 1969 another chapter was written in aviation history with the development of Concorde, the first supersonic airliner. Concorde was developed by an Anglo-French team at a cost of £360 million. Capable of flying faster than the speed of sound, it was expected to revolutionise air travel. But it was an expensive aircraft to buy and there were worries about the noise levels it produced over built-up areas. Only 16 orders were received for the plane and today flying by Concorde remains an expensive luxury. By contrast there was enormous interest in the American Boeing 747 'Jumbo Jet' which went into service in 1970. This huge aircraft carried 362 passengers (later models were even larger). It was an instant commercial success, particularly on long-haul routes such as those to the Far East, Australia and the USA.

The impact of radio

> On Halloween in 1938 radio listeners to the American CBS network were startled by an interruption to the familiar dance tunes;
> *Ladies and gentlemen, I have a grave announcement to make. Incredible as it may seem, strange beings who landed in New Jersey tonight are the vanguard of an invading army from Mars.*

The voice was that of the actor Orson Welles who was taking part in a dramatisation of H.G. Wells' science fiction classic, *The War of the Worlds*. Thousands of people across the eastern states of America became convinced they were listening to a real newscast. Reports of gigantic Martian machines firing death rays down crowded city streets created mass panic. Police switchboards were jammed with terrified callers, some even claiming to have seen the Martians! People crowded onto the roads in their cars in an attempt to evacuate the cities; those without transport gathered together in the streets or took refuge in their local churches. In Pittsburgh a man returned home in the middle of the broadcast to find his wife about to commit suicide in the bathroom. So great was the impact, the police had to halt the broadcast to prevent real deaths and injuries from occurring.

The ability of radio to reach and convince a mass audience to this extent shows just how far the 'wireless' had come since its humble beginnings as a communications device. It was now the world's most powerful news, information and entertainment medium.

SOURCE 9

At nine o'clock on Saturday morning, December 30th 1922, I arrived at the offices of the General Electrical Company in Kingsway. A notice in the entrance hall indicated that there was indeed a company for me to be general manager of – 'British Broadcasting Company, 2nd Floor'... This was it, or the beginnings of it... in those days when I said I was general manager of the BBC most people would ask what the initials meant.

John Reith, *Into the Wind*, 1949.

Shrinking the World

G.E.C. Radio

GECoPHONE
RADIO RECEIVERS AND LOUD SPEAKERS
MADE IN ENGLAND

SUPREMACY IN RADIO — G.E.C. RADIO

SOURCE 10

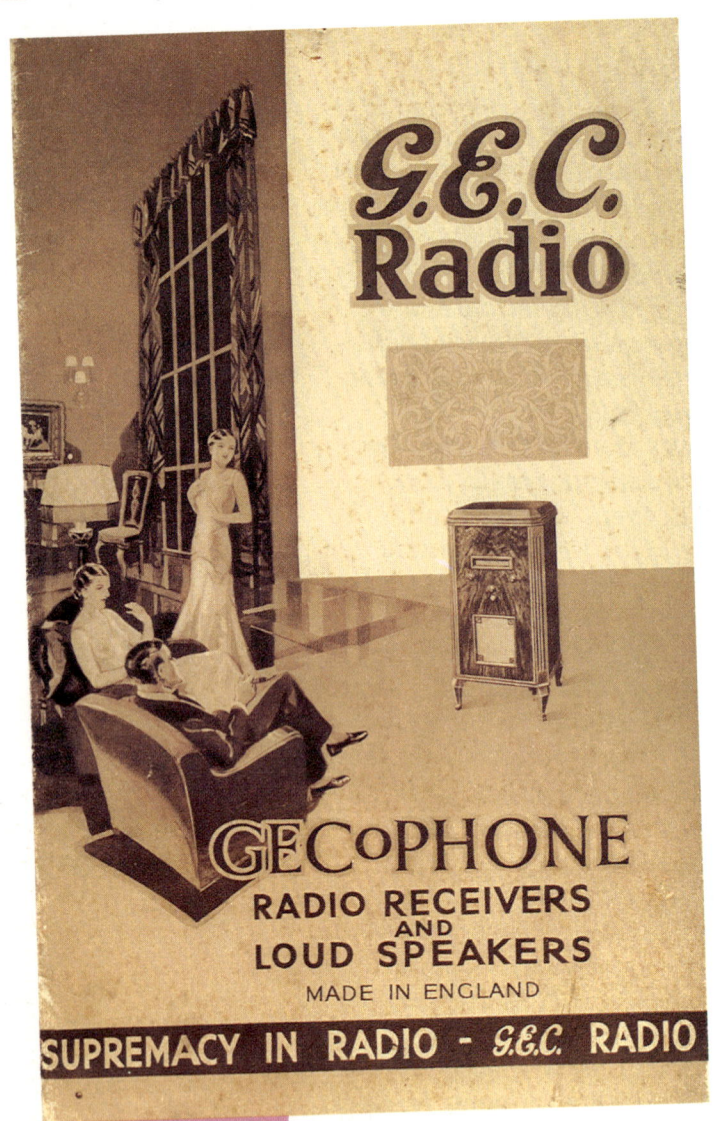

By the 1930s millions of radio receivers had been made and sold. This advertisement from 1932 shows the radio as the focus of attention in the living room. Thirty years later the television would occupy that position. Will television ever be replaced?

The BBC

The pioneers of wireless did not anticipate that it would be used for broadcasting purposes. But soon after 1918 a number of radio firms joined forces with amateur radio enthusiasts to begin wireless broadcasting. The first regular broadcasts came from Writtle near Chelmsford in 1921. They were transmitted by a group of Marconi Company engineers and came on the air once a week for just 30 minutes. In 1922 the British Broadcasting Company (BBC) was granted a licence to take over all public broadcasting. The general manager of the new company was John Reith (**Source 9**). In 1926 the BBC was taken into public ownership and was re-named the British Broadcasting Corporation. John Reith became its first Director General, a position he held until 1938. In its early years, Reith was the controlling influence on this important new institution in British life. In the 1920s and 1930s the influence and popularity of radio was huge (**Source 10**). By 1940 three quarters of the population could receive broadcasts and nine million licences had been purchased. However, at ten shillings (half the cost of the cheapest wireless set) the radio licence was not cheap and more than three million households had no access to radio.

Radio broadened the experience of millions of people. Classical music, plays and dramatised stories brought the listening public into contact with 'high' culture. Discussions and school broadcasts helped to make people better educated and informed. Regular news programmes were very effective in keeping the nation up to date with national and world events. The power of radio was demonstrated during the General Strike of 1926 when regular BBC bulletins were the only source of reliable information about the progress of the strike.

Radio also set out to entertain its listeners. Dance music, comedy shows, quizzes and sports programmes had mass appeal. As more and more people bought record players, radio helped to create the first hit records. Radio helped to weld the nation together by bringing important news to millions of people at the same time. In 1936, for example, King Edward VIII spoke to the nation explaining why he had decided to abdicate. In 1939 Britain's declaration of war on Nazi Germany was announced on the radio. The wireless helped to create 'national' sporting occasions by broadcasting commentaries on such events as Wimbledon, and the FA Cup Final at Wembley.

John Reith exercised strict control over what could be broadcast. Variety shows and popular music were kept off the air on Sundays when religious programmes dominated. Comedians had to keep their acts 'clean' and presenters had to speak 'correct' English. Working class accents and regional dialects were frowned upon. Not everyone enjoyed the rather highbrow tone of many of the BBC's programmes. They tuned to radio stations on the Continent such as Radio Luxembourg and Radio Normandy which offered entertainment with more popular appeal. By 1936 six million people in Britain regularly deserted the BBC in favour of the European stations.

During the Second World War, BBC radio took on a special significance. At first the government, through the Ministry of Information, tried to control the content and tone of BBC broadcasts (**Source 11**). But the BBC resisted this type of interference and fought hard to retain its independence. The BBC was strongly patriotic and did much to boost public morale by broadcasting Churchill's stirring speeches. But it also understood the need to provide a reliable news service, and entertainment to take people's minds off the emergency. The BBC reported defeats as well as victories and this was an important factor in building trust and confidence in Churchill's leadership. Regular news based on hard facts was vital for public morale during the crisis of wartime.

The decline of radio?

In the late 1940s the popularity of radio was at its peak. From the early 1950s television began to rob radio of its mass audience. In 1953 the Coronation of Queen Elizabeth II was watched by a television audience of 20 million, while only 12 million listened to the events on the radio (**Source 12**). Another threat came from 'pirate' radios. These were unlicensed stations which broadcast from ships moored outside British territorial waters. During the 1960s stations such as Radio Caroline captured the attention of Britain's youth by broadcasting non-stop pop music.

But radio was far from dead. It showed its versatility by adapting to changing tastes and finding new audiences. In 1967 the BBC launched its campaign to

SOURCE 11

At the beginning of the War, as the Nazis rapidly took control of Continental Europe, there was panic within the Ministry of Information. The BBC came under attack by the Ministry for failing to be sufficiently patriotic. This source comes from an internal memorandum at the Ministry.

There must be some sign of guts in the voices of announcers. This has been suggested for months and yet nothing seems to happen. They can show hate of the Germans and contempt of the Italians in their voices, or if they cannot they must get someone who can ... Entertainments should be coloured. I know the BBC don't like this, but more valuable propaganda can be got across when it appears to be unconscious than directly. In other words dirty cracks against the Germans could be put into musical sketches ... A circular should be sent round to leading politicians asking them not to refer to Herr Hitler unless the word 'Herr' is spat out or sneered.

SOURCE 12

The spectacular Coronation of Queen Elizabeth II in 1953. For the first time a major event was watched on the television by more people than listened on the radio. Many people bought or rented a television set in order to get an armchair view of this historic moment. Seen in black and white on a tiny screen the broadcast would not be considered impressive today. But forty years ago televisions were technological marvels and on Coronation Day those houses which had one were crowded with friends and neighbours eager to experience the thrill of the live broadcast.

win back young listeners with its own pop music station, Radio 1 (**Source 13**). It re-organised its other stations and made programmes targeted at different audiences. Radio 4, for example, offers a comprehensive news service rivalling that than of any television station. In 1967 local radio was launched. This has proved to be very successful in providing a range of services for local people. Local news, job vacancies, entertainment guides, weather, consumer affairs and help-lines have all proved popular. Local radio encourages public participation in broadcasting from the simple phone-in to enabling people to make their own programmes.

In 1972 the first commercial radio stations were established. These operated along similar lines to BBC local radio but raised their revenue through advertising. BBC and independent stations together provide local radio services for about 90 per cent of Britain's population.

SOURCE 13
Tony Blackburn, one of the first Radio 1 disc jockeys, opens the new pop music station in October 1967.

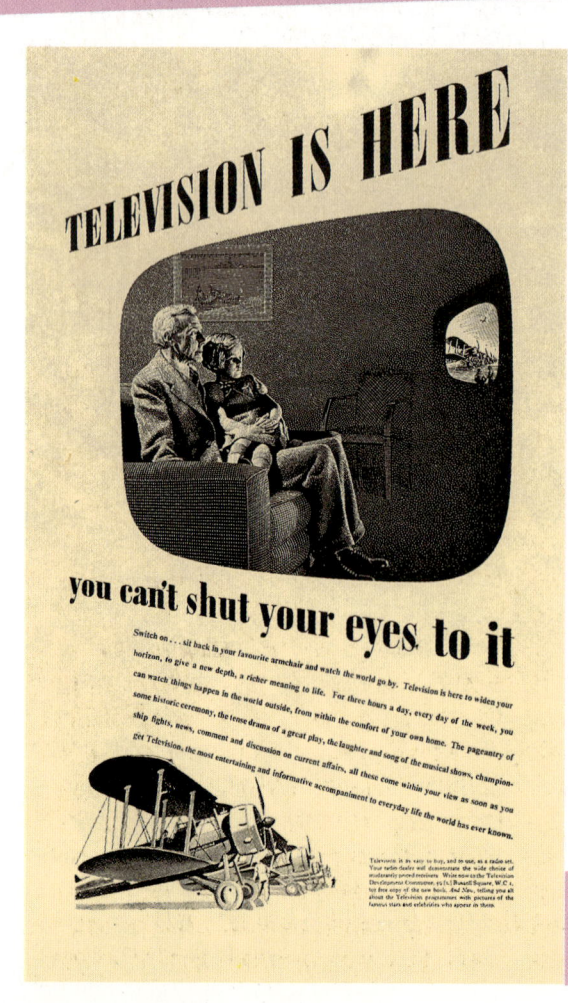

The impact of television

When the Second World War broke out, television broadcasting was suspended and the BBC didn't resume its service until 1946. During the 1950s the popularity of television grew rapidly. Television was promoted as the marvel of the modern age, capable of expanding the knowledge and experience of its viewers (**Source 14**). Television lured audiences away from cinemas and reduced the appeal of radio (see **Datapoint: Television takes over** opposite).

By 1965 13 million television sets were in use in Britain. Before 1954 there was just one TV channel, operated by the BBC. Viewers bought a licence to watch television programmes and in this way the BBC got its revenue. In 1954 the

SOURCE 14
Advertisement: 'Television is Here'

Shrinking the World 211

SOURCE 15

A 17 inch television set of the type in common use in the 1950s. By today's standards the design and features of these early sets were primitive. How will your TV compare with those being produced in 40 years time?

Knowledge and understanding

Use pages 202 to 211 investigate the following questions.

1 Describe the main technological advances which have led to the development of mass communications.

2 Look at the list below. What was the importance of these developments to the growth of modern air travel?
a the jet engine
b radar
c package holidays
d the Jumbo Jet

3 Look at the Datapoint: The impact of air travel. What have been the results of the increase in air travel in the last 50 years?

4 What was radio originally used for? What new use began to be developed in the 1920s?

5 Describe all the ways in which radio could affect the lives of ordinary people.

6 What was the special importance of radio during the Second World War?

7 'After 1953 radio was unable to match the appearance of television and has been in decline ever since'. Do you agree?

Independent Television Authority (ITA) was set up. The ITA licensed commercial television companies to broadcast in different regions. In 1955 commercial television broadcasting began. A second BBC channel (BBC2) went on the air in 1964. Three years later the first colour transmissions were introduced. In 1982 Channel 4 was launched and breakfast television first appeared on British screens in the following year. Satellite and cable services, video recorders, computer games, and information services such as Teletext and Oracle have increased the scope of television, making it a uniquely versatile source of entertainment and information.

Television in society

In 1982 a survey showed that people occupied almost half their leisure time watching television. For many people the main function of TV is to provide entertainment. Films, game shows, sport, soap operas, chat shows, music programmes, comedies and drama are all part of our TV diet. Television has made the home the centre of mass entertainment.

There is also a more serious purpose to television. It provides a regular news service to keep people up-to-date with local, national and world events. High quality documentaries about such things as wildlife, science and politics, helps to expand our knowledge and understanding of the world in which we live. Television provides an educational service, making programmes for schools

DATAPOINT

Number of British cinemas 1914-79

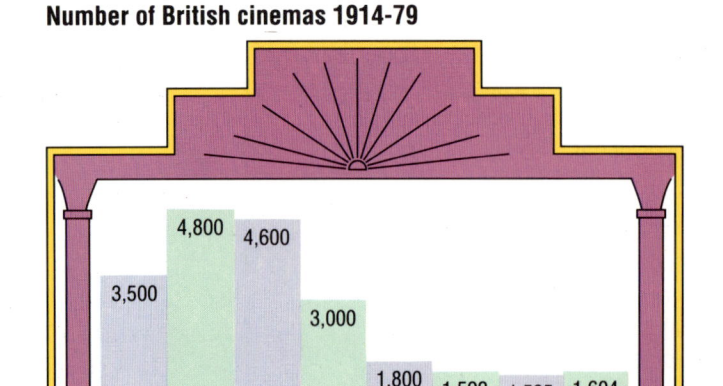

Year	Cinemas
1914	3,500
1938	4,800
1951	4,600
1960	3,000
1966	1,800
1970	1,592
1976	1,525
1979	1,604

Weekly cinema attendance in Britain 1928-76

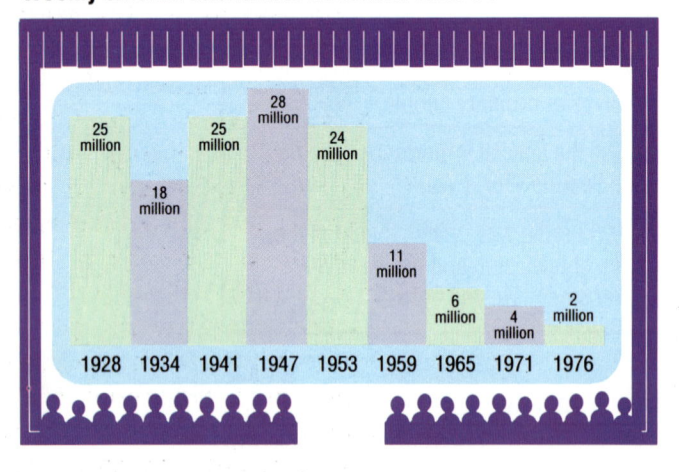

Year	Attendance
1928	25 million
1934	18 million
1941	25 million
1947	28 million
1953	24 million
1959	11 million
1965	6 million
1971	4 million
1976	2 million

Number of television licences in Britain 1947-68

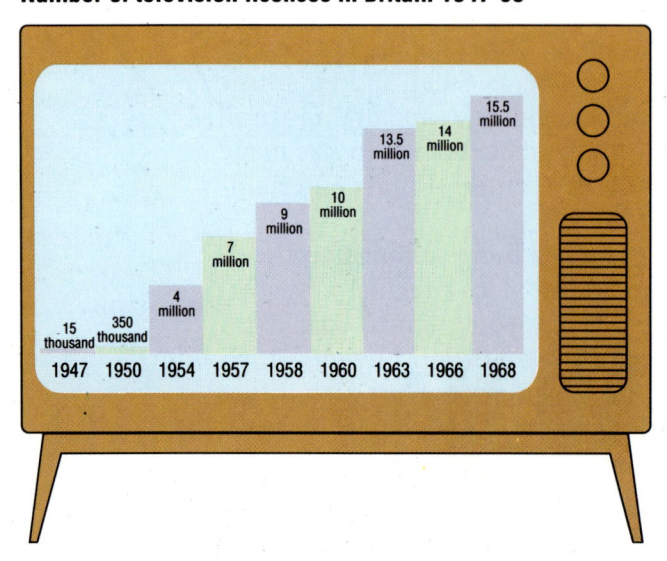

Year	Licences
1947	15 thousand
1950	350 thousand
1954	4 million
1957	7 million
1958	9 million
1960	10 million
1963	13.5 million
1966	14 million
1968	15.5 million

and colleges. In 1969 the Open University was set up to provide opportunities in Higher Education for people who could not attend normal college courses. The teaching of Open University students is done substantially through television programmes.

When the power of television joined forces with the world of advertising, a consumer revolution was begun. The introduction of commercial television has helped to shape and change people's tastes and habits. Manufacturers can bring their products to the attention of millions in a single commercial. By placing pressure on mass audiences to buy the latest products, television advertising has helped to encourage a 'consumer society'.

Critics of television have claimed that it discourages other social activity such as conversation. TV has been blamed for poor reading standards and for the increase of violence in society. Campaigners claim that there is too much sex, violence and bad language on the television and that it has helped to lower standards of behaviour in society. However, whether or not these criticisms are valid, there is no doubt that since 1945 television has become a major feature of our modern world. Television is the main source of entertainment and information in the lives of most people. Compare this with the situation 50 years and 100 years ago. This familiar household object has transformed society and demonstrates the tremendous power of technology.

Shrinking the World

Popular culture: cinema

> The first form of public amusement to have truly mass appeal was the cinema. From its beginnings as a novelty feature on Music Hall programmes, cinema grew to a position in the 1940s where it regularly attracted audiences of 20 million every week.

The first films were short and had no story-line. They showed commonplace action such as a moving train, people dancing, or waves rolling onto the shore. In spite of this they were hugely popular. Soon films began to be made with characters and plots. There were no words or soundtrack however. The silent action was accompanied by a live pianist and words which appeared on the screen. The silent era lasted until 1927 when the first 'talkie' was made. The great silent stars such as Charlie Chaplin and Mary Pickford were immensely popular (**Source 17**). When Chaplin visited London in 1921 he brought city centre traffic to a standstill as crowds swarmed into Piccadilly to catch a glimpse of their hero. When the romantic film star Rudolph Valentino died in 1926 there were scenes of hysteria particularly amongst his legions of female fans; several of them even committed suicide! Yet the 'golden age' of the cinema was only just beginning. Colour movies with dialogue made cinema-going more popular than ever. By 1937 there were 4700 cinemas in Britain. The largest cinema chains were Gaumont-British, ABC (Associated British Cinemas) and Odeon. By 1939 over half the population went to the cinema once a week. The cinema became the centre of many people's social life. It attracted children to the Saturday matinees and courting couples to the evening performances. It was a place where families could share an evening out and where women could go unaccompanied by men. Cinema brought glamour into peoples lives and allowed them to escape into other worlds. Even the names of the 'Picture Palaces' – Scala, Trocadero, Plaza, Rivoli

SOURCE 16

Before cinema, the Music Hall was the most common form of popular entertainment. Every town had at least one of these theatres running nightly programmes of live variety entertainment including singers, dancers, magicians an acrobats.

One of the best-loved music hall entertainers was the singer Miss Vesta Tilley whose stage gimmick was to dress as a man.

SOURCE 17

Charlie Chaplin, probably the greatest of the silent screen film stars.

– conjured up exotic and romantic images.

The ability of cinema to take people away from the routine of their daily lives was particularly important at times of crisis. During the depression years of the 1930s cinema played a vital role in maintaining the morale of the unemployed. It provided a touch of magic even in the most desperate times (**Source 19**).

The influence of America

British popular culture has been strongly influenced by America during the 20th century. This was particularly evident in the cinema. The centre of world feature-film production between the wars was Hollywood. Its 'dream factories', the huge studio complexes of the major film companies, produced the stars and the films everyone wanted to see (**Source 22**). By 1926 the proportion of British films shown in British cinemas was less than 5 per cent. In 1927 the government attempted to reverse this trend with the Cinematograph Films Act. This required cinema owners to show a minimum quota of British films. By 1935 the proportion was 20 per cent. British-based directors such as Alfred Hitchcock and Alexander Korda were encouraged by this measure and produced some of the finest British films in the history of cinema. In spite of this, America continued to dominate; Leslie Howard and Charles Laughton were known to many British filmgoers, but neither of these fine British actors could compete with the fame of Walt Disney's most enduring creation – a cartoon mouse by the name of Mickey!

SOURCE 18

King Kong: the most spectacular special effects movie of its time. Audiences in 1933 flocked to see the giant gorilla who falls in love with an actress, played by Fay Wray. The final sequence, with King Kong on top of the Empire State building being attacked by fighter planes, is one of cinema's most famous scenes.

SOURCE 19

Cinema-going remained very popular even in the most difficult days of the Depression. This American investigator, working in Britain, offers some reasons for this.

The appeal of the movie is that it satisfies the desire for the new experience and a glimpse of other worlds and at times an escape from the present environment. This satisfaction is doubly important to the man whose world is severely limited because of ... unemployment ... at the cinema, all of these limitations drop away, and for three hours he rides the plains of Arizona, tastes the night life of Paris or New York, makes a safe excursion into the underworld, sails the seven seas or penetrates the African jungle. Famous comedians make him laugh and forget his difficulties and discouragements. It does not surprise me that the cinema noticed very little falling off of trade in Greenwich or in other communities more subject to unemployment during the severest seasons of that scourge.

E.W. Bakke, *The Unemployed Man*, 1933.

SOURCES 20 AND 21

Although Hollywood, in the United States, was the centre of world film production, many of its stars came from Europe. In 1930 Bela Lugosi brought Dracula to the screen. His portrayal of the vampire was copied by other actors in dozens of later Dracula movies.

The German-born actress Marlene Dietrich caused a sensation in the same year with her performance as a cabaret singer in *The Blue Angel*.

SOURCE 22

[The domination of Hollywood] can be explained in various ways. There was the climate of the west coast, with its abundant sunshine, which made the outdoor shooting so essential to the early films so much easier. There was also American business know-how. Sooner, and more efficiently than anyone else, the American film industry created a distribution system that was linked both to a smooth production flow and to organised outlets (chains of cinemas). In the early days, the US had more and better films to offer. Since the films were silent there was no language barrier ... [The American film industry] was also helped by the First World War, which left the country untouched and caused no major [disruption] in production.

Keith Roberts, 'Hollywood and the Star System'.

SOURCE 23

Walt Disney and Mickey Mouse in 1928. Mickey has become the most famous cartoon character of all time and the name Disney is known to millions of people around the world. Some of Disney's full length cartoon features such as *Snow White*, *Dumbo* and *The Jungle Book* are among the most famous films ever made and Walt Disney still holds the record for winning the most Oscars. The Disney stores and giant theme parks are part of a huge family entertainment business which spans the globe.

Cinema in wartime

The power of cinema was first harnessed during the First World War. By 1914 there were already 3000 cinemas in Britain and the government quickly put them to use in encouraging support for the war effort (**Source 24**). During the Second World War the potential was even greater. Three-quarters of the adult population during wartime went to the cinema. Films provided a vital escape from the daily stress of the War and helped to maintain morale. Government newsreels showed the progress of the War and helped people to visualise the news they received from the radio. Every feature-film performance was accompanied by short propaganda films. These concentrated on the positive efforts being made by ordinary people towards winning the War. Audiences watched short documentaries about women factory workers, the Land Army and the emergency services. The message, that everyone was working together to secure victory, was a reminder to anyone in the audience not 'doing their bit' that they should get involved.

The decline of cinema

From the 1950s the popularity of cinema quickly declined as more people bought television sets and stayed at home for their entertainment. Many cinemas were forced to close down and were demolished. Others were converted to different uses: nightclubs, shops and, above all, bingo halls. By 1963 over 14 million people belonged to bingo clubs up and down the country. Some cinemas tried out new gimmicks, such as 3D films and Smell-o-Vision, in an attempt to win back audiences. Once the novelty wore off, though, cinema was still fighting a losing battle with television.

In recent years cinema-going has become more popular. Audiences have been won back with the impressive special effects of films such as *Star Wars* which work best on the big screen. New multi-screen complexes offering complete entertainment facilities under one roof are attractive to families, couples and groups of friends, and have helped to bring people back to the cinema.

SOURCE 24

In 1916 the government set up the Department of Information in an effort to gain control of public opinion through propaganda. The new Department comprised four separate sections, one of which was the Cinema Division.

The Cinema Division represented the harnessing of the new mass medium to propaganda purposes ... Propaganda trailers using animation, silhouettes, documentary footage and re-enactment were distributed through commercial newsreel networks and reached massive audiences to ridicule the Germans, promote economy campaigns and boost war savings.

John Stevenson, *British Society 1914-45*, 1984.

SOURCE 25

Some of the most successful films of recent years have been big screen versions of popular TV series. Another way of getting audiences back into the cinemas has been to produce sequels to box office hits. This photo is a still from *Star Trek IV*.

Read all about it!

In 1969 media tycoon Rupert Murdoch launched the *Sun* newspaper. During the 1970s it out sold rivals such as the *Daily Mirror* to become the most successful daily newspaper in Britain. The tabloid format of the *Sun* and its rivals has become familiar to millions of readers. Such papers are bought as much for their entertainment value as their news content. 'Quality' newspapers such as *The Times*, *The Daily Telegraph* and *The Guardian* report serious news about politics, international relations and the economy, but the tabloids have an entirely different focus.

SOURCE 26
A popular newspaper from the turn of the century.

The birth of the popular press

During the 20th century the daily newspaper has become one of the most powerful means of mass communication. In 1939 one survey reported that 69 per cent of people over 16 read a national daily newspaper. Today, around 15 million daily papers are bought in Britain. The rise of the popular press began in 1896 when Alfred Harmsworth (later Lord Northcliffe) launched the *Daily Mail*. The newspaper was very different to its competitors such as *The Times*. It was cheap, carried short news items and included gossip, sport, fashion and crime stories. There were lots of pictures and cartoons, alongside dozens of advertisements. Within four years the *Daily Mail* had increased its circulation five times and was selling almost a million copies a day. Harmsworth sparked a newspaper revolution and imitators soon followed. In 1900 the *Daily Express* appeared on news stands to be joined three years late by the *Daily Mirror*.

The popular press was created by three principal forces:

1 The new reading public

The Education Act of 1870 had brought elementary education to the masses. Millions more people could now read, but *The Times* and other established newspapers were too serious and too detailed to be read easily. By 1900 there was a big demand for a cheap and easy-to-read newspaper.

2 Low price

In the 1850s the government had removed taxes from newspapers making them much cheaper. Harmsworth brought prices down further by charging companies to advertise their products in his mass-circulation paper. In this way the newspaper made profit from its advertising revenue rather than its sales. Harmsworth was therefore able to offer the *Daily Mail* at the easily affordable price of a half-penny.

3 Technology

The mass production of newspapers was made possible by some major advances in technology. The gathering of news became much faster with the development of the electric telegraph, the telephone and the wireless. Meanwhile, printing was revolutionised by the invention of the rotary press, which raised the print rate to 200,000 copies per hour, and the Linotype machine, which could set the text of a page ten times faster than a hand compositor.

Impact of the popular press

Cheap newspapers which sold in their millions were very effective in shaping public opinion. They were used to stimulate popular enthusiasm for many things from the two World Wars to the Royal Family and the football pools. Newspaper reporting helped to encourage a sense of national identity amongst the people of the British Isles. The daily news was delivered consistently to a nation of readers whether they lived in Cardiff, Belfast, Aberdeen or London. However, some people became concerned that the news was being manipulated to reflect the opinions of the great newspaper barons who controlled most of Britain's dailies. Lord Northcliffe, Lord Beaverbrook and Lord Rothermere dominated the newspaper publishing business and each took a personal interest in what was printed.

The concentration of newspaper power in the hands of a few individuals had consequences for the smaller papers. Although the circulation of daily newspapers increased from 4.5 million in 1910 to 15.5 million in 1947, the number of national dailies fell from 12 to 9. The number of local morning newspapers declined from 41 in 1921 to 25 in 1947. Fourteen local evening papers closed down in the same period.

Newspaper advertising had a huge impact on the world of commerce. By 1938 an estimated £100 million was being spent each year on advertising. This created 'brand name' products like Pears Soap and Bovril. It shaped consumer tastes and encouraged the development of a consumer society. In turn, advertising influenced the development of the newspaper business. Mass circulation became a necessity if advertisers were to be attracted to a paper.

Recent developments

Britain's daily newspapers continue to sell in their millions. the *Daily Mirror*, the *Sun*, the *Daily Express* and the *Daily Mail* together sell around 12 million copies per day. In their battle to attract readers, newspaper owners employ a range of tactics including free gifts, competitions offering huge cash prizes, and sensational 'exclusives'.

Many technical changes have also taken place, with computers bringing about a second revolution in the gathering and printing of Britain's daily news. The most visible result of this has been newspapers in full colour, but the industry itself has also changed. The printing presses of Fleet Street have fallen silent and papers are now produced in modern factory units close to motorway links.

> **SOURCE 27**
>
> Compare the sensationalism of this copy of the *Sun* from the 1980s with the style and appearance of the *Daily Express* of 1900 (Source 26).

Youthquake!

During the 1950s a distinctive 'youth culture' appeared in Britain. Until that time teenagers had only been identified as an age group. Now they began to develop a separate social identity.

Teenagers were part of the so-called 'affluent society' in which British people enjoyed full employment, high wages, the welfare state and increased leisure time. In 1957 the Conservative Prime Minister Harold Macmillan declared 'most of our people have never had it so good.' Certainly young people had never before experienced such prosperity. By 1959 there were five million teenagers in Britain each spending an average of £3 per week. Manufacturers increasingly targeted teenagers with products designed to appeal to youthful tastes. Fashion clothing, cosmetics, transistor radios and records were all produced to capture a share of the lucrative teenage market.

The increased spending power of teenagers was only one feature of their development. They were also physically more mature than preceding generations. Motorbikes and motor-scooters encouraged personal mobility and contributed to an increased sense of independence. And there were greater opportunities for foreign travel.

The affluence and maturity of teenagers encouraged them to assert their independence. Many rejected the values and attitudes of the older generation and identified with fashions, film stars and music which their parents found unattractive. The Teddy Boys with their long jackets, drainpipe trousers and slicked back hair were the first to develop a distinctive youth identity. Later groups such as Mods, Rockers, Hippies and Punks adopted different fashions but were following the same teenage urge to 'be different' from mainstream society. In the 1950s teenage film heroes, such as James Dean and Marlon Brando, portrayed rebellious young men battling against the hypocrisy of the adult world. The titles of their films such as *Rebel Without a Cause* and *The Wild One* reflected the teenage challenge to accepted tastes, ideas and standards of behaviour. Above all, youth culture came to be identified with music. The new '45' single sold in millions and the music being played was rock 'n' roll.

The impact of rock 'n' roll

The revolution in popular music came from America. While clean-cut 'crooners' like Frank Sinatra and big band dance music remained very popular, teenagers came increasingly to reject this 'Mom and Dad' music. Dance bands and popular singers had been around for decades and were part of an established and acceptable cultural scene.

Teenagers looked for something different; something which would help to establish their separate identity. They turned first to 'black music', in particular rhythm and blues. White musicians began to experiment with the 12-bar structure of this music and when they

SOURCE 28

Elvis Presley, the 'King'.

SOURCE 29

Saturday night at the dance hall in Tottenham, North London, 1957. Dancing the jive to rock 'n' roll music required agility and physical fitness!

combined it with elements of country and western, 'rock 'n' roll' was born. In 1953 a disc jockey named Alan Freed began to broadcast a regular rock 'n' roll programme from a radio station in Cleveland, Ohio. The programme was an instant success. Teenagers adored it, their parents hated it; Freed rapidly became the most popular DJ in America.

In April 1954 a former country and western singer, Bill Hayley, recorded *Rock Around the Clock*, one of the first rock 'n' roll records to reach a mass audience. Three months later an ex-truck driver named Elvis Presley released his first single, *That's Alright Mama*. Presley became a millionaire by the age of 21 and was quickly hailed as the 'King of rock 'n' roll' (**Source 28**). He became one of the 20th century's most famous people and spent over 1000 weeks in the British charts.

Presley's style and music inspired British rock 'n' roll artists including Tommy Steele, Billy Fury and Cliff Richard. Rock 'n' roll fever gripped British teenagers. In dance halls the jive took over (**Source 29**) and screaming crowds mobbed the stars whenever they made live appearances. Teenage television shows such as the *Six-Five Special, Oh Boy!* and later, *Ready Steady Go!* were created to cater for the new musical tastes of the young. Since 1955 popular music has been dominated by rock 'n' roll and music derived from it.

The swinging sixties

In the 1960s British musical talent rocked the world. The Beatles became the pop sensation of the decade (**Source 30**). A BBC survey in 1964 revealed that Liverpool's 'Fab Four' were Britain's most popular tourist attraction. In America 'Beatlemania' swept the nation and thousands flocked to see their live performances. By 1965 the Beatles had sold 225 million records worldwide and were so successful that they were awarded the MBE for services to British exports! Their main rivals were the Rolling Stones. They cultivated a tougher image, dressed casually and grew their hair long. They recorded songs like *Let's Spend the Night Together*, reflecting youth's more casual attitude towards sex and causing dismay within 'respectable' society. Music was perhaps the most important element in the 'youth culture' of the 1960s. By the end of the decade the BBC had acknowledged this fact with the creation of Radio 1 (see page 210).

But the sixties were not just about music. Fashion designers produced clothes and accessories which helped to create a distinctive teenage identity. In the 1960s London became the fashion capital of the world thanks to designers

Shrinking the World

Knowledge and understanding

Use pages 212 to 221 to investigate the following questions.

1. Explain the importance of cinema during times of crisis such as the Great Depression and the Second World War.

2. Use Source 22 to explain why the USA became the centre of world feature-film production.

3. Look at the Datapoint: Television takes over. How would you account for the dramatic fall in cinema attendance after 1953?

4. Account for the development of a 'youth culture' in the 1950s.

5. What were the main features of youth culture in the 1950s and 1960s?

SOURCE 30

The Beatles. The best known and most successful pop group of all time. Between 1963 and 1966 they had 11 consecutive number one hit singles in Britain. A further six consecutive number ones followed from 1967 to 1969.

like Mary Quant. This was the era of the fashion boutique, the most famous of which was Barbara Hulanicki's *Biba* store. Carnaby Street became the fashion centre of London selling the essential items for the young person's wardrobe including brightly coloured hipsters, trouser suits, kaftans, beads and, most popular of all, the miniskirt. British designer Mary Quant launched the miniskirt from her boutique on the King's Road in Chelsea. It caused a sensation. Super-slim models such as Jean Shrimpton and Twiggy popularised the new high-rise hemline, making it the fashion symbol of the sixties. Young women wore miniskirts to proclaim their new-found independence and freedom.

1960 also marked the beginning of the so-called 'permissive society' and a more relaxed attitude towards sex. The contraceptive pill introduced in 1961 began a sexual revolution which appealed particularly to young people. Many observers, however, believed that the miniskirt and the pill represented a decline in moral standards and criticised young people as irresponsible and immoral.

SOURCE 31

The Isle of Wight festival, August 1969. An estimated 500,000 fans converged on the island for three days of music. Bob Dylan, Jimi Hendrix and the Doors were among the big-name acts to appear. Festivals like this showed the independence and affluence of youth in the sixties.

PRESIDENTS OF THE UNITED STATES OF AMERICA

President	Party	Took office
William McKinley	Republican	1897
Theodore Roosevelt	Republican	1901
William Taft	Republican	1909
Woodrow Wilson	Democrat	1913
Warren G. Harding	Republican	1921
Calvin Coolidge	Republican	1923
Herbert Hoover	Republican	1929
Franklin D. Roosevelt	Democrat	1933
Harry S. Truman	Democrat	1945
Dwight D. Eisenhower	Republican	1953
John F. Kennedy	Democrat	1961
Lyndon B. Johnson	Democrat	1963
Richard Nixon	Republican	1969
Gerald Ford	Republican	1974
Jimmy Carter	Democrat	1977
Ronald Reagan	Republican	1981
George Bush	Republican	1989
Bill Clinton	Democrat	1993

PRIME MINISTERS AND GOVERNMENTS OF BRITAIN

Prime Minister	Government	Government formed
Marquis of Salisbury	Conservative	1895
A.J. Balfour	Conservative	1902
Sir Henry Campbell-Bannerman	Liberal	1905
H.H. Asquith	Liberal	1908
H.H. Asquith	Coalition	1915
David Lloyd George	Coalition	1916
A. Bonar Law	Conservative	1922
Stanley Baldwin	Conservative	1923
Ramsay MacDonald	Labour	1924
Stanley Baldwin	Conservative	1924
Ramsay MacDonald	Labour	1929
Ramsay MacDonald	Coalition	1931
Stanley Baldwin	Conservative	1935
Neville Chamberlain	Coalition	1937
Winston Churchill	Coalition	1940
Winston Churchill	Conservative	1945
Clement Attlee	Labour	1945
Sir Winston Churchill	Conservative	1951
Sir Anthony Eden	Conservative	1955
Harold Macmillan	Conservative	1957
Sir Alec Douglas-Home	Conservative	1963
Harold Wilson	Labour	1964
Edward Heath	Conservative	1970
Harold Wilson	Labour	1974
James Callaghan	Labour	1976
Margaret Thatcher	Conservative	1979
John Major	Conservative	1990

RUSSIAN LEADERS

Russian Empire
Nicholas II	Tsar of Russia	1894

Provisional Government (1917)
Prince Lvov	Prime Minister	March–July
Alexander Kerensky	Prime Minister	July–Nov.

Soviet Union (USSR)
Vladimir Ilyich Lenin	General Secretary	1917
Josef Stalin	General Secretary	1924
Nikita Khrushchev	General Secretary	1953
Leonid Brezhnev	General Secretary	1964
Yuri Andropov	General Secretary	1982
Konstantin Chernenko	General Secretary	1984
Mikhail Gorbachev	General Secretary	1985

Russian Federation
Boris Yeltsin	President	1991

Index

air travel 202, 205–7
Algeria 174–77
Arafat, Yasser 135
arms race 143, 145
Asquith, H.H. 8–9, 15, 18, 24, 25, 26, 79
atomic bomb 95, 99, 104, 143
Attlee, Clement 99–100, 160, 169, 170

Baldwin, Stanley 28, 29, 31
Bangladesh 166, 179
Bay of Pigs 155
Beatles 220
Begin, Menachem 136
Benelux 157, 158
Berlin
  blockade 106–8
  Wall 154–55
Bevan, Aneurin 85, 86–7, 91, 92
Beveridge Report 84–6, 91, 92
Bevin, Ernest 100, 103, 105
'Black and Tans' 39
'Bloody Sunday' 49–50
Booth, Charles 76
British Broadcasting Corporation 208–9, 211
British Union of Fascists 187–88

Campaign for Nuclear Disarmament (CND) 106
Carson, Sir Edward 37
Carter, Jimmy 136
Castro, Fidel 113, 114–15
'Cat and Mouse Act' 10
Churchill, Winston 29, 30, 40, 79, 85, 94, 95, 96, 99, 100, 101, 102
cinema 213–16
Cold War 101, 102–3, 156
Collins, Michael 39, 40, 41
colour bar 190
Common Market 157, 159, 160
Congo 142
'coupon' election 125
Cuban Missile Crisis 113–19
Czechoslovakia, invasion, 1958 161

Davison, Emily Wilding 10
devolution 56–9
Diem, Ngo Dinh 120, 121
'dole' 80
'Domino Theory' 120
Dubček, Alexander 161

Easter rising 42–4, 48, 54–5
Eden, Anthony 110, 111, 112
Education Act, 1944 91
Eisenhower, Dwight D. 112, 120
European Coal and Steel Community (ECSC) 157–58

European Defence Community (EDC) 158–59
European Economic Community (EEC) 159, 160, 161, 162, 163
European Free Trade Association (EFTA) 160
European Union, see European Economic Community
evacuation 82–3

Fabian Society 21
Fawcett, Millicent Garrett 6, 13

Gandhi, Mohandas 167
Gaulle, Charles de 162, 163, 176–77
General Strike 28–33
Great Depression 65–7, 69, 71–3, 80

Hardie, Keir 21, 22
Heath, Edward 161, 163
Henderson, Arthur 23, 27
Hitler, Adolf 70
Home Rule 35
Ho Chi Minh 120, 121
Hungarian Rising, 1956 161
Hyndman, Henry 21

immigration 178–79, 180–81, 183–88, 191–92, 195–99
India
  independence 168, 170, 172–73
  migration from 179, 183, 184
  nationalism 167
Industrial Revolution 62
IRA 34, 36, 38, 39, 41, 44–5, 48, 49, 53
Ireland
  Civil War 41
  internment 49
  Ireland Act, 1949 53
  partition 40
  Peace People, the 51–2
  religion 38
  the 'Troubles' 36, 45, 47
Irish Volunteers 38
Iron Curtain 100
Israel 133–37

Jarrow Crusade 69
Jewish migration 180, 185–88
Jinnah, Muhammed Ali 168, 169, 170
Johnson, Lyndon B. 102, 122

Kennedy, John F. 113, 114, 115, 117, 121, 154
Khruschev, Nikita 112, 113, 114, 115, 117, 161
Kilbrandon Commission 58
Korean war 138–41

Labour Party 20–4, 27–8, 77

Index

League of Nations 128, 133
Liberal Party 25–6
Liberal welfare reforms 77–9, 93
Lloyd George, David 24, 25, 26, 40, 77, 79
Local Government Act, 1929 80

MacArthur, General Douglas 139
MacDonald, James Ramsay 21, 23, 24, 27, 29
Macmillan, Harold 160, 161, 162, 219
Mao Zedong 102, 138, 139
Marshall Aid 105, 153
Marx, Karl 21
Meibion Glyndwr 59
means test 69, 80
Monnet, Jean 157, 158
Mosley, Oswald 187–88
Mountbatten, Lord Louis 36, 170, 171
Mugabe, Robert 148, 149
My Lai massacre 123, 125

Nagy, Imre 161
Nasser, General 110, 111, 134
National Assistance Act, 1948 85
National Front 192–93
National Health Service 85, 86, 88–9, 195
National Insurance Act, 1922 78
National Insurance Act, 1946 85
NATO 109, 110, 156
National Union of Women's Suffrage Societies,
    see suffragists
Nehru, Jawaharlal 167, 169
New Deal 68
newspapers 217–18
Nixon, Richard 122, 125
Northern Ireland 35, 45, 53
Northern Ireland Civil Rights Association 47
Notting Hill riots 190–91, 200–1
nuclear disarmament 104, 143–44, 145

Organisation for the Maintenance of Supplies 28, 30, 31
Osborne Judgement 23

Pakistan 166, 168, 170, 171, 184
Palestine 133–37
Palestine Liberation Organisation (PLO) 135, 136, 137
Pankhurst, Emmeline 6, 13
pensions 78, 81
Plaid Cymru 56, 57, 58
Potsdam Conference 99, 102
Powell, Enoch 193–94
Public Assistance Committees 80

Quant, Mary 221

Race Relations Acts 194–95
radio 203–4, 207–10
'red scare' 27
Representation of the People Act, 1918 15, 26
Rhodesia, see Zimbabwe
Rock 'n' roll 219–20
Rome, Treaty of 159
Roosevelt, Franklin D. 68, 94, 95, 98, 129

Rowntree, Seebohm 76, 82

Sadat, Anwar 136
Samuel Commission 29
satellites 202–3, 204
Schuman, Robert 157–58
Scotland 56–9
Scottish National Party (SNP) 56, 57, 58
Sinn Fein 38
Six Day War 134–35
Smith, Ian 148, 149
Social Democratic Federation 21
Special Areas Act 69
Stalin, Josef 94, 95, 96
Suez Crisis 110–12
suffragettes 6, 8, 13, 18–9
suffragists 6
Sunningdale Conference 51

Taff Vale Case 22
telephones 202–3
television 204, 210–12
Tet offensive 122
Trade Union Act, 1913 23
Truman Doctrine 103
Truman, Harry S. 94, 98, 138, 139

Ulster Volunteer Force (UVF) 38
Unemployment Act, 1934 69
Unemployment Insurance Act, 1920 80
United Nations 128–49
  Children's Fund (UNICEF) 145
  in the Congo 142
  disarmament 143–45
  formation 128, 129, 132
  General Assembly 130
  in Korea 138–41
  in the Middle East 133–37
  Secretary Generals 131
  Security Council 130

Valera, Eamonn de 39, 41, 52, 53
Vienna Summit 114, 115
Vietcong 120–21, 122, 125
Vietnam war 120–27

Wales 56–9
Wall Street Crash 65–6
Warsaw Pact 156, 161
Welfare State 81, 85, 89
Wheatley's Housing Act 27
Wilson, Harold 105, 162
Wireless, see radio
Women's Social and Political Union, see suffragettes
World Bank 145–46

Yalta Conference 94, 95, 96, 102, 106
Yom Kippur War 136

Zaire, see Congo
Zinoviev letter 27
Zimbabwe 147–49